THE LAY SAINT

THE LAY SAINT

CHARITY AND CHARISMATIC AUTHORITY IN MEDIEVAL ITALY, 1150–1350

MARY HARVEY DOYNO

CORNELL UNIVERSITY PRESS
Ithaca and London

Visit our website at cornellpress.cornell.edu.

First published 2019 by Cornell University Press

Library of Congress Cataloging-in-Publication Data

Names: Doyno, Mary Harvey, 1973– author.
Title: The lay saint : charity and charismatic authority in
    medieval Italy, 1150–1350 / Mary Harvey Doyno.
Description: Ithaca [New York] : Cornell University Press
    2019. | Includes bibliographical references and index. |
    Summary: "The Lay Saint explores the numerous
    saintly cults dedicated to recently deceased members of
    the laity that grew up in the communes of late
    medieval Italy and shows how they both challenged
    and ultimately solidified the church's institutional and
    charismatic authority"—Provided by publisher.
Identifiers: LCCN 2019020872 (print) | LCCN 2019981416
    (ebook) | ISBN 9781501740206 (cloth) |
    ISBN 9781501740213 (pdf) | ISBN 9781501740220
    (epub)
Subjects: LCSH: Catholic Church—Italy—History—To
    1500. | Christian saints—Cult—Italy—History—To
    1500. | Laity—Catholic Church—History—To 1500. |
    Sanctification—Catholic Church. | Italy—Church
    history—476–1400.
Classification: LCC BX2333 .D69 2019 (print) | LCC
    BX2333 (ebook) | DDC 282/.450902—dc23
LC record available at https://lccn.loc.gov/2019020872
LC ebook record available at https://lccn.loc.gov/
2019981416

Contents

ILLUSTRATIONS

ACKNOWLEDGMENTS

I am grateful to have the chance to thank at last all of the people whose support was critical for completing this book. As an undergraduate, I was lucky to be launched into the study of medieval Italy by Robert Brentano and Adnan Husain; I remain ever grateful for their example and encouragement. In graduate school I had the good fortune of working with Caroline Walker Bynum, Consuelo Dutschke, Carmela V. Franklin, Martha Howell, Joel Kaye, Adam J. Kosto, and Robert Somerville. At a critical stage of this book's production, Amanda Irwin Wilkins and Andrea Scott provided me with a wonderful home in the Princeton Writing Program; I constantly make use of the lessons I learned from them in both my teaching and my writing. Many thanks as well go to Paula Findlen for my year at Stanford. I am also grateful for the support of the Sacramento State Research and Creative Activity Faculty Awards Program.

The colleagues I found at the American Academy in Rome have remained the ideal of an enriching intellectual community. For all that they gave both Michael and me that year (and since), I thank Mike Chin, Roger Freitas, Jefferson Friedman, Lella Gandini, Vivien Greene, Maria Elena Gonzalez, Lester K. Little, Jessica Maier, Elizabeth Marlowe, Kristina Milnor, Victoria Morse, Bill North, Dana Prescott, Emma Scioli, Jonah Siegel, Bradley Wester, and Nancy Yousef.

The friendships that came out of graduate school have meant so much to me that it feels like thanking siblings. I am beyond grateful for the support, guidance, and unwavering loyalty I have found with Leah DeVun, Jessica Goldberg, Anna Harrison, Anna Trumbore Jones, Paola Tartakoff, Ashli White, and Ellen Wurtzel. I have also benefited in too many ways to count from friendships with Pamela Bloch, Deborah Cohler, Sam Collins, Heather Rose Dodge, Robin Donovan, Ariel Coyote Ford, Jennifer Heindl, Hillary Miller, Jeff Miner, Sonya Posmentier, Karen Skinazi, Harvey Stark, Barbara Voss, and Heather Wood.

My Faculty Success Program comrades have been a crucial weekly community, offering sane and compassionate guidance and a vital sense that even though writing is a solitary endeavor, I am, in fact, never alone. Thank you, Abigail Andrews, Lauren Duquette-Rury, Kate Graber, Rachel Haywood-Ferreira, and Maria Alejandra Perez.

Maureen Miller has been a constant sounding board, a careful reader, and a crucial tie to a larger medieval community. I am grateful for all that she has given me. Anna Trumbore Jones read (multiple times) everything in this book. Her generosity as well as her smart and thoughtful eye amaze me. She has provided me with a model of friendship and support that I strive to imitate.

The completion of this book would have been unimaginable to me without the extraordinary intellectual and professional guidance I found in Caroline Walker Bynum and Joel Kaye. The direction they offered in graduate school was crucial but it has been the ongoing ideas, support, and cheering they have so willingly given me that allowed this project to finally come to its end. Their example continues to navigate me through my work as a scholar and teacher.

I send much love and gratitude to my family for their support. My siblings, Annie, Eli, and Lucy; my sisters-in-law Sonia and Kim; my in-laws, Jane and Herm, and my parents, Lisa and David, have all given more to me than can be expressed here. I fell in love with Italy and its history when my parents first took me there as a teenager. And I learned how to articulate that enthusiasm over the many nights in high school and college that my father worked with me on my writing at our kitchen table. I cannot thank them enough for all they have given me.

Carmela Franklin not only gave me valuable instruction in all things medieval when I was a graduate student but some smart and anxiety-relieving advice about the realities of being an academic mom. Her advice that one has a career that develops over time and that can change course in wonderfully unforeseen ways has stayed ever present in my mind as I began to build my own family. The arrivals of Daisy, Henry, and Bessie have made all of this work matter in ways I could not have imagined. Finally, nothing is imaginable without Michael. I dedicate this book to him.

THE LAY SAINT

Introduction

If you have had the good fortune of visiting the Cloisters Museum in New York, it is a good bet that you walked right by one of its more curious items. In the midst of that collection's numerous medieval treasures is a late twelfth-century holy-water font that depicts the merchant turned penitent and later civic holy man, Ranieri of Pisa (d. 1160). Originally placed in Pisa's cathedral, this font twice depicts Ranieri extending his larger-than-life-size hand to bless a devotee. While on one side, Ranieri blesses a woman, on the opposite side he blesses a cleric. Since this font would presumably have held water made holy through the blessings of cathedral priests, its depiction of late twelfth-century Pisa's newest civic saint offers an alternative understanding of Christian religious hierarchy: it is the layman, and not the priest, who offers the blessings.

The specter of Ranieri of Pisa blessing a cleric on a cathedral holy-water font illuminates much about the threat and opportunity offered to both church and city officials by the phenomenon of lay civic sanctity in the communes of northern and central Italy. At its core, *The Lay Saint* explores the relationship between lay religiosity and the solidification of the Christian church's institutional and charismatic authority. It explores how church officials responded to having their hierarchy and authority challenged from within and by means of their own ideals. And finally, it considers how that response shaped notions of what constituted not only an ideal lay Christian but also an ideal member of a civic community.

Between the twelfth and early fourteenth centuries, in the independent citizen-governed communes of Italy, numerous civic cults dedicated to contemporary (that is, recently deceased) laymen and laywomen appeared. Joining long-established cults for early Christian martyrs and holy bishops were new cults dedicated to midwives, goldsmiths, domestic servants, and merchants (to name just a few of the lay saints' occupations). These new cults promoted the idea that it was these laymen and laywomen who had lived model Christian lives and personified civic ideals. Although only one lay saint from the Italian communes would be canonized by the Roman church in the Middle Ages—Omobono of Cremona (d. 1197), who was canonized by Pope Innocent III in 1199—the *vitae*, miracle collections, civic statutes, tombs, and altars dedicated to pious men and women provide convincing evidence that their cults were of great local importance.

And yet, *The Lay Saint* will argue that the phenomenon of contemporary lay civic sanctity had a meaning and significance that went well beyond the confines of particular Italian cities. The interest shown not only by Pope Innocent III but also by countless secular clerics, regular canons, and mendicant friars who documented the religious lives and miraculous acts of these extraordinary laymen and laywomen demonstrates the importance the church saw in helping to shape the content and quality of an ideal lay life. This study contends that the rise of lay sanctity in the Italian communes illuminates a complex debate that was taking place between the laity, the church, and civic authorities over the source of religious power and charisma. It shows how claims that extraordinarily pious laymen and laywomen had earned spiritual gifts (or charisma) that allowed them to perform miracles during their lifetimes destabilized the power structure on which the church depended. It illustrates how promotion of these cults by both the papacy and the mendicants had more to do with controlling models of lay religion than with responding to religious trends. And finally, it demonstrates how conceptions of the ideal layman as civic charity worker and the ideal laywoman as visionary were favored and promoted by church authorities because they maintained a central tenet of the institutional church's authority: only those within that hierarchy could function as conduits of God's power; only those within church orders could perform charismatic acts.

Living the *Vita Apostolica* in Communal Italy

To understand the religious and political context out of which the phenomenon of the contemporary civic lay saint emerged, it is necessary to begin with the religious principle that each of the lay saints examined in this book followed: that the *vita apostolica*, or the life of Christ's first apostles as described in the Gospels, was the ideal Christian life. In the opening pages of the first chapter of his groundbreaking study of religious movements in the later Middle Ages, Herbert Grundmann describes the irony that such a principle emerged from the eleventh-century church reform movement.[1]

Grundmann notes that the church's attempt to establish the preeminence of its temporal as well as its spiritual authority—based overwhelmingly on the idea of apostolic succession—had raised a number of questions all of which at their core focused on "the idea of the 'worthiness of the priest.'"[2] One of those questions—"whether each and every Christian might not be called by the command of the gospels and the example of the apostles to model his or her life on the gospels and apostolic standards"—motivated the *vita apostolica*'s immense popularity in the high and later Middle Ages.[3]

Embraced by a wide range of medieval Christians, from monks to laywomen to kings, the *vita apostolica* was, as Grundmann describes it, a "religious *way of life*."[4] More recently, scholars have referred to a "lay penitential movement," in order to describe the many ways in which urban laymen and laywomen took up the *vita apostolica* in the twelfth and thirteenth centuries.[5] But these urban lay penitents (a classification that could be applied to each of

---

1. Herbert Grundmann, *Religious Movements in the Middle Ages*, trans. Steven Rowan (Notre Dame: University of Notre Dame Press, 1995).

2. Grundmann, *Religious Movements*, 7.

3. On the *vita apostolica*, see M.-D. Chenu, "Monks, Canons, and Laymen in Search of the Apostolic Life," in *Nature, Man and Society in the Twelfth Century: Essays on New Theological Perspectives in the Latin West*, ed. and trans. Jerome Taylor and Lester K. Little (Toronto: University of Toronto Press, 1997), 202–38; and Ernest W. McDonnell, "The *Vita Apostolica*: Diversity or Dissent," *Church History* 24 (1955): 15–31.

4. Grundmann, *Religious Movements*, 8.

5. On the lay penitential movement, see the collection of primary sources edited by Gilles Gérard Meersseman, *Dossier de l'ordre de la pénitence au XIIIe siècle* (Fribourg: Éditions Universitaires, 1961); also see Alfonso Pompei, "Il movimento penitenziale nei secoli XII–XIII," in *L'Ordine della penitenza di San Francesco d'Assisi*, ed. O. Schmucki (Rome: Istituto Storico dei Cappuccini, 1973): 9–40; Giovanna Casagrande, *Religiosità penitenziale e città al tempo dei comuni* (Rome: Istituto Storico dei Cappuccini, 1995); Augustine Thompson, *Cities of God: The Religion of the Italian Communes, 1125–1325* (University Park: Pennsylvania State University Press, 2005), 69–102; and the essays collected in both Lino Temperini, ed., *Santi e santità nel movimento penitenziale francescano dal duecento al cinquecento* (Rome: Analecta Tor, 1998); and Mariano D'Alatri, ed., *Il movimento francescano della penitenza nella società medioevale* (Rome: Istituto Storico dei Cappuccini, 1980).

the lay saints presented here) adhered to a way of life that began well before the *vita apostolica* movement. Since the early fourth century, "penitent" had been a term used to describe Christians who had dedicated their lives to performing penance.[6] A "voluntary penitent" was a person who had been admitted into a loosely defined order of penitents through a liturgical ceremony. In that ceremony, the penitent would swear to follow a rigorous prayer schedule and adhere to regular periods of fasting and abstinence. The penitent would also vow to follow certain restrictions placed on work and the handling of money and to abstain from military service. In the later Middle Ages, laypeople designated as penitents seem to have abided by similar restrictions and have understood their rigorous ascetic program as an attempt to follow the *vita apostolica* without formal, institutional support.[7]

In 1221, Cardinal Hugolino of Ostia (the future Pope Gregory IX) assembled the *Memoriale propositi fratrum et sororum de penitentia in domibus propriis*, which was an amalgamation of already existing guidelines for how one ought to live as a penitent in the secular world.[8] This document called for lay penitents to wear distinctive but modest clothing; to adhere to regular periods of prayer, fasting, and abstinence; to care for their larger communities and each other; and not to engage in any violent acts. Even though Hugolino drew from a variety of guidelines for the lay penitential life and thus was not presenting new strictures, his issuing of this document, as I argue in Chapter 7, was an attempt to bring a more concerted regulatory structure to a way of life that was gaining immense popularity but remained largely outside of the church's direct control.[9] Although scholars have long tried to find a mendicant source for the *Memoriale*, more recent work has advocated for seeing Francis and his first followers not as having established a lay penitential order but rather as

---

6. E. Amann and A. Michel, "Pénitence," in *Dictionnaire de théologie catholique*, vol. 12 (Paris, 1933), 803.

7. André Vauchez, *The Laity in the Middle Ages: Religious Belief and Devotional Practices*, trans. Margery J. Schneider, ed. Daniel E. Bornstein (Notre Dame: University of Notre Dame Press, 1993), 119. Vauchez has noted that the penitents of communal Italy were in some respects an extension of the phenomenon of *conversi*, laymen who had a connection with a monastery but still remained tied to and within the secular world. On *conversi* in medieval Italy, see Duane J. Osheim, "Conversion, Conversi, and the Christian Life in Late Medieval Tuscany," *Speculum* 58 (1983): 368–90. Of course, anyone (layman, laywoman, monk, nun, or cleric) who performed penance could be called a penitent. Especially in the twelfth and thirteenth centuries, however, if a person was identified as a "penitent," he or she was most likely a member of the laity. To some extent, to call a monk a penitent would have been seen as redundant; monks and nuns lived lives that were by their definition dedicated to penance.

8. For the text of the *Memoriale*, see Meersseman, *Dossier*, 92–112. Also see Thompson, *Cities of God*, 77–82; and Alison More, "Institutionalizing Penitential Life in Later Medieval and Early Modern Europe: Third Orders, Rules, and Canonical Legitimacy," *Church History* 83 (2014): 297–323.

9. Thompson notes how "hardly a single line of the 'Memoriale' lacks a model in an earlier rule or penitential canon"; *Cities of God*, 78.

having been members of this lay religious movement.[10] In other words, Francis and his friars were themselves lay penitents.

In addition to Francis and his first Friars Minor, lay groups as diverse as the beguines in northern Europe, the Humiliati in Milan, and the Flagellants in Perugia have all been identified as part of this movement. In fact, any layperson seeking to live a more dedicated ascetic life while remaining attached to and involved in the secular world could be categorized as a lay penitent and thus part of a wider association that modern scholars have deemed a movement. The diversity of names used to identify penitents in central and northern Italy—*conversi/conversae, fratres et sorores de poenitentia, penitenti, pizochere, beati/beatae, bizzoche*—underscores a fundamental diversity in how penitents organized their lives.[11] Some lived communally with other penitents. Some stayed in their family homes. And some removed themselves from others altogether, living alone either in a cell or hermitage.

The issue of lay penitents' affiliation (and by extension, lay saints' affiliation) with the mendicant orders remains ambiguous. Although some individual lay penitents and some penitential communities had associations with mendicant friars, those connections are not evidence that during the thirteenth century lay penitents were early members of an institutionally defined Franciscan or Dominican Third (or lay) Order, despite what many of the mendicant hagiographers we will encounter in this study would have us believe. Those orders would not take shape until the late thirteenth (the Franciscans) and early fifteenth (the Dominicans) centuries.[12] And even though some Franciscans writing before the late thirteenth century described lay penitents with associations to their order as members of a "third order," a formal lay wing

---

10. Casagrande, *Religiosità penitenziale*, 75–161. In his study of Francis of Assisi, Vauchez emphasizes the fact that "Francis was and remained a layman." In fact, as Vauchez writes, Francis was an emblem of a new type of Christian that appeared in western Europe at end of twelfth century: the religious layman; André Vauchez, *Francis of Assisi: The Life and Afterlife of a Medieval Saint*, trans. Michael F. Cusato (New Haven: Yale University Press, 2012), 298–99.

11. On the names used to identify penitents, see Romana Guarnieri, "Pinzochere," in *Dizionario degli istituti di perfezione*, ed. Guerrino Pelliccia and Giancarlo Rocca (Rome: 1980), 1723–24; and Alfonso Pompei, "Terminologia varia dei penitenti," in *Il movimento francescano della penitenza*, ed. D'Alatri, 11–22.

12. On the institutionalization of the penitential movement, see Alison More, *Fictive Orders and Feminine Religious Identities, 1200–1600* (Oxford: Oxford University Press, 2018), and "Institutionalizing Penitential Life." Also see Maiju Lehmijoki-Gardner, "Writing Religious Rules as an Interactive Process: Dominican Penitent Women and the Making of Their *Regula*," *Speculum* 79 (2004): 660–87; and her introduction to Maiju Lehmijoki-Gardner, ed., *Dominican Penitent Women* (New York: Paulist Press, 2005), 1–36. Also see André Vauchez, "Penitenti laici e terziari in Italia nei secoli XIII e XIV," in his *Ordini mendicanti e società italiana XIII–XV secolo* (Milan: Mondadori, 1990), 206–20; Mario Sensi, "Anchoresses and Penitents in Thirteenth- and Fourteenth-Century Umbria," in *Women and Religion in Medieval and Renaissance Italy*, ed. Daniel Bornstein and Roberto Rusconi (Chicago: University of Chicago Press, 1996), 56–83.

of the Order of Friars Minor only began to form after Pope Nicholas IV issued the 1289 bull *Supra montem*, which, in addition to repeating the guidelines that had been set in the *Memoriale*, called for much stricter oversight of lay penitents by members of the church, awarding most of that responsibility to the Franciscans.[13]

The confusion in modern scholarship about the nature of lay penitents' association with the mendicants largely stems from the work done by both the Franciscans and the Dominicans from the late thirteenth century onward to create anachronistic historical narratives that made their connections with lay penitents seem to be an unambiguous part of their order's original agenda.[14] Much of this book aims to identify the layers of mistaken institutional affiliation as well as to understand the purposes and uses of those errors. Thus, while I pay close attention to how the growing power of the mendicants helped to shape new lay Christian ideals in communal Italy, I also argue that the history of civic lay saints is distinct from and sometimes at odds with that of the mendicant orders.

Thus, even though the lay penitents of urban Italy were part of a broader lay interest in the *vita apostolica* sweeping across medieval Europe, their fundamentally independent identity distinguishes them from other examples of lay religious enthusiasm. Unlike the beguines of northern Europe or members of the Humiliati or Flagellants who enjoyed varying degrees of institutional identity and support, lay penitents in communal Italy were by and large without a religious affiliation any more specific than their identity as Christians and members of a particular parish church.[15] In short, the celebrated lay penitents I present in this study emerged from a broad categorization of laymen and laywomen embracing a rigorous penitential life. And, as I shall show, it is precisely because of this fact that they came to represent such a profound threat as well as opportunity for the medieval church.

---

13. Giovanna Casagrande, "Un ordine per i laici: Penitenza e penitenti nel Duecento," in *Francesco d'Assisi e il primo secolo di storia francescana*, ed. Maria Pia Alberzoni et al. (Turin: Einaudi, 1997), 237–55.

14. On this issue, see Bert Roest, *Franciscan Literature of Religious Instruction before the Council of Trent* (Leiden: Brill, 2004), 197–204; and his *Reading the Book of History: Intellectual Contexts and Educational Functions of Franciscan Historiography, 1226–ca.1350* (Groningen: Stichting Drukkerij C. Regenboog, 1996), 92–99. Also see Lehmijoki-Gardner, "Writing Religious Rules"; and More, "Institutionalizing Penitential Life."

15. For example, the support the Parisian beguines found in King Louis IX's beguinages; see Tanya Stabler Miller, *The Beguines of Medieval Paris* (Philadelphia: University of Pennsylvania Press, 2017). I am also referring here to Pope Gregory IX's bull *Gloriam virginalem*, which, as More has noted, allowed beguines to change from "an unofficial state to a legitimate, if non-canonical status"; see More, *Fictive Orders*, 30.

My use of the term "lay" deserves further clarification. The most basic definition of a layman or laywomen in medieval Europe was someone who had not taken clerical orders.[16] If a monk had not been ordained, he was still a member of the laity. A nun, however, was always both a member of a religious order and a laywoman. However, scholars have adopted a broader definition of the term to describe the prominent place occupied in late medieval religious history by Christians who were in neither clerical nor monastic orders. When André Vauchez described "a new lay religious order" in his study of the medieval laity, he wrote that such an "order" manifested itself in a diverse array of expressions of religious enthusiasm, such as crusades, pilgrimage, devotion to the Eucharist, *imitatio Christi*, and conjugal chastity.[17] Thus, Vauchez uses the term to refer to a population of individuals who were neither priests nor monks nor nuns—that is, people who had taken neither clerical nor monastic vows.

It is that wider understanding of the term that I will use here. In order to understand the significance of this broader usage, however, we need to return to the institutional context from which it arose. Scholars have long pointed to a so-called "birth of the laity" as having occurred alongside the growth of an institutional church.[18] As the clergy came to be regarded as a separate body within Christendom, those who were not ordained and not members of religious orders came also to have an identity as a distinct population.[19] The papacy's attempts to ban clerical marriage, simony, and lay investiture in the late eleventh century contributed both to the hardening of the distinction between

16. Yves Congar, "Laïc au Moyen Âge," in *Dictionnaire de spiritualité* (Paris: Beauchesne, 1976), 79–83.

17. For an introduction to the range of high and late medieval lay piety, see Vauchez, *The Laity*; Richard Kieckhefer, "Major Currents in Late Medieval Devotion," in *Christian Spirituality: High Middle Ages and Reformation*, ed. Jill Raitt (New York: Crossroad, 1987), 75–108; Guy Lobrichon, *La religion des laïcs en Occident: XIᵉ–XVᵉ siècles* (Paris: Hachette, 1994); and Jean Leclercq, François Vandenbroucke, and Louis Bouyer, *The Spirituality of the Middle Ages* (London: Burns & Oates, 1969). On popular piety, see Étienne Delaruelle, *La piété populaire au Moyen Âge* (Turin: Bottega d'Erasmo, 1975).

18. Jacques Fontaine, "The Practice of Christian Life: The Birth of the Laity," in *Christian Spirituality: Origins to the Twelfth Century*, ed. Bernard McGinn and John Meyendorff (New York: Crossroad, 1985), 453–91; Lobrichon, *La religion des laïcs*; André Vauchez, "Il posto dei laici nell'ecclesiologia medievale," in *Esperienze religiose nel Medioevo* (Rome: Viella, 2003), 51–65. It is important to emphasize that as early as the third century the church hierarchy saw the laity as having a religious identity that was distinct from clerics; see Hippolytus of Rome, *The Treatise on the Apostolic Tradition* (Ridgefield, CT: Morehouse, 1992).

19. On the development of a distinctive "clerical culture," see Maureen C. Miller, "Religion Makes a Difference: Clerical and Lay Cultures in the Courts of Northern Italy, 1000–1300," *American Historical Review* 105 (2000): 1095–130.

priests and laymen and to the carving out of a distinctively lay devotional space.[20]

The independent communes of medieval Italy provided particularly fertile ground in which such lay devotion could grow and it is here that the phenomenon of contemporary lay sanctity flourished. When the independent civic governments first appeared in late eleventh- and early twelfth-century northern and central Italian cities, they were most often established and run by a city's aristocratic elites.[21] As these cities continued to grow and prosper economically during the twelfth century, a hitherto absent voice—that of the non-noble but wealthy population of successful merchants and artisans—began to demand a say in the political, economic and cultural life of their cities. Modern historians have often described this political turn as the rise of the *popolo*, using the name well-off merchants and artisans gave to their political party.[22]

In his rich study of religious life within the Italian communes, Augustine Thompson has noted the "heightened religious identity" of *popolo*-dominated communes.[23] Thompson's argument fits into his study's larger point that these cities were far from secular organizations; rather, they had a deep investment in cultivating the religious life of their inhabitants and the Christian identity of their polities.[24] Thus, as communes developed more so-called "lay" governments by turning away from the bishop as the main civic authority, new *popolo*-dominated administrations actually increased or emphasized civic reli-

---

20. This has been discussed by numerous scholars; for example, see Georges de Lagarde, *La naissance de l'esprit laïque au déclin du Moyen Âge*, 3rd ed., 5 vols. (Louvain: Nauwelaerts, 1956–63); and Vauchez, *The Laity*, 3–26.

21. For the development of the communes, see Philip J. Jones, *The Italian City-State from Commune to Signoria* (Oxford: Oxford University Press, 1997); J. K. Hyde, *Society and Politics in Medieval Italy: The Evolution of Civil Life, 1000–1350* (London: Macmillan, 1973); Daniel Waley, *The Italian City-Republics*, 3rd ed. (New York: Longman, 1988); Elisa Occhipinti, *L'Italia dei comuni: Secoli XI–XIII* (Rome: Carocci, 2000); and Maureen C. Miller, *The Bishop's Palace: Architecture and Authority in Medieval Europe* (Ithaca: Cornell University Press, 2000).

22. For a good introduction to the rise of the *popolo*, see Andrea Zorzi, "The Popolo," in *Italy in the Age of the Renaissance, 1300–1550*, ed. John M. Najemy (Oxford: Oxford University Press, 2004), 145–64. Also see John C. Koenig, "The Popolo of Northern Italy (1196–1274): A Political Analysis" (PhD dissertation, University of California at Los Angeles, 1977); and E. Artifoni, "Tensioni sociali e istituzioni nel mondo comunale," in *La storia: I grandi problemi dal medioevo all'età contemporanea*, vol. 2, *Il medioevo*, ed. N. Tranfaglia and M. Firpo (Turin: UTET, 1986), 461–91.

23. Thompson, *Cities of God*, 128.

24. Ibid., 3. Thompson laments the dearth of modern scholarship that has recognized the extent to which the medieval communes were "simultaneously religious and political entities." He notes how little even the most comprehensive history of the Italian communes says about religion; Thompson points specifically to Jones, *The Italian City-State* and notes that Jones only devotes 17 out of 673 pages to religious life in the communes.

gious identity.[25] One of the ways in which they did this was through the cultivation of cults dedicated to members of their own civic population.

Although a distinct and complex history stands behind the development of each communal government, there are some generalizations that can provide a valuable context for the explosion of lay saints' cults over the late Middle Ages. First, *popolo* parties seem often to have originated in collective associations, such as merchant and artisan guilds as well as neighborhood associations that were formed to protect the interests of their members.[26] As these merchants and artisans gained economic power, they also began to demand more political power, using their increasing presence in a commune's general council to fight not only for greater economic opportunities but also to limit the privileges and abuses of the nobility. Although these associations were called *popolo* (of the people), it would be a mistake to see them as representing the entire population of a city. The merchants and artisans who ran the *popolo* were of an elevated economic status. They did not emerge from the city's substantial population of lesser merchants, artisans, or day-laborers. Nevertheless, it was during the thirteenth century, when the communes were largely under the control of the *popolo*, that we see civic governments working most explicitly to establish recently deceased pious laymen and laywomen as civic patrons. These new saints, who—as Vauchez has noted—tended to come from the middle segments of the population, seem to have appealed to members of the *popolo* as an embodiment of some of their political and cultural ideals.[27]

By the mid-fourteenth century, however, as most cities were reeling from the economic downturn brought on by famine and plague, the era of the *popolo* had come to an end. Most communes had fallen under the control of *signori* or oligarchic regimes. The fall of *popolo*-dominated communes was a crucial factor that led to the decreasing number of cults dedicated to contemporary laymen and laywomen over the fourteenth century. As cities came under the purview of individual families, patron saints representing a broader contingent of the city's working population had less appeal. And yet, as *The Lay Saint* argues, this changing political context was only part of the reason that the phenomenon of the contemporary lay civic saint waned over the fourteenth century. Lay penitents' reputations for extraordinary piety and great works of charity clearly could and did have a political meaning and use in the late medieval Italian communes.

---

25. Thompson, *Cities of God*, 136–37.

26. Zorzi, "The Popolo," 146–47.

27. André Vauchez, *Sainthood in the Later Middle Ages*, trans. Jean Birrell (Cambridge: Cambridge University Press, 1997), 173–83. It is important to note that while most of the lay saints I shall study did come from middle status families, a few came from families of a much higher and lower status.

Nevertheless the relatively independent lives those laymen and laywomen lived, as well as the claims their cults made that it was precisely through their extraordinary dedication to the *vita apostolica* that they had become living holy men and holy women—that is, living miracle workers—was something that, from at least the early thirteenth century, left the institutional church not only uneasy but also intent upon containing, controlling, and ultimately changing.

Lay Sanctity

Vauchez was the first scholar to see the numerous civic cults dedicated to members of the laity across late medieval Italy as a distinct phenomenon and to describe their common features: an emphasis upon asceticism, pilgrimage, and charitable activities.[28] Vauchez also noted both the social background of these lay saints and the important role the secular clergy played as the first patrons of these cults.[29] Vauchez's work has been instrumental not only in introducing lay civic sanctity into the scholarly conversation but also in identifying how much the nature of sainthood changed in the later Middle Ages.[30]

Vauchez's so-called Mediterranean saints of the twelfth and thirteenth centuries (deemed saints either officially by the church or unofficially by a local population) held several characteristics in common.[31] They tended to come from the laity or the mendicant orders and, almost without exception, lived in a city or town.[32] Furthermore, while northern European saints often came from the nobility and were kings or bishops, southern European saints were more likely to come from families of middle status and to have been mendicants or merchants.[33]

---

28. André Vauchez, "A Twelfth-Century Novelty: The Lay Saints of Urban Italy," in *The Laity*, 51–72. In addition, Vauchez also explores the subject of lay civic sanctity in "Lay People's Sanctity in Western Europe: Evolution of a Pattern (Twelfth and Thirteenth Centuries)," in *Images of Sainthood in Medieval Europe*, ed. Renate Blumenfeld-Kosinski and Timea Szell (Ithaca: Cornell University Press, 1991), 21–32; and "La difficile émergence d'une sainteté des laïcs à Venice aux XIIe et XIIIe siècles," in *Genova, Venezia, il Levante nei secoli XII–XIV*, ed. G. Ortalli and D. Puncuh (Venice: Istituto Veneto di Scienze, Lettere ed Arti, 2001), 335–48.

29. Vauchez, "A Twelfth-Century Novelty," 51–72.

30. In addition to his *Sainthood* and *The Laity*, also see Vauchez's *Saints, prophètes et visionnaires: Le pouvoir surnaturel au Moyen Âge* (Paris: Albin Michel, 1999).

31. Vauchez, "Lay People's Sanctity," 27.

32. Vauchez, *Sainthood*, 183–87. Also, see Michael Goodich, *Vita Perfecta: The Ideal of Sainthood in the Thirteenth Century* (Stuttgart: Anton Hiersemann, 1982), 19; and Donald Weinstein and Rudolph M. Bell, *Saints and Society* (Chicago: University of Chicago Press, 1982), 169–70.

33. Vauchez emphasizes this distinction but he does so by relying on documents gathered and created expressly for canonization inquiries. Thus this distinction only holds for the saints whom episcopal and papal authorities considered for canonization.

The perception that southern European sanctity had a particularly lay and urban identity builds on ideas about medieval religious movements that Grundmann articulated in the 1930s.[34] Grundmann argued that the religious enthusiasm of the later Middle Ages originated in part in the eleventh- and twelfth-century lay (and often female) religious movements of the burgeoning urban centers of Italy and the Low Countries—that is, the *vita apostolica* movement. In response to Grundmann's pioneering work, a wealth of modern studies have focused not only on the content and ideals of late medieval women's spirituality and sanctity but have also taken specific notice of the many examples of Italian laywomen who were penitents and saints.[35] As *The Lay Saint* argues, it was unaffiliated women's participation in the lay penitential movement and the many cults they earned for their efforts over the thirteenth century that motivated church authorities (most often in the form of Franciscan and Dominican hagiographers) to articulate new ideals for a perfected lay Christian life; ideals that by the mid-fourteenth century had brought an end to the phenomenon of the contemporary lay civic saint.

Although earlier (largely Carolingian) notions of an ideal lay life did not present one's lay status as an inherent obstacle to a perfected life, to be celebrated as a lay saint between the late twelfth and early fourteenth centuries, regardless of one's gender, meant to have overcome or to have altered many aspects of a secular life that were seen as antithetical to a holy life.[36] Because the laity had families and trades, they were believed to have a particularly difficult road to sanctity. Both Vauchez and Dyan Elliott have studied how in the later Middle Ages lay people began to transform their lives through the rejection of their trades or the adoption of conjugal chastity, in order to fit into a monastic or even a clerical religious ideal.[37] This manipulation of lay life fits into what Giles Constable has seen as a monasticization of medieval culture

---

34. Grundmann, *Religious Movements*.

35. In addition to Anna Benvenuti Papi's pivotal study *"In castro poenitentiae": Santità e società femminile nell'Italia medievale* (Rome: Herder, 1990), see Maiju Lehmijoki-Gardner, *Worldly Saints: Social Interaction of Dominican Penitent Women in Italy, 1200–1500* (Helsinki: Suomen Historiallinen Seura, 1999); Mario Sensi, *Storie di bizzoche tra Umbria e Marche* (Rome: Edizioni di Storia e Letteratura, 1995); Jacques Dalarun, *"Dieu changea de sexe pour ainsi dire": La religion faite femme, XIᵉ–XVᵉ siècle* (Paris: Fayard, 2008); and the essays collected in *Women and Religion in Medieval and Renaissance Italy*, ed. Bornstein and Rusconi. Also see the illustrated collection of essays on individual Italian female saints in Enrico Menestò and Roberto Rusconi, eds., *Umbria: Sacra e civile* (Turin: Nuova Eri Edizioni Rai, 1989).

36. For earlier models of lay sanctity, see Vauchez, "Lay People's Sanctity"; Matthew Kuefler, *The Making and Unmaking of a Saint: Hagiography and Memory in the Cult of Gerald of Aurillac* (Philadelphia: University of Pennsylvania Press, 2014); and Adrian Cornell du Houx, "Journeys to Holiness: Lay Sanctity in the Central Middle Ages, c.970–c.120" (PhD dissertation, University of Lancaster, 2015).

37. Vauchez, *Sainthood*, 356–58; Vauchez, *The Laity*, 185–204; and Dyan Elliott, *Spiritual Marriage: Sexual Abstinence in Medieval Wedlock* (Princeton: Princeton University Press, 1993).

starting in the twelfth century.[38] But as lay people began to live more like monks, the parameters of sanctity began to expand; by the late twelfth century, one did not necessarily have to withdraw from the secular world to be a saint. Although identifying the right ratio between an active and contemplative life was always a key part of negotiating lay religious ideals, *The Lay Saint* shows that the rise of the contemporary lay civic saint did not always mean that all aspects of a lay life needed to be transformed or rejected. In some lay saints' cults, a conversion that included the refutation of one's working identity is evidence of sanctity. In others, it is a rigorous and charitably minded work life that fuels such saintly claims.[39]

In addition to Vauchez's and Grundmann's work, modern treatments of lay sanctity in the medieval Italian communes have by and large focused on the role and function of patron saints as well as civic religion more broadly understood.[40] Diana Webb has studied the development and function of patron saints (both ancient and contemporary) in the communes and provided in her translation of the *vitae* of several Italian urban lay saints a tremendous resource for those interested in the phenomenon of contemporary lay civic sanctity.[41]

---

38. Giles Constable, *The Reformation of the Twelfth Century* (Cambridge: Cambridge University Press, 1996), 7.

39. The integration of work and religious ideals had long been a part of the beguine communities of northern Europe; see Miller, *The Beguines of Medieval Paris*.

40. To cite just a few examples from a rich collection of scholarship, see Vauchez, "Patronage des saints et religion civique dans l'Italie communale à la fin du Moyen Âge," in *Patronage and Public in the Trecento*, ed. Vincent Moleta (Florence: Leo S. Olschki, 1986); Chiara Frugoni, "The City and the 'New' Saints," in *City States in Classical Antiquity and Medieval Italy: Athens and Rome, Florence and Venice*, ed. Kurt Raaflaub et al. (Stuttgart: Franz Steiner, 1991), 71–91; Hans Conrad Peyer, *Città e santi patroni nell'Italia medievale*, ed. Anna Benvenuti (Florence: Le Lettere, 1998); A. M. Orselli, *L'Idea e il culto del santo patrono cittadino nella letteratura latina cristiana* (Bologna: Zanichelli, 1965); and Lester K. Little, *Indispensable Immigrants: The Wine Porters of Northern Italy and Their Saint, 1200–1800* (Manchester: University of Manchester Press, 2015). In addition, see Janine Larmon Peterson, *Suspect Saints and Holy Heretics: Disputed Sanctity and Communal Identity in Late Medieval Italy* (Ithaca: Cornell University Press, 2019); and the work of Paolo Golinelli. On civic religion in the Italian communes, see Gerald Parsons, *Siena, Civil Religion and the Sienese* (Aldershot: Ashgate, 2004); Mauro Ronzani, "La 'Chiesa del comune' nelle città dell'Italia centro-settentrionale (secoli XII–XIV)," *Società e Storia* 6 (1983): 499–534; Diana Norman, *Siena and the Virgin: Art and Politics in a Late Medieval City-State* (New Haven: Yale University Press, 1999); and the essays in André Vauchez, ed., *La religion civique à l'époque médiévale et moderne (Chrétienté et Islam)* (Paris: École Française de Rome, 1995); as well as Joanna Cannon and Beth Williamson, eds., *Art, Politics, and Civic Religion in Central Italy, 1261–1352* (Aldershot: Ashgate, 2000).

41. Diana Webb, *Patrons and Defenders: The Saints in the Italian City States* (London: Tauris Academic Studies, 1996); and Diana Webb, ed., *Saints and Cities in Medieval Italy: Selected Sources Translated and Annotated* (Manchester: Manchester University Press, 2007). Moreover, Webb's interest in the social background of lay saints has expanded our understanding of the role money and wealth played not only in these cults but also in the late medieval communes in general; see Diana Webb, "A Saint and His Money: Perceptions of Urban Wealth in the Lives of Italian Saints," in *The Church and Wealth*, ed. W. J. Sheils and Diana Wood (Oxford: Ecclesiastical History Society, 1987), 61–73. On this subject, also see Sofia Boesch Gaiano, "Lavoro, povertà, santità fra nuove realtà sociali e luoghi comuni

Thompson has mined the *vitae* of lay saints as well as communal documents attesting to the beginnings of their cults in order to demonstrate how the so-called "secularized" communes "needed their own divine legitimacy" and sought that through the promotion of new patron saints.[42] Finally, Joanna Cannon and Vauchez's study of the civic cult that grew around Margaret of Cortona (d. 1297) makes clear that any thorough study of lay sanctity demands simultaneous attention to the religious, political, and cultural context from which that cult sprung.[43]

In contrast to these studies, *The Lay Saint* does not attempt to trace the rise of particular types of behavior among the laity, the role of patron saints, the everyday religious ideals and beliefs of laymen and laywomen, or the trajectory of a single cult. I take as a given that the growth of saintly cults for lay communal residents was an indication of the laity's embrace of and enthusiasm for the ideals of the *vita apostolica*. Moreover, instead of approaching lay saints' cults as illustrative of an emerging lay religious order, one of this book's central arguments is that lay saints' cults were a crucial component of the institutional church's attempt to *establish* that lay religious order. As an embrace of the *vita apostolica* became an increasingly attractive option for the urban laity, the church developed new means of distinguishing its religious authority and charisma from those it oversaw. This was especially true as more laywomen took up the *vita apostolica* and were venerated for their efforts. Thus, instead of mapping out lay religious beliefs and practices, *The Lay Saint* focuses on how myriad church and communal authorities chose to represent ideal examples of lay religious life, how those representations changed over time in response to a changing political and religious context, and finally how those representations had at their core a desire to check yet capitalize on claims of lay religious power and charisma.

Despite the opposition I am sketching between those within the church hierarchy and those outside of it, I recognize the danger of seeing the medieval church as a monolith. Even though one might be able to characterize

---

agiografici," in *Cultura e società nell'Italia medievale: Studi per Paolo Brezzi* (Rome: Istituto Storico Italian per il Medio Evo, 1988), 117–29.

42. Thompson, *Cities of God*, 108.

43. Joanna Cannon and André Vauchez, *Margherita of Cortona and the Lorenzetti: Sienese Art and the Cult of a Holy Woman in Medieval Tuscany* (University Park: Pennsylvania State University Press, 1999). Cannon has also produced a number of articles looking at the visual evidence connected to both Margaret of Cortona and other lay saints; for example, see her "Marguerite et les Cortonais: Iconographie d'un 'culte civique' au XIVᵉ siècle," in *La religion civique à l'époque médiévale et moderne*, ed. A. Vauchez, 403–13. On Margaret of Cortona's cult and the intersection of politics and patron saints, see Daniel Bornstein, "The Uses of the Body: The Church and the Cult of Santa Margherita da Cortona," *Church History* 62 (1993): 163–77.

"the church" as having made significant strides to increase its power and authority between the eleventh and thirteenth centuries, it was not an institution that acted with one motive or one voice. Nevertheless, while I shall aim to describe the variety of responses from church authorities to the emerging cults of contemporary laymen and laywomen in the Italian communes, I shall also maintain that the very status of those earning saintly cults—who were neither nuns nor priests, monks nor bishops—accentuated a dichotomy between those who were within the institutional church—either through clerical or monastic orders—and those who remained outside of that hierarchy.

The Lay Saint

Although between 1150 and 1350 there were hundreds of cults celebrating recently deceased laymen and laywomen, primary sources documenting lay saints' lives as well as the beginnings of their civic cults survive for far fewer individuals. In the chapters that follow, I have chosen to explore the religious lives and civic cults of sixteen individuals: Ranieri of Pisa (d. 1160), Omobono of Cremona (d. 1197), Raimondo "Palmerio" of Piacenza (d. 1200), Ubaldesca of Pisa (d. 1205), Bona of Pisa (d. 1207), Umiliana de' Cerchi of Florence (d. 1246), Andrea of Siena (d.1251), Rose of Viterbo (d. 1251), Zita of Lucca (d. 1278), Pier "Pettinaio" of Siena (d. 1289), Margaret of Cortona (d. 1297), Giovanni of Urbino (d. 1304), Vanna of Orvieto (d. 1307), Enrico of Treviso (d. 1315), Margaret of Città di Castello (d. 1320), and Peter Crisci of Foligno (d. 1323). My criteria for selection rest on two factors: these were all laymen and laywomen who had lived active lives (that is, they were not primarily hermits or recluses) within their cities, and who have the most extensive surviving medieval sources.

Thus, to that end all of these sixteen cults included *vitae* written within a generation or two of the death of their saints.[44] Moreover, all of these saints spent the majority of their life outside of a cell or enclosure and were physically engaged with the people and concerns of their cities.[45] Although some

---

44. Although all of the *vitae* I shall study were written by contemporaries, or near contemporaries of these saints, medieval copies of those texts do not always survive. In some cases, such as the *vitae* of Raimondo "Palmerio" of Piacenza and Pier "Pettinaio" of Siena, I have had to rely on early modern translations of the original medieval Latin texts.

45. As a result, I am not including an urban hermit penitent such as Verdiana of Castelfiorentino. Verdiana lived for nearly thirty years in a cell attached to the walls of her city. For Verdiana, see Benvenuti Papi, "In castro poenitentiae," 263–303 and passim; and Silvia Nocentini, ed., *Verdiana da Castelfiorentino: Contesto storico, tradizione agiografica e iconografia* (Florence: Sismel, 2011).

of the lay saints I include did at times withdraw from the world into their homes or private cells, their lives were marked by tending to the sick and the poor, wandering the streets preaching penance and peace, making pilgrimages to holy sites, and working in their respective professions. These sixteen cults therefore describe men and women who all, in varying forms and to varying degrees, had to contend with the realities of lay urban life. In other words, men and women whose embrace of the ideals of the *vita apostolica* movement sometimes conflicted with their civic lives. This means that I include the cult of Umiliana de' Cerchi of Florence but not of Fina of San Gimignano (d. 1253).[46] Although Umiliana lived enclosed in her family's Florentine tower for much of her short life, she also spent several years dedicated to giving as much of her time and resources as possible to her city's needy, first as a wife and then as a widow. Fina, by contrast, suffered from a physical paralysis that left her unable to move. Her entire religious life was contained within her family's home. Margaret of Città di Castello also appears in this study. Even though this blind and severely handicapped lay saint did spend much of her life praying and performing penitential acts within the various homes she found after having been abandoned by her parents, the account of her navigating her Umbrian city to find those refuges endows her narrative with a more active urban quality than we find in Fina's cult.

My interest in how church and commune made sense of a holy lay life also means that I am fundamentally concerned with how lay sanctity was constructed. When I note that Fina lived her life in a state of paralysis, what I am actually relating is that this is how her hagiographer describes her. For most of the saints I study, we have no other source beyond a *vita* or *legenda*. Most of what we know about lay saints is therefore a matter of what their hagiographers wanted us to know. As a result, when I give details about lay saints' lives, I understand that these details are doing argumentative work. No information given in hagiography can be considered a "fact." Each point is intended to illustrate to readers that these lives were not only extraordinary Christian lives, but also holy ones. Although this makes accessing the lived reality of our saints quite difficult—if not impossible—*The Lay Saint* aims to show how hagiography can offer a tremendous opportunity to see the multitude of motivations driving the ways in which church authorities came to define a holy lay life.

My approach to studying lay sanctity has, as a result, been influenced by scholarship that emphasizes the importance voice, gender, genre, and social

---

46. On Fina, see Benvenuti Papi, *"In castro poenitentiae."*

status play in the construction of medieval *vitae*.[47] Over the past generation, scholars have articulated how readers can use a number of interpretive tools both to recognize the constructed nature of saints' *vitae* and to rely on those texts to reveal aspects of a saint's individual spirituality.[48] Much of this book considers how each hagiographer's political, social, religious, and gender concerns contributed to the filter through which he wrote. In short, I remain aware throughout that saints and their cults depend entirely upon the people and societies that venerated them in the first place. As Aviad Kleinberg has noted, sainthood is a social phenomenon that requires an audience.[49] This study keeps both the conduits and audiences of lay sanctity as its focus.

The Lay Saint is not, however, only a study of hagiography. Lay saints' cults were constructed through a variety of media: sermons dedicated to recently deceased lay saints; communal statutes calling for the annual celebration of ideal laymen and laywomen; tombs that were often embellished with paintings or sculptures documenting the lay saint's life; and finally, written and visual accounts of the living and posthumous miracles ascribed to the saint. By considering a wide spectrum of evidence for the veneration of these laymen and laywomen, *The Lay Saint* maintains that the celebration of contemporary lay individuals had both a political and a religious purpose. While the church saw an opportunity to recast what it meant to live a committed lay religious life, communes used the celebration of these laymen and laywomen to sanctify and—as a result—legitimize their new forms of civic government.

It is important to note, of course, that this is not an exhaustive study. There are, without doubt, saints that other scholars would have considered it essential to include. One of those deserves specific comment. Angela of Foligno (d. 1309), the widow turned Franciscan penitent whose extraordinary peniten-

---

47. Catherine M. Mooney's work has been key here. As she made clear in her study of Angela of Foligno's *Memorial*, everything the reader learns about Angela's religious life comes through the filter of her scribe; see "The Authorial Role of Brother A. in the Composition of Angela of Foligno's Revelations," in *Creative Women in Medieval and Early Modern Italy: A Religious and Artistic Renaissance*, ed. E. Ann Matter and John Coakley (Philadelphia: University of Pennsylvania Press, 1994), 58; also see the essays in Catherine M. Mooney, ed., *Gendered Voices: Medieval Saints and Their Interpreters* (Philadelphia: University of Pennsylvania Press, 1999).

48. In addition to the essays collected in Mooney's *Gendered Voices*, see John Coakley, *Women, Men, and Spiritual Power: Female Saints and Their Male Collaborators* (New York: Columbia University Press, 2006).

49. Aviad M. Kleinberg, "Shared Sainthood," in *Modelli di santità e modelli di comportamento: Contrasti, intersezioni, complementarità*, ed. Guilia Barone et al. (Turin: Rosenberg & Sellier, 1995), 168; also see Kleinberg, *Prophets in Their Own Country: Living Saints and the Making of Sainthood in the Later Middle Ages* (Chicago: University of Chicago Press, 1992).

tial and spiritual life earned her a following of devotees during her lifetime made up primarily of Franciscan friars, is the Italian lay saint who has arguably garnered the most attention from modern scholars.[50] However, she is missing from this study for two reasons. First, there is no evidence that she was venerated as a civic saint in medieval Foligno. Second, the complex story of Angela's connection to friars associated with the so-called spiritual wing of the Franciscan Order dominates so many of the sources documenting the beginnings of her cult (as well as so much of modern scholarship on her) that to disentangle Angela the lay penitent from Angela the Franciscan penitent would require its own dedicated study.[51]

Charisma, Charity, and Religious Authority

A key part of both the methodology and the argument driving *The Lay Saint* depends upon chronological development. In the seven chapters that follow I trace the development of a series of lay saints' cults from the late twelfth through the first half of the fourteenth centuries. In Part One, I begin by showing how the laity's embrace of the *vita apostolica* movement produced in twelfth-century lay saints' cults the idea of the charismatic layperson: someone whose penitential commitment endowed them with the power to perform living miracles that could cure both individuals and institutions. I argue that the papacy's initial response to such claims of extraordinary lay religious charisma and power aimed to change what it meant to live an ideal lay life: to be a lay saint no longer meant to perform healing or institution-changing miracles, but rather to be dedicated to prayer, delivering charity, and fighting heresy. In the rich political context of the rising *popolo* communes, however, the definition of an ideal lay life transformed further. As lay sanctity became a political tool for communal governments, more radical understandings of a holy lay life resurfaced. I contend that as *popolo*-dominated communes spread across northern and central Italy, the idea of a contemporary lay saint as living miracle worker resurfaced. However, the

---

50. For example, see Jacques Dalarun, "Angèle de Foligno a-t-elle existé?" in *"Alla signorina": Mélanges offerts à Noëlle de La Blanchardière* (Rome: École Française de Rome), 59–97; Giulia Barone and Jacques Dalarun, eds., *Angèle de Foligno: Le dossier* (Rome: École Française de Rome, 1999); Catherine M. Mooney, "The Changing Fortunes of Angela of Foligno, Daughter, Mother, and Wife," in *History in the Comic Mode: Medieval Communities and the Matter of Person*, ed. Rachel Fulton and Bruce W. Holsinger (New York: Columbia University Press, 2007), 56–67.

51. David Burr provides a summary of this work in *The Spiritual Franciscans: From Protest to Persecution in the Century after Saint Francis* (University Park: Pennsylvania State University Press, 2001), 334–44.

miracles described in these mid to late thirteenth-century cults ultimately expressed a conservative understanding of the power of lay religion. In a communal context, a lay saint's miracles alleviated unequal aspects of society and reinforced emerging notions of the good urban citizen without demanding, or even implying, that such inequities should be toppled or should not exist in the first place.

In Part Two, I posit that even though the papacy's and the communes' responses to and manipulation of cults celebrating contemporary male lay saints present one thread of the history of lay sanctity, women's appearance in this phenomenon makes up another. I argue that women's involvement in the *vita apostolica* and lay penitential movements posed a double threat both to the medieval church and to society more broadly; although a lay saint's charismatic activity already had the potential to threaten the authority and power of the institutional church, a woman living an uncloistered and unaffiliated lay religious life threatened medieval gender norms. I show how, in the first half of the thirteenth century, laywomen received cults only if their hagiographers mitigated their lay status and their charismatic authority (most often by emphasizing the connections, however loose, these women had to established religious orders and male religious authorities). By the second half of the century, however, this arrangement broke down.

I demonstrate in Part Three that as the mendicants were increasingly pushed into a position of guardianship over not just lay penitents but specifically female lay penitents, new lay religious ideals emerged. Just as I argue that Innocent's motivation in canonizing Omobono of Cremona was to limit and ultimately reconfigure claims of lay religious charisma, I see a similar impetus behind the mendicants' promotion of laywomen's cults. By the late thirteenth century, to earn a cult as a laywoman meant to be a visionary above all else. While laymen's cults continued to emphasize a civically engaged lay religious ideal, the many cults dedicated to women in this era valorized the model of an internal life of compunction and visions over an external life of charity and charismatic healing. And even though a changing political context in the communes was partially responsible for the apparent disappearance of the contemporary lay saint over the fourteenth century, a more persuasive explanation can be found, I contend, in the ways in which these new lay religious ideals paved the way for the institutional creation of the mendicant third orders. By the middle of the fourteenth century, to live an ideal lay life meant to be a lay member of an established religious order. The category of the lay religious had essentially disappeared.

The combination of the laity's embrace of the *vita apostolica* and the saintly cults that emerged to celebrate extraordinary examples of that embrace raised a troubling question for the medieval church. What happens when an institution's hierarchy is inverted; when those people the institution claims to have authority over assert a power and charisma that have the potential to render that institution moot? Neither simply representative of the intensity of lay devotion nor a result of the church's recognition of that fervor, the rise of the contemporary lay civic saint in communal Italy illustrates both the risk and potential the lay penitential movement posed. Even though Ranieri of Pisa's cathedral font might celebrate a layman blessing a cleric, over the thirteenth and early fourteenth centuries church and communal authorities found the means of reimagining an ideal lay religious life. And although that reimagining would take many different forms in response to an ever-changing religious and political context, always at its core was the desire to contain and control claims of lay religious power and lay religious charisma. Because, if an extraordinary commitment to a life of penance could render a layperson holy and give him or her the ability to effect miraculous change through touch, then, we can imagine, church authorities might have asked themselves: what use are we?

PART ONE

Creating a Lay Ideal

CHAPTER 1

From Charisma to Charity

Lay Sanctity in the Twelfth-Century Communes

Sometime in the late eleventh century, Gualfardo, an Augsburg merchant, came to Verona on business, remained in the city and its surrounding countryside for the next thirty years, and upon his death was celebrated as one of that northern Italian city's patron saints. Our knowledge of the layman comes from a *vita* that was likely written within a decade of his 1127 death.[1] That *vita* describes how after resolving to remain in Verona to live a pious life and give his earnings to the poor and sick, Gualfardo spent the next twenty years living as a hermit in the forest that surrounded the city.[2] A group of sailors eventually found the former merchant on the banks of the Adige River and convinced him to return to his adopted city. Gualfardo's final ten years were spent as an ascetic in a cell within the Church of San Salvar, providing the Veronese with miraculous cures. Those cures seem to have most often been wrought through contact with Gualfardo's hands. When Gualfardo waved his hands over the afflicted body parts of the lame, crippled, and blind, they were healed. And when the sick were washed with water the saint had used to wash his hands, their

---

1. *Vita S. Gualfardi solitarii, Acta Sanctorum quotquot Toto Orbe Coluntur . . . Editio nova*, ed. Jean Bolland et al. (Paris: Palmé, etc., 1863–), April III, 827–32 (hereafter *AASS*). For more on Gualfardo, see Vauchez, "A Twelfth-Century Novelty," 54; and Maureen C. Miller, *The Formation of a Medieval Church: Ecclesiastical Change in Verona, 950–1150* (Ithaca, NY: Cornell University Press, 1993), 79–80.

2. *Vita S. Gualfardi solitarii*, 828.

illnesses disappeared. Gualfardo's hands were so integral to his burgeoning saintly reputation that once, when he returned to the Adige River after his move back to Verona's city center, the river's fish greeted him by licking his hands.[3]

At around the same time that Gualfardo was curing his fellow Veronese and being welcomed by its fish, another northern Italian layman, Allucio of Pescia (sometimes called Allucio of Campilgiano), was also gaining a following for his miraculous facility with the natural world. Allucio, his twelfth-century *vita* reports, spent his youth working as a shepherd. One day, in the midst of a menacing storm, he sheltered a herd of heifers. In thanks for his service to them, the animals encircled him, protecting him until his family found him, dry and free from injury, the next day.[4]

In addition to celebrating his special capacity with animals, Allucio's *vita* also pays particular attention to the saint's charitable efforts, describing the many hospices and churches he founded, the hungry he fed, and the sick and lame he cured. The accounts of such work emphasize how Allucio's charity responded to an imbalanced social order. The reader is told that Allucio had once urged the bishop of Florence to build a bridge in Pescia across the Arno River after he had discovered that a group of nobles were profiting from the lack of a crossing. Moreover, when a hungry mother approached Allucio and asked him to "hold the hand of compassion" over her and her sons, the *vita* describes how he led the woman to a mill so that he could ask the miller if he would help feed her. When the miller replied that he had hardly any bread except for a bit of millet, Allucio encouraged the man to "give according to what you have," for, as he noted, "God pays in return for all good things" and is "able to multiply our provisions." When the miller returned to his chest and discovered it to be full with bread, "he rendered great thanks to God, increased his faith . . . and paid it more generously to the paupers."[5]

Both Allucio's and Gualfardo's *vitae* make clear that it was these laymen's extraordinary dedication to a penitential life—living with the fewest possessions possible, following a rigorous routine of prayer, and dedicating their lives to helping others—that earned them a saintly status. Their *vitae* see evidence of that status in the laymen's ability to perform miracles during their lifetimes—

---

3. Ibid., 829.

4. Allucio's *vita* survives in a fourteenth-century manuscript written on the occasion of the 1344 translation of his relics. Réginald Grégoire has argued that the *vita* was most likely first written in 1182 around the time of the first translation of Allucio's remains; see "Temi tipologici della vita di Sant'Allucio (†1134)," in *Un santo laico dell'età postgregoriana: Allucio da Pescia (1070 ca.–1134): Religione e società nei territori di Lucca e della Valdinievole*, ed. C. Violante (Rome: Jouvence, 1991), 15–54. For Allucio's *vita*, see *Un santo laico*, 20–27.

5. *Un santo laico*, 22.

they heal the sick with their hands, and multiply food supplies to feed the hungry. But Gualfardo's and Allucio's cults were far from the only lay civic cults that were appearing across northern and central Italy during the twelfth and thirteenth centuries. André Vauchez has argued that the veneration of laymen like Allucio and Gualfardo served not only as evidence of the growing importance the laity played in late medieval religious life but also of the way in which lay religious activity in this period emphasized asceticism, pilgrimage, and charitable activities.[6]

And yet, while Gualfardo's initial pilgrimage to Verona, and both men's adherence to a life of penance and charity appear to be evidence of Vauchez's threefold emphasis (asceticism, pilgrimage, and charity), when we look more closely at these laymen's connection to the natural world and the miracles they performed, we see that they are primarily being celebrated for their charisma—the spiritual gifts that their extraordinary commitment to a penitential life allowed them to exhibit. In short, instead of drawing attention to their pious deeds (asceticism, pilgrimage, and charity)—and seeing those acts as the ultimate evidence of saintliness—these *vitae* present the laymen's virtuous exploits as the steps necessary to produce the ultimate evidence of holiness: the ability to effect miraculous change.

In this chapter, I shall focus on another twelfth-century Italian urban lay saint, the merchant turned penitent, Ranieri of Pisa (d. 1160). It is within the first written and visual sources created to celebrate Ranieri that we find the most extensive evidence of a twelfth-century layman being celebrated more for his work as a living holy man than for his pious activities. In short, in the earliest cults of laymen in the Italian communes it is spiritual gifts or charisma, specifically the performance of miracles, and not pious actions like a dedication to penance, a rigorous prayer schedule, or charity work that stand as the most compelling proof for sanctity.[7] The first sources created for Ranieri's cult give us an opportunity to see not only a detailed portrait of this kind of lay charisma but also how threatening such claims must have been to the institutional church in the late twelfth century. By making an explicit connection between a layman's extraordinary embrace of a penitential life and his ability to function as a new manifestation of Christ, Ranieri's *vita* presents a powerful argument about the effects of lay sanctity. Ranieri's penance brings about local as well as global change: it grants him spiritual gifts that allow him to heal both his city and his church.

---

6. In addition to noting lay saints' shared social background, Vauchez also points to the important role the secular clergy played as the first patrons of these cults; see his "A Twelfth-Century Novelty."

7. I am referring to Paul's definition of charisma—"a manifestation of the Spirit"—found in 1 Cor. 12:4–10.

Although asceticism, pilgrimage, and charity would become defining characteristics of late medieval lay religion and would eventually come to dominate the cults of thirteenth- and fourteenth-century lay saints, Ranieri's early cult demonstrates how such a threefold identity was not emphasized in early lay saints' cults but rather emerged out of Pope Innocent III's efforts to redirect and reconceive of an ideal lay life. In *Quia pietas*, his 1199 bull of canonization for the merchant Omobono of Cremona (d. 1197), Innocent makes clear that a rigorous dedication to penance does not endow a layman with spiritual gifts. In Innocent's portrait, a layman's penance does not give him the power to heal with his touch, let alone reform the church. Instead, penance is one of a number of pious acts, along with prayer, charity work, and the fight against heresy that the lay saint executes in an exemplary manner. Far from performing the charismatic acts of a living holy man, in the papacy's eyes, the lay saint attends to the spiritual and physical failings of his fellow lay population largely by demonstrating his piety and obedience to the institutional church.

Radical Reform: Ranieri of Pisa

The earliest evidence we have for a cult dedicated to Ranieri of Pisa is a *vita* and miracle collection, both likely written within a year of his death in 1160. The author of these texts was one of the saint's disciples, Benincasa, who also served as the guardian of Ranieri's tomb in Pisa's cathedral and may have been a canon there as well.[8] Relying upon events he witnessed as well as conversa-

---

8. For an introduction to Ranieri and his Pisan cult, see *Intercessor Rainerius ad patrem: Il Santo di una città marinara del XII secolo*, ed. Patrizia Castelli and Maria Luisa Ceccarelli Lemut (Pacini: Pisa, 2011), and *L'Invenzione di Ranieri il taumaturgo tra XII e XIV secolo: Agiografia ed immagini*, ed. Patrizia Castelli and Maria Luisa Ceccarelli Lemut (Pacini: Pisa, 2013). Ranieri's *vita* survives in two medieval manuscripts that scholars agree were both of Pisan origin but written independently of each other—one at the beginning of the thirteenth century (the Livorno copy), and the other in the mid-fourteenth century (the Pisa copy). The *vitae* in these manuscripts are largely the same, suggesting that they were copied from a common source. However, the manuscripts differ most noticeably in their miracle collections. While the later Pisan copy disperses a number of accounts of miracles Ranieri performed during his lifetime throughout the *vita*, the earlier Livorno copy places all of its accounts of living as well as postmortem miracles after a description of the saint's burial. The Livorno manuscript was discovered and edited by Réginald Grégoire in the 1980s: *San Ranieri di Pisa (1117–1160) in un ritratto agiografico inedito del secolo XIII* (Pisa: Pacini, 1990) (hereafter *Vita sancti Ranierii*). Both Grégoire and Lily Richards have argued that the Pisan manuscript is part of a second stage of the saint's cult in the early fourteenth century; see Grégoire, *San Ranieri di Pisa*, 38; and Richards, "San Ranieri of Pisa: A Civic Cult and Its Expression in Text and Image," in *Art, Politics, and Civic Religion in Central Italy*, ed. Cannon and Williamson, 179–219. Gabriele Zaccagnini has produced the most thorough account of the issues regarding Ranieri's *vita*; see *La "vita" di san Ranieri (secolo XII): Analisi storica, agiografica e filologica del testo di Benincasa: Edizione critica dal codice C181*

tions he had with Ranieri, Benincasa traces the stages of the layman's saintly life from his youth as the son of Pisan nobles and work as a merchant, to his first attempts at adopting a penitential life and eventual moment of conversion while on a business venture to the Holy Land. Finally, Benincasa recounts the many miracles Ranieri performed once he returned to Pisa as well as those that took place at his tomb after his death.[9]

The *vita* tells us that Ranieri's penitential transformation was sparked by meeting Alberto of Corsica, another Pisan layman, who, after the death of his brother, had given all of his possessions to the poor and lived as a hermit at the church of San Vito in Pisa. Moved by Alberto's example, Ranieri began to follow a rigorous schedule of prayer as well as of fasting, and eventually joined Alberto at San Vito, where we can assume (although Benincasa does not identify him as such) they lived as lay brothers (often called *conversi*).[10] Benincasa makes clear that even though he had taken up a life of penance, Ranieri continued to work as a merchant. However, that professional life came to an end after a particularly eventful trip to the Holy Land. Benincasa writes that during a Good Friday service in the Church of the Holy Sepulchre, Ranieri received a vision of the Virgin Mary, which spurred him to strip off his clothes and replace them with what the text describes as a *pilurica*, likely some kind of hermit's garb.[11] For the next seven years, Ranieri remained in Jerusalem, living as a dedicated penitent and hermit, experiencing frequent visions of the Virgin as well as of Christ.

Penance plays a crucial role as well in Ranieri's religious life after his conversion. Benincasa dedicates much of the first half of the *vita* to descriptions of the seven years of rigorous penance Ranieri performed in Jerusalem. Benincasa argues that such penitential work allowed Ranieri to become a new

---

dell'Archivio Capitolare di Pisa (Pisa: Gisem, 2008). Colin Morris, who provides a useful discussion of the manuscript history of Ranieri's *vita*, disagrees, arguing that the two manuscripts are essentially two editions of the same *vita*, and only differ in how they have edited and incorporated miracle stories from the original (and no longer extant) account of miracles; see Colin Morris, "San Ranieri of Pisa: The Power and Limitations of Sanctity in Twelfth-Century Italy," *Journal of Ecclesiastical History* 45 (1994): 599. It is not clear if this Benincasa was the same canon Benincasa who was the imperialist replacement to Archbishop Villano between 1167 and 1170; see Grégoire, *San Ranieri di Pisa*, 97; and Morris, "San Ranieri of Pisa," 589.

    9. Grégoire lists all of the references Benincasa makes to his interactions with Ranieri; *San Ranieri di Pisa*, 89–91.

    10. On *conversi*, see Osheim, "Conversion, *Conversi*."

    11. *Vita sancti Ranierii*, 120–21. Grégoire notes that this garment serves as a distinctive element for Ranieri's iconography and suggests the Italian *pelosa* (hairy) as one way of reading *pilurica*; moreover, he notes that Niermeyer identifies it as a twelfth-century term for a mantle: see J. F. Niermeyer, *Mediae latinitatis lexicon minus* (Leiden: Brill, 2002), 946. In later depictions of Ranieri, the saint's *pilurica* is depicted as a full-length hair shirt; see George Kaftal, *Iconography of the Saints in Tuscan Painting* (Florence, Sansoni, 1952).

manifestation of Christ. Thus, when Ranieri donned the hermit's *pilurica* in front of the congregation of the Church of the Holy Sepulchre, Benincasa points out to his reader that a priest had announced that "God was stripped on Calvary, and is now stripped in the Temple for the salvation of the Christian people . . . without doubt he is in this temple."[12] Moreover, Benincasa notes how once when Ranieri was attending a Christmas sermon at Tyre, the bishop of Sidon had announced to an audience that God was "now among us and has put on the flesh of one of you, for the salvation of all Christians." He added, in case his readers had missed the point, that at that moment all eyes had fallen on Ranieri.[13]

Thus, Ranieri's rigorous dedication to penance not only makes him a new manifestation of Christ but also, as he is often called in Benincasa's text, a *habitaculum*, or dwelling-place of God; a role that allows Ranieri to be a healing balm for a compromised institutional church.[14] The reader is made aware of the church's deficiencies when Benincasa writes that during the saint's seven years in Jerusalem, God had announced that He had "given over the priests into the hands of Satan."[15] Horrified by the words coming out of his mouth (as he was relating what God had said to him), Ranieri became reassured when God informed him that it would be through this layman's efforts that all Christians would be set free.[16] As Benincasa's *vita* notes, it was through the saint's penitential acts, his great mortification of the flesh, that he had earned a "royal

---

12. *Vita sancti Ranierii*, 127: "Audite audite, fratres mei, obsecro, fratres audite: rem magnam et inauditam tempore isto, uobis qui huc conuenistis refero. Quam quia uobis referre nolebam, iterum uox nominatim me uocans terruit. Cumque adhuc reluctarer, mortis minas interminans, uice tertia me resurgere coegit: Perge, et dic populo quia Deus in caluaria expoliatus est, et est nunc expoliatus in templo pro saluando christiano populo. Querite ergo, fratres, ad inuicem, quia procul dubio est in templo isto."

13. *Vita sancti Ranierii*, 123–24: "Sidonis episcope uice archiepiscopi illius qui tunc Romam abierat missam canentem lectoque euangelio predicto episcopo pulpitum seu anbonem ascendentem, ita ad populum, multis aliis ibi existentibus pisanis, fari exorsus est: 'Audite fratres karissimi, in ueritate sciatis, quia inter nos nunc Deus est qui unius uestrum carnem induit, pro omnibus christianis saluandis.' Et uerbum iterans pluries dixit. Nostri omnes qui aderant presentes, de tam altissimo uerbo ceperunt obnixe mirari. Alterutrum sese respicientes, oculos tamen propensius ad beatum / Rainerium uertebant."

14. For example, see *Vita sancti Ranierii*, 105: "Cumque ab eo exigerem ut congruam pro meis peccatis iniungeret satisfationem, quia audierat a verbo Domini peccatum sibi patefactum, respondit: Deus in te frater suum habitaculum permundabit, non tibi iniungo aliquid: quidquid boni feceris, erit tibi pro satisfatione et ad meritum eterne vite."

15. *Vita sancti Ranierii*, 148: "Dum in Domini sepulcro, pro ecclesia et sacerdotibus quodam tempore Deum obnixe precaretur, ut lux fulgeret populi, confenstim uerbum Domini per os eius respondit ei: 'Ego sacerdotes in manu Sathane tradidi.'"

16. *Vita sancti Ranierii*, 148: "Respondit . . . 'Surge et noli sicut mortuus esse, quia non ideo te feci, et pre aliis te elegi. Incipe iam nunc penitentiam pro populo agere. Panem opirum et aquam, in cibo tuo tantum habe: pro populo ipso sine interpellatione exora me, usque dum tecum illuc ueniam, ubi populum meum christianum liberabo per te.'"

priesthood," an honor that would ultimately allow him to cure the ills of the church.[17]

Scholars have paid particular attention to what Vauchez describes as a strong "reformist current" running through this *vita*.[18] After all, Ranieri not only points to some of the clergy's deficiencies but also advocates for laymen's right to preach. As Colin Morris has pointed out, if, according to Benincasa, Ranieri is the manifestation of Christ on earth and his penitential practices in Jerusalem function to redeem a corrupt church, this layman commands a vital role in God's providential plan.[19] And yet, scholars have also concluded that although Ranieri's *vita* seems to criticize the church, the text ultimately does not wage a radical attack on either the priesthood or the church.[20] God's assurance that all Christians would be released from Satan's grip through the saint's efforts, as well as the notion that the saint's penance had made satisfaction for all Christians essentially mollifies any call for radical reform.[21] Moreover, Morris has noted that the fact that Ranieri's cult remained a local, instead of a universal phenomenon also checks any potentially radical messages. To support his argument, Morris points to the striking similarities between the delicate balance of criticism and sanction of the church that Benincasa ascribes to Ranieri's religious life and the descriptions Francis of Assisi offered of his mission nearly sixty years later.[22] Even though both saints emphasized their special vocation from God to repair, but not dismantle, the present-day church, claimed universal ministries, and were presented as second Christs, the most significant disparity

---

17. *Vita sancti Ranierii*, 141: "Et est sacerdos mortificatione carnis. Unde beatus apostolus ait: Obsecro uos per misericordiam Dei, ut exibeatis corpora uestra, hostiam uiuentem, sanctam, Deo placentem. Quicumque Deo hostiam offert, sacerdos est secundum hunc modum, et bone mulieres corpora sua crucifigentes, sacerdotis nomine censentur. Unde et Petrus ait: Uos estis ergo genus electum, regale sacerdotium. Ideo mulieres et uiri crismate fronte et uertice unguntur, ut aduersus diabolum simus reges et sacerdotes pugnantes semper, et orantes. Et Ioannes in Apocalipsi sua: Et fecit nos Deo nostro regnum, et sacerdotes." Vauchez points to this particular claim in Ranieri's *vita*; see *The Laity*, 63. Thompson, however, has cautioned modern readers not to see in this passage an assertion of a quasi-clerical status for Ranieri. Benincasa was arguing that Ranieri had earned an "intensification" of the grace originally received through baptismal and confirmation anointing, something that, as Benincasa adds, was also available to women, who had crucified Christ in their bodies; *Cities of God*, 186.

18. Vauchez, *The Laity*, 63.

19. Morris, "San Ranieri of Pisa," 593–94.

20. Something that Vauchez notes various heretical sects were doing in the mid-twelfth century; see *The Laity*, 63; also see, Morris, "San Ranieri of Pisa," 594.

21. Vauchez, *The Laity*, 63. If the *vita* is a call for reform, Vauchez reasons, it is only a qualified one: while the clergy might be in the hands of Satan, the pious behavior of one layman has the potential to restore priests, leaving no need for the overthrow of the institutional church.

22. Morris, "San Ranieri of Pisa," 594–95.

between the two was their patrons.[23] Although Francis found support in the Roman curia and gained an international reputation, Ranieri's cult would be forever limited by its resolutely Pisan identity.[24]

The impulse to compare these two laymen as well as to see Francis as the more successful "lay" saint is hard to resist. Nevertheless, such an approach asks us to read history backwards. No other (non-royal) contemporary layman had earned an international saintly reputation before Francis. To assess Ranieri as a less successful version of what was to come obscures the way in which the claims made in Ranieri's cult cut a path that allowed for Francis's dramatic accomplishments. Even though Ranieri's *vita* may not call for the overthrow of the institutional church, the religious authority it ascribes to a pious layman puts forward a powerful argument for the potential, both on a universal and local level, of the lay religious life. As his *vita* argues, Ranieri's extraordinary commitment to penance allowed him to transcend his status. It had earned him a "royal priesthood," that not only rescued corrupt priests but, as the second half of the *vita* makes clear, also cured the ills of Pisa.

Benincasa's *vita* describes how, once back in Pisa, Ranieri spent the remainder of his life crisscrossing the city with a group of disciples, serving the poor and performing numerous miracles to heal the sick. A number of factors seem to have motivated Ranieri's return home. First, the Virgin again appeared to him in Jerusalem, this time to announce that the saint's final resting place would be within her church in the city.[25] Second, Ranieri had also recently learned that another Pisan had been made pope (Eugenius III).[26] But it is Ranieri's own penitential work that seems most instrumental in bringing him back to Pisa. Benincasa writes that Ranieri's understanding (via a divine vision) that the penances he had performed over the past seven years had "satisfied me [God] for my Christian people," was crucial in motivating him to leave Jerusalem.[27] As Benincasa adds, this was the life God had always intended for Ranieri: while still in Jerusalem, God had told Ranieri that although he knew that the layman longed to lay his hands on the sick to cure

---

23. As Morris points out, the first few lines of Benincasa's dedication have much in common with Francis's letter "to all Christians, religious, clerks and laity, men and women, all who live in the whole world." See Morris, "San Ranieri of Pisa," 594; and *Vita sancti Ranierii*, 101.

24. Although Ranieri's cult is still present in Pisa, I have found no indication that it spread beyond the city either during the Middle Ages or afterwards. Morris also notes the particularly local nature of this cult; see Morris, "San Ranieri of Pisa," 590 and 595.

25. *Vita sancti Ranierii*, 124–25.

26. Ibid., 153–54.

27. Ibid., 150: "Septem uero completis annis, ita ei Deus de hac penitentia dixit: 'Ecce pro populo meo christiano michi satisfecisti.'"

them, in this land (that is, in Jerusalem), such an honor was reserved for Mary. But, as God went on to reassure Ranieri, he would lead him "to where by your ministry I shall cure many sick."[28] Benincasa points to how such work earned Ranieri a substantial following. The *vita* ends with a description of the large procession of both clerics and lay people that followed the saint's body into Pisa's cathedral, where it was displayed for several days before being placed in a tomb that had been paid for by the city's consuls.[29]

Thus, Benincasa crafts a portrait of Ranieri's sanctity that has both an expansive and more limited significance. His ability to function as a civic holy man, healing his fellow Pisans with his hands, came from the penance he performed in Jerusalem, where his seven-year diet of bread and water gave him the power to right the wrongs of the church. In fact, bread and water connect Ranieri's experiences in the Holy Land with his actions at home. After using bread and water in Jerusalem to prove the rigor of his penitential commitment, in Pisa they are the currency through which the saint brought about cures on an individual basis.[30] The *vita* describes story after story of Ranieri blessing bread and water that exorcises and heals his fellow Pisans: possessed boys, epileptic priests, and a man suffering from pleurisy are all cured through the bread and water Ranieri has blessed.[31]

Bread and water are also key in Ranieri's posthumous cult.[32] As Ranieri's body was placed in his tomb, devotees not only scrambled to grab a piece of his *pilurica* or hermit's garb but also placed bread in his hands so it might receive his divine blessing.[33] Moreover, the *vita* describes numerous times when the saint's devotees arrived at his cathedral tomb with the bread and water they believed would bring about the healings and cures they sought; a fourteenth-century copy of the *vita* contains a formula for blessing the bread and water left at Ranieri's tomb.[34] And finally, throughout the *vita* Benincasa refers to the saint as *Raynerius ex Aqua*. While the *ex Aqua* may very well denote that Ranieri's

28. Ibid., 152: "Uoluit Ierosolimis sanctus Raynerius quibusdam infirmantibus ut curarentur, manus inponere; sed prohibuit eum Deus, dicens illi: 'Uide ne feceris quia hunc ego in terris istis honorem tantum mee matri seruaui et donaui. Ego te ducam illuc ubi tuo ministerio multos habentes sum curaturus.' Quod et hodie in infinitis inpleri absque ulla anbiguitate cognouimus."

29. Ibid., 173–77. Unfortunately, Ranieri's first tomb no longer survives. A second tomb, most likely the work of Tino di Camaino, is now in the Museo dell'Opera del Duomo in Pisa. For more on this monument, see G. Bardotti Biasion, "Gano di Fazio e la tomba-altare di Santa Margherita da Cortona," *Prospettiva* 37 (1984): 2–19.

30. *Vita sancti Ranierii*, 148.

31. Ibid., 180, 181, and 185–86.

32. Morris has also noted how bread and water figure in both Ranieri's living and posthumous miracles; see "San Ranieri of Pisa," 596.

33. *Vita sancti Ranierii*, 175.

34. Morris "San Ranieri of Pisa," 596, n. 25.

family came from somewhere within the Pisan *contado* (a commune's subject countryside) along the Arno River, it could also reflect the many miracles involving water that took place at the saint's tomb.[35]

Thus, at the same time that Benincasa argues that a layman's penance of subsisting on bread and water restores the church, he also makes clear that, within Ranieri's own city, bread and water function as the prime conduit for this saint's sanctity, allowing him to effect healing miracles both while alive and posthumously. From this perspective, the resolutely local identity of Ranieri's cult takes on a new significance. Instead of being something that limits this layman's saintly reputation, Benincasa's text essentially argues that it is precisely within a local context that a layman's spiritual gifts or charisma is manifested. At the same time that Ranieri's penitential diet in Jerusalem allowed him to serve more globally as another Christ and fix the ills of the church, in Pisa, those materials are the means for him to cure Pisans' physical ills. The local identity of Ranieri's cult is therefore dependent upon and connected to its global significance.

The *vita*'s emphasis upon Ranieri's ability to redeem a corrupt clergy and perform blessings upon bread and water also endows this layman with an authority that appears priestly. The text's emphatic note that it was through his physical penance that Ranieri had earned a "royal priesthood" makes the argument explicit.[36] The priestly dimension of Ranieri's cult is also present in the depictions of the saint found on a sculpted font that scholars believe was once placed near his first cathedral tomb. Created likely within a year of Ranieri's 1160 death by a follower of Guglielmus, the sculptor credited with much of the stonework inside Pisa's cathedral, the font portrays Ranieri twice, both times extending his hand to bless a devotee.[37] On one side, Ranieri blesses a woman (figure 1), while on the opposite side he blesses a cleric (figure 2). Behind the woman and cleric stand three men, all of whom carry objects: a vase (figure 3), a bowl (perhaps to hold bread), and a rod decorated with a fleuron.

As I have already noted, we can presume that the font would have held water made holy through the blessings of cathedral priests. Thus, just as Benincasa had reported that a layman's experience in Jerusalem had redeemed and made satisfaction to God for a corrupt clergy, the font shows Ranieri again upending church hierarchy. A miracle story found in Ranieri's *vita*

---

35. Grégoire, *San Ranieri di Pisa*, 58–59.

36. Thompson argues that this does not connote a "quasi-clerical" status but rather "an intensification of . . . the grace of his baptismal and confirmation anointings." See *Cities of God*, 186. I see Benincasa playing more explicitly with the idea that Ranieri's extraordinary penitential activity has allowed him to move beyond his lay status.

37. On this font, see Bonnie Young, "A Saint on a Holy-Water Font," *Metropolitan Museum of Art Bulletin* (1965): 362–66.

FIGURE 1. Workshop of Master Guglielmus, "Holy-water Font" ("Ranieri Blessing Woman"), New York, The Cloisters Collection. © The Metropolitan Museum of Art. Image Source: Art Resource, NY.

makes explicit the anxiety such a reordering could engender. Before Ranieri cures the epileptic priest who has sought out the layman's miraculous cures, the saint asked the priest whether or not he believed that God had sent him to bring about this cure. Benincasa is careful to show that Ranieri only healed the priest once such an assurance has been given.[38]

Regardless of whether or not Ranieri's Pisan contemporaries were concerned about the nature of the religious claims being made in his cult, we can imagine that such assertions did alarm the papacy. After all, if one man's penitential commitment had the power not only to transform him into a holy man who could dole out cures for his urban neighbors but also to restore a corrupt clergy, what use was there for a church hierarchy in the first place? Such

---

38. *Vita sancti Ranierii*, 181.

FIGURE 2.   Workshop of Master Guglielmus, "Holy-water Font" ("Ranieri Blessing a Priest"), New York, The Cloisters Collection. © The Metropolitan Museum of Art. Image Source: Art Resource, NY.

aspects of lay sanctity that we find in Ranieri's cult are missing in the many thirteenth-century lay saints' cults that would emerge in communal Italy. Therefore, instead of categorizing Ranieri as a proto, but ultimately less successful, version of Francis, it makes more sense to ask why later cults did not award their protagonists the same kind of religious power and charisma that we see Benincasa give to Ranieri. By asking such questions we can begin to see the effect twelfth-century claims about the potential of an ideal lay life would ultimately have on conceptions of lay sanctity and lay religion in the later Middle Ages.

"A Lily among Thorns": The Canonization of Omobono of Cremona (d. 1197)

Within a generation of Ranieri's death, Omobono of Cremona, another merchant who had also adopted a rigorous religious life, was canonized by Rome. Pope Innocent III's bull of canonization, *Quia pietas*, issued on January 12, 1199,

FIGURE 3. Workshop of Master Guglielmus, "Holy-water Font" ("Devotee of Ranieri"), New York, The Cloisters Collection. © The Metropolitan Museum of Art. Image Source: Art Resource, NY.

less than two years after the saint's death, stands as one of the earliest attempts by the church to identify what constituted an ideal lay life.[39] Scholars have often interpreted Innocent III's decision to canonize Omobono—made quite early in his papacy—as a move aimed at assuaging factional violence as well

---

39. The bull is included in *Die Register Innocenz' III*, vol. 1, ed. O. Hageneder and A. Haidacher (Vienna: Böhlau, 1964), 528–30, 761–64. It is also included in Daniele Piazzi's collection of sources relating to Omobono: *Omobono di Cremona: Biografie dal XIII al XVI secolo: Edizione, traduzione e commento* (Cremona: Diocesi di Cremona, 1991), 14–19. For more on this bull, see Roberto Paciocco, "'Virtus morum' e 'virtus signorum': La teoria della santità nelle lettere di canonizzazione di Innocenzo III," *Nuova Rivista Storica* 70 (1986): 597–610. For how Innocent's canonization of Omobono illustrates the development of papal authority in late medieval saints' cults, see Vauchez, *Sainthood*, 36–37 and 112; André Vauchez, "La canonisation de Saint Homobon," in *Innocenzo III: Urbs et Orbis*, vol. 1, ed. Andrea Sommerlechner (Rome: Instituto Storico Italiano per il Medioevo, 2003), 435–55.

as stemming the tide of Cathar activity in Cremona.[40] Similar to his decisions to reintegrate the *Humiliati* into the church as well as to embrace Francis of Assisi and his Friars Minor, the canonization of Omobono has been seen as one of Innocent's many maneuvers to placate potentially hostile religious movements by bringing them under the patronage and, thus, the control of the church.[41]

Embedded within this scholarly assessment is an assumption that Omobono stands as an emblematic example of the lay religious life, or more specifically of the lay religious enthusiasm that was sweeping through late medieval cities; an example made all the more compelling by Innocent's legitimation. But missing from this response is a recognition of the extent to which Innocent's canonization bull for Omobono as well as the earliest life we have for the saint, *Cum orbita solis*, most likely written around 1200 by Cremona's bishop, Sicard, aim to prescribe rather than describe the content of an ideal lay life.[42] In both Innocent's bull and *Cum orbita solis*, an ideal lay life is no longer one in which a dedication to penance transforms a pious layman into a manifestation of Christ, able not only to right the wrongs of a compromised priesthood but also to take on priestly duties and dispense living miracles to heal his civic community. Rather, in these early sources describing Omobono, lay sanctity is defined above all by a dedication to prayer, peacemaking, charity work, and

---

40. See André Vauchez, *Omobono di Cremona (†1197): Laico e santo, profilo storico* (Cremona: Nuova Editrice Cremonese, 2001), 16–22; Webb, *Saints and Cities*, 46–47; and Diana Webb, "The Pope and the Cities: Heresy and Anticlericalism in Innocent III's Italy," in *The Church and Sovereignty c.590–1918: Essays in Honor of Michael Wilkes*, ed. Diana Wood (Oxford: Basil Blackwell, 1991), 135–52.

41. On Innocent and the *Humiliati*, see Frances Andrews, *The Early Humiliati* (Cambridge: Cambridge University Press, 1999); and Brenda Bolton, "Innocent III and the *Humiliati*," in *Innocent III: Vicar of Christ or Lord of the World?*, ed. James M. Powell (Washington, DC: Catholic University of America Press, 1994), 114–20.

42. Vauchez's work with the Omobono sources has been a guide for other scholars. His studies of both the development of the saint's civic cult in the thirteenth and fourteenth centuries and of the manuscript history of Omobono's three anonymous medieval *vitae* (*Cum orbita solis* ca. 1200, *Quoniam historiae* ca. 1240–1270, and *Labentibus annis* ca. 1270–1300) have largely set the terms for how modern scholars approach the saint. Vauchez's most thorough treatment can be found in *Omobono di Cremona (†1197)*; also see his "Le 'trafiquant céleste': Saint Homebon de Crémone (†1197), marchand et 'père des pauvres,'" in *Horizons marins, itinéraires spirituels (V*ᵉ *–XVIII*ᵉ*)*, ed. H. Dubois, J.-C. Hocquet, and A. Vauchez (Paris: Sorbonne, 1987), 115–22; and "Le culte de saint Homebon du XIIᵉ au XVIᵉ siècle: Intentions des promoteurs et modalités de sa reception," in *Il pubblico dei santi: Forme e livelli di ricezione dei messaggi agiografici*, ed. Paolo Golinelli (Rome: Viella, 2000), 129–39. Daniele Piazzi's collection of sources, *Omobono di Cremona*, has also proved vital for the study of the saint as well as the religious history of late medieval Cremona and it is upon his editions of the Latin texts regarding Omobono that I shall rely (hereafter *Cum orbita solis, Quoniam historiae, Labentibus annis*, and *Quia pietas*). Moreover, I have found Webb's translations of Innocent's bull, *Quia pietas*, and one of the later thirteenth-century *vitae*, *Labentibus annis*, as well as her thorough introduction to the manuscript history of all of the medieval *vitae* extremely helpful. I shall be relying upon her translations of those two sources in the discussion that follows; see Webb, *Saints and Cities*, 46–61.

the fight against heresy, activities that emphasize Omobono's obedience to the institutional church, the inherent sinful nature of lay life, and finally, the limits of lay religious enthusiasm.

Although Innocent addresses *Quia pietas* to the clergy and people of Cremona, he makes clear that this pious layman came to his attention not because of any popular outcry but rather because Cremona's religious authorities had alerted him to Omobono's activities and reputation. Innocent writes that he had first learned of Omobono from Cremona's bishop Sicard, who along with other religious men and "honorable persons of his diocese" had described to him the life and deeds as well as "the manner of dying of a certain blessed man, in name and in fact Omobono."[43] Sicard's own chronicle corroborates Innocent's claim: the bishop writes that he had traveled to Rome to seek and was granted canonization for this "most faithful and devout" man.[44]

Having established that his knowledge of Omobono came to him through the channels of a church hierarchy, Innocent dives into describing the saint's pious activities, giving no information about Omobono's social background, marital status, or trade—features of the layman's biography that would be added in *vitae* written for the saint in the late thirteenth century. Instead, Innocent organizes *Quia pietas* to highlight four aspects of Omobono's religious life: his dedication to following a rigorous schedule of prayer, his charity work, his efforts to promote civic peace, and finally, his work to fight heresy in Cremona. By pointing to a set of concrete activities that formed the foundation for Omobono's extraordinary piety, Innocent not only offers his audience a set of obtainable (and controllable) criteria for emulating such a life but also emphasizes the extent to which every aspect of this layman's piety recognized and reinforced obedience to the church.

That obedience was on full display when Omobono prayed in Cremona's churches. Innocent writes that Omobono was always "present at the office of matins," and frequented "the office of the mass and the other hours with the utmost devotion." This layman was so dedicated to his prayers, Innocent claims, that "whatever work he [Omobono] did, standing, sitting or lying down, his lips seemed to move continually in prayer."[45] Thus every action Omobono

---

43. Webb, *Saints and Cities*, 55; and *Quia pietas*, 16: "Sane veniens ad praesentiam nostram venerabilis frater noster Sicardus, episcopus vester, multis viris religiosis et aliis honestis personis de sua dioecesi comitatus, cuiusdam beati viri et re et nomine Homoboni vitam et actus necnon et modum transitus eius humiliter nobis aperuit, in quibus et sanctae ipsius degustavimus conversationis odorem Deumque mirabilem et omnia opera eius in fide cognovimus et praedicavimus gloriosa."

44. Sicard's chronicle can be found in *Monumenta Germaniae Historica, Scriptores*, vol. 31, ed. O. Holder-Egger (Hanover, 1903), 177; cited by Webb, *Saints and Cities*, 46.

45. Webb, *Saints and Cities*, 55; *Quia pietas*, 16: "adeo in lege Domini meditabatur die ac nocte, et ei serviens in timore et secundum prophetam media nocte surgens ad confitendum ei matutinis semper

performed, Innocent seems to argue, was done in the midst of praying. Omobono even dies mid-prayer: having risen early for matins, the saint "prostrated
himself in his accustomed manner in prayer before the Cross," and passed
away lying on the church's floor "while the angelic hymn was being sung."[46]
Innocent's characterization of this layman as a model member of the church
is clear: not only does Omobono assiduously maintain a rigorous schedule of
prayer but he also dies lying on the ground of a church, a dramatic gesture of
obedience and subservience.

Innocent also mentions that in addition to the information he had gleaned
from Sicard, his knowledge of both Omobono's life and miracles had been confirmed by the testimony of a Cremonese priest, Osbert, who had served as
Omobono's spiritual father and confessor for twenty years. Noting that Osbert had confirmed what others had said about "the obedience which he [Omo-
bono] showed in prayers, vigils and other fruits of penitence," Innocent
writes that Osbert had testified that Omobono had always done more than
"what was laid upon him."[47] Innocent uses Osbert's testimony to reinforce the
relationship constructed throughout the bull between Omobono's piety and
his obedience. Omobono is an ideal Christian because he is both compliant
and dutiful. And, as Innocent emphasizes in the bull, it is the layman's priest
who is there to confirm that the obedience Omobono showed "in prayers, vigils and other fruits of penitence," always having done more than what was
expected or "laid upon him," was what made him special.

This is the only time Innocent uses the word "penitence" in the bull, a word
that appears countless times in Ranieri's *vita*. In Innocent's hands, the word
seems to have a more circumscribed meaning than we saw it convey in Ran-

---

laudibus interesset. Missae quoque officium et alias horas cum summa devotione frequentans, ita as-
siduis orationibus insistebat, ut in certis horis aut incessanter oraret aut horas ipsas aliquando
praeveniret—nisi forte ipsum sollicitudo, quam super pace reformanda per civitatem tamquam pacifi-
cus vir gerebat, aut occasio eleemosynae pro pauperibus acquirendae seu alia iusta causa in aliis operibus misericordiae detineret—, qui nimirum ante crucem dominicam ex assuetudine se prosternens,
opus quodlibet faciendo, stando, sedendo, iacendo, ad orationem labia movere continue videbatur."

46. Webb, *Saints and Cities*, 55; *Quia pietas*, 16: "Deducto autem sic vitae sanctae curriculo, cum
ad matutinale officium, prout dictum est, in festivitate sancti Brictii surrexisset, circa Missae primor-
dia idem se ante crucem dominicam more solito in oratione prosternens, dum cantaretur hymnus
angelicus, beato fine quievit."

47. Webb, *Saints and Cities*, 56; *Quia pietas*, 18: "Fidem namque, quam super conversatione ipsius
absque figmento hypocrisis fraudolento divinum iudicium, ut dictum est, manifeste ostendere videbatur, per testimonium dilecti filii Osberti, presbyteri sancti Egidii Cremonensis, praesentis cum episcopo memorato, recepto ab eo firmavimus iuramento. Sub cuius obtestatione, videlicet iuramenti,
ipse, qui patrinus eius existens per viginti annos et amplius confessionem eius saepe receperat, quae
de illius sancti conversatione praemisimus, cum ipso episcopo et aliis supradictis iuratis similiter as-
seruit esse vera. Et de oboedientia, quam in orationibus, vigiliis et aliis paenitentiae fructibus, in qua
sibi ab eo imposita erat, plus iniuncto satisfaciens exhibebat, non reddidit certiores."

ieri's *vita*. Whereas Benincasa used both Ranieri's performance of penance and his status as a penitent to argue that Ranieri was a new manifestation of Christ, whose penitential extremes had earned him a spiritual charisma that could both restore a corrupt clergy and heal his civic community, for Innocent, penitence is a passive exercise: it is a byproduct of what Omobono does when he prays or holds vigils. While the bull repeatedly mentions how much Omobono prays, it never describes what kind of, if any, change those prayers brought about. Omobono's prayers do not transform him into a new manifestation of Christ, they do not right the wrongs of the church, and they do not bring about any miraculous cures. In short, they do not endow this layman with the kinds of spiritual gifts or charisma that we see Ranieri's penance having given him.

In marked contrast to the plethora of living miracles Benincasa describes Ranieri performing on behalf of his fellow Pisans, Innocent only credits Omobono with postmortem miracles. And instead of enumerating those miracles "one by one," Innocent writes that he is recounting only one, since it stood out for its "strengthening of the Catholic faith."[48] A possessed woman was brought to Omobono's tomb and left "freed by the merits of the saint."[49] Innocent prepares his reader for a focus on the saint's postmortem miracles by stating at the beginning of the bull that it takes both "works of piety in life and miracles after death" for someone to be designated a saint in "the Church Militant."[50] Although scholars have pointed to how this statement illuminates the measures Innocent was taking to standardize the canonization process as well as bring it fully under papal authority, his words also make clear the parameters he was setting for an ideal lay life.[51] An extraordinary layman like Omobono could prove himself through "works of piety," not healing miracles

---

48. Webb, *Saints and Cities*, 55; *Quia pietas*, 16: "Que vero, quot et quanta miracula fuerint subsecuta et quot advenientibus ad sepulcrum eius sanitatis beneficia sint impensa, cum longum sit enumerare per singula, unum inter cetera ad assertionem catholicae fidei duximus expressius adnotandum."

49. Webb, *Saints and Cities*, 55–56; *Quia pietas*, 16: "Cum enim quaedam daemoniaca mulier ad sepulchrum eius deducta fuisset, ne aliqua fraus lateret, eadem primo fuit aqua non benedicta respersa, qua se patienter aspergi permittens, aquam secundo respuit benedictam. Et ut res evidentiori experimento pateret, oblatam non consecratam absque aliqua praescentia sibi recipiens praesentatam, eucharistiam consecratam subsequenter abhorruit nec receipt: quae et meritis eiusdem sancti liberata recessit."

50. *Quia pietas*, 14: "opera scilicet pietatis in vita et miraculorum signa post mortem, ut quis reputetur sanctus in militanti ecclesia, requiruntur." On Innocent's introduction of the idea of the "interdependence of moral virtues in life, *virtus morum*, and supernatural phenomena occurring after death, *virtus signorum*, as a means of validating each other" (Bolton's words), see Brenda Bolton, "Signs, Wonders, Miracles: Supporting the Faith in Medieval Rome," in *Signs, Wonders, Miracles: Representations of Divine Power in the Life of the Church*, ed. Kate Cooper and Jeremy Gregory (Martlesham: Boydell & Brewer, 2005), 165.

51. For more on Innocent's transformation of canonization process, see Vauchez, *Sainthood*, 23–57.

as Benincasa described Ranieri having performed after returning to Pisa. In Innocent's estimation, therefore, a layman's ability to change matter, that is, to perform miracles, only takes place after death.[52] The pious layman remains charismatically passive during his lifetime; he prays and performs penance but neither of those actions makes him a catalyst for miraculous change.

It is in Innocent's description of Omobono's efforts to aid his fellow laymen, however, that we see this saint become a more active figure. If he was not praying, Innocent writes, Omobono was busy acquiring alms for the poor, giving them shelter in his own house, providing for their burials, and working for peace within Cremona.[53] In short, Omobono was constantly acting on behalf of his fellow layman. Omobono was particularly successful battling heretics in Cremona, Innocent writes, because he held himself "aloof from the society of worldly men," among whom he "bloomed like a lily among thorns."[54] Thus what makes Omobono special—what, in Innocent's estimation, marks him as exceptionally pious—was the way in which he kept himself distinct from other laymen. Embedded within this argument is the assumption that to be an ordinary layman or laywoman meant to be a "thorn."

The notion that the laity were flawed "thorns" also features prominently in Omobono's earliest *vita*, *Cum orbita solis*. Innocent's assertion in *Quia pietas* that Cremona's bishop, Sicard, traveled to Rome to plead Omobono's case has led scholars to wonder not only if *Cum orbita solis* was written by Sicard but also if it was presented to the pope as part of a plea for the layman's canonization.[55] Regardless of the circumstances of its creation, the text's liturgical form

---

52. Bolton has also noted how Innocent's "most skeptical statements were reserved for those miracles *in vita*, still occurring in his own day, which held such sway in popular religion and hagiography." See her "Signs, Wonders, Miracles," 164.

53. Webb, *Saints and Cities*, 55; *Quia pietas*, 16.

54. Webb, *Saints and Cities*, 55; *Quia pietas*, 16.

55. Sicard's episcopacy was marked by his commitment to promoting his city's saints; he translated two of the city's patrons, Saint Archelaus and Saint Himerius, into new cathedral shrines in 1196. On Sicard, see Leonard E. Boyle, "Sicardus of Cremona," in *New Catholic Encyclopedia*, vol. 8 (New York: McGraw-Hill, 1967), 190–91; and Webb, *Saints and Cities*, 46–47. Scholars base their conclusion on several factors: the fact that the text makes no mention of Omobono's canonization, its likely origin as a liturgical text (it is divided into nine readings, the first six devoted to Omobono's life and the last three to the miracles performed after his death), and finally the mention made by the anonymous author of a mid-thirteenth-century *vita* of Omobono that his new *vita* was meant to include information about the saint revealed during the canonization proceedings, which as a result did not make it into *Cum orbita solis*. Vauchez, *Omobono di Cremona (†1197)*, 26; and Piazzi, *Omobono di Cremona*, 27–28. For the mention of *Cum orbita solis* by the anonymous author of *Quoniam historiae*, see *Quoniam historiae*, 50. Vauchez's and Piazzi's argument has not been accepted without question, however. In the introductory remarks to her recent translation of the bull, Webb takes a more cautious approach, noting that there are details in *Quia pietas*—most notably the miracle of the possessed woman—that are not included in *Cum orbita solis* and thus must have come from another source. Webb wonders if *Cum orbita solis* was written (perhaps by Sicard) to mark the 1202 transla-

suggests that it was created by members of Cremona's religious authority with the intention of being read in that city's churches.[56] And like Innocent's bull, it emphasizes Omobono's dedication to performing prayer, penance, and charity as well as fighting heresy.

But unlike the bull, this first *vita* pays particular attention to Omobono's life as a merchant. In the first liturgical reading, we are told that the layman turned to blessed contemplation from a familiarity with a "perverse and miserable business."[57] In the third, the author notes that in his conversion to a life of penance, Omobono abandoned the commerce of this world and became a merchant of heaven.[58] And in the fifth reading, the author celebrates the saint's conversion using language that emphasizes the evil of Omobono's working past: "O theft, o blessed pillage! O commerce, o glorious violence! The blessed Omobono stole the kingdom of heaven through faith. He pillaged with penitence, he purchased with alms."[59] The *vita's* hostility exemplifies a lack of sympathy toward the work of merchants that was often seen in medieval religious texts.[60] Whether as an echo of or as a source for Innocent's bull, the author of *Cum orbita solis* also makes the point that Omobono is all the more remarkable for distinguishing himself from other members of the laity: Omobono has rejected his former working life to embrace a life of prayer, penance, and charity. He is saintly because, to borrow Innocent's words, he stood as a "lily among thorns," overcoming the inherent sinful nature of his life as a lay merchant.

Although we cannot definitively say whether or not Sicard wrote *Cum orbita solis*, both the fact that it was produced in Cremona during his episcopate and that he traveled to Rome to plead Omobono's case strongly suggests that he had some role in its creation. Sicard's motive for supporting Omobono might seem obvious: what bishop would not want one of his own canonized? Moreover, what bishop would not welcome the papacy's efforts to stamp out heresy through the celebration of a pious and institutionally obedient contemporary? I would suggest, however, that just as Innocent was probably spurred to support Omobono as a means of containing claims about lay religion that were being articulated in the twelfth century, Sicard's support of

---

tion of Omobono's body from his parish church (where he died) to the cathedral; see her *Saints and Cities*, 49.

56. Bolton discusses the liturgical form of this life in "Signs, Wonders, Miracles," 161–62.

57. *Cum orbita solis*, 30: "a contubernio perversae miseraeque negotiationis ad officium beatae contemplationis."

58. Ibid., 32.

59. Ibid., 34: "O furtum, o rapina beata! O commercium, o violentia gloriosa! Furatus est beatus Homobonus regnum caelorum per fidem, rapuit per paenitentiam, mercatus est per eleemosynam . . ."

60. Vauchez, *Omobono di Cremona (†1197)*, 28–29.

Omobono was also likely motivated by a desire to control another vocal lay movement in early thirteenth-century Cremona: the *popolo*.

In 1197, the same year that Omobono died, members of Cremona's *popolo* revolted against communal authorities and elected their own nominee for *podestà* (the chief magistrate of a commune).[61] Although the *popolo* would not assume full control of the commune until the late thirteenth century, this event marked the beginning of a violent struggle between its older elite population and its wealthiest merchants and artisans that would last throughout the century.[62] By 1229, the *popolo* had created a formal organization, the *Societas populi*. And in 1256 members of that society had not only begun to construct their own civic headquarters, the Palazzo Cittanova, but were also refusing to acknowledge the commune's jurisdiction.[63]

In 1210, Bishop Sicard had awarded a third of all the offices and honors of the commune to members of the *popolo*.[64] While scholars have traditionally seen this move by Sicard as a concession aimed at ending the violence and responding to the desire of members of the *popolo* (the *popolani*) for a voice in their communal government, John Koenig has proposed a different interpretation.[65] In his work on the rise of *popolo* governments in the northern communes, Koenig notes that Sicard's legislation actually weakened the *popolo* as a political movement. While Sicard's concessions gave the *popolani* a role in the communal government as a social class, they did not give it one as a political party. The bishop's provision called for a third of all communal seats to be filled by the people of the city but did not guarantee them to members of the *popolo*'s organized political party. Moreover, Sicard's legislation outlawed any political allegiances that were "against the commune."[66] As the only internal opposition to Cremona's civic government at this time, such a provision was clearly aimed at the *popolo*. Finally, Sicard's legislation also called for a massive increase in the power held by the *podestà*, effectively giving this one office control of the communal government. As Koenig reasons, if the *popo-*

61. For the history of this revolt, see U. Gualazzini, *Il "populus" di Cremona e l'autonomia del comune* (Bologna: Zanichelli, 1940).

62. From the 1230s on, members of Cremona's *popolo* refused to recognize the city's communal government and began to organize their own governmental bodies; see Barbara Sella, "Cremona," in *Medieval Italy: An Encyclopedia*, ed. Christopher Kleinhenz (New York, Routledge, 2004), vol. 1, 265; also see her doctoral dissertation, which gives a good introduction to Cremona's medieval history: "Piety and Poor Relief: Confraternities in Medieval Cremona, c.1334–1499" (PhD dissertation, University of Toronto, 1996).

63. Sella, "Cremona," 265.

64. Ibid; and Lauro Martines, *Power and Imagination: City-States in Renaissance Italy* (Baltimore: Johns Hopkins University Press, 1979), 47.

65. Koenig, "The Popolo of Northern Italy," 459.

66. Ibid., 460–61.

lani controlled only a third of the votes, the position of *podestà* was assured to remain in the hands of the city's noble families.[67]

Relying upon Koenig's interpretation of the sources, it is hard not to interpret Sicard's actions as ultimately aimed at preserving the civic power of the old aristocracy of Cremona. To what extent then did his promotion of Omobono serve the same ends? Did Sicard see the promotion of Omobono's cult as a means of exerting control over those who would have been its expected devotees: the *popolani*? The emphasis in both Innocent's bull and *Cum orbita solis* on Omobono's orthodoxy, his adherence to a rigorous prayer schedule and civic charity, and his need to give up his worldly business for a "heavenly commerce" shifts the notion of what a lay saint can do. In these sources, the power of a holy layman is limited to reforming himself and other members of the laity. Both sources celebrate Omobono's ability to transcend and transform the sin inherent in a worldly life. They do not award their protagonist spiritual gifts or charisma. In short, Omobono cannot bring about miraculous change through his own actions.

Moreover, both sources emphasize Omobono's role as an obedient layman. In addition to the explicit statements Innocent makes about the great obedience Omobono showed in his devotional life, *Cum orbita solis* makes a more subtle argument about lay obedience in a section devoted to miracles. Just as was true in *Quia pietas*, *Cum orbita solis* does not mention Omobono having performed living miracles. Instead it devotes several readings to describing all of the many kinds of illnesses and ailments that were cured through prayers to the saint after his death. But before listing these miracles performed in Omobono's name, the *vita* devotes an entire reading to a more general description of the nature of miracles.[68] In the seventh reading, after noting that in both the early and contemporary church it is God who performs miracles among the faithful, Sicard points out how easy it is for one to be duped by a false apostle or by fake righteousness.[69] He follows these points with a question: what could be more marvelous (*mirabilius*) than the transubstantiation of bread into flesh and wine into blood? This most miraculous of acts, he reminds his reader, is effected by a priest. Finally, Sicard writes, while at the end of the

---

67. Ibid.

68. Bolton has also discussed this reading on miracles, see her "Signs, Wonders, Miracles," 161–64.

69. *Cum orbita solis*, 36: "Mirabilis Deus, qui mirabiliter in cunctis operatur, mirabilius in his quae praeter naturae cursum eveniunt, ut fides sanctorum sit posteris in argumentum et vita recte vivendi conversationis exemplum corroborat ea miracula operibus, scilicet hominibus inusitatis, evenientibus non contra naturam, quae semper est oboediens Creatori suo, sed praeter naturam, cui in propriam non convenit taliter operari . . . Proinde in primordio nascentis Ecclesiae, ut fides nasceretur in eis, signa in fidelibus frequentabat Altissimus. Sed et nunc, canescente."

world "false Christs" will use "signs and wonders" to torment the elect, nothing remains ambiguous about one's sanctity when the Catholic faith and a virtuous life are strengthened by the subsequent performance of miracles.

Two points stand out from this reading. First, that, in addition to God, it is ordained members of the clergy who perform living miracles like the transubstantiation of the Eucharist. And second, that there is a particular order to how all others perform miracles: miracles come after, and thus corroborate, a saintly life. Sicard concludes the seventh reading by noting that since the virtuous aspects of Omobono's life had already been covered, he will move on to describing the miracles.[70] Thus, in this author's estimation, miracles are not themselves evidence of sanctity. Although false Christs and apostles might claim to perform miracles during their lifetimes, those outside of church offices only bring about miraculous change after their deaths.

Innocent's bull and Omobono's first *vita* therefore remove and reconceive some of the more radical claims made for a holy layman that we saw expressed in Ranieri's cult. In Innocent's hands, Omobono's piety neither rights the wrongs of a compromised church nor endows the layman with powers or abilities associated with priestly rather than lay status. Instead, the pope makes clear that an ideal layman is someone who overcomes the sinful nature of lay life and directs his power at aiding and healing his civic community. Moreover, both bull and *vita* also present Omobono as only having a posthumous power to effect miracles. Omobono does not lay his hands on his fellow Cremonesi, and he does not bless their bread or water. Unlike Ranieri, Omobono only cures from the tomb.

The sources for the beginnings of Omobono's cult show us the ultimately conservative interest that pope and bishop took in a lay penitent who had acquired a saintly reputation within his urban community. Just as modern scholars have long celebrated Innocent's reintegration of the *Humiliati* and his embrace of Francis of Assisi as agile and shrewd attempts to coopt the late medieval explosion of new religious movements that were often critical of the institutional church, his canonization of Omobono was, in effect, an attempt to redirect and reconceive ideas about lay sanctity circulating in the twelfth-century communes. Moreover, Bishop Sicard's interest in Omobono should be understood in conjunction with his efforts to limit the power of the growing *popolo*. Both men, I would argue, used their celebrations of this Cremonese merchant to articulate what proper lay religious enthusiasm ought to look like. An ideal layman attends to his own community but only in certain ways: he administers charity; he fights heresy; but he does not heal with his hands.

---

70. Ibid., 38.

Such a reimagining of an ideal lay life would influence the ways in which the cults of other thirteenth-century pious laymen and laywomen were to be conceived of as fundamentally local rather than global affairs. By celebrating Omobono's ability to distinguish himself from the "thorns" of lay life, his canonization bull and first *vita* fix the lay saint's cult to its local civic context. Innocent and Sicard reimagine the effect of lay sanctity by simplifying the meaning of Omobono's penance. In Ranieri's *vita*, the layman's extraordinary penitential commitment gives him both a local and global significance; Ranieri has the spiritual gifts or charisma—the ability to perform living miracles—that aid both city and church. In the early Omobono sources, however, penance is not a catalyst for miraculous change. Instead, penance is something that is performed as proof of piety, on par with a rigorous schedule of prayer, the struggle against heresy, and charity work. In short, it is not an act that garners one charisma.

In the chapters that follow I shall describe how, over the course of the thirteenth century, communal governments would capitalize on the notion that to be a lay saint meant to be deeply engaged in the welfare of one's city. Nevertheless, there would be one layman in communal Italy who would move far beyond his local context and assume a reputation for global change. The story of Innocent III's dream of seeing Francis of Assisi holding up a crumbling church vividly illustrates that it was the Franciscans in particular, and not lay saints in general, who were able to take on the role of saviors of the institutional church.[71] Francis can repair a broken church precisely because, with Innocent's blessing, he and his friars became an institutionally legitimate order within the church. And with that new status, Francis gained a more global or church-wide significance; he could, as Innocent's dream illustrated, support a crumbling church. The lay saints of urban Italy, as Innocent's canonization of Omobono made clear, were to move away from twelfth-century models of lay sanctity that emphasized the layman's ability to effect living miracles. Instead, they were to turn their attention to their local populations. In Innocent's estimation, the ideal layman remakes the laity by leading them away from heresy, away from civic strife, and away from the "perverse and miserable business of commerce." The ideal layman dedicates himself to asceticism, pilgrimage, and charity; he does not deliver priests from the hands of Satan, as Ranieri had.

---

71. This story, perhaps made most famous in the frescoes found in the upper church of the Baslica of San Francesco in Assisi, likely first appeared in the *Legenda trium sociorum* and in Thomas of Celano's second life of Francis in the early 1240s; see Holly J. Grieco, "Pastoral Care, Inquisition, and Mendicancy in the Medieval Franciscan Order," in *The Origin, Development, and Refinement of Medieval Religious Mendicancies*, ed. Donald Prudlo (Leiden: Brill, 2011), 117–19.

This new threefold concentration for the lay religious life essentially demanded that the good layman be externally rather than internally focused. To be an ideal lay Christian meant to be most concerned with the state of others rather than with one's own spiritual development. Again, a comparison with Francis is helpful. As Kenneth Baxter Wolf has argued, Francis's embrace of poverty and charity had much more to do with the transformation of the self than it did with an actual administration of aid to the needy.[72] In short, Francis's new religious life was essentially a move at self-transformation. While Benincasa's portrait of Ranieri touches upon the idea of self-transformation—the motivation found in meeting Alberto of Corsica and the many steps Ranieri went through to become a dedicated penitent illustrate this change—that idea is missing in the early Omobono sources and, as we shall see, does not reappear in lay saints' *vitae* until the late thirteenth century. When such ideas about using a penitential commitment to remake a layman's internal reality do return, as we will see most vividly in the descriptions of Margaret of Cortona's religious life, the church would see this as another moment to step in and redefine the lay religious life, this time by placing lay penitents under the guardianship of the Franciscans and encouraging the creation of the mendicant third orders.

Thus, in the papacy's hands, an ideal layman must rise above his inherently sinful nature, attend to his own civic community, and demonstrate only a posthumous power to perform miracles. Moreover, instead of presenting the local dimension of lay sanctity as an effect of a more far-reaching global impact, as we see in Ranieri's *vita*, the earliest sources associated with Omobono's cult present the city as the boundary of a lay saint's power. The lay saint does not, as we hear of our twelfth-century lay saints, dispense living miracles through his touch, his blessing, or his living presence. By setting such limits the church had taken a key first step in making charity and civic involvement the defining aspects of a good Christian life. It had also set the stage for more politically and socially radical understandings of lay religion to emerge in the thirteenth-century communes.

---

72. Kenneth Baxter Wolf, *The Poverty of Riches: St. Francis of Assisi Reconsidered* (Oxford: Oxford University Press, 2003).

CHAPTER 2

Charity as Social Justice

The Birth of the Communal Lay Saint

Like Benincasa's *vita* of Ranieri of Pisa, the *vita* of Raimondo "Palmerio" of Piacenza (d. 1200), written in 1212 by Rufino, a canon from Piacenza's Church of the Twelve Apostles, describes a saint whose conversion to a religious life occurred over several years.[1] A native of Piacenza and son of a well-off artisan, Raimondo first began to embrace a more dedicated religious life after the death of his father left him free to give up his trade and travel (accompanied by his mother) to the Holy Land.[2] Rufino describes how mother and son visited various sites, marveled at what they saw, and were eager to return home to "inflame the cold hearts of worldly men and women with divine love."[3] On the voyage home, however, Raimondo's mother died. When he returned to Piacenza, his remaining family convinced him to take up the life that had been expected of him: he married and returned

---

1. The *vita* can be found in *AASS*, July VI, 645–57 (*Bibliotheca hagiographica latina antiquae et mediae aetatis* (hereafter *BHL*) 7068); hereafter referred to as *Vita S. Raymundi*. Luigi Canetti's *Gloriosa civitas: Culto dei santi e società cittadina a Piacenza nel medioevo* (Bologna: Pàtron, 1993) remains the most extensive study of both Rufino's *vita* and the development of Raimondo's cult in Piacenza. In addition to looking at the hagiographic issues raised by Rufino's *vita*, Canetti also places Raimondo's cult within the context of Piacenza's ancient cults.

2. *Vita S. Raymundi*, 646.

3. Ibid., 647: "Elapsis interea diebus non paucis, cum sacra omnia jam loca circuissent, de repetenda patria cogitarunt; ut quaecumque viderant mirabilia, cum hominibus piis ac religiosis communicarent, et frigentia cum virorum, tum mulierum secularium corda divino amore succenderent."

to his former trade. But, as Rufino describes, Raimondo still longed for a more dedicated religious life. God, Rufino writes, knew that "the conjugal yoke and the care of children" were getting in the way of Raimondo's spiritual ambitions. To clear his path, God took Raimondo's wife and all but one of his children in quick succession.[4] The saint responded by entrusting his remaining son to his in-laws, selling his possessions, and setting off once again on pilgrimage, this time to Rome.

Under the portico of St. Peter's in Rome, Raimondo's understanding of a committed lay religious life began to change. Rufino writes that Christ, dressed as a pilgrim, appeared to Raimondo and instructed him that acts of charity and not pilgrimages would be of the most value at the Last Judgment.[5] Pointing out that Raimondo's own city was teeming with the poor and sick as well as with abandoned widows and those simply "overcome by various misfortunes," Christ told Raimondo that it was up to him to return to Piacenza in order to "lead the rich to almsgiving, the unquiet to peace, and erring and sinful women to a right way of living."[6] Although Rufino reports that Raimondo at first resisted, claiming he was "not equal to such an undertaking," and begging that he not be bound to his "bitterly divided" and "strife-torn" fellow-citizens, the second half of the *vita* details how passionately the saint took up Christ's command.[7]

Raimondo's work in Piacenza—founding a hospice to house and aid the city's poor and needy, helping the city's prostitutes find husbands or convents, rescuing abandoned children, pleading cases in court on behalf of poor defendants, and calming civic rivalries—serve as Rufino's most potent evidence for this layman's sanctity. Raimondo's focus on charity illustrates the ideal lay religious life that Innocent III had advocated for in Omobono of Cremona's

---

4. Ibid., 649: "At benignus omnium Conditor cum sciret, non posse famulum suum toto pectore ad studia vitae spiritualis incumbere, utpote conjugii vinculo, curaque liberorum, adstrictum servituti, misertus ejus est, et aliqua illum voluit libertatis parte donare: filiolos enim ejus omnes anno uno ex hac vita sustulit . . ."

5. Ibid., 650.

6. Webb, *Saints and Cities*, 76; *Vita S. Raymundi*, 650: "Nolo itaque, fili mi, deniceps ut per orbem vageris: sed patriam tuam Placentiam repete; ubi tot pauperes, tot infirmi et variis oppressi calamitatibus misericordiam implorant meam, et non est qui adjuvet. Ibis tu, eroque tecum ego, et gratiam dabo, qua possis ad eleemosynam divites, dissidentes ad pacem, aberrantes denique, et vagas praesertim mulierculas, ad rectam vivendi normam adducere." On the criticism that was aimed at pilgrims and pilgrimage in the Middle Ages, see Giles Constable, "Opposition to Pilgrimage in the Middle Ages," *Studia Gratiana* 19 (1976): 125–46.

7. *Vita S. Raymundi*, 650: "Respondit voce demissa fidelis Dei Servus: Domine, par ego non sum rei tantae suscipiendae, homo utique rudis, sine litteris, sine agendi industria, peccatis plenus. Noli me, obsecro Domine, ad cives illos meos legare: vides enim, quam infense divisi sint inter se, quam discordes. Non audient me; frustra laborabo: novi mores eorum. Tum, numquid non ipse asseruisti, Domine, acceptum non esse hominum in patria sua?"

canonization bull. Like Innocent's presentation of Omobono, the portrait we find of Raimondo in Rufino's *vita* equates lay piety with acts of civic charity, and gives no indication that this layman performed miracles during his lifetime.

Raimondo's charity work exemplifies Vauchez's claim that by the thirteenth century "saints of charity and labor" were prominent in late medieval Italy.[8] In Kenneth Baxter Wolf's study of Francis of Assisi's commitment to poverty, he notes the similarities as well as the differences between Vauchez's saints and Francis.[9] Looking at Raimondo, Wolf points out that both Francis and Raimondo lived in the expanding cities of northern Italy, gave up the lives their families had expected them to lead, and dedicated themselves to living a penitential life largely by following the *vita apostolica*. But as Wolf notes, although Raimondo's story makes clear that Francis was far from the first layman to take up a life of penance, prayer, and poverty in the Italian communes, the poor man from Assisi's decision to transform himself into a beggar marks "a decisive shift away from the new civic saint paradigm" that Raimondo exemplified.[10] Francis, Wolf argues, ultimately "decided to follow a different path," one which allowed him to focus more on his own "ascetic self-denial" than on "the needs of the urban underclass."[11] In short, unlike other laymen celebrated for their embrace of a penitential life, Francis was more interested in becoming poor than in aiding the poor.

Scholars have not considered, however, the extent to which the church's sanction of Francis's "different path" depended upon its earlier approval of a normative lay ideal in Omobono. It was only after Innocent had articulated that the steps to an ideal lay life were to be found in external acts—prayer, penance, charity work, and the struggle against heresy—that Francis's internally focused lay life became a viable option. But such support came with a condition: Francis and his followers had to be tonsured. Only as a religious order under the church's oversight could these (former) laymen earn the church's approval to be manifestations of their spiritual ideals.

This chapter will argue that during the thirteenth century, and contemporaneous with the rise of the Franciscan Order in communal Italy, the path to sanctity that remained a true lay option, the path that men like Omobono and Raimondo first exemplified, began to veer in a new direction. In Raimondo of Piacenza's *vita*, in two later thirteenth-century *vitae* for Omobono of Cremona as well as in a *vita* written to celebrate another Cremonese layman, the

---

8. Vauchez, *Sainthood*, 199–207.
9. Wolf, *The Poverty of Riches*, 69–76.
10. Ibid., 75.
11. Ibid.

silver and goldsmith Facio of Cremona (d. 1271), we see the creation of a new lay ideal that drew not only on the conservative portrait articulated by Innocent and Sicard in their initial celebration of Omobono but also on the more radical understanding of the lay religious life expressed in Ranieri of Pisa's cult. While Raimondo himself was never credited with performing living miracles (as Ranieri had been and lay saints in the second half of the thirteenth century would be), it is in his early cult that we see the first step in the creation of a new lay ideal. In Raimondo's *vita*, the lay saint's charity work became the work of social justice.

This new paradigm of an ideal lay life, what I will call the communal lay saint, came to its fullest expression once civic authorities became the primary patrons of contemporary lay saints' cults. As merchants and artisans came to dominate civic governments (in the form of *popolo*-dominated regimes), the pious layman's commitment to serving his civic lay population through works of charity found a receptive audience. In these cults, the penitential commitment of an extraordinary layman was once again presented as transforming him into a living miracle worker. But this time, the lay saint's charisma was not focused on healing a broken church but rather on identifying, soothing, and sometimes fixing the economic and social inequalities of a commune.

Raimondo Palmerio of Piacenza: The Prudent Servant of God

Rufino's 1212 *vita* of Raimondo survives only in a form that, as Diana Webb has noted, is the result of a "double-process of translation."[12] With the original Latin text lost, the seventeenth-century Bollandist editor Peter Bosch retranslated into Latin a 1525 Italian translation of the *vita* made by a Dominican friar for the community of nuns living at the site of Raimondo's former hospice.[13] The fact that only one copy of Raimondo's *vita* has come down to us must be, to some extent, a result of the fact that he was never canonized by

---

12. Webb, *Saints and Cities*, 62.

13. Webb notes that even if the sixteenth-century effort were a faithful translation of the original text, the Latin that comes down to us in Bosch's translation is a far cry from that of a thirteenth-century cleric. But as Webb and other scholars have done, I shall rely upon Bosch's text, since as Webb herself reasons, there is nothing in terms of content that "is not acceptable as a product of Rufino's time and place." Webb, *Saints and Cities*, 62–63. In addition to Webb, both Vauchez and Canetti have accepted the *Acta sanctorum* text as a viable source; see André Vauchez, "Raimondo Zanfogni, detto Palmerio," in *Bibliotheca sanctorum* (Rome: Istituto Giovanni XXIII nella Pontificia Università lateranense, 1961–70), vol. 11, 26–29; and Canetti, *Gloriosa civitas*, 167–75.

Rome. The curia was likely not interested in pursuing Raimondo's canonization in the early 1200s as Piacenza was under papal interdict.[14] The collection of postmortem miracles that Rufino appended to the *vita* suggests, however, that within the city there was an active cult during the thirteenth century.[15]

In the introduction to her translation, Webb notes that Rufino's *vita* presents a "remarkably straightforward account of a practical saint."[16] Webb elaborates by noting that Rufino makes no mention of any miracles performed by Raimondo during his lifetime, gives only a passing reference to the saint's penitential routine, and recounts just one visionary experience (when Christ appeared to him in Rome).[17] If we compare these experiences with the detailed descriptions Benincasa provided of the penance to which Ranieri of Pisa subjected his body while he was in Jerusalem, Rufino's account of the regulations and habits that made up Raimondo's devotional life seem rather paltry. Nevertheless, we must consider how far this portrait of penitential restraint and practicality reflects the direction in which *Quia pietas* and *Cum orbita solis* (the first sources for Omobono of Cremona's cult) had sent conceptions of the ideal lay religious life in the early thirteenth century. To that end, when Rufino reports that Raimondo modeled himself on Tobit and was thus "sparing in his food, assiduous in almsgiving, fasting and prayer, and tireless in attendance at the divine office," we are getting a vision of lay sanctity that draws upon a papally sanctioned prototype.[18] Like Omobono, Raimondo's penance was moderate, allowed him to attend to his civic community, and always kept him following the church's devotional schedule.

Moreover, Rufino repeatedly emphasizes Raimondo's obedience to authority—both familial and ecclesiastical—which was also a key theme in Innocent's portrait of Omobono. Rufino makes clear that from the time Raimondo was an adolescent he considered family duty before he allowed himself to embrace the spiritual life for which he longed. Rufino writes that

---

14. Webb, *Saints and Cities*, 64; and Vauchez, "Raimondo Zanfogni," 28.

15. In spite of both the scarcity of evidence and challenges present in the surviving *vita*, Raimondo has garnered a fair amount of attention from scholars; see Diana Webb, "Raimondo and the Magdalen: A Twelfth-Century Italian Pilgrim in Provence," *Journal of Medieval History* 26 (2000): 1–18; Vauchez, *Sainthood*, 198; and for the early modern history of Raimondo's cult, see Simon Ditchfield, *Liturgy, Sanctity, and History in Tridentine Italy: Pietro Maria Campi and the Preservation of the Particular* (Cambridge: Cambridge University Press, 1995), 195–203.

16. Webb, *Saints and Cities*, 64.

17. Ibid.

18. Ibid., 72; *Vita S. Raymundi*, 649: "Vitam suam in opera Dei Famulus ad exemplum sancti Tobiae instituebat, in victu parcissimus, in eleemosynis assiduus, in jejuniis, in oratione, in Officiis divinis indefessus." In my citations of Raimondo's *vita*, when I am relying on Webb's translation, I shall cite both her text and the Latin from the *Acta sanctorum*.

when Raimondo was twelve years old and still "under his father's authority," the saint felt compelled to take up the family profession even though he was "born for bigger and better things."[19] It was not until his father died two years later that Raimondo was "at liberty" to give up his "lowly trade" in order to concentrate on his spiritual desires.[20] And finally, Rufino notes that the layman would not allow himself to leave on pilgrimage after the death of his father until he had obtained permission from his mother, who not only sanctioned the saint's pilgrimage but also decided to join him.[21]

Rufino's Raimondo falls in line with the ecclesiastical hierarchy as well. Before mother and son left for Jerusalem, they "made the necessary arrangements" with their own kin as well as with the bishop. Rufino even embeds a purported transcription of their plea to the bishop, leaving no doubt in his readers' minds that mother and son had followed the proper protocol for embarking on such a journey.[22] And once back from his pilgrimage, Raimondo remained obedient to the church. Christ had cautioned Raimondo to check in with Piacenza's bishop so that he might explain his new duties before he began his charity work.[23] As Raimondo walked back into Piacenza, he was followed by a large crowd that was "struck dumb" by the sight of the saint dressed all in blue and carrying a large wooden cross over his shoulder. As Rufino reports, Raimondo followed Christ's order, neither looking at nor speaking to anyone before he had met with the bishop.[24] And again, Rufino transcribes Raimondo's exchange with the bishop, even though it largely re-

---

19. Webb, *Saints and Cities*, 67; *Vita S. Raymundi*, 646: "eum vero ad aetatem annorum circiter duodecim accrevisset, apud opificem quemdam a patre elocatus est, non ut litteris doctrinaeve daret operam; sed ut artem ejus servilem atque ignobilem exerceret, in eaque disceret mercaturam facere. Hoc opificium quale fuerit, comperiri certo argumento non potuit: sunt, qui sutorium fuisse velint, opinione ducti, non scientia. Id tamen est verum, quaecumque demum ars illa fuerit, optimo Adolescentulo non parum illam displicuisse; ut qui ad majora utilioraque, quemadmodum patebit infra, natus esset: puer ipse interea, atque in patria potestate constitutus, tolerare illam necesse habuit; ut ita Domini, honorem erga parentes obedientiamque divina lege praecipientis, mandato obtemperaret."

20. Webb, *Saints and Cities*, 67; *Vita S. Raymundi*, 646: "Jam annos pubertatis, sive adolescentiae, quae ab anno aetatis quarto decimo ducit initium, B. Raymundus attigerat, cum pater eius ex hac brevi vita ad patriam caelestem transiit. Tum vero sanctus Adolescentulus liberum sese esse considerans, obscuro isti opificio statuit valedicere, non ut otium sectaretur, aut se vitiis prostitueret, quod vulgus assolet adolescentium; verum ut Salvatori suo, per consecratam divinis obsequiis toto animo vitam, propius adhaereret."

21. Webb, *Saints and Cities*, 67; *Vita S. Raymundi*, 646: "Proficisci tamen ante noluit, quam annuisset mater vidua, ac bene sibi precata esset"; and "Fili mi; simul ibimus ad sanctissimum Sepulcrum, a quo sola me poterit mors divellere."

22. Webb, *Saints and Cities*, 68; *Vita S. Raymundi*, 647: "Tum vota exsecuturi, res ad peregrinationem necessarias disponunt; et post amicos cognatosque ex officio salutatos . . . Pater ac pastor reverendissime, deliberatum nobis est hinc peregre ad sanctum Sepulcrum abire; manibus igitur ad modum crucis compositis id poscimus, quod solent hujuscemodi peregrini."

23. *Vita S. Raymundi*, 651.

24. Ibid.

peats what the text has already described Christ as having said to the saint in Rome.[25]

And yet, although the *vita* emphasizes the obedience Raimondo demonstrated both to his family and to his bishop, it also makes clear the degree to which the saint as well as his mother saw many of their obligations and responsibilities as burdens that kept them from pursuing a more rigorous religious life. For example, when the saint informed his grieving mother that he would soon leave Piacenza for the Holy Land, she burst into joyful tears telling her son that since she had been "released from the bonds of matrimony" and had no other children, she would join him on his pilgrimage.[26] For both Raimondo and his mother, familial responsibilities were a servitude that prevented them from fully pursuing a religious life. Rufino notes that Raimondo had once tried to convince his wife to live with him in chastity. She refused, telling him that as long as she was a wife she would continue to act like one and not like a nun.[27] Ever "the prudent servant of God," as Rufino calls him, Raimondo believed such a response to be due to "his wife's imperfection and peril," and "so that they might live without sin," decided not to press the subject, hoping to maintain a domestic peace.[28] The couple would have one more child, but Raimondo found that this new addition once again reduced him "to servitude."[29] After Raimondo's wife died, he entrusted his remaining child to his in-laws. Rufino presents these losses as gains. He writes that the saint was finally "emancipated from the marital yoke."[30]

---

25. After informing the bishop that his mission will direct him to collect "alms for the needy," gather up "poor pilgrims," and reconcile "those in conflict," he adds that he would do none of this without the bishop's "good will." As Rufino reports, the bishop offered Raimondo his blessing, promising to protect him in whatever way he could. See *Vita S. Raymundi*, 651.

26. Webb, *Saints and Cities*, 67–8; *Vita S. Raymundi*, 646: "Haec audiens piissima mater, uberrimis perfusa lacrymis, complectitur Filium, et in haec verba prorumpit: O carum et unicum lumen meum . . . nam et ego, cum vinculo conjugali solutam nunc me viderem, nec alium habere filium, nisi te, educatum pridem nec jam amplius puerum; me vero aetate maturam esse, omnino decreveram, quidquid mihi superesset vitae, id officiis divinis, sacrisque locis adeundis totum impendere . . ."

27. Webb, *Saints and Cities*, 73; *Vita S. Raymundi*, 649: "At illa, rebus caelestibus parum addicta, procaciter admodum, Cum fuero monialis, inquit, tum monitis hisce tuis parebo: nunc abs te ducta cum sim, uxorem agere certum est, non viduam aut sanctimonialem."

28. Webb, *Saints and Cities*, 73; *Vita S. Raymundi*, 649: "Noluit prudens Dei Famulus, spectata conjugis imperfectione ac periculo, importunius eam urgere; ut pacifice porro inter se et absque peccato viverunt."

29. Webb, *Saints and Cities*, 73; *Vita S. Raymundi*, 649: "Ita factum divina providentia, ut alium denuo filium gigneret. Hunc bonus Raymundus, cum se reductum ad servitutem videret . . ."

30. Webb, *Saints and Cities*, 73; *Vita S. Raymundi*, 649: "At benignus omnium Conditor cum sciret, non posse Famulum suum toto pectore ad studia vitae spiritualis incumbere, utpote conjugii vinculo, curaque liberorum, adstrictum servituti, misertus ejus est, et aliqua illum voluit libertatis parte donare: filiolos enim ejus omnes anno uno ex hac vita sustulit . . . Ita bonus Raymundus, maritali jam jugo exsolutus, perpetuae castitatis et continentiae propositum confirmavit."

In expressing such sentiments, Rufino's portrait of Raimondo echoes early descriptions of Omobono. Neither Innocent III's canonization bull, *Quia pietas*, nor Omobono's first *vita*, *Cum orbita solis*, give much detail about Omobono's life as a merchant or husband. Nevertheless, they do make clear that this Cremonese saint's lay status functioned as an impediment to his sanctity. Innocent called Omobono a "lily among thorns," and the author of *Cum orbita solis* celebrated the saint's conversion with language that suggested an antagonism to lay work. Rufino's descriptions of Raimondo as having been finally freed from the servitude brought on by marriage and family frames lay status in a similarly negative manner.

If we look more closely at Rufino's text, however, we see that despite these remarks, the *vita* does not wholeheartedly embrace the same negative assessment of lay life that we saw in the earliest Omobono sources. At the same time that Rufino presents the saint's familial responsibilities as burdens, he also constructs an argument around the spiritual and saintly opportunities they present. When Rufino first mentions marriage, he reports that the saint's relatives had encouraged Raimondo to marry, arguing that if he were to live unmarried and alone he would have "a hard life" with no one to care for him. "Married people too could serve God," they added.[31] Rufino reports that Raimondo "allowed himself to be persuaded, the divine goodness permitting it," so that he could "experience what trials those joined in marriage undergo, in feeding and bringing up children and looking after a household."[32] Thus, even though Raimondo clearly saw marriage and family life as impediments on his penitential path, we see in this *vita* an attempt to craft a more complex understanding of the realities of lay life. As distracting and burdensome as they might be, such obstacles offered this layman occasions to prove his spiritual commitment.[33]

---

31. Webb, *Saints and Cities*, 71; *Vita S. Raymundi*, 648: "Elapsis a reditu ejus in patriam diebus aliquot, Raymundo haec suggerere coeperunt consanguinei: Raymunde frater, si caelebs ac solus ita pergis vivere, laborabis multum; cum neminem habeas, qui res tuas curet. Auctores itaque tibi simus, ut uxorem ducas, cogitesque, Deo servire posse etiam conjugatos; quandoquidem institutum ab ipso matrimonium est."

32. Webb, *Saints and Cities*, 71; *Vita S. Raymundi*, 648: "Sivit bonus Raymundus haec sibi persuaderi, permittente id etiam divina bonitate, ut experiretur et Famulus ejus, quas matrimonio juncti regenda conjuge, alendis instituendisque liberis, re domestica administranda patiuntur miserias."

33. Dyan Elliott's exploration of sexual abstinence in medieval marriage touches upon the idea that marriage itself was sometimes seen as increasing opportunities for spiritual growth. She notes how John of Marienwerder presents Dorothea of Montau's marriage as having given her opportunities for greater spiritual rewards; see Elliott, *Spiritual Marriage*, 195–265, esp. 205 and 229.

Preaching in a "Homely Fashion"

It is in Rufino's descriptions of Raimondo's working life that we see him most clearly alternate between portraying the responsibilities of lay life as a liability and an opportunity. At first Rufino seems concerned to defend the fact that Raimondo worked at all. He writes that the saint worked "without fraud and without avarice," solely to feed his family and have alms to offer the poor.[34] But Rufino complicates that defense as soon as he makes it. Although his work could keep him from his "spiritual purposes," Raimondo was constantly adapting his work responsibilities to feed his religious goals. Rufino reports that Raimondo set aside as many hours as he could to study scripture and devote himself to "conversation with religious men."[35] These experiences allowed the saint, who was uneducated, to seem "most knowledgeable about those things that had to do with God and with the Catholic religion."[36] Each feast day, Raimondo would travel to a workshop in Piacenza and preach—in what Rufino describes as "a homely fashion"—so as to "divert worldly men" and "instruct them in the works necessary to fulfill the divine commands."[37] So effective were Raimondo's words that the men in those workshops began to look to the saint as a "spiritual father and guide" and together "formed a sort of religious order."[38]

Rufino seems aware in his descriptions that Raimondo's preaching walks a fine line between orthodoxy and heresy.[39] He emphasizes that Raimondo's

---

34. Webb, *Saints and Cities*, 72; *Vita S. Raymundi*, 648: "in quo quidem integerrime versatus est, sine dolo, sine avaritia: tantum ut se, ut uxorem, ut filios aleret, essetque, unde pauperibus eleemosynas largiretur."

35. Webb, *Saints and Cities*, 72; *Vita S. Raymundi*, 648: "Quoniam vero ipsi ars illa non placebat, ut quae ab instituto suo spirituali avocaret animum, horis, quas opus urgendo nancisci poterat, subsecivis, et festis praesertim diebus (ut erat cognoscendae legis divinae ac sacrarum Litterarum studio concitatus) id operam dabat, ut cum viris religiosis, probitate ac doctrina conspicuis, conferret sermonem."

36. Vauchez speculates that Raimondo was illiterate; "Raimondo Zanfogni," 26.

37. Webb, *Saints and Cities*, 72; *Vita S. Raymundi*, 648: "Ea re tantum profecit, ut etiam sine litteris, non tamen sine dono divinae sapientiae, scientissimus appareret eorum, quae ad Deum religionemque Catholicam pertinebant. Porro ut homines profanos, atque eos imprimis, qui eamdem secum profitebantur artem, a lascivis confabulationibus, ludisque vanis averteret, ipse festo quoque die certam sibi officinam deligebat, ubi magno caritatis ardore sodalibus suis veram sanctae Dei legis doctrinam familiariter praedicaret, eosque edoceret operum ad praecepta divina exigendorum, ac virtutum ante omnia sectandarum, fugiendorumque vitiorum rationem."

38. Webb, *Saints and Cities*, 72; *Vita S. Raymundi*, 649: "Domesticis tamen suis illis et humilibus exhortationibus apud eos, quos in eodem opificio habebat socios, tantum effecit, ut ordinem quemdam religiosum referrent, nec aliter ad bonum Raymundum, quam ad patrem suum ducemque spiritualem, recurrerent."

39. Although the orthodoxy of lay preaching remained a contentious subject in late medieval Europe, Innocent III had specifically given his approval in 1201 to the lay Humiliati to preach words of "exhortation" but not articles of faith or sacraments of the church. For a brief summary on the

feast-day sermons were not public events and he gives no details about their content."[40] Rufino does note that when news of Raimondo's powerful sermons spread through the city, many people began to urge the saint "to hold meetings in public places, even in the main piazza, but Raimondo refused," claiming that if he did so "error could creep up on him."[41] According to Rufino, Raimondo stated that such preaching was properly the work of priests and learned men.[42]

In these passages we see Rufino move between two quite different understandings of lay sanctity. While he notes how Raimondo's lay status hindered opportunities for a full religious life, he also emphasizes the way in which those same obstacles intensified the significance of that commitment. Raimondo's piety allows him to take on tasks (preaching) and create organizations (forming a kind of "religious order" with his fellow workers) that extend his authority beyond the traditional boundaries of a lay life. Nevertheless, as Rufino is quick to add, Raimondo's preaching was not doctrinal but instead "homely," taking place in private and concentrating on the performance of good works.

Such a back and forth between alternate understandings of an ideal lay religious life could leave the reader to wonder what Rufino's ultimate message was concerning the power and potential of lay sanctity. Is a perfected lay life one that, following the model of Omobono's early cult, is obedient to church hierarchy and fundamentally focused on external matters such as charity and the fight against heresy? Or is Rufino's presentation of the spiritual opportunities Raimondo finds in the limits of his lay status as well as in his preaching and spiritual leadership a portrait of lay religiosity that sees the lay saint as ultimately dismantling ecclesiastical authority and hierarchy?

---

issue, see Vauchez, *Francis of Assisi*, 306–7. For Innocent's approval of the preaching of lay Humiliati (his June 7, 1201 letter *Incumbit nobis*), see Meersseman, *Dossier de l'order de la pénitence*, appendix 1; also see Andrews, *The Early Humiliati*.

40. *Vita S. Raymundi*, 648. Vauchez talks about how Rufino casts Raimondo's preaching as acceptable because it was "private exhortation" rather than public preaching; see *The Laity*, 64.

41. Webb, *Saints and Cities*, 72; *Vita S. Raymundi*, 649: "Non multo post tempore optimi Raymundi fama usque adeo percrebuit; ut festis diebus, cum primum rescissent, in qua tum ipse domo aut officina versaretur, ad eam plurimi verba ipsius ardentia excepturi concurrerent. Quidam etiam hortabantur illum, ut loco publico, atque adeo in ipso foro, conciones haberet."

42. The *vita's* distinction between public and private preaching is a bit odd since Innocent had elsewhere defined preaching as a public act, noting that private preaching was something heretics did; see Beverly M. Kienzle, "Holiness and Obedience: Denouncement of Twelfth-Century Waldensian Lay Preaching," in *The Devil, Heresy and Witchcraft in the Middle Ages: Essays in Honor of Jeffrey B. Russell*, ed. Alberto Ferreiro (Leiden: Brill, 1998), 268.

The Birth of the Communal Lay Saint

We can begin to answer these questions and form a more precise picture of Rufino's understanding of an ideal lay religious life by looking at the second half of the *vita*. Here, after we hear about how Christ appeared to Raimondo in Rome, described the ongoing suffering in Piacenza, and urged the saint to return home so that he might alleviate such misery, the *vita* no longer lingers on either the challenges or the opportunities of being a layman. Instead it focuses on describing the content and effects of Raimondo's charity work. And it is in these descriptions that we see Rufino integrate ideas about the inherent worth and religious potential of a lay life that were voiced in Ranieri of Pisa's *vita* with the archetype of a holy lay life that Omobono's canonization bull and first *vita* had proposed. The result is a layman whose religious dedication leads him to work so tirelessly for the welfare of his civic community that his concern for the social welfare and justice of his fellow city-dwellers trumps any discussion of the limits of a lay religious life. In short, it is in the last half of Raimondo's *vita* that Rufino begins to construct a portrait of what would become, over the course of the thirteenth century, the model communal lay saint. A role that both laymen and laywomen would seek to fill and communal governments would seek to patronize.

Rufino writes that upon Raimondo's return to Piacenza, the layman began to look for a suitable place to live, store alms, and help the most needy. The canons of the Church of the Twelve Apostles served as his first patrons, providing a building next to their church for Raimondo to establish a hospice for both men and women.[43] From the beginning of his descriptions of Raimondo's charity work in Piacenza, Rufino seems especially eager to emphasize that this layman's charitable activities were often directed at poor people whose high social status or infirmity prevented them from begging—those who in later thirteenth-century *vitae* would be called *pauperes verecundi*.[44] Raimondo was therefore not only helping those in need but also those in shame. Raimondo's reputation for charity grew to such an extent, Rufino writes, that all of the afflicted, that is, "the poor both public and private," looked to the saint as

---

43. *Vita S. Raymundi*, 651. On Raimondo's hospital, also see Giovanni Poggi, "Raimondo Palmerio e il suo ospedale nella Piacenza del sec. XII," *Rivista di Storia della Medicina* 12 (1968): 212–16.

44. For more on the "shameful poor," see Richard Trexler, "Charity in the Defense of the Urban Elites in the Italian Communes," in *The Rich, the Well-Born, and the Powerful*, ed. F. C. Jaher (Urbana: University of Illinois Press, 1973), 64–109; also see O. Z. Pugliese, "The Good Works of the Florentine 'Buonomini di San Martino': An Example of Renaissance Pragmatism," in *Crossing the Boundaries: Christian Piety and the Arts in Italian Medieval and Renaissance Confraternities*, ed. K. Eisenbichler (Kalamazoo: Medieval Institute, 1990), 108–20.

their "father and defender."[45] His hospice became particularly known for taking in repentant prostitutes and placing them under the care of what Rufino notes were respectable matrons.[46] After they had lived at the hospice for some time, Raimondo would ask the women what sort of life they wanted. For those who wanted to marry, he provided a dowry. And for those who wanted to maintain their chastity, Raimondo assisted in getting them admitted to convents.[47]

Raimondo's work on behalf of his civic community did not end there. The saint also gained a reputation for helping all who were "unjustly oppressed by others." In particular, Rufino describes how the reports of those who could not afford to bring legal cases to court moved Raimondo to take up his wooden cross and plead for justice for these neighbors.[48] At the courts, Raimondo begged the judges to "love and do justice to the poor," since they would be judged by Christ "with that judgment with which you have judged."[49] Rufino claims that Raimondo was so successful that he earned the trust of the city's magnates and *podestà*, who sought his advice "as if he were a prophet."[50] Rufino also describes how Raimondo comforted prisoners in their cells, begged judges to pardon those who had sincerely repented, and worked to convince his fellow Piacentians not to engage in "Trojan" or other dangerous "gladiatorial games."[51] And finally, Rufino notes that Raimondo worked to maintain peace not only between rival factions within the city but also between Piacenza and its longtime enemy, Cremona.[52]

---

45. Webb, *Saints and Cities*, 79; *Vita S. Raymundi*, 651: "Beati vero Raymundi tantum brevi crevit existimatio, ut eum afflicti omnes, infirmi, pauperes tam occulti quam publici, patris ac tutoris loco haberent."

46. For more on medieval prostitution and repentant prostitutes, see Ruth Mazo Karras, "Prostitution in Medieval Europe," in *Handbook of Medieval Sexuality*, ed. Vern L. Bullough and James Brundage (New York: Garland Press, 1996); and Jacques Rossiaud, *Medieval Prostitution*, trans. Lydia G. Cochrane (Oxford: Basil Blackwell, 1988). Webb, *Saints and Cities*, 79–80; *Vita S. Raymundi*, 651.

47. Webb, *Saints and Cities*, 80; *Vita S. Raymundi*, 651–52.

48. *Vita S. Raymundi*, 652.

49. Webb, *Saints and Cities*, 81; *Vita S. Raymundi*, 652: "Tum surgens ab oratione, cruce humero imposita, ac toto corde abreptus in Deum, pergebat ad tribunal; ubi manu crucem apprehendens, sic apud injusto judices perorabat: Diligite, atque ergo inopes servate justitiam, o vos judices, qui judicatis terram: mementote, quo judicio judicaveritis, eodem et vos ab eo, qui pro vobis exspiravit in cruce, judicatum iri: mementote, post hanc vitam non judicaturos vos, sed judicandos esse."

50. *Vita S. Raymundi*, 652: "Tantum vero vitae sanctimonia verbis ejus virtutis addebat et ponderis, ut cum a magnatibus, tum ab urbis praefecto perlibenter audiretur; et id impetraret auditus, ut ex ejus consilio res ab ipsis plurimae conficerentur. Imo vero si quid urbi vel difficultatis acciderat vel periculi, B. Raymundum iidem, tamquam prophetam, consulebant, et quod agendum erat, ad ejus saepe decernebant arbitrium."

51. Ibid., 653.

52. Ibid.

In the midst of describing Raimondo's charity work, Rufino devotes significant space to noting the outrage the saint felt once he realized how unwilling Piacenza's wealthy were to support their needy neighbors. When the saint would find those whose "shame or disease prevented [them] from begging," he would seek donations from his fellow city-dwellers by carrying his wooden cross on his shoulders as he walked through the streets yelling: "Woe to thee, O avaricious rich, for the supreme sentence will be pronounced against you."[53] Rufino reports that Raimondo's pleas were successful only up to a point: "the good and generous" were inspired, "the avaricious and hard-hearted" were terrified, but most stopped short of sharing their wealth with their needy neighbors.[54]

Rufino does not shy away from presenting Raimondo's anger and vocal protests over his fellow Piacentians' miserly ways. Raimondo again took to the streets, carrying his cross, and yelling at all he passed:

> Help, help, hard and cruel Christians, for I am dying of hunger while you have plenty . . . I don't have just one mouth, for I could suffer hunger not unwillingly; but there are as many mouths as you see here, perishing for want of food. I beg you, by the most holy Cross, have pity on the poor of Jesus Christ.[55]

While Raimondo's tireless dedication to providing charity to his civic community serves as unmistakable evidence for his sanctity, Rufino's focus on Raimondo's invectives against his fellow city-dwellers also functions as proof that this layman was holy. It is within these arguments that we see Rufino assimilate the two distinct models of an ideal lay life that preceded Raimondo: Raimondo's lay status endows him with the ability to identify the injustices within his city, to find both the needy and the hardhearted, but it is his obedience to Christ's commands that turns him away from his internal focus (specifically

---

53. Webb, *Saints and Cities*, 78; *Vita S. Raymundi*, 651: "Hoc igitur obtento, coepit bonus Raymundus investigare per urbem egenos, quos vel pudor ingenuus, vel morbus mendicare non sinebat; nactusque debitam quorumdam notitiam, tota palam urbe stipem illis conquirere, et crucem humero praeferens, clamare contenta voce: Beati misericordes, quoniam ipsi misericordiam consequentur: vae vobis, avari divites, quia suprema in vos sententia pronuntiabitur!"

54. Webb, *Saints and Cities*, 79; *Vita S. Raymundi*, 651: "Quibus quidem verbis et accendebantur boni ac liberales, et avari durique terrebantur, itaque largas ab utrisque eleemosynas obtinebat."

55. Webb, *Saints and Cities*, 79; *Vita S. Raymundi*, 651: "Hoc ut audivit B. Raynundus exarsit caritate scilicet, atque adversus opulentorum duritiam commovit sese, et arrepta in humerum sancta cruce, ac jussis sequi se miseris, per compita procedens, clamitabat: Succurrite, succurrite, Christiani crudeles ac duri; quia ego fame morior, dum vos interim abundatis . . . At ille progrediens, Non unum hoc, ait, os mihi est, quod quidem inedia vexari non invitus patiar; sed ora tot sunt, quot hic videtis, fame pereuntia. Per sanctissimam igitur crucem hanc obtestor, miseremini pauperum Jesu Christi."

away from embarking on more pilgrimages), motivating him to demand that his fellow city-dwellers act upon the inequality plaguing their community.

Raimondo's *vita* thus offers a new understanding of an ideal lay religious life that recognizes as well as maintains the authority and hierarchy of the church. Instead of seeing the pious layman as a miraculous healer of both the church and the city, as Benincasa had encouraged his readers to see Ranieri, Rufino presents Raimondo as providing a kind of roving social conscience for Piacenza.[56] Raimondo's commitment to charity leads him to criticize other laymen's greed and to work to redeem those men and women who have been shamed by either a financial fall or sexual transgression. In Rufino's portrait, for a layman's commitment to the *vita apostolica* to rise to the level of sanctity, it must have at its core an external motivation: the *vita* seems to be arguing that Raimondo carries his cross through Piacenza not to aid his own spiritual growth but to encourage other Piacentians to "lead the rich to almsgiving, the unquiet to peace, and erring and sinful women to a right way of living" as well as to "love and do justice to the poor."

In short, by emphasizing Raimondo's obedience to familial and religious authorities but still seeing great spiritual potential and opportunity in his lay status, Rufino constructs a portrait of the contemporary lay saint that justifies an external turn: at Christ's urging, Raimondo gives up the pilgrimages that would serve his own, internal, spiritual progress in order to focus on a deep and sometimes critical engagement with a city's social welfare. As his city's conscience, Raimondo not only continues the kind of criticism of lay life that we saw expressed in the earliest sources for Omobono but also maintains an idea trumpeted in Ranieri's *vita*: that a holy layman can heal a broken system. The genius of Rufino's *vita* is found in how he depicts Raimondo as protecting both church and commune from blame. Neither institution is as broken as is the broader civic society. Thus it is not the church or the commune that is the cause of these Piacentians' hardships but rather other members of the laity, those "cruel and hard Christians" who refuse to offer aid. Such a portrait places us back within Innocent's conception of the holy layman as someone who fixes the deficiencies within his own lay population.

The political history of Piacenza in the late twelfth and early thirteenth century provides some clues for why Rufino might have conceived of lay civic sanctity in this way. Rufino begins the text by noting that Raimondo was both a native of the city and had parents who were neither wealthy nor poor but

---

56. Wolf describes Raimondo as the "conscience of Piacenza"; see *The Poverty of Riches*, 74–75.

instead were "private citizens."[57] To describe them this way is to suggest that they occupied an economic middle ground: they were neither at the lowest social status nor members of the nobility. In fact, Rufino was likely signaling to his readers that Raimondo's parents were members of Piacenza's *popolo*.[58] Like Cremona, Piacenza endured a long battle waged by its new class of merchants and artisans for political control in the late twelfth and early thirteenth centuries.[59] Although the most significant period for this revolt came in the 1220s (twenty years after Raimondo's death, and eight years after Rufino wrote his *vita*), confrontations between the city's older nobility and the growing *popolo* began in the 1190s.[60] Rufino's interest in Raimondo's social background, his vivid depiction of Raimondo's pleas to the wealthy to help the city's less fortunate, and his keen sense of the harsh realities of urban life likely reflect the turbulent politics of this period in Piacenza's history.[61]

But although the political context of late medieval Piacenza seems an obvious factor in Rufino's decision to emphasize Raimondo's external turn, to what extent was this author also trying to navigate the dangerous terrain of the laity's embrace of the *vita apostolica*? If a layman could reach a perfected state through his rigorous adoption of the life of the apostles, or at least the late medieval conception of that life, by going on frequent pilgrimages, practicing an intense routine of penance, and seeking God through his prayers, what need was there for the institutional church? As I have noted, we can imagine such a question vexing Innocent III and leading him to write his canonization bull for Omobono. But if that bull offered a solution that aimed to change the nature of lay religiosity, Rufino's portrait of Raimondo offers a more complex resolution to the inherent tension of lay sanctity. By having a holy lay life keep at its core a focus upon external matters (charity relief, peacemaking, and civic justice), and by presenting such a focus as both protecting and sustaining the need for the church as well as the commune, the lay saint does not threaten but serves to sustain the institutional church's authority.

---

57. *Vita S. Raymundi*, 646: "Beatus Raymundus, quod quidem ad patriam attinet, Placentinus fuit, in ipsa natus urbe Placentia. Parentes habuit nec illustres origine, neque viles admodum; sed cives privatos, eosque, si rem spectes domesticam, nec pauperes nec opulentos."

58. On Raimondo's social origins, see Vauchez, *The Laity*, 59; and Canetti, *Gloriosa civitas*, 176–77. Rufino admits that he cannot be sure, but notes that many claim, that Raimondo's father worked as a cobbler; see *Vita S. Raymundi*, 646. Webb has wondered if Rufino left out any specific mention of what kind of trade Raimondo and his father practiced and that this aside is a later addition to the text; see *Saints and Cities*, 63.

59. For a general history of medieval Piacenza, see *Storia di Piacenza*, vol. 2 (Piacenza: Cassa di Risparmio di Piacenza, 1980).

60. See Canetti, *Gloriosa civitas*, 235–43; and Koenig, "The Popolo of Northern Italy," 68–136.

61. Thompson has noted that in 1204 a conflict between the city's ecclesiastical and secular authorities lead to the clergy leaving the city for three years; Thompson, *Cities of God*, 104.

By the middle of the thirteenth century, an emphasis on charitable works as well as a concern for social justice had become the most prevalent indicators of a perfected lay life, suggesting the extent to which Rufino's conception of an ideal lay life solved the inherent problems raised by the laity's embrace of the *vita apostolica*. The cults that were to grow up in the later thirteenth century around Zita of Lucca (d. 1278), as well as around Andrea Gallerani (d. 1251) and Pier "Pettinaio" (d. 1289), both of Siena, all present an ideal layperson as organizing his or her religious life around efforts to reform urban communities. In contrast with Raimondo, however, these communal lay saints do not berate and beg their fellow city-dwellers to effect that social change; instead they perform miracles while they are still alive to bring about that change. If we return to Cremona to look at the growth of Omobono's cult during the second half of the thirteenth century, as well as at the appearance of a cult dedicated to the celebrated gold and silversmith of that city, Facio (d. 1271), we see how Raimondo's version of lay sanctity was put in concert with the political and social context of rising *popolo* governments. The result was two cults (Omobono's in the later thirteenth century, and Facio's) that revive notions of the lay saint as living holy man and miracle worker.

The Later Lives of Omobono

During the thirteenth century, two additional *vitae* (both anonymous) were written for Omobono of Cremona. Scholars date the first, *Quoniam historiae*, to between 1200 and 1240, and the second, *Labentibus annis*, to between 1270 and 1300.[62] Although both of these new lives repeat details about the saint that likely came from Innocent's bull, *Quia pietas*, and the earlier *vita*, *Cum orbita solis*, they do not share those sources' negative assessment of lay life and instead play with ideas about lay sanctity that appear in the *vitae* of both Ranieri of Pisa and Raimondo of Piacenza. In particular, as we saw expressed in Raimondo's cult, they emphasize the spiritual potential that the challenges of work and family present. And similar to Ranieri of Pisa's cult, they see the ideal layman as a living miracle worker. Moreover, even though these two *vitae* take different approaches to describing Omobono's life, with *Quoniam historiae* focusing upon Omobono's penitential habits and *Labentibus annis* emphasizing the saint's ability to perform living miracles, both construct a holy lay life in a manner that reconceives Innocent's portrait of the lay saint. The Omobono

---

62. For a discussion of how scholars have dated these *vitae*, see Vauchez, *Omobono di Cremona* (†1197), 37–54; Piazzi, *Omobono di Cremona*, 49, 56–59, and 68–69; and Webb, *Saints and Cities*, 46–53.

who emerges in the later thirteenth-century texts is a lay saint whose actions are grounded in the political and social context of a *popolo*-dominated commune and who uses living miracles to demonstrate his holy status.

The anonymous author of *Quoniam historiae*, claiming that this *vita* offers details about the saint's life that were revealed during the canonization process and thus absent from the first *vita*, divides the text into short vignettes, each of which uses descriptions of various aspects of Omobono's religious life as evidence for his sanctity.[63] Such an organization suggests that this life was used for preaching.[64] With the focus it places upon the details of Omobono's penitential acts, *Quoniam historiae* functions as a kind of manual for lay people seeking more rigorous religious lives, and it reintroduces ideas about the lay religious life that were expressed in Raimondo's *vita*—a positive approach to the realities of a lay life as well as the belief that lay burdens and limitations can deepen and enrich spirituality.

Quoniam historiae makes these points by describing in depth the saint's penitential routine. The reader learns that Omobono followed a rigorous schedule of fasting: he fasted for all of Lent, went without his regular meals three days a week, limited himself to bread and water on Good Friday, and on the vigils of saints' feast days gave the food he would have eaten to the poor.[65] The reader is also given extensive descriptions of Omobono's struggles with the devil, his demanding schedule of prayer, and the tormenting belt and hair shirt he wore to aid his efforts to mortify the flesh. Although this *vita* offers many details about Omobono's everyday religious life that were not mentioned in either Innocent's bull or *Cum orbita solis*, *Quoniam historiae* still maintains the focus upon the saint's obedience to the church that we saw emphasized in those earlier sources. To that end, within the descriptions of Omobono's routines the *vita*'s author makes clear the extent to which the church structured Omobono's penitential life: Omobono was careful to confess his sins to his parish priest every week and listened closely to the weekly sermons, always trying to practice the teachings they offered.[66]

But although an emphasis on Omobono's obedience echoes ideas found in this saint's early cult, the interest *Quoniam historiae* shows in both the details

63. For *Quoniam historiae*, see Piazzi, *Omobono di Cremona*, 49–58; *Quoniam historiae*, 50.

64. Webb makes this point as well; *Saints and Cities*, 50. The earliest copy of this *vita* is nestled between the sixth and seventh *lectiones* of *Cum orbita solis* in an early thirteenth-century manuscript: Venice, Biblioteca Marciana, MS. Lat. 2798; for a full discussion of this manuscript, see Piazzi, *Omobono di Cremona*, 30–42; and Vauchez, *Omobono di Cremona (†1197)*, 39–54. The sixth *lectione* marks the end of this first *vita*'s description of Omobono's life, while the seventh *lectione* is the first of two that describe the saint's postmortem miracles.

65. *Quoniam historiae*, 50.

66. Ibid.

of Omobono's lay life—his wife, his children, and his work—and the benefit such responsibilities could bring to a lay religious life is new. In a paragraph that begins by offering a physical description of the saint—he was tall but slight and had a dark complexion—*Quoniam historiae* tells its audience that Omobono was a merchant but had first worked as a tailor, presenting details of this saint's lay life in a matter-of-fact manner.[67] Moreover, just as Rufino portrayed Raimondo's lay life as offering the saint greater opportunities to deepen his religious commitment, the author of *Quoniam historiae* makes use of the particulars about Omobono's work and family to help him convey the intensity of the saint's penitential practices. For example, he notes that if Omobono was working in his vineyard when he heard church bells ring to mark a canonical hour, the layman simply stopped what he was doing and began to pray.[68] In addition, if Omobono were to come upon a sick person in the street, the saint would give away his own coat, later telling his family that a thief had stolen it.[69] And while the author mentions how frustrated Omobono's wife became when she discovered her husband's habit of giving away their food and clothes to the poor, instead of depicting Omobono's marriage as keeping him from fulfilling his charitable impulses, the author uses the disagreement between husband and wife to enliven his narrative: he writes how Omobono became the holy thief (*beatus fur*), hiding the bread, wine, and meat in various spots (under the bed, in the window) before taking it to the poor.[70]

Despite the several mentions of Omobono's charity work, the *vita* appears more concerned to present such work as having strengthened the saint's spiritual life than as having addressed a critical social need. Such an approach marks a diversion from the vision of lay sanctity expressed in Rufino's life of Raimondo. Unlike Raimondo's *vita*, in which the reader is told that Christ explicitly instructed Raimondo to work for others rather than continuing to embark on pilgrimages to benefit his own spiritual profile, *Quoniam historiae* sees Omobono's charity work as something that at its core not only demonstrates but

---

67. Ibid., 54.

68. Ibid., 50.

69. Ibid., 52.

70. Ibid.: "Murmurabat etiam familia sua ex hoc quod pauperibus erogabat portionem suam, quam comedere debebat, modica tamen particula sibi retenta, ut superius dixi . . . Furabatur et panes, vinum, carnes, nummos et quidquid pauperibus fore utile sibi videbatur et sub lecto suo vel in foraminibus domus vel in fenestris abscondebat et privatim ad domum pauperum et infirmorum deportabat. De quo cum familia eius perciperet et sub clave panem, vinum, carnes et his similia reponebat, sed beatus fur et contra clavem furabatur, ut de absconditis pauperes recrearet." Omobono was, of course, far from the only saint to endure wrath from his family when he gave away their goods; see Caroline Walker Bynum, *Holy Feast and Holy Fast: The Religious Significance of Food to Medieval Women* (Berkeley: University of California Press, 1987), 80, 121–22, and 124–29.

also enriches the saint's spiritual development. Thus, when the text reports on Omobono's generous distribution of alms to the poor, the reader does not hear about how desperately the Cremonese needed such aid but instead about the lengths to which the saint went in order to steal and hide food from his disapproving family.[71] Moreover, when the reader is told how Omobono had once offered his cloak to a poor and naked man whom he found in his vineyard, the *vita* seems more interested in describing how Omobono explained his actions to his family rather than detailing how this man ended up in such a condition in the first place.[72] Instead of using Omobono's charity work as an opportunity to criticize the harsh economic reality of late medieval civic life, *Quoniam historiae* remains more interested in describing the particular steps this layman took to remake himself into a saint. It seems likely that hagiographic models beyond communal Italy played a role in establishing those steps. *Quoniam historiae's* portrait of Omobono brings to mind the tales of charity and penance made famous in the *vitae* of such saints as Martin and Alexius.

But the local political context was also at play here. In his study of the many medieval *vitae* created for Omobono, Daniele Piazzi has noted how well the model presented in *Quoniam historiae* would have spoken to the merchant and artisan population that was dominating Cremona's civic and political life by the mid-thirteenth century.[73] Like so many other northern Italian cities, Cremona had experienced a dramatic period of growth in the late twelfth century.[74] Its position on the Po River and its production of fustians (a coarse cloth typically worn by laborers) were key factors for this growth. In the late twelfth century, Cremona had expanded its walls to enclose both a *città vecchia*, where the city's *milites*, or its noble and merchant elite, lived, and a *città nuova*, populated largely by members of the *popolo*, the city's lesser merchants and artisans. As I have already noted, Bishop Sicard's decision to award a third of city offices to *popolani* was likely an effort to weaken this new faction. Nevertheless, by 1229, Cremona's *popolo* faction had set up a separate communal government, complete with its own statutes and elected officials, and in 1256, it had built the Palazzo Cittanova to be its headquarters.

The fact that *Quoniam historiae* was likely composed between 1200 and 1240, a time of intense political battles between the city's older guard and its rising merchant and artisan class, lends support to Piazzi's point. Moreover, the ab-

---

71. *Quoniam historiae*, 52.
72. Ibid.
73. Piazzi, *Omobono di Cremona*, 58
74. For a brief history of medieval Cremona, see Sella, "Cremona," 263–67. Also see Gualazzini, *Il "populus" di Cremona*.

sence of any negative assessment of Omobono's lay responsibilities also argues for seeing this *vita* as written to appeal particularly to Cremona's rising *popolo*. But while the *vita* presents the saint's civic charity work as a key aspect of his sanctity, if we compare it to the final thirteenth-century life for Omobono, *Labentibus annis*, which talks extensively about the saint's social context, we see how very little *Quoniam historiae* actually says about late medieval Cremona. Instead of wanting to reflect the social and political realities of thirteenth-century Cremona, the author of *Quoniam historiae* seems most interested in providing a model of a dedicated lay penitential life; a model that aims to circumscribe the internal focus integral to any rigorous religious life. Thus, even though *Quoniam historiae* does not explicitly argue for turning one's attention away from one's own spiritual progress and toward the welfare of a civic community, as we saw when Christ instructed Raimondo to stop his pilgrimages and return to care for the needy in Piacenza, the specific details this *vita* gives about Omobono's penitential life still present an ideal lay religious life as penitentially restrained and externally directed. Omobono fasts, but only on particular days. He gives his and his family's goods and food away but earns an income from his vineyards. He wears a tormenting hair shirt and belt but adheres to the priest's commands. At the same time that *Quoniam historiae* recognizes the lay penitent's need for some internal focus, it is careful to present that focus as circumscribed by obedience to a church hierarchy as well as to a civic order.

Not long after the appearance of *Quoniam historiae*, another *vita* was added to Omobono's hagiographic portfolio. Scholars have dated the writing of *Labentibus annis* to sometime during the last third of the thirteenth century.[75] As is the case for *Cum orbita solis* and *Quoniam historiae*, the author of this *vita* has remained anonymous.[76] Above all else, the portrait of Omobono presented in *Labentibus annis* emphasizes the saint's identity as a model member of his civic community. Although the *vita* mentions the penitential practices the saint followed, these acts do not constitute the author's main evidence for Omobono's sanctity. Instead, the author of *Labentibus annis* locates Omobono's holy reputation in his ability to turn the impediments of his lay life into spiritual opportunities that respond to the needs of his fellow city-dwellers, largely through the performance of living miracles. By pre-

---

75. Vauchez, *Omobono di Cremona (†1197)*, 48.

76. *Labentibus annis* has been preserved in four medieval manuscripts, the earliest dated to 1301; on the manuscript history, see Piazzi, *Omobono di Cremona*, 59–60; and Vauchez, *Omobono di Cremona (†1197)*, 47–54. We do know that it was used as the model for the *vita autentica* written by the canons of Cremona's cathedral in 1570. For more on Omobono's *vita authentica*, see Piazzi, *Omobono di Cremona*, 79–92.

senting Omobono as a layman whose rigorous religious life gave him the means to effect cures that heal the economic and social disparities of his urban community, the author of *Labentibus annis* gives Omobono an agency that ought to remind us of Ranieri of Pisa. And yet, unlike Ranieri, this lay saint's living miracles pose no threat to the church's authority. In this final thirteenth-century *vita* for Omobono, we have a layman who performs miracles that simultaneously emphasize his role as holy man, obedient member of the church, and civic charity worker. In short, we have the fully realized communal lay saint.

From its very beginning, *Labentibus annis* announces its focus on Omobono's civic context. The first lines of the *vita* bemoan the sad state of the city during the saint's lifetime. Whereas in *Quia pietas* Innocent called Omobono a "lily among thorns," the author of *Labentibus annis* refers to the saint as a "rose" produced by God to inflame and lead away from sin not only the people of Cremona, whom he describes as "blinded by the great falsehoods of heretics," but also those in the surrounding region.[77] From the larger city, the author narrows his focus to describing Omobono's neighborhood, family, and professional context, details about the saint that speak to the particular social context of late medieval Cremona as well as seem aimed to encourage a contemporary lay audience to identify with this portrait of Omobono.

To that end, the author writes that the saint's parents lived among "other citizens of middling and popular rank" in an area surrounding the church of Sant' Egidio, which he notes had become quite densely populated.[78] These details would have served as key social and political identifiers for a late thirteenth-century audience. The Sant' Egidio neighborhood was part of the *città nuova*, the area created by the expansion of the city walls in the late twelfth century and populated by merchants and artisans (citizens of "middling and popular rank"). We learn that Omobono was a member of the "de' Tucenghi" family, which, the author notes, had practiced a variety of trades but most recently had been known to be tailors. Omobono's father lived both "on the

77. *Labentibus annis*, 60: "Labentibus annis ab incarnatione mille centum nonaginta septem, cum Cremona urbs magnis haereticorum esset decaecata fallatiis, qui quasi spinae saepius bonorum etiam animas lacerabant, rosam in spinis attulit Deus, quae non quidem Cremonam urbem, verum adiacentem patriam sui odoris fragrantiam de peccati foetore ad virtutis redolentiam adductam servaret de vitiosis animum ad honeste beateque vivendum accenderet sui Conditoris cognitione et hiis spretis falatiis quae fere omnium hominum vanas sollicitant mentes."

78. Ibid.: "Illo itaque tempore in ea civitate iuxta basilicam incliti confessoris Egidii, tum civium frequentia tum aedificiorum structura cives, illam non indecoram partem effecerant. Eo loco inter concives ceterasque prosapias, quas medriocris status popularis fortuna fovebat, habitabat quaedam prosapia de Tucengo tunc dicta, cuius domus antiqui variis pro tempore mercaturae artis officiis praedicti etiam resarciendorum vestimentorum arte vivebant; eorum quos et sartores vulgo appellare solemus."

produce of his labors," and on the income generated by the land he owned outside of the city.[79]

Similar to the account of the beginnings of Raimondo of Piacenza's religious life, the author of *Labentibus annis* describes Omobono as having lived a relatively pious life until the death of his father prompted him to take up a more comprehensive religious commitment. After his father's death, Omobono "became his own master," and began to think about the shortness of life as well as "the falsity of the world and its fleeting goods." Such thoughts prompted him to give up his "great preoccupation with increasing his fortune."[80] And although he had always been "assiduous in attending church, in prayer and fasting" and had always given the wealth he made from his trade to the poor and needy, the spiritual clarity brought by his father's death led him to make a significant change: he stopped working. The author notes that this greatly upset Omobono's wife, whose nagging gave the saint a chance to explain his new orientation. When she demanded to know why he "no longer lived by his trade" but was instead giving all of their goods away "to wretched people," he told her that "fleeting earthly goods were like a flow of water," and that he "who stored up treasure in heaven by aiding the poor of Christ" was a happy man.[81]

But even though *Labentibus annis* makes clear that Omobono turned away from his worldly duties, this *vita* does not use detailed descriptions of Omobono's penitential practices to illustrate or prove his sanctity. The reader is simply told that Omobono assiduously attended church, followed a rigorous schedule of prayer and fasting, and devoted himself to helping Cremona's needy; no specifics are given about these activities. Instead, *Labentibus annis*

---

79. Ibid.: "Ex hac prosapia de Tucegno antiquus vir cum uxore sua suis laboribus vivens, ibi domo quam eius attavi possederant, habitabat; cui et agrorum satis ampla possessio non longe a moenibus eius urbis victus necessaria ministrabat."

80. Ibid.: "Cum qua uxore plurimos annos vivente patre cum omni ad parentes oboedientia permanens; statuto die mortuo patre, sui iuris effectus, considerare coepit breves hominis dies et falacem mundum eiusque bona fugacia nihilque sanctius fieri quam quod evangelicus sermo testatur: 'Thesaurizate vobis thesauros in caelo, ubi neque aerugo neque tinea demolitur.' Hoc ergo iamplurimos dies intentus proposito, quo dudum in illo grandis sollicitudo augendarum fortunarum callere consueverat, tepere iam coepit, nec socios sequi, nec operam solito artificio consummare . . ."

81. Ibid., 62: "Cum vero eius sic mutatum uxor a propositis maritum videret et industriam et artem solita reliquisse, seque quasi in contemptum hominibus saeculi vitam dedisse, illi non parum molesta effecta est dicens: 'Quae te, Homobone, quondam prudens vir iam coepit insania, cum nec arti nec exercitio, quibus honorifice vivebas, attendas, sed eis destitutis omnia bona nostra consumis in miserabilibus ea errogando personis, ex quibus non minimum unquam servitium expectamus!'. Et multa adversus virum sanctum improperia contumeliasque fundebat. Ille vero patienter ferens, illi praedicabat fugentia bona terrena velut aquarum lapsus et felicem illum thesaurum, qui subveniendo pauperibus Christi congregatur in caelis. Huius uxoris saepe varias temptationes accipiens, semper cum patientia et humilitate vincebat."

takes as its primary focus a number of miracles Omobono performed while still alive, stressing the way in which the saint's penitential acts gave him the ability to move beyond the inherent limitations of his lay status and attend to the needs of his fellow city-dwellers as a living holy man.

For example, the first living miracle described in *Labentibus annis* concerns Omobono's rigorous schedule of prayer. Noting that it was the saint's custom to go to his neighborhood church of Sant' Egidio every night, the author writes how the church's priest, Osbert, whom we know from Innocent's bull had served as Omobono's confessor for twenty years, always came to open the church doors for the saint. One day, Osbert was not there. After Omobono had waited for some time, "by God's will" the doors miraculously opened on their own. The author writes how this sequence of events repeated several times, making Osbert come to see that "this was the work of God and that this was a holy man."[82] The author also describes several miracles of food multiplication that Omobono performed for the benefit of his fellow Cremonese.[83] Once, during a famine, Omobono received his usual bread delivery but found a crowd of the "poor and needy" had gathered around his house. The saint gave away his family's bread to the crowd but was saved from his wife's punishment when she opened their cupboard to find it full of loaves "of an incomparable firmness and quality, as many in number as Omobono had given away."[84] Moreover, after informing the reader that the saint had kept a "little vineyard" in order to support himself and tend to the poor, the author

---

82. Ibid.: "Erat autem huic sancto homini consuetudo singulis noctibus ad ecclesiam suam accedere, ut ibi continue matutinali interesset officio. Unde presbyter Osbertus quidam nomine, qui tunc illius ecclesiae curam gerebat, vir et ipse bonus ac timens Deum, cum huiusmodi Homoboni devotionem vidisset, singulis noctibus cum pulsaret campanam pro Matutinis, veniebat ut ei aperiret et in ecclesiam ipsum induceret. Unde cum quadam vice ante sonitum campanae Homobonus venisset et aliquandiu stetisset ante ecclesiam expectans ante valvas, ecclesiae portae nutu Dei per se ipsas in conspectu sancti Dei apertae sunt . . . ex quo intellexit sacerdos hoc opus esse divinum et hunc sanctum virum existere, cum illud postmodum in annis viginti sex, quibus sacerdos ille ecclesiam rexit, pluribus vicibus accidit quod superius narratum est."

83. In her study of the religious significance of food to medieval women, Bynum notes that while the confluence of food and religion is most often seen in the lives of female saints, medieval men were often associated with miracles of food multiplication. Bynum cites the work of Herbert Thurston, who has noted that food multiplication miracles seem to occur as much to male saints as to female saints. As Bynum points out, Thurston includes modern saints as well as medieval ones; see Bynum, *Holy Feast and Holy Fast*, 76 and 332, n. 21.

84. *Labentibus annis*, 62–63: "Quadam vero die dum tempore famis quandam mensuram panis, ut fieri solet, furni magister ad sancti viri detulisset domum, cognovissentque egeni et pauperes plurimi hunc panem ad Homobonum patrem pauperum pertinere, portantem secuti sunt usque ad domum viri Dei; quem in domo repertum suppliciter petunt ut eis, more solito, ex hoc pane pias eleemosynas largiatur. Quibus annuens, ne uxor perpendeat, quae forte tunc aberat, maiorem partem distribuit panis. Venta vero uxore, cum hora esset cenae, ad arcam vadens uxor duplex genus panis videt in arca. Nam quot panes dederat Homobonus, tot erant incomparabili bonitate et pulchritudine cum reliquis."

describes how one day Omobono took a jug of wine to the men who worked his land. On the way to the vineyard, Omobono gave away all of the wine to the poor people he passed, leaving him afraid of his wife's reproaches and unwilling to return home. But after filling the jug with water, and making the sign of the cross over it, Omobono found it full of wine.[85]

The portrait of an ideal lay religious life in *Labentibus annis* demonstrates a dramatic departure from the depiction of Omobono we saw in both Innocent III's canonization bull and the saint's first *vita, Cum orbita solis.* Omobono's working and married life are not details either to be ignored or disparaged but aspects of the saint's life that offered him more opportunity to practice and articulate his new religious orientation. After Omobono comes to realize "the brevity of human life and the falsity of the world and its fleeting goods," *Labentibus annis* does not launch into a diatribe against a merchant's work, as his first *vita* had, but instead presents his decision to give his earnings to the poor and needy as an ideal response.[86] And when his wife complains about his actions, this *vita* describes how Omobono saw her distress as both a trial to endure and as opportunity to explain his new religious commitment.[87]

Thus from the text's first lines, the author of *Labentibus annis* makes clear the importance Cremona plays in understanding Omobono's story. We are told of the saint's family background, the social makeup of his neighborhood, and the ways in which his family earned a living. While the *vita* looks to Omobono's own spiritual development as part of its argument for his sanctity, it sees his holiness as most clearly articulated in miracle stories that describe his connection with and duty toward his civic community instead of his own penitential practices. The focus of a lay penitential life has moved away from an internal focus on self-improvement, as we saw emphasized in *Quoniam historiae,* toward an externally minded penitential commitment that rights the wrongs of an unequal society without drawing attention to any larger systematic problems. Although Innocent may very well have seen the living miracles of a layman as endowing him with a power that could ultimately threaten the church's authority, *Labentibus annis* delivers a new vision of the miracle-working layman that speaks to the particular civic context of the late medieval communes and renders the holy layman an unthreatening force. Omobono's penance does not turn him into a new manifestation of Christ, bent on restoring a broken church, as Ranieri of Pisa's had, but rather allows him to become the ultimate model of social responsibility: the layman who can heal inequality through his living miracles.

---

85. Ibid., 64.
86. Ibid., 60.
87. Ibid.

Omobono's Civic Cult

Although there was a flurry of activity around Omobono initiated by Pope Innocent III's 1199 canonization and the saint's first *vita*, *Cum orbita solis* (likely written by Bishop Sicard in the autumn of 1198), most of our evidence for his civic cult comes from the fourteenth century.[88] Around 1310, a statue of the saint clutching a pouch of money he famously distributed to Cremona's poor occupied a niche on the outside back wall of the cathedral (figure 4).[89]

Bishop Sicard had moved some of Omobono's remains from Sant' Egidio, where the saint had so often prayed, died, and was first buried, to the cathedral in June 1202. It was not until 1356, however, that these remains were installed in the cathedral's crypt.[90] It was also in 1356 that Bishop Ugolino Ardengherio founded a fraternal organization in the saint's name, the "consortium sancti Homoboni."[91] And while Cremona's Bishop Rainerio di Casole (1296–1312) required all parishes within the diocese to celebrate the feast days not only of their titular saints but also of Omobono and Cremona's sixth-century bishop Imerio, we do not see Omobono named as a civic patron in civic statutes until 1339.[92]

Scholars have attributed the lag between the church's initial promotion of Omobono and the growth of his civic cult to the antagonism that existed between the city and the papacy through much of the thirteenth century.[93] After the death of Sicard in 1215, Cremona's reputation as a Ghibelline stronghold and a haven for Cathars created an environment in which a saint championed by the papacy and its ecclesiastical ally might not have captured the interest of civic authorities. It was only after 1270, when Cremona had fallen firmly into Guelf hands, that we see the city beginning to promote Omobono's cult; the first evidence of that interest comes in the Sala degli Alabardieri within the communal palace, where in frescos likely produced between 1270

---

88. Vauchez, *Omobono di Cremona (†1197)*, 73.

89. Today, this sculpture can be found on the cathedral's façade. The sculpture of Omobono stands to one side of the Virgin holding a baby Jesus. A sculpture of Cremona's other patron saint, the sixth-century Bishop Imerio, which was also originally created for a back niche, also flanks the Virgin; Alfredo Puerari, *Il duomo di Cremona* (Milan: Cassa di Risparmio delle Provincine Lombarde, 1971), 114–18.

90. Vauchez, *Omobono di Cremona (†1197)*, 77.

91. Ibid., 76–77; and Vauchez, *Sainthood*, 129. Vauchez also notes that Omobono's image had begun to show up on Cremona's coins a few years before civic statutes produced in 1339: *Sainthood*, 129, n. 3.

92. *Statuta et ordinamenta comunis Cremonae, facta et compilata currente anno MCCCXXXIX*, ed. Ugo Gualazzini (Milan: Giuffrè, 1952), 92–94, 190–91.

93. Vauchez makes this point most thoroughly in *Omobono di Cremona (†1197)*, 78–81.

FIGURE 4. "Omobono of Cremona," ca. 1310, Cremona Cathedral. Photo by Michael Howerton.

and 1280, Omobono is depicted next to Cremona's other patron saint, Bishop Imerio.[94]

And yet, although communal authorities do not seem to have shown an interest in Omobono until the late thirteenth century, evidence from Omobono's parish church, Sant' Egidio, suggests that an active cult did remain there throughout the century. In his 1245 *Liber epilogorum in vitis sanctorum*, the Dominican hagiographer Bartolomeo da Trento mentions the construction of an *ecclesia testudinata* adjacent to Sant' Egidio, a structure that scholars have speculated constituted of a *martyrium* or centrally planned octagonal building not unlike the early Christian churches of Santo Stefano Rotondo in Rome or Jerusalem's Church of the Holy Sepulchre.[95] This structure, no longer ex-

94. See Marco Tanzi and Andrea Mosconi, *Il Palazzo Comunale di Cremona e le sue collezioni d'arte* (Milan: Electa, 1981).

95. Vauchez discusses these remains (*Omobono di Cremona (†1197)*, 77) but draws most of his information from Giorgio Voltini, "La prima chiesa di Sant' Omobono: Architettura e fonti storiche," in *Omobono: La figura del santo nell'iconografia, secoli XIII–XIX*, ed. Pietro Bonometti (Milan: Silvana, 1999), 133–39. For Bartolomeo da Trento's text, see *Liber epilogorum in gesta sanctorum*, ed. Emore

FIGURE 5. "Omobono of Cremona," ca. 1200, Cremona, Church of S. Omobono (the former S. Egidio). Photo by Michael Howerton.

tant but known through recent archaeological work at Sant' Omobono (the former Sant' Egidio), held not only a sculptural depiction of the saint created around the time of his canonization (figure 5) but also the cross that Omobono had frequently prayed in front of, as well as some of his remains that were not moved into the cathedral.[96]

Scholars believe that this *ecclesia testudinata* was begun quite early in the thirteenth century, likely around 1202 (the same year that some of Omobono's remains were translated into the cathedral), and was administered, until at least 1521, by a combination of a community of canons and lay *fratres*.[97]

Paoli (Florence: Sismel, 2001), 343–44. I am taking *testudinata* as a variant of *testitudo* or "vaulted hall, nave"; see Niermeyer, *Mediae latinitatis lexicon*, 1340–41.

96. Vauchez, *Omobono di Cremona (†1197)*, 76–77 and 126. This statue, likely made between 1200 and 1230, can now be found on the façade of Sant' Omobono (the former Sant' Egidio). For more on the statue, see Puerari, *Il duomo di Cremona*, 103–35.

97. Vauchez, *Omobono di Cremona (†1197)*, 78; and F. Aporti, *Memorie di storia ecclesiastica di Cremona*, vol. 1 (Cremona, 1835), 112. Although there were two structures present on this site, it was not until 1356 that Sant' Egidio was officially renamed Sant' Edigio e Sant' Omobono to recognize the separate identities of the dual structures.

In his *Liber epilogorum*, Bartolomeo da Trento also mentions that Omobono's cult was particularly associated with the release of prisoners, noting the *insignia* (likely a kind of *ex voto* or material offering) found in "his church" (*sua ecclesia*) that referenced these miracles.[98] Such information points us tantalizingly toward the saint's popular cult; a subject that we hear almost nothing about in our earliest sources. While Innocent discussed one postmortem miracle performed in Omobono's name (the freeing of the possessed woman), neither his canonization bull nor Sicard's first *vita* gives us a sense of how the Cremonesi interacted with Omobono during his lifetime or his tomb after his death. Did his fellow Cremonesi seek him out for miraculous cures during his lifetime? Did his cult become associated with particular types of cures or miracles, as Bartolomeo da Trento suggests? *Labentibus annis* seems intent on filling in some of these gaps in our knowledge about Omobono by describing his many living miracles. But we are still left to wonder why some of the saint's remains were kept at Sant' Egidio. Do Bartolomeo da Trento's remarks suggest that there were two centers of Omobono's cult, one that was managed by Cremona's episcopal authority and one that remained at his parish church? To what extent might we see the writing of *Quoniam historiae* and *Labentibus annis* as attempts to integrate these strands?

In other words, does the lag between Omobono's canonization and his appearance as a civic patron of Cremona suggest a divided, or at least, a diverse cult? Did the cult advocated for in Innocent's bull and Sicard's first *vita*—the cult that had its headquarters at the city's cathedral—reflect a portrait of lay sanctity at odds with how Omobono was celebrated at the newly expanded Sant' Egidio after his death? Might Omobono have had a reputation as a living healer, as Ranieri of Pisa had? Might he have voiced more trenchant social and political criticisms, along the lines of Raimondo of Piacenza? The extant sources do not allow us to answer these questions. But the evidence of a thirteenth-century cult at Sant' Egidio suggests that such questions ought to be asked. Those questions seem ever more pressing when we turn to explore the cult of another Cremonese lay saint: Facio.

Facio of Cremona and His Holy Hands

A 1272 cathedral obituary notes the death of Facio of Cremona, a gold and silversmith, who, we are told, lived a life dedicated to arduous penitence, dili-

---

98. Bartolomeo da Trento, *Liber epilogorum*, 343–34: "Fitque ei a Cremonensibus testudinata ecclesia et decenter sepelitur. Multisque miraculis claret, maxime in redemption capitvorum, sicut insignia in sua ecclesia demonstrant."

gent prayer, and many pilgrimages.[99] The obituary notes the outpouring of devotion the clergy and people of Cremona showed at Facio's cathedral tomb.[100] The immediate interest in this pious artisan was so large that a cathedral priest, Don Pre Iohannes, assembled a collection of the fifteen miracles the saint had reportedly performed during his lifetime and the fifty miracles that took place in the first three months after his death.[101] A *vita*, which included mention of most of Facio's living miracles, was written a few years later by another cathedral cleric, and repeats the obituary's assessment of Facio: he was to be venerated for his great commitment to fasting, abstinence, and his regular prayer schedule, as well as for the many pilgrimages he undertook and the work he did to defend the faith.[102] By the mid-fourteenth century, he was being named, alongside Omobono, as a civic patron in communal statutes.[103]

To some extent, all three of our earliest sources for Facio's cult—the cathedral obituary, the miracle collection, and the *vita*—portray this artisan as embodying the model of the holy layman that Innocent had created in his canonization of Omobono. But if we look more carefully at the many living miracles these sources ascribe to Facio, we see how Innocent's prescription of an ideal lay life had been altered over the thirteenth century. While Facio remained obedient and subservient to an ecclesiastical hierarchy, the numerous living miracles he performed through physical contact harkens back to an earlier model of lay sanctity. Just as Ranieri of Pisa had brought cures to his fellow Pisans via his touch, Facio is repeatedly credited with acting as a living holy man, by healing numerous Cremonese with his hands. But unlike Ranieri and Omobono, Facio does not have to give up his work to reach a spiritual ideal: rather, he is celebrated for redirecting his profits and his artisan skills for the benefit of the poor and unfortunate within his civic community.

---

99. *L'obituario della cattedrale di Cremona (obituarium ecclesias cremonensis)*, ed. Francesco Novati (Milan: Bortolotti, 1881), 34–35.

100. Ibid.

101. Vauchez has published an edition of Facio's *vita* (hereafter *Vita Beati Facii*) that includes the fifteen living miracles and nine of the postmortem accounts. His edition also includes an extensive introductory essay discussing the manuscript history of the *vita* and miracle collection as well as the development of Facio's cult; see André Vauchez, "Sainteté laïque au XIIIe siècle: La vie du bienheureux Facio de Crémone (v. 1196–1272)," *Mélanges de l'École Française de Rome* 84 (1972): 13–53.

102. *Vita Beati Facii*, 39. Both the *Vita Beati Facii* and the miracle collection survive in only one, sixteenth-century manuscript that includes a list of signatures of those clerics who between 1582 and 1756 had used this manuscript in the city's cathedral to celebrate Facio's January 18 feast day. Vauchez notes that there are mentions of a thirteenth-century copy in the archives of Cremona's l'Ospedale Maggiore through the nineteenth century. Unfortunately this copy has disappeared; see Vauchez, "Sainteté laïque au XIIIe siècle," 14.

103. *Statuta et ordinamenta comunis Cremonae*, 92–94, 190–91.

Facio was not a native of Cremona but had fled to the city as a young man when his political party had fallen out of favor in his hometown of Verona.[104] When Facio first arrived in Cremona, he was already living as a penitent, practicing a rigorous lay religious life and working as a gold- and silversmith. Not long after coming to Cremona, however, Facio returned to Verona in an attempt to reconcile with his former enemies, and as the *vita* reports, be able to free his mind for greater divine contemplation.[105] His enemies in the city promptly threw him into prison. It was during this time in prison that a cadre of devotees began to seek out Facio for his growing reputation as a thaumaturge. Both the *vita* and miracle collection recount two miracles that Facio performed in prison. In the first, a woman came to the artisan's prison cell with her dying baby, whom she reported had refused to nurse for some time. After Facio made the sign of the cross over the baby and instructed it to "suck those breasts!" the baby began to nurse and was restored to health.[106] In the second account, we learn that Facio had sent bread that he had blessed to a Humiliati woman whom he had been told was possessed by a demon. After receiving Facio's blessed bread, the woman came to see him in prison; while there she was finally freed from the tormenting demon after Facio made the sign of the cross over her and sprinkled her with holy water.[107] The *vita* goes on to describe Facio's eventual release from prison, his return to Cremona, and the long life he lived in his adopted city—a life, the *vita* makes clear, that was dominated by his dedication to penance, prayer, and charity. Two lay charitable organizations founded by Facio speak to that dedication: the lay confraternity of Santo Spirito and a hospice in his home dedicated to serving the city's poor (the origins of Cremona's L'Ospedale Maggiore).[108]

---

104. Vauchez, "Sainteté laïque au XIIIe siècle," 21–22. There are two extant charters produced in Verona that mention a *Facinus aurifex* (or Facio, the goldsmith): in a 1221 charter a man is identified as a companion of Facio's (*socii Facini aurificis*), while in 1222, a man names Facio as his financial proxy. As Vauchez has noted, we cannot be certain that this is the same Facio for whom a cult would develop in Cremona, but it seems likely. See Lorenzo Astegiano, *Codex diplomaticus Cremonae, 715–1334*, vol. 1 (Torino, 1896), 243 and 245. For the *vita's* description of the trouble Facio ran into in his native Verona, see *Vita Beati Facii*, 36.

105. *Vita Beati Facii*, 37.

106. Ibid.: "Unde cum quaedam domina haberet filium suum unius anni et plus pene iam mortuum, quia per octo dies non suxerat mammas . . . curcurrit ad carcerem ac devote petivit a beato Facio ut benediceret filio suo morienti, qui mox facto in eum crucis signaculo dixit: In nomine illius benedicti pueri de Bethleem, suge mammas, fili mi, dixitque matri: date sibi pectus; et cum mater porrigeret sibi mamillam, statim puer cepit sugere, et sic de die in diem convalescere, donec ad perfectam sanitatem fuit mira celeritate reductus."

107. Ibid., 37–38.

108. On the origins of Cremona's L'Ospedale Maggiore, see Vauchez, "Sainteté laïque au XIIIe siècle," 16–20; and F. Soldi, *La carità di Cremona* (Cremona: Pizzorni, 1959).

Although the descriptions of Facio's charitable work constitute some of the *vita*'s most salient evidence for his sanctity and place him within the model of lay piety proposed in Innocent's canonization bull, those descriptions also relate the physical and environmental cures or miracles that Facio performed in the midst of that work, a subject not found in either *Quia pietas* or Omobono's first *vita*, *Cum orbita solis*. Thus, we hear about how Facio straightened twisted and deformed bodies, restored sight to the blind, and healed the sick.[109] We also hear about how he calmed the sea as he and members of his confraternity made their way to or from a pilgrimage, and how he stopped the overflowing Po from consuming Cremona.[110] Some of these accounts suggest that it was the simple proximity to the saint that allowed Facio's holy power to heal (when, for example, a devotee was cured of his bodily ailment by spending the night next to Facio),[111] but most describe the goldsmith using physical gestures to bring about his cures: Facio cures a woman's blindness by blowing three times into her eyes; he ends the agony brought on by a foot fistula by making the sign of the cross and then blowing three times on the foot; and he is able to remove a thorn stuck in one man's throat by again blowing three times, in this case into the man's mouth.[112]

Facio's *vita* thus not only places a particular stress upon the miracles this layman performed during his lifetime but also emphasizes how integral Facio's actions were to those cures. Facio himself must act by blessing bread, making the sign of the cross, or blowing on a compromised body part to bring about the cure. Facio's method of performing miracles ought to recall Ranieri of Pisa's *vita*, where we hear story after story of limbs straightened, mouths fed, and dying children healed through Ranieri's blessings and touch. The living miracles that dominate both Facio's miracle collection and *vita* thus revive an understanding of a holy lay life that places particular emphasis on the healing potential of physical contact between the saint and his devotee; an aspect of lay sanctity emphasized in our earliest sources (remember the fishes licking Gualfardo of Verona's hands) but ignored in Innocent's bull. Whereas Omobono (in all three of his thirteenth-century *vitae*) and Raimondo are celebrated for delivering charity to their civic communities—feeding, clothing, and sheltering the needy, and, in *Labentibus annis*, producing food multiplication miracles while alive—any miracles of bodily healing that were credited to them took place after their deaths. Devotees primarily sought cures from Omobono and Raimondo through prayers and visits to these laymen's tombs.

---

109. For example, see *Vita Beati Facii*, 43–48.
110. Ibid., 41.
111. Ibid., 43–44.
112. See esp. ibid., 44, 45, and 47.

Like Ranieri of Pisa, however, Facio performs healing miracles during his lifetime and does so either through bread he has blessed or through gestures of blessing.

The active performance of healing miracles is not the only aspect of Facio's saintly cult that looks like a move away from the model of lay sanctity proposed by Innocent: Facio's *vita* also celebrates the fact that this layman continued to work. Unlike *Cum orbita solis*, which commends Omobono for abandoning his "perverse and miserable business" to attend to "blessed contemplation," Facio's *vita* makes several references to his reputation as a highly skilled artisan and, without missing a beat, posits a connection between the excellence he demonstrated in his trade and the excellence he showed in his religious life.[113] Integral to Facio's great reputation as a goldsmith, the *vita* makes clear, was the fact that he used his profits to feed and support the needy of Cremona.[114] The positive spin on Facio's professional life completes ideas we saw germinating in both Raimondo of Piacenza's *vita* and in the two later thirteenth-century *vitae* of Omobono, *Quoniam historiae* and *Labentibus annis*. Raimondo preaches penance in "workshops," where the workers who followed his exhortations began to resemble religious orders. And while *Quoniam historiae* presents a matter-of-fact attitude toward Omobono's work, *Labentibus annis* sees Omobono's decision to stop working after his father's death as a step in his penitential progress that allowed him to dedicate himself more fully to his prayer and charity work but does not denigrate his former working life. Thus, over the thirteenth century, lay saints' *vitae* had come to adopt a new understanding of the lay working life. The fullest expression of that changing attitude came in Facio's *vita*, in which lay work does not hinder but rather aids lay religion.

But Facio's early cult also emphasized Facio's obedience to Cremona's religious authority, a trait that Innocent had celebrated in Omobono. Both the *vita* and miracle collection describe trips Facio made at the behest of the city's bishop to visit and enact cures at several convents within the diocese where nuns were either suffering from a prolonged drought or from demonic possession.[115] In several pious bequests made by Cremonese to the Santo Spirito confraternity, which Facio had founded, the brothers of that institution are not only called *consortium fratris Facii* and *consortium Sancti Spiritus* but also *consortio maioris ecclesiae*, suggesting an association between Facio's institution

---

113. Ibid., 36–37.

114. For example, the *vita* claims that Facio worked as a goldsmith not out of vanity but as a means to have more money to fund his confraternity, Santo Spirito, as well as his hospice; see *Vita Beati Facii*, 37. The *vita* also sees Facio's income as funding for his charitable activities; see ibid., 39.

115. Ibid., 41–42.

and the cathedral.[116] In addition, the description of Facio's death simultaneously reminds us of Omobono's death and emphasizes Facio's role as an obedient layman: Facio died after he had received the Eucharist and listened to psalter as well as other readings.[117]

And yet, while Facio was clearly obedient to a church hierarchy, Facio's penitential commitment endows him with a religious authority that goes beyond the traditional limits of the laity and suggests a blurring of religious status. Facio blesses bread, makes the sign of the cross above the suffering, and blows on his devotees to bring about cures, acts that suggest that this layman has earned clerical privilege. Such a blurring ought to remind us of Ranieri of Pisa's cult, in which his *vita* repeatedly associates him with blessed water and bread, and depictions of the Pisan saint on a cathedral font show him blessing a priest. In addition, Facio's *vita* does not shy away from portraying the goldsmith and his fellow members of Santo Spirito as constituting a lay religious order, repeatedly referring to Facio and his companions as *fratres*.[118]

And finally, unlike Omobono's cult, Facio's cult seems to have been embraced not only by Cremona's ecclesiastical authority but also by the commune without delay. He was immediately buried in the cathedral and shows up alongside Omobono as a civic patron in the city's next set of communal statutes. The collection of living and postmortem miracles leaves no question that some kind of popular cult existed for this layman both during his lifetime and immediately after his death. Facio's confraternity, Santo Spirito, was also supported by the papacy. In July 1263, Pope Urban IV recognized both Facio's confraternity and another fraternal organization associated with Cremona's cathedral as a charitable *consortium* dedicated to defending the faith and liberating the church from heretics—a move aimed at stemming what the papacy saw as the heretical element among Ghibelline aristocrats, who were frequently joining these organizations.[119] If the papacy was giving its approval to an organization founded and run by a lay holy man like Facio, how can we make sense of the return to a more radical understanding of lay sanctity that we see in his cult? To some extent, the absence of direct involvement from the papacy matters here. On one hand, the thirteenth-century *vitae* for Raimondo and Omobono suggest that at the same time that communes were increasingly

---

116. Vauchez, "Sainteté laïque au XIIIe siècle," 34, n. 2.

117. *Vita Beati Facii*, 42.

118. The *vita* also notes that the members of this *ordinem Spiritus Sancti* wore capes, had beards, and threw themselves into rigorous work in a way that, as the *vita* notes, "is characteristic of men." Ibid., 38.

119. Vauchez transcribes Urban's bull, which has not been preserved in his registers. See Vauchez, "Sainteté laïque au XIIIe siècle," 26–27.

ruled by *popolo* factions, civic governments were also taking the lead in promoting lay saints' cults. But, on the other hand, we must also recognize that the living holy layman that we see presented in Facio's *vita* was someone who was still working within the conception of the lay religious life established by Innocent. Facio's touch ultimately supports a strong church, and by doing so, neutralizes the potentially threatening nature of an extraordinary lay religious life. Facio might effect miraculous cures. He might take on a religious charisma that had the potential to render a church hierarchy moot. But as his *vita* makes clear, his charisma ultimately supports and sustains the institutional church—both his touch and his breath respond to the bishop's command. While he might create quasi-religious orders, he does so to attend to the city's poor and sick. And finally, he dies as an obedient, churchgoing layman.

Facio's Cross

A silver cross, purported to be the work of Facio, can be found today in Cremona's cathedral treasury. The cross is an ornately decorated depiction of a crucified Christ flanked by Mary and John on its front and the Virgin Assunta on its back. Both sides include four roundels with portraits of various saints: flanking the crucified Christ are saints Peter and Paul, with Jerome below Christ and Omobono above Him. On the cross's posterior side, the early Christian martyrs Marcellino and Pietro accompany the Virgin Assunta, while a portrait of Saint Dominic sits below and a portrait of Cremona's sixth-century bishop Imerio sits above her. An inscription informs the viewer that this cross was a gift of the blessed Facio to the cathedral. Scholars have concluded, however, that this is a fifteenth-century object and thus neither the work of the saint nor that of any thirteenth-century silversmith.[120]

Although not a medieval production, the cross's purported identity as a liturgical object made by the saint speaks to an essential aspect of Facio's early cult. The cross conveys the idea that Facio had hands that could craft magnificent works of silver and gold at the same time as it reminds its audience that those hands could also perform miracles. Facio, the cross seems intent on reminding us, did not give up his identity as an artisan but instead used it to fund charitable activities and, in the case of the cross, to create liturgical instruments, categorizing this layman's work not as "perverse and miserable business" but as something that enriched the church. This cross quite literally

---

120. On this cross, see *Omobono: La figura del santo*, ed. Bonometti, 117–19; Puerari, *Il duomo di Cremona*, 135–38.

objectifies the positive attitude we see in his *vita* and miracle collection toward his identity as a producer—both of precious works of gold and silver and of miracles—an identity that is conveyed in his very name, which is a play on the vernacular verb *fare*, meaning to do or to make.

The portrait of Omobono, placed so prominently above the crucified Christ, also makes clear how much this layman, whose sanctity was recognized by Rome, served as the model for all laymen seeking to live rigorously religious lives. And yet, the cross's very existence and purported circumstances of creation speak to the ways in which that papally sanctioned model had not entirely eradicated some of the more radical understandings of an extraordinary layman's religious power. Thus, while it is easy to see the documents connected with Facio's early cult as well as this fifteenth-century cross as working within the parameters set by the papacy for what constituted a holy lay life, these sources also adopt some of the ideals first articulated in Ranieri of Pisa's *vita* regarding the inherent value and spiritual potential contained within lay status. In this way, Facio's *vita* and miracle collection resist the idea found in those early Omobono sources that being a layman was something that needed to be reformed and redeemed. Facio is not so much a lily among thorns, as Innocent had described Omobono, but an example of what a perfected lay life could look like. The cross, as a perfected object of the lay world, reinforces that point.

We might ask to what extent the Omobono sources (both Innocent's canonization bull and the series of thirteenth-century *vitae*) had paved the way for a lay saint like Facio. In other words, does Facio stand as a culmination of the work that was taking place over the late twelfth and thirteenth centuries to describe how one could be simultaneously lay and holy? On one hand, it is easy to see Facio's early cult as working within the parameters set by the papacy for a holy lay life. On the other hand, even though Facio's *vita* and miracle collection hit such key points as the goldsmith's dedication to prayer, penitence, charity, and obedience, they also adopt, as well as extend, ideals first articulated in Ranieri of Pisa's *vita* about the inherent value and spiritual potential contained within one's lay status. In this regard, Facio's early cult resists the idea found in early Omobono sources that one's lay status was something that needed to be reformed and redeemed. We see in Facio the idea that lay sanctity could be a careful balance between institutional obedience and charismatic power.

I see two factors influencing this development. The first can be seen in Innocent's canonization bull for Omobono. Here the pontiff outlined the first of what would become two paths for those laity drawn to the *vita apostolica* in the early thirteenth century. *Quia pietas* saw the ideal lay religious life as one focused on charity, pilgrimage, penitential acts, and the fight against heresy—all externally focused actions. The second path, which was born in 1210 when Innocent accepted Francis and his companions into the church, allowed for an internal focus. A Franciscan friar could orient his religious life toward becoming poor, instead of only helping the poor—but only as a member of the newly minted Franciscan Order.

The second factor came in the mid-thirteenth century, when lay sanctity had become entangled within its local context. As we saw not only in Raimondo's *vita* but also in the later thirteenth-century *vitae* of Omobono, the lay saint's social status and urban identity was no longer an impediment to sanctity but instead a defining feature of it. Rising *popolo* governments began to take an interest in their pious contemporaries. As a result, lay saints' *vitae* reimagined how lay status and lay work interacted with a rigorous lay religious life. When lay sanctity became entangled in its local context, claims for lay power began, once again, to emphasize the charisma a life dedicated to penitence could produce: lay saints were again portrayed as living holy men, dispensing miracles that healed their local communities. Facio of Cremona stands as the most fully articulated example of such an understanding of the communal lay saint. If we turn to the cults of contemporary laymen that developed in thirteenth-century Siena, we can see how one particularly self-conscious civic community used this conception of the ideal layman to craft a new definition of the ideal citizen.

CHAPTER 3

Civic Patron as Ideal Citizen

The Cult of Pier "Pettinaio" of Siena

We do not know much about the lives of medieval comb-makers. Like so many members of the lay population, their appearance in the historical record is limited. Pier "Pettinaio" or Pier "the comb-maker" seems to be an exception.[1] Pier lived in Siena until his death in 1289, earning first a pious, and then a saintly reputation for his efforts to follow a rigorous schedule of prayer, to deliver charity to his fellow city-dwellers, and finally to resist the more aggressive commercial practices espoused by other urban artisans and merchants. In the century after his death, knowledge of and interest in the comb-maker extended beyond the confines of his Tuscan commune. In the prologue of his *Arbor vita crucifixae Iesu*, Ubertino da Casale notes that he had found many virtuous men in his travels through Tuscany, and mentions "Pier, a man full of God" in particular.[2] Pier also appears in Dante's *Purgatorio*: the Sienese noblewoman Sapia Tolomei

---

1. Pier "Pettinaio" has been studied by Carol Agricoli, *Pier Pettinaio nella Siena duecentesca: Biografia ragionata in cerca di trace nella Siena di otto secoli fa* (Siena: Il Leccio, 2014); Alessandra Bartolomei Romagnoli, "Pier Pettinaio e i modelli di santità degli ordini mendicanti a Siena tra duecento e trecento," *Hagiographica* 21 (2014): 109–54; and Webb, *Saints and Cities*, 191–241. Also see Thompson, *Cities of God* (esp. chaps 5 and 7) and André Vauchez, "Pietro Pettinaio," in *Bibliotheca sanctorum*, vol. 10 (Rome: Istituto Giovanni XXIII nella Pontificia Università Lateranense, 1968), 719–22.

2. Ubertino da Casale, *Arbor vitae crucifixae Iesu* (1485; reprint, Turin: Bottega d'Erasmo, 1961), 4.

credits Pier's prayers for keeping her out of hell and granting her a place in purgatory.[3]

More extraordinary, however, are the numerous mentions we find of Pier during his lifetime in Sienese communal records. These documents show not only that Pier was actively involved in his community but also that his fellow Sienese relied on him to address a broad range of civic challenges: how to restore usurious and illicit profits,[4] how to manage the commune's annual release of prisoners,[5] and how to distribute alms.[6] After his death, Pier continued to matter to the Sienese. Indeed, within a few weeks of his death, both the Sienese government and local Franciscans designated time to celebrate Pier's extraordinary piety and money to create monuments to support his cult. Numerous records produced by both Siena's financial magistracy, the Biccherna, and its General Council, the Consiglio Generale, document the initial money the commune donated for the construction of Pier's tomb in the church of San Francesco as well as the ongoing contributions the civic government made to support the comb-maker's feast day.[7]

Pier was also the subject of a sermon most likely written within a month of his death in December 1289 by the Franciscan friar Bindo Scremi da Siena.[8] Bindo uses the sermon to offer proof of Pier's sanctity as well as to give his audience an opportunity to grieve their recent loss. In example after example of Pier's perfection, Bindo reminds those listening that they had wit-

---

3. Dante Alighieri, *The Divine Comedy of Dante Alighieri: Purgatorio*, trans. Allen Mandelbaum (New York: Bantam, 1982), canto 13, lines 124–29.

4. *Libri dell'entrata e dell'uscita della repubblica di Siena detti del camarlingo e dei Quattro provveditori della Biccherna* (hereafter Biccherna), 19 (1258) (Siena: Academic Senese degli Intronati, 1963), 18; and Archivio di Stato di Siena (ASS), Biccherna, 94, f. 9r, July 1264.

5. ASS, Deliberazioni del Consiglio Generale, 29 (January 6, 1285), ff. 25r–25v.

6. ASS, Biccherna, 90 (1285), f. 12r.

7. Communal documents that record the interest taken in supporting Pier's cult include ASS, Deliberazioni del Consiglio Generale, 38 (December 19, 1289), f. 62; Biccherna, 102 (December 1289), f. 150v; Biccherna, 113 (December 1296), 233r; Biccherna, 121 (December 1307), 196v; Biccherna, 171 (December 1331), 152r; Biccherna, 234 (December 1354), 125r; Biccherna, 248 (December 1369), 197v. Most of these sources have been listed in the following two articles: F. Cristofani, "Memorie del B. Pietro Pettinagno da Siena," *Miscellanea Francescana* 5 (1890): 3–52; and A. Lisini, "Notizie sul B. Pier Pettinagno," in *Miscellanea storica senese*, vol. 4 (Siena: C. Nava, 1896), 42–45.

8. Pesaro, Biblioteca Oliveriana, MS 1300, ff. 168c–171a. I have not consulted this manuscript and will rely upon Cesare Cenci's transcription; see Cenci, "San Pietro Pettinaio presentato da un predicatore senese contemporaneo," *Studi Francescani* 87 (1990): 5–30; also see Cenci, "Fonte anonima di un anonimo predicatore francescano senese," *Archivum Franciscanum Historicum* 87 (1994): 135–39. On Bindo da Siena as the most likely author of this sermon, see Cenci, "'San' Pietro Pettinaio presentato da Fra Bindo da Siena," *Archivum Franciscanum Historicum* 99 (2006): 189–211. In his 2006 article, Cenci also identifies a second redaction of this sermon that was most likely created in the early fourteenth century for use in another Tuscan city.

nessed Pier's charitable deeds and had heard his pious words. Bindo uses the temporal proximity of his Sienese audience to frame his argument for the comb-maker's sanctity; their personal loss, Bindo argues, has become the city's gain. Although the immediacy of Bindo's celebration of Pier is striking and gives us an unusually intimate glimpse of sanctity through the lens of a community mourning one of its own, the sermon gives us little detail about the actual content of Pier's religious life.

That content would not be recorded for another forty years, when in the early 1330s a *vita* celebrating and memorializing Pier appeared. Written by another Sienese friar, Pietro da Monterone, Pier's *vita* was an effort to secure the city's ongoing support of Pier's cult in the wake of a financial crisis and presented Pier's sanctity as intrinsically linked to the comb-maker's behavior as a businessman and communal resident.[9] Pietro's portrait of Pier aimed not only to capitalize on the fusing of political and religious concerns that was so ubiquitous in late medieval Siena but also to articulate how the cult of a saintly communal resident could both reflect and contribute to the city's grandeur and importance.

The development of Pier's cult—both during his lifetime and in the half century after his death—offers us a rich example of the state of lay civic sanctity in the late thirteenth-century commune. Pier organized his life in ways that adhered to the model of contemporary lay sanctity that we saw established in the cults of Omobono and Facio of Cremona as well as Raimondo of Piacenza. But, it is likely that Pier's particular version of a saintly self-fashioning was a response to the emergence of a cult dedicated to another Sienese lay saint, Andrea Gallerani (d. 1251), a nobleman whose holy reputation as well as renown as the (purported) founder of the Domus Misericordiae was growing in the second half of the thirteenth century.[10] Nevertheless, as the extant documents make clear, while Pier may have organized his life to fit his experience of what made a contemporary lay saint, as I shall show, his fellow Sienese both interacted with him during his lifetime

---

9. Pietro da Monterone, *Vita del Beato Pier Pettinajo senese del terz'ordine di San Francesco volgarizeata da una leggenda latin del 1333 per F. Serafino Ferri Agostiniano di Lecceto l'anno 1508*, ed. Luigi de Angelis (Siena, 1802) [hereafter *Vita Pier*], vii. Although sources refer to the saint as both "Pier" and "Pietro," in order to distinguish between the saint and the author of the *vita* (Pietro da Monterone), I shall call the author of the *vita* "Pietro" and the saint "Pier."

10. Nancy Caciola discusses the idea of saintly "self-fashioning" in "Through a Glass Darkly: Recent Work on Sanctity and Society," *Comparative Studies in Society and History* 38 (1996): 301–9. Caciola cites Gábor Klaniczay, who has noted how Margaret of Hungary seemed to organize her religious life in such a manner as to follow the "script" she found in the life of her aunt, Elizabeth of Hungary; see his "Legends as Life-Strategies for Aspirant Saints in the Later Middle Ages," *Journal of Folklore Research* 26 (1989): 151–71.

and memorialized him after his death in ways that aided this saintly construction.

Perhaps it was the strength of that fashioning—a joint effort by the layman and his urban community—that delayed the production of a *vita* until nearly half a century after Pier's death. With a saintly reputation profoundly fused to the city itself, it was not until economic hardship threatened that relationship that a full narrative account of Pier's life and achievements needed to be written. As this chapter will show, when that *vita* finally appeared it reflected the deliberate campaign by the Nine (Siena's hugely successful late thirteenth- and early fourteenth-century *popolo* government) to articulate a civic ideology that married political concerns with religious ones. To that end, we see in Pier's *vita* how the celebration of a contemporary lay patron became an opportunity to think about the role everyday men and women played in the creation of an ideal civic community. As the *vita* repeatedly argues, Pier's extraordinary spiritual rigor produced the model of good communal citizenship.

But we also see in this *vita* an expanded understanding of the content and role of lay charisma. As in the late thirteenth-century *vitae* of Omobono and Facio of Cremona, Pier demonstrates his sanctity by performing miracles during his lifetime. Pier's living miracles are more numerous as well as more dramatic than those performed by our Cremonese lay saints, however. Pier lays his hands on the sick *and* raises the dead. Moreover, Pier's spiritual gifts are a means for deepening his own spiritual development—the *vita* continually describes Pier as having passed from an active to a contemplative life and as falling into ecstatic states.

Pietro's portrait of Pier's lay sanctity therefore ultimately complicates the dual model of lay spirituality and religion that I have argued was created by Innocent III's canonization of Omobono of Cremona. In this *vita*, the lay penitent is fully involved in aiding his civic community through acts of charity as well as of good citizenship. And yet, Pier's sanctity derives from more than just his external actions. At the same time that the *vita* celebrates Pier's external actions, it also celebrates his internal focus: his embrace of the contemplative life, his prophetic powers, and his ecstatic states. Thus, in the years immediately before the mendicants took over guardianship and control of the lay penitential life—Pier died the same year that Pope Nicholas IV issued *Supra montem*—the cult of a pious Sienese comb-maker shows us not only a new equation between the ideal lay Christian and the ideal lay citizen but also an expanded notion of the content and power of lay spirituality.

Becoming Siena's Holy Man

The extant evidence we have for Pier's life in Siena paints a picture of a lay-man involved in the financial, religious, and charitable life of his commune. It also paints a picture of a civic community that relied upon the pious comb-maker to help with the sometimes difficult merging of economic and spiri-tual interests.

The two earliest mentions we have of Pier show how the Sienese comb-maker worked during his lifetime to repair the ill effects of nefarious financial transactions on behalf of his fellow city-dwellers. In the 1258 Biccherna register—the yearly account book produced by Siena's financial magistracy—"Piero Pectinario" is recorded as having returned fifty-one soldi to the com-mune on behalf of an unnamed man who, as the entry notes, had earned that money through usury.[11] In 1264, another Biccherna account book records that the comb-maker had returned fifteen lire to cover money another unnamed man had taken from the commune through his office.[12] Although the 1264 account does not specify how or why the money was taken, it seems likely that this entry refers to some kind of abuse of political office. The 1258 Biccherna entry is more puzzling for a number of reasons. First, Pier is cited as having restored usurious profits for an individual who remains anonymous. An act of restitution was seen as a pious act that not only secured one a proper burial but also protected one's heirs from further financial claims—it is odd, therefore, to see a beneficiary remain anonymous.[13] Second, while it was common to see merchants make provisions for restitution in their wills and

---

11. Biccherna, 19 (1258), 18: "Item LI. sol. quos dicti tres habuerunt et receperunt a Piero Pectinario, quos ipse dicebat se habuisse a quodam homine, qui eos restituit Comuni pro usuris." Since the Third Lateran Council in 1179, European Christians could only be absolved from the sin of usury by making full restitution for their profits. See John Gilchrist, *The Church and Economic Activity in the Middle Ages* (London: Macmillan, 1969), 173 and 194–96. Unless illicit profits were returned to the original debtor, or to an ecclesiastical authority, canon law called for the usurer to be denied a proper burial. On the theory of restitution in the later Middle Ages, see Benjamin N. Nelson, "The Usurer and the Merchant Prince: Italian Businessmen and the Ecclesiastical Law of Restitution, 1100–1550," *Journal of Economic History* 7 (1947): 104–22; John W. Baldwin, *Masters, Princes, and Merchants: The Social Views of Peter the Chanter and His Circle* (Princeton: Princeton University Press, 1970), vol. 1, 302–7; and Julius Kirshner and Kimberly Lo Prete, "Peter John Olivi's Treatises on Contracts of Sale, Usury and Restitution: Minorite Economics or Minor Works?" *Quaderni Fiorentini per la Storia del Pensiero Giuridico Moderno* 13 (1984): 233–86.

12. ASS, Biccherna, 94 (1264), f. 9r: "Item XV lib. quos predicti quattuor receperunt a Piero Pec-tenario quos ipse solvit pro quodam homine, qui eos illicite subraxerat a Comuni pro quodam offitio quod habuit."

13. In his study of how canon law influenced the practical application of restitution in late medi-eval Florence, Nelson has noted that a usurer could select a "discreet person" to perform the restitu-tion on his or her behalf but does not cite specific evidence of such a phenomenon; see Nelson, "The Usurer and the Merchant Prince," 110.

testaments, it is rare to see such transactions appear in civic documents.[14] Nearly thirty years after this episode, Siena's communal government, the Nine, would begin a protracted battle with the city's episcopal authority to claim jurisdiction over usury, eventually convincing church authorities to limit their prosecution of usury to cases involving testaments.[15] Long before Siena began this battle with the church, however, Pier saw the commune as the appropriate authority to which he should direct this restitution. Thus, in both Biccherna records we see Pier acting to help his fellow Sienese right their financial wrongs and doing so under the aegis of the commune.

Three charters produced in the 1270s and 1280s also make clear that, for much of his adult life, Pier had an association with the Domus Misericordiae (also known as Casa della Misericordia or Santa Maria della Misericordia), medieval Siena's largest hospital.[16] In 1272, Pier's name appears among the lay brothers of the Domus named in a communal charter that exempts those brothers from both military service and any taxes aimed at supporting the poor.[17] Pier is again named as one of that institution's lay brothers in an episcopal charter from 1278 recognizing land newly acquired by the Domus.[18] And finally, in his 1284 testament, Bartolomeo di Vincenzo, the Domus's rector, stipulated that, after his death, Pier was to be consulted on where Vincenzo should

---

14. For work that looks at the restitution of usury through wills and testaments in the late medieval and Renaissance Italy, see F. L. Galassi, "Buying a Passport to Heaven: Usury, Restitution and the Merchants of Medieval Genoa," *Religion* 22 (1992): 313–26; Marvin B. Becker, "Three Cases Concerning the Restitution of Usury in Florence," *Journal of Economic History* 17 (1957): 445–50; and Steven Epstein, *Wills and Wealth in Medieval Genoa, 1150–1250* (Cambridge, MA: Harvard University Press, 1984).

15. William Bowsky, *A Medieval Italian Commune: Siena under the Nine, 1287–1355* (Berkeley: University of California Press, 1981), 110–12. Florence experienced a similar battle in the fifteenth century when rising anticlericalism initiated the commune's efforts to assert its jurisdiction over matters involving the restitution of usury; see Becker, "Three Cases," 445–50. Gilchrist looks at a similar battle waged by Florence in the mid-fourteenth century; see his *The Church and Economic Activity*, 112–13.

16. For more on the Domus, see Mario Ascheri and Patrizia Turrini, eds., *La misericordia di Siena attraverso i secoli: Dalla domus misericordiae all'arciconfraternita di misericordia* (Siena: Protagon Editori Toscani, 2004); Giuliano Catoni, "Gli oblati della Misericordia: Poveri e benefattori a Siena nella prima metà del trecento," in *La società del bisogno: Povertà e assistenza nella Toscana medievale*, ed. Giuliano Pinto (Florence: Salimbeni, 1989), 1–17; and Diana Norman, "When Charity Fails: Andrea Gallerani and Memory of the Misericordia in Siena," in *The Kindness of Strangers: Charity in the Pre-Modern Mediterranean*, ed. Dionysios Stathakopoulos (London: Centre for Hellenic Studies, 2007), 91–118.

17. ASS, Diplomatico, R. Università, May 17, 1272; cited by Paolo Nardi, "Origini e sviluppo della casa della Misericordia," in *La misericordia di Siena attraverso i secoli*, ed. Ascheri and Turrini, 68 and 88, n. 32.

18. ASS, Diplomatico, R. Università, February 1278; cited by Nardi, "Origini e sviluppo della casa della Misericordia," 68 and 88, n. 37; and transcribed by Giovanni Antonio Pecci, *Storia del vescovado dela città di Siena* (Lucca, 1748), 235–37.

be buried and how his estate was to make restitutions for his usurious gains.[19] Thus by the mid-1280s, Pier had become a prominent enough member of Siena's largest charitable organization that its director singled him out for combined religious and financial advice.

During the last decade of his life, Pier's pious efforts were also being noticed by the commune, which began to award him duties that capitalized on his emerging identity as a civic holy man. Although the earliest communal sources mentioning Pier's work to return illicit profits do not indicate whether or not the commune had actively sought Pier's help, civic documents from the 1280s make clear that, by this time, the Sienese government had begun to assign Pier specific civic tasks. In January 1284, records from the deliberations of the commune's General Council tell us that Pier was placed on a committee to choose which poor or "afflicted" prisoners (*ex pauperibus et afflictis*), who had not committed any violent crimes, were to be released in the government's annual show of clemency.[20] Siena had relied on such committees of prominent citizens to do this work from at least the late 1270s.[21]

The commune used Pier in other ways as well during this period. A 1285 Biccherna register records that the commune gave money to Pier and the notary Ser Compagno to distribute to the poor and religious of the city.[22] We know from Pier's ca. 1330 *vita* that Ser Compagno was one of the eight companions with whom Pier lived for some time.[23] Ser Compagno's name is again mentioned

---

19. ASS, Diplomatico, April 23, 1284. Bartolomeo's testament is also discussed by Nardi, "Origini e sviluppo della casa della misericordia," 68; and by Daniel Waley, *Siena and the Sienese in the Thirteenth Century* (Cambridge: Cambridge University Press, 1991), 146.

20. ASS, Deliberazioni del Consiglio Generale, 29, ff. 25r–25v, January 6, 1285: "Bartolomeus Mainetti consuluit et dixit quod ex carceratis et Comunis Sen. debeat relaxari et offerri V et eis qui debeant eligi per pierum pettenarium, Compagnum Episcopi et dominam Agnesem. Inter quos sit et esse debeat Castraleone et sint ex pauperibus et afflictis et quod detenti non sint pro homicidio, nec pro furtis, nec pro proditione et rubbaria stratarum et incendia et qui fuerint oblati, sint liberi et absoluti ab omnibus bapnis et condepnationibus . . ." I am using a transcription of this document made by Cristofani, "Memorie del B. Pietro Pettinagno," 51–52. Thompson also refers to the 1285 deliberations; see *Cities of God*, 199. De Angelis mentions that the commune placed Pier on one of these committees in 1282 as well; see *Vita Pier*, 84, n. 1.

21. On the annual release of prisoners, see John Koenig, "Prisoner Offerings, Patron Saints, and State Cults, at Siena and Other Italian Cities from 1250 to 1550," *Bullettino Senese di Storia Patria* 108 (2001): 222–96. Koenig has identified communal documents from other years identifying Pier as a member of this committee, suggesting that the commune may have begun using the comb-maker in this capacity as early as the 1270s.

22. ASS, Biccherna, 85 (1285), f. 12r: "Item ccc lib. per apodixam XV Piero Pectinario et Compagno mantellato, quos solverunt religiosis et aliis personis pauperibus, prout eis visum fuit, sicut commissa est per consilium Campane Comunis Senensis." Transcribed by Lisini, "Notizie sul B. Pier Pettinagno," 45.

23. A "Compagno Martini" is also listed among the *frati* of the Domus Misericordiae in the 1278 bull issued by Bishop Bernardo of Siena; see ASS, Diplomatico, R. Università, February 1278; cited by Nardi, "Origini e sviluppo della casa della Misericordia," 68 and 88, n. 37, and transcribed by Pecci, *Storia del vescovado*, 235–37.

alongside Pier's in a Biccherna register from 1286: the commune had commissioned Pier, Ser Compagno, and Talomeo Battaglia (another of Pier's companions named in the *vita*) to paint pictures (*picturis*) near the city gates.[24]

While it was not unusual for the Italian communes to rely on both lay penitents and professed religious to fulfill communal duties, Pier's involvement in the financial, political, and cultural life of his commune seems unusual for its simultaneous specificity and ambiguity.[25] Pier was placed on committees to determine which prisoners to release, he was charged with distributing alms to the poor, and finally he was tasked with painting images on city gates, yet his role or particular civic position was never specified. He seems to function as a living civic holy man: someone to whom both the commune and individual Sienese turned to for advice and action. I have found no parallel examples in other communal records—Pier's involvement in his civic community and government as a living civic holy man appears exceptional. For example, Andrea Gallerani, the founder of the Domus, is mentioned in communal documents only once during his lifetime: a Biccherna record from February 1251 notes that the commune had given Andrea money to help him in his efforts to aid the *pauperes verecundi* (or the shameful poor), whose high social status kept them from begging.[26] Ambrogio Sansedoni, the popular Dominican preacher who died in 1287 and would garner a civic cult on par with, if not larger than, Pier's, only began to appear in the communal record after his death when the commune gave money for the building of his tomb and the annual

---

24. ASS, Biccherna, 94 (1286), f. 198r: "Item, l lib. Ser Pier Pectenario et Ser Compagno del Veschovo et Talomeo Battaglia, pro picturis quas feccerunt fieri ad Portas per ordinamentum XV." Transcribed by Lisini, "Notizie sul B. Pier Pettinagno," 45. I have been unable to find any information about the circumstances behind this commission or the content of the images. In his study of early Sienese artists, Hayden Maginnis notes that there is evidence from at least the early fourteenth century that the Nine commissioned paintings on or near city gates. The most famous of these was a *Coronation of the Virgin* by Simone Martini (no longer extant) on the Porta Romana; see Maginnis, *The World of the Early Sienese Painter* (University Park: Pennsylvania State University, 2001), 131–32.

25. See the work of Frances Andrews: "Monastic Observance and Communal Life: Siena and the Empoyment of Religious," in *Pope, Church and City: Essays in Honour of Brenda M. Bolton*, ed. Frances Andrews, Christoph Egger, and Constance Rousseau (Leiden: Brill, 2004), 357–83; and "Living Like the Laity? The Negotiation of Religious Status in the Cities of Late Medieval Italy," *Transactions of the Royal Historical Society* 20 (2010): 27–55; as well as her edited volume, Frances Andrews with Maria Agata Pincelli, eds., *Churchmen and Urban Government in Late Medieval Italy c. 1200–c.1450: Cases and Contexts* (Cambridge: Cambridge University Press, 2013). Most relevant for understanding Pier's role as a lay penitent working for the commune is Giovanna Casagrande's article "Religious in the Service of the Commune: The Case of Thirteenth- and Fourteenth-Century Perugia," also in *Churchmen and Urban Government*, ed. Andrews with Pincelli, 181–200.

26. *Libri dell'entrata e dell'uscita della repubblica di Siena detti del camarlingo e dei Quattro provveditori della Biccherna*, libro XII (1251) (Siena: Lazzeri, 1935), 74. On the office of the Biccherna in Siena, see William Bowsky, *The Finance of the Commune of Siena 1287–1355* (Oxford: Clarendon Press, 1970), esp. 1–15.

civic celebrations (including a *palio*, or horse race) to celebrate his feast day.[27] Thus Pier seems to have held an unusual position within his civic community: a holy artisan to whom both individual Sienese and the commune itself turned, during his lifetime, to solve the tricky intersection of religious ideals and urban financial realities as well as to execute their more general charitable and pious endeavors.

Saintly Self-Fashioning: Pier and the Gallerani Shutters

If Pier organized his life in such a way as to fill the role of roving lay holy man for late thirteenth-century Siena, how did the comb-maker construct such an identity in the first place? In other words, what model or whose example was Pier likely following? While it is not out of the question that Pier heard stories about other communes' lay saints, such as Omobono of Cremona or Raimondo of Piacenza, it is more likely that a local example was his prime influence. Pier's involvement with the Domus Misericordiae came at a time when Siena was experiencing a growing interest not only in that pious institution but also in its purported founder, the nobleman Andrea Gallerani (d. 1251). Although there is no direct evidence linking Andrea to the founding of the Domus, by the 1270s the Sienese had come to connect the memory of the pious nobleman with the origins of the charitable institution.[28]

Gallerani was a member of a prominent Sienese noble family that held extensive land both within the city and in its *contado* (Siena's subject countryside).[29] Pier and his fellow late thirteenth-century Sienese would have been familiar with Andrea's noble lineage as well as with the story of his religious conversion.[30] As a young adult, Andrea had been exiled from Siena after

---

27. Webb, *Patrons and Defenders*, 278–79. For an introduction to the life of Ambrogio Sansedoni, see Waley, *Siena and the Sienese*, 142–46.

28. See Norman, "When Charity Fails," 95–96; Norman cites the studies by Nardi "Origini e sviluppo della casa della Misericordia," in *La misericordia di Siena attraverso i secoli*, ed. Ascheri and Turrini, 65–93.

29. The family had increased its already sizable fortune during the early thirteenth century through their work as international merchants. Hayden Maginnis has noted that in a property assessment taken in 1316–20, three Sienese families (the Salimbeni, Bonsignori, and Gallerani) owned 20 percent of the city's real estate; see Maginnis, *The World of the Early Sienese Painter*, 28. For more on the Gallerani family as international merchants, see Georges Bigwood, *Les livres des comptes des Gallerani*, 2 vols., ed. and rev. Armand Grunzweig (Brussels: Palais des Académies, 1961–62).

30. The medieval *vita* for Andrea is found in Siena, Biblioteca Comunale degli Intronati, K. VII. 2. Webb has translated the *vita* in *Saints and Cities*, 141–59. Webb points out that the *Acta sanctorum* adopts a different organization for the chapters of the *vita* than the fourteenth-century manuscript. Her translation follows the order found in the fourteenth-century manuscript.

a murder conviction.[31] Upon his return, a vision of the Virgin Mary precipitated his conversion to a life dedicated to aiding the sick and poor of Siena.[32]
Although he was buried in the church of San Domenico in 1251, his cult did
not begin to flourish there or in the rest of the city until the early 1270s.[33] In
1274, Siena's bishop offered an indulgence to anyone who visited Andrea's San
Domenico tomb on the saint's feast day.[34] In addition, the first *vita* for Andrea
was most likely written in the 1270s.[35] And finally, scholars have proposed the
early 1270s as the production date for a pair of painted wooden shutters used
to cover the niche containing Andrea's remains.[36]

Though we cannot know if Pier's decision to join the Domus was motivated by Andrea Gallerani's growing cult in the 1270s, that cult was clearly
enjoying a surge in popularity at this time. And for Pier, as well as for other
Sienese, the most obvious manifestation of the cult would have been the
San Domenico shutters. Those shutters present a portrait of lay sanctity

---

31. Thompson has written that the man Andrea had killed was a blasphemer, but I have been
unable to find any mention of this in the medieval sources; see *Cities of God*, 196. Webb has noted the
same error; see *Saints and Cities*, 141.

32. Webb, *Saints and Cities*, 144–45.

33. Thompson claims that Andrea's cult sprang up immediately after his death, but this is not
supported by any evidence I have been able to find; see *Cities of God*, 196.

34. A transcription of the indulgence is printed in *AASS.*, Mar. III, 50; it is also transcribed in
Pecci, *Storia del vescovado*, 233–34.

35. I base this conclusion both on the fact that the 1270s is the earliest period for which we have
any evidence for an active cult for Andrea and on internal evidence from the *vita's* concluding list of
miracles performed in Andrea's name after his death. In one account, we learn that a mother vowed
her son to Andrea after the boy was cured of an illness. The account mentions that the mother had
been spurred to pray to Andrea after hearing "Brother Ambrogio" preaching about Andrea's miracles. "Brother Ambrogio" refers to Ambrogio Sansedoni, the popular Dominican preacher. Although
Ambrogio was not recognized as a *beatus* by Rome until the sixteenth century, within a year of his
1287 death civic and ecclesiastical authorities were treating him as a civic saint: the commune had
donated money for the construction of his tomb, and the bishop had authorized an account of his
miracles to be written. It would be reasonable then to expect the author of Andrea's *vita*, himself
most likely a Dominican, to have referred to the distinguished Dominican as "Blessed" or "Saint" after
his death. It therefore likely that a text referring to Sansedoni as "Brother Ambrogio" would have
been written before his death. For the miracle, see Webb, *Saints and Cities*, 152.

36. Siena, Pinacoteca Nazionale. The panel is illustrated in Vauchez, *Sainthood*, pl. 21, and in
James H. Stubblebine, *Guido da Siena* (Princeton: Princeton University Press, 1964), 36. Long thought
to be solely the work of Guido da Siena (dates unknown), L. Bellosi has convincingly argued that
while Guido da Siena was responsible for the interior panels, the exterior panels (visible when the
shutters were closed and Andrea's relics were hidden) were the work of Dietisalvi di Speme (active
until 1291); see L. Bellosi, "Per un contesto cimabuesco senese: a) Guido da Siena e il probabile Dietisalvi di Speme," *Prospettiva* 61 (1991): 6–20; and Raffaele Argenziano, "La prima iconografia del Beato
Andrea Gallerani fondatore della Domus Misericordiae di Siena," in *La misericordia di Siena attraverso i
secoli*, ed. Ascheri and Turrini, 53. For more on the shutters, see Joanna Cannon, "Dominic *alter Christus*? Representations of the Founder in and after the *Arco di San Domenico*," in *Christ among the Medieval
Dominicans: Representations of Christ in the Texts and Images of the Order of Preachers*, ed. Kent Emery Jr.
and Joseph Wawrykow (Notre Dame, IN: University of Notre Dame Press, 1998), 26–48.

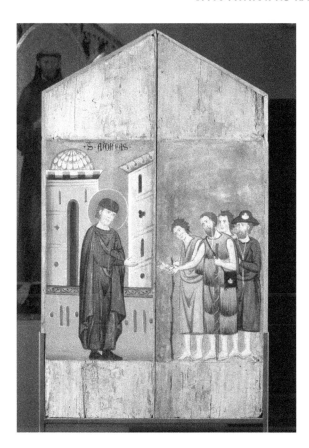

Figure 6. "Blessed Andrea Gallerani," ca. 1270, closed diptych, Siena, Pinacoteca Nazionale. Scala/Ministero per i Beni e le Attività culturali/Art Resource, NY.

that underlines Andrea's institutional independence at the same time as they make an equation between lay piety and urban harmony; a portrait that may have reflected and inspired the civic persona Pier Pettinaio was cultivating.

If Pier had stood in front of Andrea's tomb when the shutters were closed, he would have seen a depiction of Andrea standing with his hand outstretched to a group of four pilgrims who carry staffs and have both a satchel and a hat with the pilgrim's badge, the scallop shell, clearly visible (figure 6). Pier and any other Sienese who gazed at this image were clearly meant to read the three structures behind Andrea as representing their city. It is possible that they were also meant to understand the illustrations on these exterior panels as both depicting and welcoming the many pilgrims who, we know from the 1274 episcopal indulgence, were visiting Andrea's tomb.[37] Those pilgrims

---

37. See *AASS.*, Mar. III, 50, and Pecci, *Storia del vecovado*, 233–34.

were of course drawn to Andrea's saintly reputation; although Andrea was never officially canonized by Rome, the shutters make clear that such an institutional stamp did not matter: Andrea appears on the exterior panels with a nimbus and "S. Andreas" inscribed above him.[38]

If Pier had been in San Domenico when the shutters were opened to reveal Andrea's remains, he would have seen how the two interior panels are divided into four registers (figure 7). In the lower register of the right-hand panel, Andrea prays in front of a crucifix. Barely still visible today is a rope connecting a bunch of Andrea's hair to an iron rod above. Andrea's *vita* notes that the saint had used this rope to stay awake as he prayed.[39] In the register directly above this scene, Reginald of Orléans (an early member of the Order of Preachers) receives a vision while he is ill in which the Virgin Mary presents him with the black and white habit of the Dominican Order, which miraculously cures him.[40] In the left-hand panels, Andrea dispenses bread with an unidentified companion to a group of poor and ill Sienese in the lower register, while above we see a depiction of Saint Francis receiving the stigmata.

Taken as a whole, these panels clearly celebrate Andrea for his generosity toward pilgrims and the poor. But what other messages might they have conveyed to thirteenth-century Siena? What exactly is the argument that they are making about lay sanctity? Joanna Cannon's study of early representations of Dominic is helpful here. Cannon has noted that in both visual and written accounts of Reginald's vision, Dominic often functions as an intermediary. In the San Domenico shutters, for example, the order's founder is shown below Reginald, praying for his recovery.[41] Dominic's decision to appeal to the Virgin and not to Christ to heal Reginald underscores the order's particular interest in Mary.[42] If we extend Cannon's ideas, we can see that on one hand, the inclusion of a scene emphasizing the Virgin's importance is not only apt

---

38. Although he was never canonized, Andrea was recognized as a *beatus* by Pope Pius VI in 1798; see Norman, "When Charity Fails," 94.

39. Webb notes that Henk van Os thought the rope was around Andrea's neck. Van Os was most likely following Kaftal; see Webb, *Saints and Cities*, 144; van Os, *The Art of Devotion in the Late Middle Ages in Europe, 1300–1500* (Princeton: Princeton University Press, 1994), 61; and Kaftal, *Iconography of the Saints*, 56–57.

40. Cordelia Warr has recently shown how the story of Reginald's vision became an important part of Dominican iconography in the late thirteenth century. Warr notes that later visual and written renderings of this episode often inserted Dominic into the story, as we can see is the case in the reliquary shutters, where Dominic prays for Reginald's recovery; see Cordelia War, "Religious Habits and Visual Propaganda: The Vision of the Blessed Reginald of Orléans," *Journal of Medieval History* 28 (2002): 43–72.

41. Cannon, "Dominic *alter Christus*?" 26–28.

42. Ibid.

FIGURE 7. "Blessed Andrea Gallerani," ca. 1270, open diptych, Siena, Pinacoteca Nazionale. Scala/ Ministero per i Beni e le Attività culturali/Art Resource, NY.

on a panel placed within a Dominican church but also relevant for a painting celebrating Andrea, whose *vita* emphasizes that he was particularly known for his prayers and devotion to the Virgin. Moreover, just as Dominic acts as a mediator between his order and the Virgin in this and other depictions of Reginald's vision, the panel also seems to suggest that a holy layman, like Andrea, could fulfill a similar role for the laity. Both the paternoster beads in Andrea's hand and the saint's physical position (kneeling in front of a crucifix) would have invited a lay audience at Andrea's tomb to see a reflection of their own devotional routine: Andrea was performing the same actions that lay devotees did as they prayed in front of the nobleman's remains. The inclusion of the rope to keep Andrea alert during his extensive sessions of prayer transforms a familiar posture into a saintly ideal at the same time that it underscores the saint's humanity. While Pier and his fellow Sienese may have seen an echo in the panels of their own devotional lives, Andrea's routine is also presented as having gone beyond the everyday and into the saintly. Andrea takes steps to counter his need for sleep—just like anyone else, he finds it hard to stay awake for midnight prayers.

To understand the full potential effect of this image, we must also consider how Pier and his fellow Sienese would have made sense of a depiction of Francis's stigmata (arguably the culmination of Francis's spiritual development) within a Dominican church. The depiction of episodes from the histories of both mendicant orders means the shutters are not evidence for an exclusive affiliation between Andrea and the Dominicans. After all, even though the shutters feature a story that emphasizes the importance of the habit for the Dominican order—it is what the Virgin offers Reginald in his vision and what Dominic wears below—the panels still depict Andrea wearing only a simple dark gray cloak and tunic that convey no particular religious affiliation.[43]

Instead of presenting Andrea as a Dominican lay saint, the shutters' internal scenes invite their audience to see Andrea's religious life as constituting a devotional path similar to, but ultimately independent from, that of both mendicant orders. They also would have presented to Pier a version of the standard communal lay saint different from the examples we have already explored. Although Andrea exemplifies the ideals of the lay religious life established in Innocent's 1199 canonization of Omobono—Andrea appears as dedicated to prayer as he was to charity—we also see here a visual argument about the potential spiritual power of a rigorous but independent lay religious life. Andrea's posture as he prays in front of the crucifix references not only Dominic's position as he prays for Reginald but also Francis's posture below the seraph. Through prayer, the panels seem to suggest, Andrea found a role as an effective intermediary (like Dominic) as well as a connection with the divine (like Francis).[44] Moreover, just as the Virgin's charity heals Reginald, Andrea's charity heals the poor and the sick of Siena. The panels make clear that alongside the great feats of the Dominicans and the Franciscans stand the religious accomplishments of the laity. Those accomplishments are equal parts concern for others and attention to one's own spiritual growth.

---

43. Andrea's *vita* also does not make an argument for the saint having had a formal affiliation with the Dominican Order. It describes the penitential habit worn by the saint simply as "poor and common garments"; see Webb, *Saints and Cities*, 149. On the importance of the Dominican habit in both visual and narrative renderings of the episode, see Warr, "Religious Habits and Visual Propaganda." Early thirteenth-century rules for lay penitents did not specify a uniform habit, but advised penitents to wear clothes made of cheap fabric, without embellishment or ornamentation; see the penitential rules collected in Meersseman, *Dossier de l'order de la penitence.*

44. Cannon has noted that while Francis is depicted in the midst of a direct contact with the divine, Dominic is shown acting as an agent or intermediary between a prospective member of order and the Virgin; see "Dominic *alter Christus?*" 27.

Thus, the evidence we have for Pier's pious activities during his lifetime—his restitution of illicit profits, as well as his work for the commune and the Domus—suggests that the comb-maker not only organized his devotional life in such a way as to combine religious and civic concerns but also that his fellow Sienese accepted and aided Pier's service in such a role. We can imagine, then, that standing in front of Andrea's tomb, Pier would have seen both a reflection and celebration of just the kind of public persona he had been working to create. That persona drew heavily upon the model of the communal lay saint that had developed over the thirteenth century: his dedication to helping his fellow laymen points to Pope Innocent's insistence that an ideal lay life include charity, while Pier's specific work with the intersection of economic and spiritual issues allowed him to smooth over some of the inherent tensions of a late medieval commune—something we saw Raimondo of Piacenza, Omobono of Cremona (in the two later *vitae*), and Facio of Cremona also do. But Pier might have also seen in these panels permission to place his own internal spiritual development at the forefront of his life as a civic holy man. The first evidence we have documenting how his fellow Sienese mourned Pier's death shows that they also saw a holy lay life as an amalgam of work to aid others and work to improve one's own spiritual state.

Mourning Pier

In a sermon that scholars have recently concluded was likely written immediately following Pier's death in December 1289 by the Franciscan friar Bindo Scremi da Siena, the admiration, love, and familiarity Pier had earned from his fellow city-dwellers serves as prime evidence for his sanctity.[45] Functioning in many ways as a eulogy, the sermon offers its audience an opportunity to grieve their recent loss as well as to hear the reasons why Pier's life was a

---

45. Pesaro, Biblioteca Oliveriana, MS 1300, ff. 168c–171a. Cesare Cenci has transcribed this manuscript; see Cenci, "San Pietro Pettinaio presentato da un predicatore senese contemporaneo"; also see Cenci, "Fonte anonima di un anonimo predicatore francescano senese," 135–39. Cenci has argued that Bindo's use of the verb *scit* as opposed to *memoratur* emphasizes the temporal proximity between the saint and the sermon's audience and stands alongside the repeated mentions that both Bindo and his audience had known Pier and witnessed his great piety, the absence of any mention of postmortem miracles suggesting a composition date of 1289. Cenci also points to a number of dating clues found in a sermon dedicated to the feast of the Annunciation found in this same codex. The author of the Annunciation sermon notes that the feast was to fall on a Friday that year. As Cenci points out, March 25th fell on a Friday in 1289, 1295, and 1300; see Cenci, "San Pietro Pettinaio presentato da un predicatore senese contemporaneo," 6.

holy one. Using as its *thema* the claim in Ecclesiasticus 45 that "Moses was beloved of God, and man, whose memory is in benediction," Bindo's sermon is remarkable not only for conveying a sense of the close relationship that existed between his audience and Pier but also for constructing a portrait of a communal lay saint, who—despite having a particular association with the Sienese Franciscans—belonged, in Bindo's eyes, to all of Siena.

Throughout the sermon Bindo makes clear that his audience had an immediate and close connection with Pier. He does this by peppering his celebration with repeated mentions of how his audience had known Pier, had heard and benefited from his words, and had witnessed his moments of spiritual ecstasy. Bindo begins the sermon by noting that to be perfect, a man must simultaneously arrange or order (*ordinatus*) himself toward God, his neighbors, and himself. And, as he explains throughout, Pier's perfect arrangement toward God, his neighbors, and himself was clear in the love showered on him by both God and man. The evidence for this point is found in the audience themselves; Bindo reminds them that they saw "in what way Pier was made perfect;" and using the present tense to emphasize his point, he notes that "the majority of the city knows him."[46]

Bindo structures the sermon as an annotated list of the many signs of both God's and man's love of Pier, using Pier's words, his moments of purposeful silence, as well as the Sienese knowledge of and experience witnessing these signs as his proof. Many among his listeners, Bindo notes, were "able to see and saw" when Pier's heart became so inflamed with love as he heard about God that he had to lie down, looking as if he were dead.[47] Bindo claims that the comb-maker's frequent conversations (*frequentia collocutionum*) both about and sometimes to God and the Virgin Mary stand as the second sign of God's love; indeed, Pier almost never mentioned temporal things and only spoke of celestial matters.[48] To prove his point, Bindo notes that when Pier was dying

---

46. Cenci, "San Pietro Pettinaio presentato da un predicatore senese contemporaneo," 24: "Sed videamus quomodo Pe(trus) perfectus fuit, qualiter ipse fuerit ordinatus et ad Deum et ad se et ad proximum. Maior pars civitatis scit. Recte ergo de ipso possumus dicere verbum propositum 'dilectus' etc."

47. Ibid., 25: "Sed Petrus qualiter habit cor? inflammatum amore Dei. Multi ex vobis videre potuerunt et vidi quia cum (de) Deo audiebat loqui vel cum aliis loquebantur frequenter, sic rapiebatur in Deum quod, extra sensum factus, remanebat in terra quasi mortuus et frigidus; et sic aliquando stabat quasi per totam diem."

48. Ibid., 26: "Vere signum magnum divini amoris est frequenter loqui de Deo, quia ex habundantia cordis os loquitur . . . Sic beatus Petrus; quia amor Christi habundabat in corde, continue quasi loquebatur de Deo et virgine Maria et rebus celestibus et nunquam quasi de temporalibus; et si sibi aliquid diceretur, statim recedebat vel alia verba de Deo assumebat."

and could no longer speak, he seemed to "speak" the *pater noster* prayer through his gestures, instead.[49]

Bindo's explanation of the third sign of God's love, the comb-maker's continual conversation (*continua conversatio*) might seem yet another way of celebrating the saint for the same virtue.[50] Bindo's elaboration that Pier's tendency always to spend his time either alone in his room or in church so that he could remain close to God and the Virgin asks the reader to think more carefully about his use of the word *conversatio*.[51] While it can mean conversation, its most common medieval usage referred to a manner of living, specifically life under monastic vows.[52] Rona Goffen proposed that the early Renaissance paintings titled *sacra conversazione* are better understood as depicting the patristic definition of *conversazione* as "community" rather than "conversation," since as she notes the figures represented in such panels are not speaking with each other.[53] Goffen also argued that the development of the pictorial genre of *sacra conversazione* was preceded by writings produced by the mendicants that tended to see the veneration of a contemporary holy man as a means for participating in a holy community.[54] Bindo's description of Pier's *continua conversatio* seemingly draws on all of these meanings simultaneously. Both Pier's manner of living (that is, his tendency to remain alone in his room or in church) and his words (constantly speaking of and to God and the Virgin) stand not only as proof of God's love but also of how that love had earned Pier a connection to a holy community. While Bindo uses the sermon to emphasize the connection contemporary Siena had with Pier, he also seems interested in arguing that Pier's perfection gave him access to a holy community. The multiple interpretations that Bindo's use of *conversatio* reinforce the benefits of venerating Pier: by celebrating him, the Sienese, who were the comb-maker's earthly community, are given access to the heavenly community that the comb-maker's piety allowed him to join.

---

49. Ibid., 26–27: "Dum enim in morte esset, pater noster in manu tenens, in gestibus pater noster dicere videbatur quod ore non poterat."

50. The emphasis we see both here as well as in Pier's *vita* on the saint's potent yet prudent use of speech seems reminiscent of Frances Andrews's argument about the "legitimating force" or "technique" that speech had in political treatises produced for the Italian communes; see Andrews, "Albertano of Brescia, Rolandino of Padua and the Rhetoric of Legitimation," in *Building Legitimacy: Political Discourses and Forms of Legitimacy in Medieval Societies*, ed. Isabel Alfonso, Hugh Kennedy, and Julio Escalona Monge (Leiden: Brill, 2004), 319–40.

51. Cenci, "San Pietro Pettinaio presentato da un predicatore senese contemporaneo," 27: "3ᵐ signum est continua conversatio."

52. See Niermeyer, *Mediae latinitatis lexicon*, 355.

53. Rona Goffen, "*Nostra Conversatio in Caelis Est*: Observations on the *Sacra Conversazione* in the Trecento," *Art Bulletin* 61 (1979): 198–222.

54. Ibid., 201–2.

Bindo points to Pier's work or action (*sua operatio*) as the final sign of God's love for the saint. And here again, Bindo turns to the words Pier shared with his fellow Sienese as proof. When Pier was not at prayer he was visiting prisoners, the infirm, or the poor, consoling the afflicted, and comforting as well as fortifying the friends of God by preaching the words of both God and the saints.[55] Bindo notes that he can make such a statement because he had heard Pier counseling a lay brother against the idea of predestination, an admission suggesting that Pier did, on occasion, preach doctrine.[56] And yet, although Bindo continues to rely on his audience's direct knowledge and experience with Pier as proof of this final sign of God's love, beyond referring to him as "Petro Pettenario" in the sermon's title and noting that he gave a tenth of his earnings to the poor, Bindo does not discuss Pier's work as a comb-maker or the work we know from communal documents that he performed on behalf of the city.[57]

Bindo does, however, bring up the subject of usury. He points to Pier's rigor in his last days (when, having lost his voice, he would perform his prayers with gestures) as evidence of the importance of living a life fully dedicated to the love of God, and he uses the life of a usurer as a contrast to this dedication. Unlike Pier, Bindo writes, the usurer comes to his moment of death having placed his love of wealth over his love of God, leaving his soul oriented in death toward the same concerns that had occupied it in life.[58]

Bindo also says very little about the different religious organizations with which we know Pier had associations. Even though he makes repeated reference to Pier's work for the city's poor and infirm, Bindo never identifies the comb-maker as a *frater* at the Domus Misericordiae. Moreover, Bindo only twice mentions Pier's connection to the Sienese Franciscans, noting that Pier had once cured his Franciscan confessor's toothache, and that Pier had (at what point in his life, Bindo does not say) fled the world to live with the friars so that he might be free to think about God.[59]

If we turn back to the beginning of the sermon, we find some clues for why Bindo would not emphasize Pier's work for the commune or his involvement with the city's Domus Misericordiae and Franciscan Order. Here Bindo writes about how the Sienese's love of Pier reached across traditional divides. In a city where it was impossible to avoid taking sides in the Guelph versus Ghibelline split, Bindo notes that Pier appealed to all; soldiers, members of

55. Cenci, "San Pietro Pettinaio presentato da un predicatore senese contemporaneo," 27.
56. Ibid.
57. Ibid., 29.
58. Ibid., 27.
59. Ibid., 26.

the *popolo*, just men and sinners, clerics and religious—all spoke highly of Pier.[60] Thus it would make sense to see Bindo's omissions as an attempt to emphasize that Pier belonged not only to the Franciscans, the Domus Misericordiae, or even the city's artisan population, but also—and most importantly—to Siena.

In the second half of the sermon, Bindo continues to rely on Pier's speech as evidence for how much his fellow Sienese loved him. However, instead of repeatedly reminding his audience that they had direct knowledge of Pier's piety, as he did in the first part of the sermon, Bindo instead assembles a portrait of Pier that emphasizes his role as a civic holy man who performed living miracles for his urban community. Bindo does this again by organizing the sermon around an annotated list of the comb-maker's virtues. Pier's honest life, his great moral and religious edification, the virtue of his actions, and finally his eternal life all stand as evidence of both his pious orientation toward his neighbors and their love for him. Each of these aspects of Pier's life gave the comb-maker opportunity to perform miracles for his fellow Sienese.

Thus, Bindo describes how Pier's *honestas vite* led him to exhibit prudence not only when he fled the company of women after the death of his wife but also when he constantly kept a finger to his lips to stop himself from saying anything that was not well considered.[61] His great moral and religious edification (his *hedificatio magna*) was evidenced by the attention—more precisely the verbal attention—that he gave to the afflicted, sick, and poor.[62] When he visited the sick, it was his words that offered them comfort and sometimes even restored them to health.[63] Finally, Bindo points to Pier's frequent battles with demons as well as three miracles he performed during his life as proof of his virtuous deeds.[64] In the first of those miracles, Siena cathedral's night custodians saw Pier walking toward the church, two candles seemingly floating in front of him. The custodians were later astounded to discover Pier inside the closed doors of the cathedral.[65] In the second, Bindo mentions the time Pier touched the tooth of his confessor, Friar Bonafinus, and cured him.[66] And in the third miracle, Bindo points to the cures Pier's words brought when he ran

60. Ibid., 24–25.

61. Ibid., 28. In the fifteenth century, Pier would often be represented with his finger over his mouth; for example, see H. W. van Os, *Vecchietta and the Sacristy of the Siena Hospital Church: A Study in Renaissance Religious Symbolism* (The Hague: Ministerie van Cultuur, 1974), 20 and pl. 5. Also see Diana Norman, "'Santi cittadini': Vecchietta and the Civic Pantheon in Mid-Fifteenth-Century Siena," in *Art as Politics in Late Medieval and Renaissance Siena*, ed. T. B. Smith and J. B. Steinhoff (Abingdon-on-Thames: Routledge, 2012).

62. I am reading *hedificatio* as *aedificatio* meaning "moral and religious edification."

63. Cenci, "San Pietro Pettinaio presentato da un predicatore senese contemporaneo," 28–29.

64. Ibid., 29.

65. Ibid.

66. Ibid.

into a friend whose son was near death; after simply telling his friend to believe firmly, take strength, and go in peace, the man returned home to find his son restored to health.[67]

Throughout the second half of the sermon, Bindo emphasizes aspects of Pier's religious life that fit into the established model of the communal lay saint. Pier exhibits prudence in both his private and public life, uses his moral teachings to deliver charitable rewards to the city's poor and needy, and performs miracles that give him the opportunity to wrestle demons, gain access to closed churches, and heal the sick. In short, the second half of Bindo's sermon celebrates Pier for the same qualities we saw emphasized in the *vitae* of other thirteenth-century urban lay saints, including Raimondo of Piacenza as well as Omobono and Facio of Cremona. And yet, Bindo's Pier is also a saint whose reputation rests on both what he does for others and what he does for his own spiritual progress. Pier's prayers to God and the Virgin Mary matter as much as his work to heal and aid others. In this way, Bindo's portrait of Pier's lay sanctity blends the two distinct paths for lay religion that were created by Innocent's canonization of Omobono of Cremona and approval of the Franciscan Order at the beginning of the thirteenth century. Pier may be devoted to helping his fellow Sienese but he also falls into ecstatic states. His lay sanctity therefore has both an external and internal identity.

Finally, the focus Bindo places upon the familiarity between his audience and his subject as well as upon the powerful influence of Pier's words allows the text to become more eulogy than sermon and asks us to reconsider the development of a cult within a local context. Bindo's words seem aimed at helping his Sienese neighbors mourn the passing of a well-known and well-loved civic holy man. But while Bindo does emphasize the contemporary nature of Pier's sanctity, he leaves out key aspects of Pier's biography: his work as a comb-maker, his work on behalf of the commune, and his association with the Domus Misericordiae. This is the information that would be crucial for constructing a saint's institutional identity. In Pier's case, however, the audience's familiarity with Pier negated the need for any such construction of identity. The sermon seems to argue that it is the audience themselves—the Sienese— and the intimate knowledge they have of Pier that constitutes his saintly identity. Pier's cult therefore transcends any particular association—he is not one faction's saint as much as he is the city's saint.

An even fuller equation of Pier's piety and his civic identity would be made nearly forty years later, when other Sienese Franciscans relied upon Bindo's

---

67. Ibid., 29–30.

sermon to craft the first narrative *vita* for the comb-maker. Although this *vita* would also celebrate the close connection Pier cultivated with his fellow Sienese and use a focus upon the saint's words to make that point, it would ultimately locate Pier's sanctity in his behavior as an artisan and communal citizen.

Civic Religion and the Nine

In 1287, two years before Pier's death, the Sienese commune began to be ruled by the Nine Governors and Defenders of the Commune and People of Siena, or the Nine, as the government was most commonly called.[68] The Nine were a *popolo* government. Most *popolo* governments were relatively short-lived, but in Siena the Nine ruled longer, in circumstances of more peace and civic growth, than any other communal regime in that city.

Much of the Nine's success and longevity has been attributed to the strong political ideology they crafted. That ideology focused on linking civic piety and patriotism to the city's prestige and strength. The Nine demonstrated their power by pouring funds into the support of public works, civic monuments, and saints' cults. Perhaps more than any other medieval commune, Siena under the Nine fashioned itself as a spiritual community as much as a civic one.[69] Nowhere was this more evident than in the Nine's support and expansion of the city's cult of the Virgin—richly and concisely articulated in two works commissioned by the Nine for the cathedral and newly built Palazzo Pubblico (the seat of the communal government): Duccio di Buoninsegna's *Maestà* for the cathedral's high altar (1308–11) and Simone Martini's *Maestà* for the Palazzo Pubblico's Sala del Consiglio (ca. 1315).[70] In both images, the city's peace, prosperity, and good government are presented as dependent upon the city's veneration of the Virgin and as a sign of her divine sanction of the city.[71]

The Virgin's cult was of course not the only cult that Siena patronized during the reign of the Nine. Less than two weeks after Pier's death in

---

68. For an introduction to the Nine, see Bowsky, *A Medieval Italian Commune*, 260–98; Waley, *Siena and the Sienese*.

69. Jones, *The Italian City-State*, 298.

70. The primary study of the Virgin's cult in Siena remains Norman, *Siena and the Virgin*.

71. For the political dimensions of this period of Sienese art, see Norman, *Siena and the Virgin*; Bram Kempers, "Icons, Altarpieces, and Civic Ritual in Siena Cathedral, 1100–1530," in *City and Spectacle in Medieval Europe*, ed. Barbara A. Hanawalt and Kathryn L. Reyerson (Minneapolis: University of Minnesota Press, 1994), 89–136; Maginnis, *The World of the Early Sienese Painter*; and Chiara Frugoni, *A Distant City: Images of Urban Experience in the Medieval World*, trans. William McCuaig (Princeton: Princeton University Press, 1991).

December 1289, the commune's General Council referred to him as a saint in a decree giving the Sienese Franciscans two hundred lire for the construction of a tomb for the pious comb-maker.[72] Although this tomb does not survive, both the references in the communal record to a *sepulchrum nobile cum ciborio et altare* (a noble tomb with a ciborium—or canopy—and altar) and the large amount of money donated have led scholars to speculate that Pier's tomb was quite elaborate and likely resembled the first tomb constructed for Ranieri of Pisa.[73]

Over the next twenty years, the commune appears to have gradually increased what was most likely an annual donation to San Francesco to mark Pier's December feast day. In 1296, the Biccherna records that Siena's *podestà* and other government officials had taken forty lire of wax and two *doppieri* (large candles) to San Francesco.[74] In 1307, the commune presented ten *doppieri* to the Franciscan church along with an additional donation of wax. And finally, in 1321 and 1323, the Biccherna records that celebrations for the December feast included donations of over one hundred pounds of wax from the commune.[75] While the annual Biccherna records do not list the subvention each year, a debate over communal expenditures in the General Council in the late 1320s makes clear not only that Pier's cult had been receiving a yearly donation but also that it was not the only cult supported by the Nine that was dedicated to a contemporary Sienese holy figure.

---

72. ASS, Deliberazioni del Consiglio Generale, 38, f. 62, December 19, 1289: "quod fratribus minoribus et conventui ipsorum fratrum de Senis detur de pecunia Comunis et solvatur usque quantitatem .CC. librarum denariorum senensium pro faciendo construi super tumulum sancti Petri Petenarii venerabilis civis senensis, unum sepulcrum nobile cum ciborio et altari . . ." This donation is also listed in Biccherna records, see ASS, Biccherna, 102 (1289), f. 150v: "Item CC lib. fratribus minorum pro sepultura Sancti Petri Pectenarii, pro reformatione Consilii."

73. There were two tombs made for Ranieri of Pisa (d. 1160) and scholars speculate that Pier's tomb may have been similar to the Pisan patron's first tomb, which consisted of a stone tomb chest, decorated with rectangular reliefs, supported on consoles, with a historiated gable above and an altar below; see Cannon and Vauchez, *Margherita of Cortona*, 66–68. Our only evidence for the first tomb for Ranieri comes from a depiction of a miracle that took place at the tomb sculpted by Tino di Camaino for the second tomb monument made for San Ranieri between 1291 and 1306. For more on these types of tomb monuments, see works by Bardotti Biasion, G. Kreytenberg, and J. Garms, which Cannon cites in Cannon and Vauchez, *Margherita of Cortona*, 67.

74. ASS, Biccherna, 113 (1296), f. 233: "Item XV lib: xiii sol. et iiii den. datis et expensis in quadraginta cereis, et duobus dopieris (*sic*) que (*sic*) dominus Potestas et dominus Capitaneus et alii officiales Comunis Sen. portaverunt ad festum Sancti Petri Pectenarii et est inde habita apodissa (*sic*) a dominis Novem." I am relying on a transcription made by Cristofani, see "Memorie del B. Pietro Pettinagno da Siena," 52. Thompson defines *doppieri* as twelve-pound candles, while Maginnis writes that the term orginally referred to "a two-branch candelabra," but in late thirteenth and early fourteenth-century sources it most likely referred to "a very large candle," see Thompson, *Cities of God*, 402–3; and Maginnis, *The World of the Early Sienese Painter*, 42, n. 95.

75. ASS, Biccherna, 142 (1321), f. 146v; and 148 (1323), f. 132 (modern pagination). These three Biccherna references are taken from Webb, *Patrons and Defenders*, 280.

Between February and April 1329, the Dominicans, Franciscans, Augustinians, Servites, and Carmelites all issued protests to Siena's General Council. The orders were reacting to the broad legislation that the Nine had brought forth and approved during the previous year forbidding government officials from attending or making offerings for any festival (*ad aliquam festivitatem*).[76] Siena had entered a period of economic hardship and belt-tightening in response to the march of Louis of Bavaria through Tuscany as well as to a drought and the resulting food shortages. These Sienese religious knew that such measures could mean the end of support for the civic cults that were associated with their orders. In each petition, representatives of the orders argued for the value that their particular saint brought to the city and urged communal officials to continue both their financial support for and attendance at each saint's feast day celebrations. All but the Carmelites were arguing for cults dedicated to contemporary Sienese.[77]

Thus, the Dominicans argued that it was precisely a poor city that could most benefit from a celestial patron like the preacher Ambrogio Sansedoni. Noting the general value saints' cults brought to the city, the Dominicans also pointed out that the veneration of saints had "conferred many advantages" upon Siena and had "brought to an end and protected the city from many evils and perils." They called for Siena to be forever associated with the cult of the native preacher.[78] While the Franciscans also mentioned Pier's native blood, their argument focused on the benefits multiple intercessors brought to a city.[79]

---

76. See André Vauchez, "La commune de Sienne, les ordres mendiants et le culte des saints: Histoire et enseignements d'une crise (novembre 1328–avril 1329)," *Mélanges de l'École Française de Rome* 89 (1977): 760; this legislation is preserved in ASS, Deliberazioni del Consiglio Generale, 106 (November 10, 1328), ff. 87v–88v. Webb has pointed to the fact that although the broad language of the measure could have been interpreted as limiting the Nine's participation in the August feast of the Assumption, it does not seem to have been taken this way; see *Patrons and Defenders*, 281–82.

77. The Sienese Carmelites were arguing for the commune to continue its patronage of the cult of St. Nicholas of Bari; see Webb, *Patrons and Defenders*, 283; and Vauchez, "La commune de Sienne," 762. For a thorough study of the addition of new cults to Siena's ancient pantheon of civic saints, see Romagnoli, "Pier Pettinaio e il modelli di santità."

78. ASS, Deliberazioni del Consiglio Generale, 107 (February 16, 1329), ff. 33–35v: "Quare, cum credatur et speretur firmiter quod veneratio sanctorum quae facta est hactenus in civitate Senarum per dictum Communem et Officiales ipsius multa commoda contulerit Communi praedicto et a multis malis et periculis cessaverit et custodierit civitatem praedictam, petunt et rogant humiliter . . . quod praefati officiales possint et debeant ire et Consilium etiam ire possit, sicut fuit hactenus consuetum, ad festivitatem S. Ambrosii nobilissimi civis vestri . . ."; cited by Vauchez, "La commune de Sienne," 761, n. 22. Bowsky cites and translates this passage but misidentifies it as referring to Pier; see *A Medieval Italian Commune*, 263.

79. ASS, Deliberazioni del Consiglio Generale, 107 (February 16, 1329), ff. 35v–37v: "Quare cum ipse beatus Petrus fuerit de civitate ista nativus et ex eius originali amore specialem curam ad civitatem habeat et ad cives, et sanctitate et meritis eius, ut debemus credere, obtineat apud Deum, et tanto magis civitas servetur incolumis quod plures apud defensorem suum, scilicet ipsum Deum, magnos

Declaring that the more advocates a city had, the more safely it would be preserved, the Franciscans argued that precisely because a man as holy as Pier had emerged from the city, Siena and its citizens had been honored. The friars concluded their appeal by calling for the *podestà*, the *capitano*, and other communal officials to be required to attend Pier's liturgical office at San Francesco. While the petitions of the Dominicans and Franciscans passed by the greatest margin, all of the orders that had issued protests were successful in garnering some communal support for their saints.[80] The council rescinded the original measure and took actions to make the commune's donations on the feast days of Ambrogio Sansedoni and Pier a regular event that no longer required annual petitions.

Thus, in the midst of the debate over the commune's financial role in the cults of its civic saints, the mendicants had reminded civic officials that these cults both protected the city from harm and offered Siena and its citizens a divine sanction. They were, in effect, arguing that the city's contemporary holy figures held a role similar to the Virgin's. In their eyes, both Siena's security and its spiritual dignity depended upon the city's participation in the cults of contemporary patrons.

The Nine's 1328 legislation was also likely a key motivation for the appearance around 1330 of the first *vita* for Pier. Although the *vita* relies on the portrait Bindo da Siena drew of Pier in his 1289 sermon, it offers much more information about Pier's work as a comb-maker as well as his participation in communal life and politics. In short, the *vita* stakes its most persuasive claim for sanctity on its characterization of Pier as an ideal member of the commune. The portrait we get in the *vita* of civic lay sanctity aims not only to capitalize on the fusing of political and religious concerns in late medieval Siena but also to articulate how an ideal lay life that equated spiritual concerns with fair business practices and piety with civic duty reflected and contributed to the city's grandeur and magnitude. Pier's *vita* therefore served as a justification for the role the extraordinary but yet ordinary city-dweller could play in helping a city achieve its greatness.

Holy Layman/Holy Citizen

The only known manuscript of the fourteenth-century *vita* written by Pietro da Montarone, a Sienese Franciscan who claims to have known Pier, was de-

---

habuerit advocatos, et cum honor sit civitati et civibus quod ex eis provenerit tantus sanctus . . ." This source has been transcribed by Cristofani, "Memorie del B. Pietro Pettinagno da Siena," 37–38; and Vauchez, "La commune de Sienne," 761, n. 25.

80. The Augustinians were arguing for the cult of their friar, Agostino Novello (d. 1309), while the Servites advocated for their friar, Giovacchino (d. 1305).

stroyed in a fire in the church of San Francesco in Siena in the late sixteenth century.[81] We are fortunate, however, that two early sixteenth-century Italian translations survive.[82] In the *vita's* proem, Pietro notes that his Franciscan superiors and fellow friars had encouraged him to write a life for Pier but does not indicate when he began this project.[83] Although it is clear that Pietro used Bindo's sermon as a source, repeating many of its episodes and points, the *vita* goes much further to present Pier as a miracle-working ecstatic, whose religious experiences and ideals produced not only an ideal layman but also an ideal member of the commune.

Pietro's portrait of Pier's early religious activities focuses on the saint's relatively uneventful youth and conversion experience. Although the comb-maker had been a "hot-tempered" and "boisterous youth," he adds that Pier had always been "immune from the vices" often associated with the young.[84] His conversion, Pietro writes, was not precipitated by a particularly sinful past nor a moment of mental and spiritual clarity: after the saint took up comb-making and had married, "the hand of the Lord" came upon him and "suddenly he changed into another man altogether."[85] The somewhat mundane

---

81. De Angelis, *Vita Pier*, vii. De Angelis speculates here that Pietro had been Pier's confessor, but I have been unable to find any information to support this claim.

82. In 1508, Serafino Ferri, an Augustinian hermit at Lecceto (near Siena), translated the original Latin into Italian; that translation was first published in 1529: Serafino Ferri, *Vita auctore Pier de Monterone (c. 1330), vita del Beato Pier Pettinaio* (Siena, 1529). The only copy I have found of the Ferri translation is in Rome, Biblioteca Vallicelliana, Stampati: S. II. 45. Ferri's translation was reissued with added notes of both a scholarly and devotional bent in 1802 by de Angelis to mark Rome's first acknowledgment of Pier's cult: on January 6, 1802, the Vatican confirmed that the comb-maker's cult had existed *ab immemorabili* in the Sienese diocese. De Angelis claims to have corrected parts of Ferri's original translation. After comparing the 1529 edition to de Angelis's text, Webb found no significant difference between the two; Webb, *Saints and Cities*, 191. I shall therefore rely on de Angelis's edition. In 1541, the Franciscan Dionisio Pulinari completed another Italian translation for the convent of S. Orsola in Florence. The Pulinari translation survives only in one manuscript now held in the convent di Giaccherino (outside of Pistoia), I.G.2; see Cenci, "'San' Pietro Pettinaio presentato da Fr. Bindo da Siena," 202–3. I have not consulted the Pulinari translation. Both of these translations unfortunately do not include the final chapter of postmortem miracle accounts that was part of the original Latin manuscript. Ferri includes short notices of a number of miracles that he claims represent the diversity of miracles and beneficiaries found in the Latin *vita*; see de Angelis, *Vita Pier*, 119. The Ferri translation does corroborate much of what we know regarding Pier's life from communal documents. When I cite particular passages of Pier's *vita*, I shall refer to both Webb and de Angelis and shall provide the Italian text where appropriate.

83. Webb, *Satins and Cities*, 194; de Angelis, *Vita Pier*, 2.

84. Webb, *Saints and Cities*, 195; de Angelis, *Vita Pier*, 5–6: "Questo Pietro nella puerizia e adolescenza sua visse sempre allegramente, essendo di condizione faceta: benchè (secondo si diceva da chi in quella età giovanile l'aveva conosciuto) fosse stato giovane furibondo ed assai tempestoso. Nientedimeno, ajutandolo la divina protezione, da quei vizj, ne'quali quell'età si suole immergere, sempre fu alieno."

85. Webb, *Saints and Cities*, 195; de Angelis, *Vita Pier*, 6: "E fatta la mano del Signore sopra di Pietro, subito fu grandemente in altr'uomo mutato, e così cominciò divotissimamente a frequentar la

characterization of Pier's conversion experience sets the tone for much of what Pietro tells us about the saint's daily devotional life. Pier adhered to a penitential routine, but it does not seem to have been particularly noteworthy. He attended church frequently, where he listened "with the greatest attention." He fasted from All Saints to Christmas, throughout Lent and, in honor of the Virgin, on Saturdays.[86] Admitting that Pier's commitment to abstinence was "hidden and discreet," Pietro does note that the comb-maker was careful to eat only "permitted things according to their season," in amounts that barely sufficed, "remained ceaselessly in prayer and contemplation," slept very little (always on a hard bed), dressed in "the cheapest fabrics," and mortified his flesh with pilgrimages to Rome, Assisi, Pisa, and Pistoia.[87]

Pietro also paints Pier as a typical urban lay penitent when he turns to describing the saint's dedication to offering charity to the poor and sick of Siena. Pier, he writes, "continually visited the hospital of Santa Maria della Scala," and like Francis, "devotedly washed the hands and feet of the sick, and cleaned and bound even horrible wounds."[88] We know from charter evidence that Pier also served as a *frater* of the Domus Misericordiae. However, just as we saw in Bindo's sermon, this is an aspect of the saint's life that is left out of the *vita*. But unlike the sermon, the *vita* pays particular attention to Pier's relationship with the Sienese Franciscans and his devotion to St. Francis.

That devotion is most clearly expressed in a vision that Pier received while he prayed in Siena's cathedral. Pier saw Christ walking down the cathedral's ash-strewn center aisle, followed by a procession of saints. He noticed that of all of the saints, only Francis of Assisi's feet perfectly fit into Christ's footprints. Realizing that Francis was the "singular imitator" of Christ, Pier decided at that moment to deepen his devotion to the order and its founder; he went to live

---

Chiesa, e quel tanto che egli della Sacra Scrittura nel divino Uffizio, o nelle sante Predicazioni con attentissimo animo udiva, non oblioso ascoltatore, tutto riponeva nel secreto del suo petto . . ."

86. Webb, *Saints and Cities*, 202; de Angelis, *Vita Pier*, 22–23; and Webb, *Saints and Cities*, 223; de Angelis, *Vita Pier*, 79.

87. Webb, *Saints and Cities*, 223; de Angelis, *Vita Pier*, 79: "e però vacava singolarmenti all'astinenza, la quale era in lui ascosa e discretissima, imperocchè di tutte le cose lecite secondo i tempi suoi mangiava, ma con tanta sobrietà e parsimonia che con fatica poteva bastare alla naturale sostentazione . . . Molto poco dormiva, e secondo l'Apostolico precetto stava senza intermissione in orazione e contemplazione, e quel poco dormiva sopra un durissimo Letto, al quale non altro che la estrema necessità lo adduceva andare. Vestiva di vilissimi panni, i quali spesso rappezzava ancora di diversi colori. Macerava spesso il corpo suo con diverse e faticose pellegrinazioni andando ora a Roma alle sante Indulgenze: ora a S. Francesco d'Assisi, alla quale Indulgenza aveva singolare devozione e fede: ora a Pisa nella santa Ascensione del Signore, ora Pistoia nella Chiesa di S. Jacopo maggiore."

88. Webb, *Saints and Cities*, 198; de Angelis, *Vita Pier*, 11: "Visitava di continuo lo Spedale di Santa Maria della Scala di Siena, dove singolarmente agli poveri di Cristo serviva . . . Le mani ed i piedi di quell'infermi divotamente lavava, e baciava, e le piaghe ancora orride nettava e fasciava, quasi come un altro beatissimo Francesco."

at San Francesco in a cell near the infirmary, and was assigned, as Pietro reports, a "devout and circumspect religious," who was to minister to his needs.[89]

Pietro also claims, in a passage describing Pier's love of poverty, that the comb-maker was a member of the Franciscans' Third Order. He writes that having given up the richly colored clothes he had worn in his youth, Pier "made himself a habit of the Third Order of St. Francis, whom he had adopted as his special advocate, out of cheap cloth."[90] While it was not uncommon in the mid-thirteenth century for Franciscan writers to refer to lay penitents as members of their "Third Order," a formal Franciscan lay wing did not exist until after 1289, the year that Pope Nicholas IV's bull *Supra montem* required all lay penitents to be placed under Franciscan guardians.[91] Pietro's ca. 1330 characterization of Pier's clothing is thus either anachronistic or hyperbole.

Later in the *vita*, Pietro offers another description of Pier's clothing that seems more in line with the reality of lay penitential habits in the mid to late thirteenth century. He writes that Pier had dressed in "the cheapest fabrics, which he often patched in different colors."[92] We know from early thirteenth-century lay penitential rules that penitents were advised to wear clothes

---

89. Webb, *Satins and Cities*, 212; de Angelis, *Vita Pier*, 48–50: "E così rimase Pietro grandemente consolato, rendendo a Gesù grazie infinite, che si era degnato mostrargli Beato Francesco suo singolare immitatore così bella e grata visione . . . E così crebbe l'Uomo di Cristo in singolar devozione di S. Francesco, avendolo infra li Santi, dopo la beata Vergine, in precipuo suo Avvocato, e singolarmente amava li Frati successori suoi, e per meglio poter con loro conversare se ne andò ad abitare nel Convento di S. Francesco e da loro benignamente recevuto, gli assegnarono una Cella vincino alla Capella della Infermeria, assegnandogli ancora un dovoto e circospetto Religioso, il quale lo servisse nelle occorrenze sue." In another passage, Pietro cites Pier's declining health as the impetus for his move. He writes that during the time Pier was living in Siena's Ovile district, he became quite ill and asked a number of friars to stay with him through the night, fearing that he might die. The friars reminded Pier that they were not allowed to spend the night outside of the convent and urged him to come to live with them at San Francesco. Pier agreed to join the friars and, as Pietro describes, spent all of his time at the convent, finding there that "his devotion to God and the merits of his excellent life increased." See De Angelis, *Vita Pier*, 44. Allison Clark has noted that there is evidence in Siena, as in many late medieval cities, that hermits lived in cells attached to churches. But Pier does not seem to have lived as a recluse at San Francesco, since the *vita* makes it clear that he continued to come and go from his cell as he pleased; see Allison Clark, "Spaces of Reclusion: Notarial Records of Urban Eremiticism in Medieval Siena," in *Rhetoric of the Anchorhold: Space, Place and Body within the Discourses of Enclosure*, ed. Liz Herbert McAvoy (Cardiff: University of Wales Press, 2008).

90. Webb, *Saints and Cities*, 198; de Angelis, *Vita Pier*, 12–13: "Levati dunque via i vestimenti colorati quali nella gioventù ventù usare soleva, secondo la decenza e dello stato, e del tempo, come dispregiatore vero di se medesimo, di vile panno si fece un abito del Terz' Ordine del B. Francesco, il quale aveva pigliato per suo singolare avvocato . . ." Thompson notes that Margaret of Cortona made herself a habit of the Franciscan Third Order, but I have not found any reference to this. Thompson is likely confusing Margaret for Pier; see *Cities of God*, 82.

91. Casagrande, "Un Ordine per i laici," 237–55.

92. Webb, *Saints and Cities*, 223; de Angelis, *Vita Pier*, 79: "Vestiva di vilissimi panni, i quali spesso rappezzava ancora di diversi colori."

made of cheap fabric, without embellishment or ornamentation.[93] As Thompson has noted, even though there was no standard lay habit before the late thirteenth and early fourteenth centuries, it was this kind of ad hoc clothing that marked the penitent.[94] Communal governments punished those who dressed as penitents (and thus could claim exemption from certain laws and taxes) but did not follow a true penitential regime.[95] Pier's tattered and mismatched clothes mattered as the outward sign of his religious commitment. They would have alerted his fellow Sienese to the fact that he was living as a penitent. And while those clothes may have also indicated that his penitential life was associated with the city's Franciscan Order, they did not constitute formal membership in a (yet-to-exist) Franciscan lay order.

If we delve deeper into the *vita*, we can see that Pietro actually paints a more nuanced, and I would argue more accurate, portrait of the kind of independent religious life that was available to lay penitents before 1289. Pietro refers to a group of eight men with whom Pier lived, all of whom he names. This living arrangement likely began sometime after the death of his wife but before he came to live at San Francesco. Pietro writes that these men "had for the love of God spurned the world" to focus their lives "on nothing but prayer and works of mercy."[96] Each Sunday, Pier and his companions met in Siena's largest hospital, Santa Maria della Scala, and "there took counsel together as to how during the next week they could most diligently serve the sick and the needy."[97] Pietro describes how the men would split up into pairs of two to make their way through various districts of the city, offering food and begging for alms. Pietro notes that Pier lived with these men "as with the best of brothers," adding that they venerated Pier "with pious affection like a father."[98] We meet two familiar names among the eight: first, the notary Ser Compagno,

---

93. See the penitential rules collected in Meersseman, *Dossier de l'order de la penitence.*

94. Thompson, *Cities of God*, 82–84.

95. Thompson cites a Florentine statute as evidence here; see *Cities of God*, 83.

96. Webb, *Saints and Cities*, 200; de Angelis, *Vita Pier*, 18: "Tutti questi avendo per l'amor di Cristo disprezzato il mondo, non ad altro che all'orazioni, ed alle opere di misericordia attendevano." The companions were Guglielmo da Pancole, the notary Ser Compagno, Frate Baldino, Tolomeo Barcigli, Mino Luglioli, Bartolomeo di Vincenzo, the notary Ser Buonfigliuolo, and Jacomo Falconi.

97. Webb, *Saints and Cities*, 200; de Angelis, *Vita Pier*, 18: "Il giorno poi delle Feste sempre cinque de'prenominati uomini di Dio si congregavano nello Spedale maggiore di Siena, ed ivi insime consigliandosi in che modo e via la futura settimana si dovesse più diligentemente servire agl'infermi ed ai poveri indigenti, e dividendosi, e ciascheduno pigliando il compagno colla tasca in collo; alcuni altri col vaso di portar minestra, andavano per diverse contrade di Siena cercando limosine, le quali caritativamente agli indigenti somministravano."

98. Webb, *Saints and Cities*, 200; de Angelis, *Vita Pier*, 16–17: "Aveva l'Uomo di Dio Pietro con alcuni massima conversazione, coi quali, come con ottimi fratelli conversava, e da essi quasi come un loro Padre era con pio affetto venerato."

whom the commune had named in 1285 to distribute alms on its behalf (along with Pier), and in 1286 to paint images on the city gates; and second, Bartolomeo di Vincenzo, the rector of the Domus Misericordiae in the 1270s and 1280s, who had asked in his testament that Pier be consulted on his burial location and on how to make proper restitution for his ill-gotten gains.

Pietro notes that, at a certain point, while Pier was living with these men, he abandoned the active life all together. While his companions would break off into pairs each Sunday to administer charity to different districts, Pietro writes that Pier and a few others remained behind to do "nothing but concentrate with Mary Magdalen on the contemplative life."[99] Pietro explains that since these men had "already won favor with God by the performance of the active life," they could concentrate "solely on the divine harvest."[100]

When Pier concentrated "solely on the divine harvest," more often than not he either performed miracles for his fellow Sienese or fell into ecstatic states. Pier, Pietro writes, was so full of love for "all the afflicted, imprisoned, and other poor persons suffering from any infirmity" that he was "privileged" by Christ to perform "healing miracles."[101] Those miracles run the gamut from Pier curing his friend Matteo's bad head cold to the saint reviving a child who died after having fallen from a high story.[102] In many of these episodes, it is the physical contact between Pier and the afflicted that initiates the cure. By placing his hands on the head of a young girl from Pistoia, Pier not only heals her ulcer but also makes any sign of the infirmity vanish.[103] Moreover, after the mother of a girl paralyzed from the waist down managed to grab some of Pier's hairs, wrap them in a cloth, and place them "with great faith and devotion" on her daughter's neck, the girl was "cured at once."[104]

---

99. Webb, *Saints and Cities*, 201; de Angelis, *Vita Pier*, 18: "Gli altri quattro fra i quali l'uomo di Dio Pietro, quei giorni non ad altro che con Maria Maddalena alla contemplativa vita attendevano, come fatti già a Dio grati per le azioni dell'attiva vita, nella sola fruizione divina si pascevano."

100. Webb, *Saints and Cities*, 200–201; de Angelis, *Vita Pier*, 18.

101. Webb, *Saints and Cities*, 206; de Angelis, *Vita Pier*, 34: "Era Pietro di tanta carità ripeno che a tutti gli afflitti, incarcerate, ed alter mendiche persone poste in qualche infermità aveva tal compassione che più dir non si potrebbe, in modo che più volte fu l'Uomo di Dio illustrato e dotato da Cristo Gesù, per la immense pieta, benignità, e carità, la quale aveva verso i poveri ed afflitti, di far miracoli sanando infermi."

102. Webb, *Saints and Cities*, 206; de Angelis, *Vita Pier*, 34; also see Webb, *Saints and Cities*, 218; de Angelis, *Vita Pie*, 65–66.

103. Webb, *Saints and Cities*, 207; de Angelis, *Vita Pier*, 37–38.

104. Webb, *Saints and Cities*, 206; de Angelis, *Vita Pier*, 35–36: "era una Fanciulla, la quale dalla cintola in giù era così totalmente perduta, che come insensibile pareva; e venendo un giorno l'amico di Dio Pietro per gran carità a consolare, e confortare a pazienza la Madre di detta fanciulla . . . accostandosegli per modo di riverenza, gli prese alcuni Capelli che pendevano dalla Testa fuori della berretta, i quali così pigliati ed involtati in certo panno, e con gran fede e devozione li pose al collo della figliuola così inferma. Ella fu liberate immediatamente . . ."

Pier's speech also brings about miracles. Pietro describes the time when Pier saw a friar who was suffering from "the intense cold" scurry out of the church of San Francesco to find a fire to warm himself.[105] Pier encouraged the friar to listen to his words, reminding him of the "immense fire and ardent love with which Jesus Christ" loved him. Pietro writes that when Pier was done speaking, the friar, "already thoroughly heated," said to the comb maker: "Leave me, leave me, my father, go away and don't keep me any longer, for I tell you truly that from the moment you began to speak to me, I became so warm that I can't bear it any more."[106] As it does in this episode, Pier's speech often serves as a catalyst for his charisma. While Pier's speech could warm a freezing friar, it was also the act of counseling others that most often launched him into an ecstatic state.

Thus, when Pier gives advice—as he is so often asked to do—to other laymen, to friars, or even to communal officials, when he calls out to the Virgin, or when he is simply talking with his friends about the sweetness of the figs they are eating, the holy comb-maker finds himself time and time again "suddenly seized by ecstasy."[107] In several of these episodes, Pietro notes that Pier looked "half-dead;"[108] in others, Pietro claims that the saint had been "elevated above the earth" or "illuminated" to such an extent that he created at night a light that suggested the midday sun.[109]

The dual focus upon Pier's words and his tendency to fall into an ecstatic state are aspects of the saint's profile that Pietro likely borrowed from Bindo's sermon. In that text, Bindo repeatedly reminds his readers that they had heard Pier's pious words and had seen his moments of spiritual exuberance. Bindo also notes that Pier often kept a finger over his mouth to keep himself from saying anything rash. Pier's ability to control his speech also figures prominently in the *vita*. Pietro writes at length about how, "out of humility," Pier had "mastered his tongue" so that "without great necessity, he never or rarely spoke and what he said was always useful, either to himself or to his neighbor."[110] Even though Pietro's mention of Pier's mastery of his tongue

---

105. Webb, *Saints and Cities*, 205; de Angelis, *Vita Pier*, 33.

106. Webb, *Saints and Cities*, 205–6; de Angelis, *Vita Pier*, 33: "lasciami, lasciami: Padre mio, andare e non mi voler più ritenere, che veramente ti dico, che dal momento che mi cominciasti a parlare, così sono riscaldato che più non posso soffrire."

107. For example see Webb, *Saints and Cities*, 201 and 204; de Angelis, *Vita Pier*, 18 and 29.

108. Webb, *Saints and Cities*, 201; de Angelis, *Vita Pier*, 18.

109. See, for example, Webb, *Saints and Cities*, 204 and 214; de Angelis, *Vita Pier*, 29 and 54–55.

110. Webb, *Saints and Cities*, 220; de Angelis, *Vita Pier*, 70: "Per tanta umiltà in tal guise dominava la sua lingua, che sense grande necessità mai, ovvero raro parlava, e quello che diceva sempre era utilità o sua, o del prossimo, e questo dono di predominare la lingua l'aveva Pietro di special grazia, con studio, e sollecitudine di sante orazioni per molti anni da Dio dimandata, e finalmente ottenuta e così secondo il consiglio del Sapiente Ecclesiastico nel parlar suo prudentemente si portava, cioè o

might be seen simply as the author repeating information found in the sermon, I would argue that this aspect of Pietro's portrait of Pier conveys an anxiety about lay religion absent in the sermon.

That anxiety is visible not only in the many mentions that Pietro makes of Pier's ability to control his speech (which is also ability to control his moments of ecstasy, since they so often were initiated by the comb-maker talking) but also in the author's references to Pier's turn to the contemplative life. From the text's first lines, Pietro seems intent on making sense of an ideal layman who was as dedicated to the contemplative life as he was to the active life of charity work (if not more so). Pietro writes that "like an angelic spirit," Pier continuously practiced the contemplative life, linking that practice to the fact that the comb-maker "was filled with the spirit of prophecy." But while he was "entirely caught up in God," Pietro goes on to note that Pier "did not confine himself to all of this, but tirelessly practiced the active life of charity toward his neighbor."[111]

Although Pietro seems intent on portraying Pier's religious life as embodying a perfect balance of the active and contemplative life—he notes that Pier was "another Martha" but did not "abandon the contemplation of heavenly things with Mary"—the author also gives his readers ample evidence that Pier's focus on his own spiritual development struck many of his contemporaries as odd.[112] Pietro writes that several men once asked Pier why "he did not apply himself to works of mercy." The men were confused about why Pier would concentrate on contemplation when anything that Pier asked for would surely be given to the poor. Pier responded by noting that there were "many paths to spiritual advancement," and that "it was no longer safe" for him to be "involved in the world." When the men challenged Pier, noting that his companion, Ser Compagno, was still involved in charity work, Pier retorted that Ser Compagno could do such work without suffering harm, while he "did not feel fit" or safe for charity work.[113] In two other episodes, Pietro portrays Pier defending his

---

sempre taceva, o sivvero parlando non altro che cose salutifere proferiva. Aveva Pietro in uso o andasse ovvero stesse tenere quasi sempre la mano sopra la bocca come uomo tutto circospetto in ogni suo parlare, e timoroso di non dire parola senza utilità."

111. Webb, *Saints and Cities*, 193; de Angelis, *Vita Pier*, 2: "Il quale, come spirito angelico, di continuo nella contemplativa vita si esercitava: donde molto spesso si trovava ripieno di spirito di Profezia, e seguitando gli Apostolici vestigj, l'umana superbia dispregiando, con ardore di fervente carità, e colla sincerissima fede degli antichi Patriarchi e Martiri di Cristo santissimi, tutto in Dio si trovava rapito. E non però su tutto questo si arrestava; ma indefessamente nell'attiva vita per le opere della misericordia inverso il prossimo si esercitava, ed in se con singolar prudenza, le penitenze durissime dei Confessori di Cristo rinnovava."

112. Webb, *Saints and Cities*, 198; de Angelis, *Vita Pier*, 11.

113. Webb, *Saints and Cities*, 222; de Angelis, *Vita Pier*, 75: "Fratelli dovete sapere, che diversi sono i modi e le vie dei spirituali guadagni, ed io per esperienza parlo e conosco omniamente, che per me

adoption of the contemplative life. In the first, Pietro writes that Pier once told a Florentine friend that, "he who wants truly to serve in the ways of God must leave the world."[114] And in the second, after hearing a pilgrim boasting about his travels, Pier responded that it is not possible "to know the world . . . if a person does not first try to know his own state and interior condition."[115]

And yet, at the same time that Pietro claims that Pier had abandoned the active life, it is precisely the manner and quality of Pier's civic life to which Pietro repeatedly turns to prove his sanctity. Pier's actions and attitudes as a husband, a comb-maker, and communal resident serve as Pietro's most striking and novel evidence for Pier's sanctity. We see then in Pietro's portrait of lay sanctity a new way of mixing external and internal concerns for the pious layman. On one hand, Pier abandons the active life and is lauded by Pietro for his contemplative and ecstatic states. But on the other hand, such an internal focus ultimately allows Pietro's audience to see the extent to which Pier was an ideal member of his civic community in his identity as a husband, an artisan, and most importantly, as a commune member.

At first, Pietro describes Pier's relationship with his wife within the familiar confines of a lay penitential commitment. He writes that Pier "paid constant and vigilant attention" to his chastity and lived with his wife "in a Christian manner."[116] Like Abraham, Pier had "knowledge of his wife solely out of the desire to have children for the service of God." Once he realized that his wife was unable to have children, the couple decided to live together "observing perfect chastity."[117]

---

non fa di più intromettermi ed implicarmi col mondo, nel quale, eccettuatane la mia perdizione, non mi sento alcun bene operare."

114. Webb, *Saints and Cities*, 226; de Angelis, *Vita Pier*, 83.

115. Webb, *Saints and Cities*, 231–32; de Angelis, *Vita Pier*, 100: "Amico non credo che ben si possan cercare, e conoscere le parti del Mondo, nè fare le laudabili pellegrinazione, se prima la persona non ricerca e conosce diligentemente lo stato e condizione sua intrinseca . . ."

116. Webb, *Saints and Cities*, 223; de Angelis, *Vita Pier*, 79: "Vegliava il servo di Cristo Pietro con molta custodia ed attentissima cura sopra la costanza del singolare tesoro della santa Cast ità"; and Webb, *Saints and Cities*, 195; de Angelis, *Vita Pier*, 6: "Fatto adunque uomo Pietro, prese Donna,dalla quale non ebbe mai prole, e colla quale cristianamente vivendo, schivava le lascivie e i vani consorzj degli altri giovani: le quali cose sogliono a molti esser causa di rovina."

117. Webb, *Saints and Cities*, 197; de Angelis, *Vita Pier*, 9–10: "Venne come si crede il servo di Cristo Pietro a tanta purità, che quasi come Abraham solamente per desiderio di aver Prole del servizio di Dio, conobbe pudicissimamente la sua compagnia, e vendendola sterile sì determinarono insieme vivendo, osservare perfetta castità, e di poi la morte di detta sua donna sempre con somma continenza visse." Dyan Elliott has noted that Pier's *vita* provides an unusual example of what appears to be the mutual agreement of husband and wife to take up a spiritual or chaste marriage; see *Spiritual Marriage*, 252. The late nineteenth-century Sienese historian A. Lisini questioned the portrayal of Pier as childless. Pointing to archival evidence, Lisini notes that Pier had at least four sons; see Lisini, "Notizie sul B. Pier Pettinagno," 42–45. Both the *vita* and the sermon dedicated to Pier

But Pietro also describes how Pier never let his religious enthusiasm cause him to compromise his duties as a husband. Pier was always so concerned "to show consideration" for his wife that he was careful never to let his prayers or charity work make him late for lunch or dinner.[118] As Pier began to sell everything he owned so that he could give the money from those items to the poor, a "tactful and prudent religious" reminded him that he needed to preserve his wife's dowry as long as she lived.[119] Ever dutiful, Pier kept his house with a vineyard while his wife was alive and, after her death, he made sure to execute her will before he offered what he had left to the poor.[120]

While medieval *vitae* often tell stories of the criticism saints faced after alienating property or selling goods that either did not belong to them or upon which their family depended (remember the description in *Labentibus annis* of how upset Omobono's wife became after the saint had given away their food), there is a distinct message in Pier's actions. Pietro emphasizes the saint's concern to adhere to the legal rules and social norms of his society. On the one hand, Pietro makes it clear that Pier lived a committed religious life, had a chaste marriage, and spurned worldly things. But, on the other hand, he wants his reader above all to understand that this comb-maker never let his religious ideals keep him from attending to his responsibilities as an urban layman.

Pietro describes Pier applying a similar rigor to his business life. Noting that Pier practiced his trade of comb-making with "such justice and purity that he seemed not to be a craftsman or a merchant of the world, but the most devout and God-fearing religious," Pietro recounts several episodes to illustrate Pier's pious behavior.[121] We learn that once, when Pier traveled to Pisa to buy materials for his combs, he found the Pisan merchants selling both good and bad quality materials. When Pier asked to be sold only good materials, the Pisan

---

chose to ignore this aspect of Pier's life. As we saw in the case of Omobono's cult, it was not uncommon for the *vita* of a male lay saint to discuss marital status, but not children.

118. Webb, *Saints and Cities*, 196–97; de Angelis, *Vita Pier*, 8–9: "sforzandosi sempre in quello, che credeva piacere a Dio, farsela grata; per la qual cosa, come accade, trovandosi in sull'ora del desinare o della cena con qualche persona a confabulare, dolcemente loro diceva: Fratelli carissimi statevi in pace, imperocchè già è l'ora, che la mia Padrona mi aspetta: sicchè non volendola turbare, voglio andare a casa."

119. Webb, *Saints and Cities*, 199; de Angelis, *Vita Pier*, 14: "Vendendo l'uomo di Dio, vivendo ancor la moglie, ciò che aveva ed abbondantemente lo spregiatore del denaro, ed amatore carissimo della povertà ai poveri per le strade, e agli incarcerati, e massimamente ai poveri vergognosi contribuiva in modo, che una volto un circospetto, e prudente Religioso fu fatto avvertito, che nel dare, almanco la dote della moglie riserbasse perchè, ella vivendo, non la poteva alienare."

120. Webb, *Saints and Cities*, 199; de Angelis, *Vita Pier*, 14–15.

121. Webb, *Saints and Cities*, 195; de Angelis, *Vita Pier*, 6: "L'arte, la quale imparò di fare i Pettini, con tanta giustizia e purità esercitava, che non artefice o mercatante mondano, ma timorato e divotissimo religioso pareva."

merchants refused, forcing Pier to buy both. Pietro writes that the merchants "behaved like men who feared damage to their business more than to their conscience." Since Pier was "already full of the love of God and neighbor," he "bought the good and bad together" and tossed the bad materials into the Arno to save someone else from having to "offend God because of this merchandise."[122]

Pietro also presents Pier as having been concerned that both he and other merchants be charged a "just price" for their goods, rather than taking advantage of a bargain. The reader is told of a time when Pier was buying the bones and horns he used to make combs from a Sienese butcher and became convinced that the butcher was underselling his goods. Pier informed the butcher that he did not "know the real value of these bones," telling him, "they're worth twenty-four soldi, not twelve; so take their value, and peace be with you."[123] Pietro describes how Pier himself was careful to sell only good quality combs and always charged "the just price, never either increased or diminished what it was worth." Pier's piety did not keep him from running a healthy business, however. If someone argued with the saint that a comb was worth less than he was asking, Pier held his ground, telling that customer that if they did not like that price, they could "leave it and go with the grace of God."[124] Scholars have noted that while Roman and canon lawyers generally agreed that a just price was a going market rate that was unaffected by monopolies, hoarding, or other activities deemed unjust, theologians doubted that relying on a market price alone could ever be just, calling on individual exchangers to be bound by conscience to aim at a fair price.[125] Pietro seems concerned to em-

---

122. Webb, *Saints and Cities*, 195–96; de Angelis, *Vita Pier*, 6: "come da uomini più tementi il danno dell'interesse, che della coscienza . . . Ma il servo di Dio Pietro ripieno già della carità di Dio e del prossimo, acciochè alcun altro non avesse materia in quella mercanzia di offendere Dio, tale quale era buona e trista insieme comprò. E così comprata se ne andò sul Ponte sopra il fiume chiamato Arno, il quale passa per detta Città di Pisa, e lì (siccome Angelo di Dio mandato a separare i buoni dai rei) elesse in una parte la mercanzia buona, nell'altra la rea, la quale così separata, la gittò nel fiume."

123. Webb, *Saints and Cities*, 196; de Angelis, *Vita Pier*, 7: "Fratello carissimo, tu non conosci bene il prezzo di queste ossa; imperciocchè, non solo dodici, ma vagliono ventiquattro soldi: e però piglia il prezzo loro e rimani in pace."

124. Webb, *Saints and Cities*, 196; de Angelis, *Vita Pier*, 7: "Facendo dunque sempre il B. Pietro i suoi pettini di ottima e miglior materia che si trovasse, a ciascuno giustamente gli vendeva, in modo che, se alcuni compratori il dimandavano: Dimmi Pietro, questo Pettine è buono? rispondeva il servo di Dio (quando non fosse il pettine molto buono) dicendo: Fratello il pettine non è nè molto buono, nè molto tristo: ma se pure il compratore diceva, Eleggimene tu uno che sia buono; allore Pietro fedelmente ne pigliava uno, dicendo: io per me piglierei questo. Ma domandandolo il compratore: Quanto ne dimandi? sempre rispondeva Pietro il giusto prezzo, e mai non accresceva nè diminuiva a quel tanto che valesse, perchè sempre dimandava il giusto prezzo. Ma se pure il compratore, secondo il costume del mondo, istava mostrando valesse manco: rispondendo il servo di Dio, diceva: Fratello o Sorella mia, il pettine tanto vale: se non ti piace, lascialo stare, e và colla grazia di Dio."

125. See Joel Kaye, *Economy and Nature in the Fourteenth Century: Money, Market Exchange, and the Emergence of Scientific Thought* (Cambridge: Cambridge University Press, 1998), 99–100; and Lester K.

phasize the extent to which Pier understood that responsibility. He demanded a just price for his own goods as well as for those he himself purchased and, at least in theory, used his own piety to regulate the city's market.

Pietro claims that Pier's business practices earned him such a following that the other merchants and craftsmen with whom he worked were left struggling to sell their own goods. Taking note of this, Pier stopped selling his goods during the day and waited until after vespers, so, as Pietro writes, "the other comb-sellers could have a better chance of selling theirs."[126] But Pier's efforts were only somewhat effective: anyone needing a comb quickly learned to wait until after vespers or to go directly to the comb-maker's house to make their purchase. Nevertheless, Pier had done what he could so that, as Pietro writes, "the other merchants should have no cause for complaint."[127] Elsewhere in the *vita*, Pietro records the advice Pier gave his friend Salvi di Orlando one day when he passed him dressing hides. Pier urged Salvi to be careful to dress the hides well so he did not damage his conscience. Pietro added that Pier had said these words "to show that one must practice one's trade in such a way as not to offend God or one's neighbor."[128] Pietro clearly saw Pier's concern for his fellow city-dwellers as well as for the norms governing their city as crucial evidence for the comb-maker's sanctity.

Although Pietro does not refer to the specific activities that we know Pier performed for his commune (restoration of ill-gotten gains, the release of

---

Little, *Religious Poverty and the Profit Economy in Medieval Europe* (Ithaca, NY: Cornell University Press, 1978), 177; Little cites J. W. Baldwin, *The Medieval Theories of the Just Price: Romanists, Canonists, and Theologians in the Twelfth and Thirteenth Centuries* (Philadelphia: American Philosophical Society, 1959), 54.

126. Webb, *Saints and Cities*, 196; de Angelis, *Vita Pier*, 7–8: "Spesse volte aveva in uso il servo di Dio Pietro il giorno del Sabbato pigliare i suoi pettini, e portarli in su la Piazza comune, acciocchè più presto gli vendesse, imperocchè in maggior parte viveva di quelli. Ma essendo già la fama sua non solo per la città di Siena, ma per lo Contado ancora divulgara, quasi tutti, che volessero comprar pettini, come ancora per la devozione, correvano a Pietro. Quinid (secondo avvenir suole) gli altri mercatanti, ovvero artefici, per questo se ne indegnavano contro Pietro pure assai, non potendo (siccome volevano) spacciare le mercanzie loro. Della quel cosa avvedendosi il servo di Cristo Pietro, ripieno di carità, acciò per causa sua non ricevesse il prossimo scandalo, incominciò a non più andare se non dipoi Vespero alla Piazza a vendere i suoi pettini, acciocchè gli altri pettinai, meglio potessero vendere i loro."

127. Webb, *Saints and Cities*, 196; de Angelis, *Vita Pier*, 8: "Ma avvedendosi di questo i compratori, tutti, massimamente quei che non avevano a camminare molto dicosto dalla Città, per comprare da Pietro, aspettavano insino dopo Vespero, ovvero andavano a trovarlo a casa; e in questo modo il servo di Dio operò; che gli altri mercatanti non si avessero a indegnare, vendendo niente di meno la mercanzia sua."

128. Webb, *Saints and Cities*, 232; de Angelis, *Vita Pier*, 100: "Andando un dì Pietro per Siena, e passando per la via dove si conciano le Pelli, e vendendo un amico suo chiamato Salvi conciare una Pelle gli disse: O Salvi fratello, avverti che conciando tu bene cotesta Pelle, tu non guasti la coscienza tua. E questo disse l'uomo di Dio, dimostrando che in tal modo si debbono fare le arti, che non si offenda Dio, nè il prossimo, e così detto andò al suo viaggio."

prisoners, donations to pious organizations, and the painting of city gates),
he does spend much of the *vita* discussing Pier's involvement in both his
civic government and the wider urban community. For example, Pietro
writes that Pier's friend Salvi once asked the comb-maker why, since he was
"so often bidden to attend the councils," he did not try to dress a bit better.
Pier told Salvi that "he who cares for the world cannot care for God." The
rejection of worldly concerns is a common theme in saints' lives. Salvi's
question, however, seems aimed at emphasizing how deeply involved Pier
was in the world of his commune, as he was "so often" being asked to attended civic councils.[129]

More often than not, Pietro's description of Pier's civic involvement focuses
on the proper and improper uses of money and repeatedly equates Pier's religious commitment with his scrupulous adherence to the rules and regulations of his city. When a new *podestà* of the city asked to see the holy
comb-maker, wanting to hear "something of God" from him, Pier obliged and
asked the *podestà* if he had come to Siena in debt.[130] When he said he had not,
Pier urged the civic official not to go into debt in the future and quickly hur-
ried away, because (as Pietro reports) he felt himself falling into an ecstatic
state.[131] Pier's simple exhortation satisfied the *podestà*, who told those around
him that he was sure that Pier "has in him the spirit and wisdom of God, for
in very few words he has given a mighty piece of advice."[132]

The issue of debt appears again in a passage describing a time when Pier
had lent money to his brother-in-law, Gezio, who held onto the money for several years. When he was finally able to repay Pier, Gezio noted that he was
adding some interest, because, as he told him, he had kept the money for so
long that he was sure he had prevented Pier from using and profiting from it.
That interest, Gezio assured Pier, was "not in usury," since, as he added, he
knew that Pier disapproved of such gains, "but by way of legitimate business
and the profit" that Pier could have made from it. Gezio reassured Pier by tell-

129. Webb, *Saints and Cities*, 199; de Angelis, *Vita Pier*, 13: "Pietro a me non pare, che conversando tu con tanti uomini da bene, ed essendo tu, per la grazia, che ti ha data Iddio, spesse volte richiesto ne consiglj, che tu debba usar così vile, e rappezzato mantello . . . che chi si cura di Dio, non può curare del mondo; e a Dio solo non al caduco mondo dobbiamo attendere, e questa esteriore apparenza, credimi, è quella cosa che distrugge il vivere umano."

130. Webb, *Saints and Cities*, 226; de Angelis, *Vita Pier*, 84–85: "il Potestà desidera udire da te al-cuna cosa di Dio. Allora il servo di Cristo parlando al Potestà gli disse: Ditemi Messer Potestà, quando veniste in questa Città portaste con voi alcun debito?"

131. Webb, *Saints and Cities*, 226; de Angelis, *Vita Pier*, 85: "E dette queste parole immediata-mente di lì si partì (credo come quello che si sentiva prossimo all'Estasi, e rapimento di spirito)."

132. Webb, *Saints and Cities*, 226; de Angelis, *Vita Pier*, 85: "Veramente credo questo sant'uomo avere in se spirito e sapienza di Dio, il quale in sì poche parole, ha parlato una grande ed utile senteza."

ing him that his "conscience need not trouble" him since he was giving it to Pier of his own free will.[133] But as Pietro makes clear, Pier did not subscribe to the distinction Gezio was making. The comb-maker saw any money added to the loan as usury and in the end refused Gezio's offer, telling his brother-in-law that since he had "honestly and faithfully" kept his money there was no "need to make satisfaction."[134]

In addition, Pietro includes episodes portraying Pier's sanctity as also emerging out of his desire to follow civic statutes. Pietro describes a time when Pier was caught after the city's curfew by two of the *podestà*'s household servants. Pier was making his way to the cathedral at midnight to pray before the image of the Virgin. The servants saw Pier walking between two lighted torches but could not see anyone holding the torches. Amazed by what they saw—and, as Pietro adds, out of reverence for Pier—they said nothing as they passed him. Pier, however, knew he had broken a city ordinance and became adamant that he be punished for his infraction. Pier walked back to the servants to tell them that since they had "taken an oath" to their superiors to report anyone found wandering the city after the curfew, they should report him in the morning so they would not have to perjure themselves.[135]

On the following day, Pier "on his own accord," turned himself in to the *podestà*, reminding the official that "anyone who is found at night going around the city must pay a certain amount of money, according to the form of the proclamation which you issued when you took office." Pietro reports that Pier gave the *podestà* the money to cover his fine, urging him to "take it and put it into the communal treasury."[136] While the *podestà* marveled "at such punctilious

---

133. Webb, *Saints and Cities*, 204; de Angelis, *Vita Pier*, 30–31: "Ecco Pietro i denari quali benignamente mi hai prestati, e che avendoli tenuti più del dovere, ed impedito il guadagno tuo, quale avresti con essi conseguito, non voglio essere ingrato; sicché non per modo di usura, la quale ben so che non ti è grata, ma per modo di lecita mercanzia e guadagno, quale con essa avresti potuto conseguire, piglia questa somma di denari de quali non bisogna ti rimorda la conscienza, dandotegli di mia libera volontà."

134. Webb, *Saints and Cities*, 204–5; de Angelis, *Vita Pier*, 32: "Carissimo mio Fratello a te debbo render grazie, che ti sei degnato integramente e fedelmente sì lungo tempo riservare la mia pecunia, e però non tu a me, ma io a te debbo satisfare: sicché ti prego di queste duecento lire ne tolga quella parte che ti piace, ovvero tutta te la riserva e adoprela secondo le tue occorrenze."

135. Webb, *Saints and Cities*, 224; de Angelis, *Vita Pier*, 81: "Ma Pietro vedendoli, chiamolli a se dicendo: Fratelli carissimi non vogliate giurare per alcuna cosa il falso: io so bene, che voi avete giurato al vostro Superiore, e promesso di denunziargli qualunque a quest'ora troverete andare per la città: sicché domattina per ogni modo, acciocché voi non pergiuriate, denunziate al Giudice come mi avete trovato."

136. Webb, *Saints and Cities*, 224; de Angelis, *Vita Pier*, 81–82: "Ma il giorno seguente andò il servo di Cristo Pietro spontaneamente a trovare il Potestà della città, al quale disse: Messere tu sai lo statuto, quale hai giurato d'osservare: contiene che ciascuno, quale di notte sarà trovato andare per la Città debbe pagare certa quantità di denari secondo la forma del bando, quale in principio del tuo

observation of the statues," he told Pier that the law had not been made for him but for "criminals and ill-livers," adding that he knew that Pier went around at night in order to do good and that from then on Pier would be exempted not only from this particular statute but also from "any impost which may be imposed" by the commune of Siena.[137] While Pier was happy to be allowed to travel around the city at night, he strongly objected to being exempted from communal taxes. Pietro records Pier's objection: "'Messer *podestà* I do not want this second privilege, because, if I make use of the amenities of this city—land, water, air, fire, the company of others, the security of this way of life, and many other common goods—it is not good for me to be exempt from the city's imposts.'"[138] Pier could not allow himself to be exempted from paying taxes, since it would in effect allow him to profit from a community he was not supporting—Pier did not want his saintly reputation to place him above the law.

To further emphasize this point, Pietro describes a time when the commune issued an additional tax on all Sienese to raise an army.[139] Pier learned of the tax several days after it was issued, when he heard his neighbors complaining. He immediately figured out what he owed and brought his payment to the tax collectors, apologizing that it was a few days late. The collectors "marveled at such justice and observance of the law" but told Pier that they had no intention of trying to collect from him, since they knew he was "not rich in things of this world" and asked only that he pray for them and for Siena.[140] Pier

---

uffizio mandasti. Ora sappi che questa notte da tuoi famiglj io fui trovato andare per la Città, e così avendo fatto contro al Bando ti ho portata la pecunia, la quale per questo debbo pagare: sicchè falla pigliare ed applicare alla Camera del Comune."

137. Webb, *Saints and Cities*, 224; de Angelis, *Vita Pier*, 82: "Ma il potestà vedendo tanta giustizia nell'uomo di Dio Pietro, e maravigliandosi di tanta osservanza degli statuti, come uomo prudente gli disse: va servo di Cristo, che già ben sono informato della vita e santità tua: piglia la tua pecunia, che la legge non è fatta per te, ma per i trasgressori, e per quelli che mal vivono: ben so che tu non vai di notte se non per ben fare: e così acciocchè tu non t'abbia di simil cosa in futuro a far coscenza, io ti assolvo da questo statuto, dandoti piena licenza e libertà di andare a qualunque ora di notte e a qua lunque loco e in qualunque modo ti piace . . ."

138. Webb, *Saints and Cities*, 224–25; de Angelis, *Vita Pier*, 82: "Messer Potestà questa seconda grazia io non la voglio, perchè non sta bene, che usando io i comodi di questa Città, cioè e terra, acqua, aere, fuoco, la compagnia degli altri, la securità del viver quieto, e molti altri comuni beni, sia alieno dalle gravezze di questa Città."

139. De Angelis, *Vita Pier*, 82–83.

140. Webb, *Saints and Cities*, 225; de Angelis, *Vita Pier*, 83: "Maravigliandosi eglino di tanta giustizia ed osservanza di Legge gli dissero: non bisogno Uomo di Dio che noi ti perdoniamo, perchè in questo tu non ci hai ingannati, e bene han fatto gli esattori a non ti dir niente, che ben sappiamo che delle cose del mondo tu non sei ricco; ma questo ci basta, e questo da te ricerchiamo, che per noi e per la nostra e tua città faccia a Dio orazione, che ci difenda da ogni male: piglia adunque la tua pecunia e riportala conte e va in pace."

objected, handing the assessors his money, stating that he would not keep money "that belongs to my commune, for it is not mine."[141]

By focusing on Pier's insistence that he be subject to all communal laws and taxes, Pietro makes an equation between the comb-maker's civic virtue and his sanctity. In Ambrogio Lorenzetti's series of frescoes, *Effects of Good and Bad Government* (ca. 1337–40), painted for the Nine's meeting chamber, the Sala dei Nove, less than a decade after the appearance of Pier's *vita*, personified virtues surround examples of the effects of good and bad government. Sitting beneath these visual allegories, the Nine would surely have seen them as constant encouragement to continue the good rule they believed they were providing their city. While scholars have long debated the allegorical meaning and political ideology, as well as the possible textual sources represented in this work, Quentin Skinner's argument that these frescoes illustrate ideologies found in early thirteenth-century, or pre-humanist, treatises justifying the new republican governments of the communes seems most in keeping with the Nine's concern to craft and control a political and cultural identity for Siena. As such, it also offers a productive path for understanding Pietro's portrait of Pier.[142]

Writers such as the anonymous author of the *Oculus pastoralis* (1220s), Orfino da Lodi (writing in the 1240s), Giovanni da Viterbo (writing in the 1250s), and Brunetto Latini (in the 1260s) produced texts that both offered advice to city magistrates and served as justifications of the Italian cities' new enterprise of self-government.[143] Drawing on the moral and political philosophy of Cicero and Sallust to mount their defense and celebration of the communes, these pre-humanists shared one voice in their identification of the immense value civic concord and justice play in leading a city to realize its *grandezza*—a word that, as Skinner notes, the pre-humanists coined to describe the combined grandeur and magnitude that every city aimed to achieve.[144] In short, the pre-humanists argued that to reach that ideal of *grandezza*, civic governments

---

141. Webb, *Saints and Cities*, 225; de Angelis, *Vita Pier*, 83: "Ai quali l'uomo giusto rispose: Carissimi miei Maggiori sempre desidero andare nella pace di Dio, ma pure questa pecunia quale è del mio Comune non la porterò, imperciocchè è sua, e non mia, e lassatala, prestamente si partì."

142. Quentin Skinner, "Ambrogio Lorenzetti's *Buon Governo* Frescoes: Two Old Questions, Two New Answers," *Journal of the Warburg and Courtauld Institutes* 62 (1999): 1–28. Some of the classic works exploring this fresco include Frugoni, *A Distant City*, esp. 118–88; Quentin Skinner, "Ambrogio Lorenzetti: The Artist as Political Philosopher," *Proceedings of the British Academy* 72 (1986): 1–56; and Randolph Starn, "The Republican Regime of the 'Room of Peace' in Siena, 1338–40," *Representations* 18 (1987): 1–32.

143. For an introduction to these works, see Quentin Skinner, "Machiavelli's *Discorsi* and the Pre-Humanist Origins of Republican Ideas," in *Machiavelli and Republicanism*, ed. Gisela Bock, Quentin Skinner, and Maurizio Viroli (Cambridge: Cambridge University Press, 1990), 121–41.

144. Skinner, "Machiavelli's *Discorsi*," 127–28.

must be committed, above all, to maintaining the *bonum commune* (or the common good). This could be done, they made clear, if communal magistrates adhered to the Roman legal principle of *ius suum cuique* (or giving to each his due).[145] In other words, if magistrates committed to privileging the commands of justice over their own personal ambitions and needs, the common good would be upheld, peace would reign, and a city could realize its *grandezza*.

To what extent, then, can we see Pietro's ca. 1330 *vita* as an attempt to shape the image of Pier as a lay civic patron in line with this pre-humanist ideology? Pier's scrupulous desire to follow all of the rules and regulations of his commune, to be subject to all of the same statutory and legal commands as any other city-dweller, and to frame each of his pious acts in terms most beneficial to his civic government all point to seeing the *vita* as an attempt to articulate how an ideal, yet ordinary, commune member could support the common good and thus contribute to the city's grandeur and magnitude.

Before describing all of the ways in which Pier maintained a meticulous adherence to Siena's curfews and tax requirements, Pietro writes:

> By means of his great prudence and discretion Pier had achieved the singular virtue of justice, compelling himself in everything to render to each according to their entitlement. First of all, to God he rendered the most passionate love, with fear and honor; to his neighbor the sincerest affection; to his own soul special purity and devotion; to his body endless toil and bare subsistence, exerting himself always to do good to himself and his neighbor, and to the utmost of his ability avoiding all evil.[146]

In rendering "to each according to their entitlement," Pietro's *vita* argues that Pier used his spiritual commitment not only to increase his love of God, and his care for his own soul but also to achieve "the singular virtue of justice."

Siena under the Nine was a civic community intensely interested in how images and figures could articulate and support its *grandezza*. The *vita* written to secure governmental support for the cult of a comb-maker seems to argue that everyday city-dwellers could also have a hand in maintaining that political ideology. If the *Maestà* paintings present Siena's prestige as dependent

---

145. Ibid., 131.

146. Webb, *Saints and Cities*, 223–34; de Angelis, *Vita Pier*, 80–81: "Era venuto Pietro servo di Cristo per la grande prudenza e discrezione sua alla singolarissima virtù della Giustizia, sforzandosi in ogni cosa rendere a ciascheduno secondo la loro ragione. A Dio prima rendendo affettuosissimo amore con filiale timore ed onore: al Prossimo sincerissima dilezione; all'anima sua singolare purità e devozione, al corpo suo continue fatiche e la sola sostentazione. Ingegnandosi a se, ed al prossimo sempre bene operare, evitando quanto poteva qualunque male."

on its close connection to the Virgin, and the Lorenzetti frescoes ultimately argue that the Nine stand behind the creation and maintenance of a good republican regime, Pietro's *vita* suggests that the city's greatness is also a product of the good business and civic behavior of a beloved artisan. The Nine may have sworn to uphold "the good and honor" of the city when they took office, but the everyday behavior of a pious comb-maker—who practices his trade with the utmost concern for others, reminds the *podestà* of the importance of avoiding debt, insists that he be punished properly after committing a civic offense, and ensures that he pays his taxes—worked to support and sustain that same goal.

The Last Communal Lay Saint

Pietro describes Pier in his ca. 1330 *vita* as having had a particular devotion to Francis, having worn a Third Order habit, and eventually having lived in a cell attached to Siena's San Francesco. And yet, as I have argued, Pietro ultimately does little to "Franciscanize" the saint. Moreover, even though concern with money and debt was prominent among Franciscans in late medieval Italy, Pietro's presentation of Pier's involvement in these issues concentrates on how such matters could poison a civic community, rather than on their inherent contradiction of Christian ideals.[147] Instead, Pietro seems most intent on constructing Pier in terms that resonated with the political and cultural context of late medieval Siena. Just as members of the Nine had sworn to uphold "the good and honor" of the city, Pietro portrays Pier's religious commitment as supporting and sustaining that same goal. On one hand, this portrait seems a smart response to the commune's efforts to limit its support for civic cults in the late 1320s. On the other hand, it also corroborates and builds upon what we see of Pier's life in the archival evidence. That evidence makes clear that Pier's religious life was often taken up with activity aimed at regulating and maintaining Siena's religious ideals.

In the first half-century of Pier's cult, we see the definition and limits of lay sanctity expanded beyond the model articulated by Innocent III. Neither Pier's activities during his lifetime nor his reputation after his death follow the model of the communal lay saint that took shape in the cults of Omobono and Facio of Cremona. As a lay penitent, Pier seems to have had an unusually prominent role in communal activities that mixed financial and pious concerns.

---

147. The classic work on the Franciscans' concern with money and debt remains Little, *Religious Poverty and the Profit Economy.*

And in both the sermon written immediately after his death and in the ca. 1330 *vita*, Pier is celebrated not only for performing miracles for his fellow Sienese but also for his prophetic powers and ecstatic moments. In many ways, Pier is the saint who breaks open the distinction between lay penitent and mendicant that I have argued was drawn in Innocent's canonization of Omobono and recognition of the Franciscan Order. Pier is celebrated for having had both an internal and external focus. His dedication to serving the poor, sick, and financially challenged of his city is celebrated alongside his prophetic, ecstatic, and contemplative powers. As Pier chastises the boasting pilgrim: one cannot know the world without first knowing oneself.

Although Innocent III's two paths for a lay religious life seem to come together in Pier, they do so within the circumscribed context of the Sienese commune. By once again having living miracles and a focus on a layman's internal spiritual life as a key aspect of a holy lay life, Pietro's portrait of Pier draws upon an understanding of lay sanctity that ought to remind us of Ranieri of Pisa's twelfth-century cult.[148] But unlike in Ranieri's cult, Pier's simultaneous commitment to his own spiritual development, the health and well-being of his lay neighbors, as well as the rules and regulations governing his city, presents him not only as posing no threat to institutional authority but as crucial to its good functioning.

In the late thirteenth and early fourteenth centuries, *vitae* for contemporary lay saints would continue to explore how a layperson's penitential commitment could deepen their spiritual identity. However, that work would increasingly be done in the context of a new institutional form of the lay penitential life and increasingly in reference to laywomen. After Pope Nicholas IV's 1289 bull, *Supra montem*, called for all lay penitents to be under the guardianship of the Franciscans, the ambiguity of religious identity that we have seen in the cults of so many thirteenth-century lay saints began to disappear. With the Franciscans (and later the Dominicans as well) overseeing lay religious, the lay saint came to belong more to the mendicants than to the city. This was a change, however, that applies overwhelmingly to the cults awarded to laywomen.

---

148. Romagnoli makes the point that Pier represents the most complete example of the normalization of tertiary charisma. See her "Pier Pettinaio e i modelli di santità," 151.

PART TWO

The Female Lay Saint

CHAPTER 4

Classifying Laywomen

The Female Lay Saint before 1289

Sometime in the late twelfth century, Ubaldesca (d. 1205), a poor fourteen-year-old girl from Calcinaia, a town twenty kilometers east of Pisa, was at home by herself baking bread when she received an angelic vision. The angel instructed her to travel to Pisa, dedicate her life to penance, and place herself under the guidance of the nuns of S. Giovanni dei Fieri (or S. Giovannino, as it was later called).[1] When Ubaldesca objected, noting that she came from a poor family and did not have the necessary dowry to enter the convent, the angel responded that it would be with virtue and not money that she would earn her entry.[2] An anonymous *vita* written in the mid-thirteenth century describes how fully Ubaldesca took up the angel's

---

1. For more on Ubaldesca, see Gabriele Zaccagnini, *Ubaldesca, una santa laica nella Pisa dei secoli XII–XIII* (Pisa: ETS, 1995); and Anthony Luttrell, "Saint Ubaldesca di Calcinaia," *Ordines Militares: Yearbook for the Study of the Military Orders* 18 (2013): 287–91. Luttrell points out that the house Ubaldesca joined was a monastery in the Kinzica area of Pisa. It would begin to be referred to as S. Giovanni or S. Giovannino during Ubaldesca's lifetime when it became a Hospitaller house associated with Pisa's San Sepulcro.

2. Catherine M. Mooney has highlighted this portion of Ubaldesca's *vita* in her exploration of the difficulties involved in the religious classification of thirteenth- and fourteenth-century religious women in Italy, noting that many Italian women were forced by economic circumstances to live either as lay penitents or semireligious. Like Ubaldesca, they simply did not have the financial means to enter a monastery; see Mooney, "Nuns, Tertiaries, and Quasi-Religious: The Religious Identities of Late Medieval Holy Women," *Medieval Feminist Forum* 42 (2006): 84–85.

command.[3] At S. Giovannino, she subsisted on a diet of bread and water, dressed in hair shirts, and slept on the ground. Such extraordinary penance produced miracles: her parents found the bread she had abandoned to rush to S. Giovannino still in the oven but perfectly baked; after a fall, she healed her own grave head injury simply by invoking Christ's name; and at a popular pilgrimage site, she turned water into wine for thirsty pilgrims. But as Ubaldesca's *vita* makes clear, this laywoman's charismatic powers were not only the result of penitential rigor but also of her new identity: in joining S. Giovannino, Ubaldesca had become a *conversa* or lay-associate of the convent. As her *vita* repeatedly emphasizes, Ubaldesca served the S. Giovannino nuns with such spirit and joy—attending to their physical needs as well as begging for alms in Pisa to support them financially—that she was able to perform numerous healing miracles on their behalf.[4]

The conversion story of Rose of Viterbo (d. 1251), another young laywoman who took up a life of penance, also comes from an anonymous *vita* written in the mid-thirteenth century. Although only fragments of this *vita* survive, those passages describe how, like Ubaldesca, Rose's life took a dramatic turn when she was still a teenager.[5] As she was recovering from a severe illness, Rose began to see visions of the dead. When the visions stopped, Rose renounced all of her possessions and asked her mother to bring a woman only identified in the text as "Lady Sita" to their house so that she could clothe Rose in "the tunic," girdle her with "the cord," and cut her hair "like a cleric's."[6] Sita, who was likely a lay penitent with some association to the Viterban Fran-

---

3. For an edited edition of that *vita* as well as a study of the text's manuscript history and the growth of Ubaldesca's cult, see Zaccagnini, *Ubaldesca, una santa laica*.

4. Ibid., 5, 172.

5. Those fragments have been transcribed and edited by P. Giuseppe Abate, *S. Rosa da Viterbo, terziaria francescana (1233–1251): Fonti storiche della vita e loro revision critica* (Rome: Miscellanea Francescana, 1952), 119–23 [hereafter *Rosa Vita I* or *Rosa Vita II*]. A second *vita*, also anonymous and which survives intact, was written in the early fifteenth century, and has also been transcribed and edited by Abate. For more on the manuscript history of these *vitae*, see Abate, *S. Rosa da Viterbo*, 31–50; and Anna Maria Fabbri, "Vita di una santa: Aspetti della *vita* di S. Rosa da Viterbo," in *Santa Rosa: Tradizione e culto*, ed. Silvio Cappelli (Rome: Vecchiarelli, 1999). In addition to Abate's collection of sources and Cappelli's collection of articles, the major scholarly studies of Rose and her early cult include Rosa Mincuzzi, "Santa Rosa da Viterbo: Penitente del XIII secolo," *Analecta Tertii Ordinis Regularis Sancti Francisci* 31 (2000): 7–120; and Darleen Pryds, "Proclaiming Sanctity through Proscribed Acts: The Case of Rose of Viterbo," in *Women Preachers and Prophets through Two Millennia of Christianity*, ed. Beverly Mayne Kienzle and Pamela J. Walker (Berkeley: University of California Press, 1998), 159–72.

6. *Rosa Vita I*, 3, 228: "Et incontinenti se nudam in terram et in crucem prostravit lugens, ac dicens matri suae: 'Mater, omnes res ac delicias huius saeculi tibi relinquo ac renuntio.' Et rogavit matrem, dicens: 'Mater, volo quod domina Sita induat mihi tunicam, et cingat mihi chordulam, et tondeat mihi capillos sicut clerico.'"

ciscans, initially demurred, declaring herself to be unworthy to perform such acts. But with Rose's encouragement, Sita ultimately carried out Rose's instructions.[7] After what appears to be an initiation ceremony into a penitential life, Rose announced to her mother that she felt the presence of the Holy Spirit and asked that her mother bring a group of neighborhood women to their house.[8] Rose proceeded to organize those women into a circle, placed herself in the middle and declared that she alone could see the most beautiful bride of Christ, who had instructed her to make a circuit of three of the city's churches carrying a *maestà* or image of Christ.[9]

Rose, as her first *vita* makes clear, had crafted a penitential as well as visionary life outside of any ecclesiastical context or oversight. Although Ubaldesca's *vita* presents her devoting her life to performing miracles while serving the S. Giovannino nuns, Rose's penitential routine as well as her charismatic activity are entirely independent enterprises. And even though both Ubaldesca and Rose would eventually earn civic cults, the vastly different trajectories of those cults illustrate how much affiliation mattered for the construction of female lay religious ideals in the thirteenth century. Ubaldesca's *vita* describes the beginnings of her cult largely through the particular patronage offered by Frate Dotto, a Hospitaller from Pisa's San Sepulcro church. The *vita* recounts how Frate Dotto was not only intent on being by Ubaldesca's side when she died in 1205 but also on burying her in San Sepulcro.[10] Frate Dotto was so devoted to Ubaldesca that, the *vita* reports, he remained next to her tomb for seven days, witnessing a multitude of devotees cured of their maladies by invoking Ubaldesca's name, as well as a vision of the saint making her way to heaven between two fiery chariots and surrounded by various saints.[11] Over the century following this Pisan laywoman's death, the efforts made by Frate Dotto, as well as the association that developed between the S. Giovannino nuns and the Hospitaller Order, and a ca. 1260 sermon delivered by Bishop

7. Mincuzzi, "Santa Rosa da Viterbo," 53.

8. *Rosa Vita I*, 4, 228: "Postmodum vero vocavit matrem suam, et dixit ei: 'Mater, vade et suscita modo omnes mulieres de contrata.' Et hoc fuit de nocte. Et mater dixit ei: 'Filia, quis remanebit tecum?' Et Virgo respondit: 'Spiritus Sanctus erit mecum.' Et mater abiit, et fecit praeceptum beatae Virginis."

9. Ibid., 5, 228–29: "Tunc omnes mulieres surrexerunt, et venerunt ad ipsam Virginem. Et Virgo dixit mulieribus: 'Venite omnes extra domum, quia beata Virgo Maria venit extra.' Et exiverunt post ipsam, et coeperunt omnes sedere; et Virgo sedebat in medio ipsarum, et incoepit dicere mulieribus: 'Audite, quia ego video Sponsam Christi speciosissimam, quam nemo vestrum videt; quae Sponsa venit ornata cum purpura et sendado, cum corona aurea in capite plena gemmis et lapidibus pretiosis. Quae Sponsa mihi praecipit quod ego ante vadam ornata ad beatum Ioannem, et postea ad beatum Franciscum, et revertar ad ecclesiam beatae Mariae.' Quae omnia altero die fecit, sicut ei praeceptum fuerat, et semper portabat maiestatem secum quocumque ambulabat."

10. Zaccagnini, *Ubaldesca, una santa laica*, 8, 173.

11. Ibid., 9–10, 173–74.

Frederico Visconti of Pisa to mark Ubaldesca's feast day, all secured her identity as one of Pisa's civic saints.[12]

But while Ubaldesca's cult was well established fifty years after her death, it would take more than a century after Rose's death for her cult to find the same legitimation. Despite the fact that Pope Innocent IV initiated a (never completed) canonization inquiry the year after Rose's death and Pope Alexander IV had a series of dreams in 1257 that led him to move Rose's body from its first tomb in the church of Santa Maria del Poggio to Viterbo's female Franciscan convent, this chapter will argue that it was not until the late fourteenth century that Rose's cult had real institutional support from the church. This was when the Franciscan friar Bartholomew of Pisa wrote the *De conformitate vitae Beati Francisci ad vitam Domini Iesu*, which included the first catalogue of Franciscan saints that listed members of the Friars Minor Third Order. By including Rose (as well as other thirteenth-century lay penitents) in his list, Bartholomew rewrote the history of not only the mendicant lay orders (since neither the Franciscan nor Dominican third orders had a full institutional form in the mid-thirteenth century) but also the relationship between lay penitents and the Franciscans.[13] In short, Bartholomew saw connections where the documentary evidence either reveals silence or antagonism between lay penitents and friars.[14]

In the preceding chapters, I have argued that the church's response to the rise of the lay penitential movement, and more specifically to the growth of cults dedicated to contemporary laymen in the late twelfth and early thirteenth centuries, was to propose its own model of the ideal lay Christian. In Innocent III's canonization bull for Omobono of Cremona, an ideal lay life is dedicated to prayer, penitence, charity, and the fight against heresy. As *popolo*-dominated communes began to patronize the cults of contemporary lay saints in the mid-thirteenth century, that model began to change. Although Innocent's portrait of Omobono sought to de-emphasize the kind of charismatic activity that had marked the cults of earlier lay saints like Ranieri of Pisa, notions of the lay saint as a living holy man and miracle worker crept back into mid thirteenth-century cults as lay saints' charismatic acts were increasingly framed as responding to inequalities within urban society. In cults such as that of Pier

---

12. For the development of Ubaldesca's Pisan cult, see ibid., 139–41; Rosalia Amico, *Il monastero di S. Giovanni gerosolimitano in Pisa: Studio storico introduttivo: Inventario dell'Archivio e appendice di documenti* (Pisa: ETS, 2007), 37–43; and Luttrell, "Saint Ubaldesca di Calcinaia."

13. On the long held (but incorrect) idea that these third orders were created around the same time as the main mendicant orders, see More, "Institutionalizing Penitential Life."

14. Mary Harvey Doyno, "The Creation of a Franciscan Lay Saint: Margaret of Cortona and Her *Legenda.*" *Past and Present* 228 (2015): 88–90.

"Pettinaio" of Siena, the ideal layman had become the ideal communal citizen. The city contained and made palatable the kind of charismatic lay penitent who had been seen as a threat to the institutional church's authority at the end of the twelfth century.

But what about laywomen? Although laywomen made up a substantial portion of the lay penitential movement in Italy and were frequently awarded saintly cults for their efforts, they have thus far been absent from this study.[15] To what extent did these early and mid thirteenth-century models for an ideal lay life apply to laywomen who garnered saintly reputations? Were they understood as having the same kinds of charismatic powers as holy laymen? Did the church work to contain their charisma in the same ways that it had for male lay saints? Did interest shown by *popolo*-run communes lead to the return of cults that emphasized the female lay saint as living miracle worker (with an emphasis on miracles that solved social issues)?

The complicated answer, expressed in simple terms, is yes and no. In this and subsequent chapters, my exploration of several laywomen who garnered cults in communal Italy before Pope Nicholas IV's *Supra montem* identifies a similar back-and-forth between radical and more conservative models of lay sanctity (that is, between the charismatic miracle worker and the charity worker) that we saw in men's cults. However, as a comparison between Ubaldesca's and Rose's conversion stories as well as the trajectories of their cults illustrates, what mattered most in the creation of the cult of the female lay saint in communal Italy was institutional affiliation and identity. This chapter will therefore argue that Rose's early cult did not take off precisely because she did not have the institutional affiliation critical for the cults of female lay saints in the thirteenth and early fourteenth centuries. She was not a *conversa* or lay associate of an established monastic house; nor was she a lay penitent whom the mendicant friars were interested in cultivating, as was true of a lay penitent such as Umiliana de' Cerchi (d. 1246), who also garnered a saintly reputation in the mid-thirteenth century. Thus, as I shall argue, Alexander IV's translation of Rose's body was more likely an effort to appease the Viterban Poor Clares who were concerned about the competition Rose's cult could potentially present for their own house, rather than evidence that the papacy

---

15. The classic studies on laywomen penitents in medieval Italy are Benvenuti Papi, *"In castro poenitentiae"*; Mario Sensi, "Anchoresses and Penitents," in *Women and Religion in Medieval and Renaissance Italy*, ed. Bornstein and Rusconi, 56–83; Sensi, *Storie di bizzoche*; and Luigi Pellegrini, "Female Religious Experience and Society in Thirteenth-Century Italy," in *Monks and Nuns, Saints and Outcasts: Religion in Medieval Society, Essays in Honor of Lester K. Little*, ed. Sharon Farmer and Barbara H. Rosenwein (Ithaca, NY: Cornell University Press, 2000), 97–122. Another good introduction to female lay penitents can be found in Lehmijoki-Gardner's introduction to *Dominican Penitent Women*, 1–36.

was working to promote Rose's memory and reputation. In contrast, Ubaldesca's identity as a lay associate of S. Giovannino and Frate Dotto's early patronage offered her cult institutional as well as male legitimacy; the independent nature of Rose's religious life ultimately retarded the growth of her civic cult.

Nevertheless, as Catherine M. Mooney has persuasively illustrated, figuring out late medieval Italian women's religious affiliations is far from an easy task.[16] Although religious women in late medieval Italy tended to pursue religious lives as laywomen, and thus exist outside of the institutional clarity of regularized orders, they also often had either shifting or competing affiliations.[17] Ubaldesca, for example, never lost her lay status, but her saintly reputation was tied first to her role as a *conversa* to the S. Giovannino nuns and then, after her death, to the connection the Hospitaller Order forged with her cult. In addition, another thirteenth-century Pisan lay saint, Bona (d. 1207), first found a spiritual guide in a canon from Pisa's San Martino church but later forged an affiliation with the monks of San Michele degli Scalzi.

I shall therefore look less in this chapter at how and why medieval women claimed particular religious connections and more at how and why hagiographers and other architects of women's cults constructed saintly identities that depended upon such affiliations. Although the cults of male lay saints could acknowledge and even make argumentative use of an ambiguous relationship between a lay saint and his city's religious hierarchy—witness the appearance of both Dominic and Francis on Andrea Gallerani's reliquary shutters—laywomen's cults could not. Ubaldesca earned a thirteenth-century cult precisely because she could be institutionally identified. And even though we might be able to see in the fragments of Rose's first *vita* evidence of a popular following, her cult lacked the kind of institutional support in its earliest phases that it needed to grow; this would only come when the Franciscans had attached her memory to their order.

In addition to exploring the institutional identity of female lay sanctity, this chapter will also consider the role gender played in the construction of female lay religious ideals. By looking at the complex hagiographic dossier connected with Bona of Pisa's early cult as well as how the Franciscans first conceptualized female lay sanctity in their *vita* for Umiliana de' Cerchi, I shall identify a similar interest in a living laywoman's charismatic power that I found in men's cults. Instead of channeling such powers primarily through an emphasis on the lay saint as charity worker, in the cults of female lay saints,

---

16. Mooney, "Nuns, Tertiaries, and Quasi-Religious," 68–69.
17. Ibid.

by contrast, laywomen's charisma was increasingly mitigated over the thirteenth century not only by the presence of male confessors, patrons, and religious authorities but also through a growing emphasis on their visionary experiences.

Although men's cults could (and often did) embrace a more flexible approach to the distinctions between laymen and clerics or laymen and monks, and used that flexibility to construct varying definitions of lay sanctity, laywomen were too resolutely lay—that is, too fully outside of the hierarchy of the institutional church as well as the power structures of medieval society more broadly understood—to undertake such explorations. Thus, this chapter asks if the very idea of the female lay saint—that is, of the ideal female lay penitent—brings to the fore tensions regarding lay charismatic power and religious authority that had always been present in cults dedicated to men. Although much of the work to answer this final question is the focus of chapter 7, this chapter in its exploration of the development of four cults dedicated to laywomen—Ubaldesca and Bona of Pisa, Umiliana de' Cerchi, and Rose of Viterbo—aims to introduce the ways in which women's participation in the lay religious movement precipitated responses that ultimately characterized the ideal lay religious life as institutionally identified, at the same time as it moved the major expression of that life out of the city streets and into women's bodies and heads.

Ubaldesca and Bona of Pisa

In 1263, Pisa's bishop, Federico Visconti, lamented in a sermon that so few recent Pisan holy men and women had been canonized by Rome.[18] The occasion for his sermon was Ubaldesca's feast day. Ubaldesca, Visconti noted (quoting from 2 Corinthians), demonstrated such glory and patience in dealing with infirmity that Christ dwelt within her. In addition to Ubaldesca, the bishop also mentioned Ranieri of Pisa, the Camaldolese monk Dominic Vernagalli (d. 1219), and Ubaldesca's contemporary, Bona of Pisa (d. 1207).[19] Visconti noted that he had been told of the many postmortem miracles ascribed to Ubaldesca, a point that has suggested to scholars that the bishop may well

---

18. *Les sermons et la visite pastorale de Federico Visconti archevêque de Pise (1253–1277)*, ed. Nicole Bériou and Isabelle le Masne de Chermont (Rome: École Française de Rome, 2001), 965–69. For more on Visconti, see Alexander Murray, "Archbishop and Mendicants in Thirteenth-Century Pisa," in *Conscience and Authority in the Medieval Church* (Oxford: Oxford University Press, 2015), 105–62.

19. *Les sermons*, 968.

have been gathering documents to launch a formal canonization inquiry in Rome.[20]

Although there is no extant evidence that a medieval canonization process was ever taken up for either Ubaldesca or Bona, Visconti's interest in these women coupled with the fact that new *vitae* appeared for both of them around the same time as the bishop's sermon suggests that in the mid-thirteenth century their cults were expanding.[21] Moreover, even though the *vitae* point to the women's penitential commitments, pilgrimages, and charity work, it is their charismatic activity—most often evidenced through the performance of living miracles—that stands out as the most compelling evidence for their sanctity. And finally, while Visconti's sermon makes no mention of either Ubaldesca or Bona having been associated with a particular Pisan religious order or institution, the *vitae* suggest that these laywomen's legitimacy and charismatic powers depended upon such connections.

Ubaldesca's *vita*, which survives only in a sixteenth-century manuscript, describes the nearly fifty-five years of service she performed as a *conversa* at the S. Giovannino convent. The *vita* reports how S. Giovannino's abbess had welcomed Ubaldesca by giving her a habit, a point that has led some modern readers to the mistaken assumption that Ubaldesca had given up her lay status.[22] The *vita*, however, makes no mention of formal vows and depicts Ubaldesca negotiating the world outside of the convent on behalf of the cloistered nuns, most notably by wandering the streets of Pisa in order to beg for alms.[23] The habit the abbess gave to Ubaldesca more likely marked the beginning of her life as a professed lay penitent or *conversa* rather than the end of her lay status.[24]

Much of Ubaldesca's short *vita* describes her intense penitential routine, the tireless service she offered the S. Giovannino nuns, and the miracles she performed. The text's ordering of this information sets up an argument about the source of Ubaldesca's sanctity: it is her rigorous penitential routine that endows her with charismatic power. Thus, we first hear about how Ubaldesca was always increasing her prayers and her fasts, how her habit

---

20. See Zaccagnini, *Ubaldesca, una santa laica*, 18–22; and Luttrell, "Saint Ubaldesca di Calcinaia," 288.

21. The Roman church did not canonize Bona until 1962. Ubaldesca was never formally canonized. Zaccagnini has produced editions of the thirteenth-century *vitae* for both women; see his *Ubaldesca, una santa laica*, and Gabriele Zaccagnini, *La tradizione agiografica medievale di santa Bona da Pisa* (Pisa: ETS, 2004). There are several thirteenth-century redactions of Bona's *vita*, which I discuss in more detail below.

22. Zaccagnini, *Ubaldesca, una santa laica*, 126–32.

23. Ibid., 172–73.

24. Ibid., 128.

was made of sackcloth, how she never slept in a bed, and how she existed on bread and water alone.[25] After providing evidence that Ubaldesca was living a life of extraordinary penance, the *vita* turns to describing how Ubaldesca served the S. Giovannino community with the greatest humility and patience—begging for alms to support them and always ready to attend to one of the forty nuns in need of her curative talents and kindness. By emphasizing Ubaldesca's acts of penance and charity, the *vita* sets up both a validation and cause for the final aspect of her holy life: the performance of living miracles.[26] The text ends with two episodes that demonstrate how Ubaldesca's charisma extended beyond the convent. In the first, Ubaldesca invoked Christ's name to heal herself after she suffered a serious head injury.[27] In the second, she made the sign of the cross over water she had fetched for a thirsty pilgrim at a well outside the church of San Pier a Grado, transforming it into wine.[28] This well would remain a potent part of her postmortem cult, with devotees flocking to its water for its purported ability to heal as late as the seventeenth century.[29]

The argument made in this *vita*—that Ubaldesca's intense penitential routine endowed her with the ability to perform living miracles—connects her to Pisa's most celebrated lay saint, Ranieri of Pisa. Like Ubaldesca, when Ranieri adopted an extreme penitential life, existing solely upon bread and water, he became endowed with spiritual gifts. Those gifts allowed Ranieri to turn the material of his penitential sustenance—the bread and the water—into agents of miraculous change. Although Ubaldesca's miracles are less dramatic than Ranieri's, the connection between a layperson's penitential activity and his or her charismatic powers is clear. Ubaldesca's penance is most explicitly expressed in the service she offered the S. Giovannino nuns. And it is that long dedication to service that endows her with the ability to heal her own grave head injury, turn water into wine, and make the well a source of miraculous healing.

The other Pisan woman whom Bishop Visconti mentions is Bona, born about twenty years after Ubaldesca to a merchant family living in the Kinzica

---

25. Ibid., 171–72.

26. Ibid., 172.

27. Ibid.

28. Ibid., 172–73. Located between Pisa and Lucca, San Pier a Grado is a pilgrimage church purported to have been the site where the apostle Peter had once come ashore. To underscore that Ubaldesca's act was in fact a miracle, the *vita* describes how she implored the woman to remain silent about the miracle they had both witnessed.

29. Paolo Tronci mentions the healing reputation of Ubaldesca's well in his seventeenth-century chronicle; cited by Natale Caturegli, "Ubaldesca, santa," in *Bibliotheca sanctorum*, vol. 12, 731–32.

neighborhood of Pisa.[30] When Bona was three years old, her father left on a business trip to Jerusalem from which he would never return. Travel would also figure prominently in Bona's own life. She undertook many pilgrimages to local Tuscan shrines, to Santiago de Compostela, and to the Holy Land. Bona made a name for herself through her dedication to charity, founding the hospice of S. Jacopo de Podio just outside of Pisa.[31] And while Bona was still quite young, she became an *oblata* or *devota* to Pisa's S. Martino canons.[32] In Bona's thirteenth-century *vitae* (there are multiple redactions, which I discuss below), one of those canons, Giovanni, is referred to as Bona's "spiritual father," offering her guidance and witnessing several of her living miracles. As an adult, Bona also attached herself (the exact nature of the connection is never spelled out) to S. Michele degli Scalzi in Orticaia, a reformed Benedictine or "Pulsani" congregation (sometimes referred to as the "barefoot monks"). It was with these monks that Bona founded the S. Jacopo de Podio hospice. Moreover, it was in this monastery that Bona found a second spiritual adviser, the house's abbot, Paolo. Just as was emphasized in Ubaldesca's cult, the hagiographic tradition associated with Bona makes clear that these associations not only supported and legitimized her lay religious life but also provided male religious figures to serve as witnesses to as well as participants in the extraordinary charismatic acts that she performed.

Bona's hagiographic tradition is complex and deserves a detailed unpacking in order to illustrate both her multiple institutional affiliations and the diversity of approaches these *vitae* took to describing her charisma.[33] Between roughly 1230 and 1260, both the Pulsani monks and the S. Martino canons produced redactions of a *vita* for Bona that Gabriele Zaccagnini has argued were based on a now-lost single original text.[34] Although the S. Martino *vita* is a longer account of Bona's life and has been traditionally favored by scholars (it is the version that appears in the *Acta sanctorum*), Zaccagnini has argued that it is actually a later (ca. 1260) redaction than the Pulsani text, which he dates to ca. 1230.[35]

30. In addition to Zaccagnini's study of Bona, for a general introduction, also see Anna Benvenuti Papi, "Donne sulla strada: L'itineranza religiosa femminile nel medioevo," in *Donne in viaggio: Viaggio religioso politico metaforico*, ed. M. L. Silvestre and A. Valerio (Bari: Laterza, 1999), 74–86.

31. Zaccagnini, *La tradizione agiografica*, 39.

32. While one redaction of Bona's *vita* refers to her simply as a *devota* of S. Martino, another, written by a canon from S. Martino, awards the more formal association of *oblata*; see Zaccagnini, *La tradizione agiografica*, 25–27.

33. My discussion of this tradition will depend on the work done by Zaccagnini, *La tradizione agiografica*, 9–15 and 93–98.

34. Ibid., 93. Both redactions have been preserved in the same late fourteenth-century manuscript; for more on that manuscript see ibid., 9–15.

35. Ibid, 94–95.

The Pulsani *vita* consists of not one but three distinct texts.[36] The first, which Zaccagnini calls B1, contains a prologue and the beginnings of what appears to have been a full redaction. The second text, B2, is much longer than B1 and contains a somewhat disordered collection of episodes from Bona's life. Zaccagnini has speculated that these episodes are the notes and testimony collected by Bona's second spiritual father, the Pulsani abbot Paolo.[37] Finally, B3 is made up of a number of postmortem miracle accounts, likely the beginning of a *libellus* or miracle book. Considering all of this material together, Zaccagnini has speculated that while B1 and the S. Martino *vita* are attempts at full redactions (with B1 incomplete and the S. Martino text complete) based on a lost original life, B3 is the beginning of a collection of postmortem miracles (all of which reappear in the S. Martino *vita*), and B2 is a copy of the notes and testimony used to write that lost original *vita*. Thus, B2 offers readers an opportunity to see how those chronologically closest to Bona described and interpreted both her religious life and her miraculous acts. It also offers an opportunity to see how later redactions (foremost the S. Martino *vita*, since B1 is incomplete) decided to change and amend that portrait.

Overall, the San Martino and Pulsani *vitae* give essentially the same narrative of Bona's life.[38] Where the texts differ most significantly, however, is in their descriptions of Bona's visionary and miracle-working life. The second Pulsani text (B2), the text that Zaccagnini argues is likely testimony and notes, presents Bona's charismatic activity as something that derives from a combination of her own agency and the fact that she was "full of the Holy Spirit." The S. Martino *vita* and the first Pulsani text (B1)—all texts likely composed after B2—present the origins of Bona's visions and living miracles in a more ambiguous manner: Bona might experience visions and be present as miracles unfold, but her role in their performance is continually downplayed. Thus, although in the earliest notes collected in reference to Bona's religious life (B2) we see an emphasis placed upon this laywoman's charismatic gifts and activities, that emphasis is muted in later writings.

Despite these differences, all three texts (B1, B2, and the S. Martino *vita*) point to a connection between Bona and the Holy Spirit as a key part of the beginning of her saintly life. When she was still a young girl (one of her *vitae* claims she was seven years old), Bona had a vision of Jesus accompanied by

---

36. These come one after the other in the fourteenth-century manuscript in which it is preserved. Editions of all three can be found in ibid., 111–52.

37. An episode within B2 describes how Paolo was concerned to create a record to preserve all that Bona said and did; B2, cap. XXXII, 136.

38. That history only varies substantially in the emphasis each gives to its order's role in Bona's religious life; see Zaccagnini, *La tradizione agiografica*, 94–98.

the Virgin Mary, Saint James, and Mary's "two sisters," a grouping that would repeatedly appear to offer her guidance and participate in the miracles she performed. While in the S. Martino *vita*, this initial vision of Christ and his companions appears to Bona after she has attached herself to the S. Martino canons, in both Pulsani texts it is the first event described. In all of the redactions, Bona is presented as having at first been frightened at the appearance of this holy group. But after Saint James reassured her that she was indeed seeing Christ and his mother, Bona turned toward Christ, who instructed her to open her mouth and "receive the holy spirit."[39] Christ proceeded to blow three times into Bona's mouth, leaving her, as the *vitae* note, "immediately full of the Holy Spirit."[40]

While all of the *vitae* mention Christ blowing the Holy Spirit into Bona, it is only in B2 that this episode continues to be referenced after the event itself. Not long after Bona had complied with Jesus's instructions, she had another vision of this group. Jesus and his companions appeared to her dressed as pilgrims and implored her to embark on what would become the first of her many pilgrimages to the Holy Land, during which Bona not only found her father but also met a hermit, Ubaldo, whose small religious community she would join for the next nine months.[41] At the end of her time in Ubaldo's hermit community, Bona again had a vision of Christ and his companions, telling her that it was time for her to return to Pisa so that she could have many children.[42] When Bona objected, citing her desire to remain a virgin, Christ responded by telling her that he was referring to spiritual and not to carnal children. To prove his point, he revealed to her a mountain full of men dressed in white robes, representing those spiritual children. Placing a gold ring on Bona's finger, Christ noted that the ring represented both his love and his grace and would allow others to address her as mother and his bride.

Even though up to this point, the outlines of this vision are largely the same in all of the redactions, it is only B2 that notes that Bona was "full of the Holy Spirit" (*Spiritu Sancto repleta*) before describing her reaction to Christ's proph-

---

39. B1, cap. IV, 113; B2, cap. II, 117; A, cap. VIII, 161. While this vision appears in the Pulsani texts (B1 and B2) at the very beginning of Bona's religious life, in the S. Martino text it comes after episodes describing how an angel instructed Giovanni to go to S. Martino in Pisa (he was studying in Paris) in order to receive Bona as a sister of the house. A, cap. II, 158.

40. This episode is essentially the same in all three redactions.

41. Zaccagnini has noted how Bona's hagiographic tradition depicts her under the spiritual guidance of a series of religious men; men who guided and gave legitimacy to her lay religious life, and who, in some sense, seem to have served as replacements for her missing father; *La tradizione agiografica*, 26 and 31.

42. B1, cap. VII, 114–15; A, cap XIII, 164–65.

ecy.[43] Moreover, it is only in B2 that the reader is told that Bona responded to Christ by noting that as his handmaiden, and on behalf of their children, she wished to take on in her own body (*in corpore meo*) all of the infirmities of those suffering.[44] Zaccagnini has argued that this episode introduces readers to the work and community that Bona would find once she had returned to Pisa and had founded the hospice of S. Jacopo de Podio; but such a connection is only explicitly made in the S. Martino *vita*.[45] While B1 makes no mention of the charitable work Bona would perform back in Pisa, B2 draws the readers' attention both to the fact and to the effect of Bona being "full of the Holy Spirit." In addition, although the S. Martino text makes an explicit connection between Bona's (spiritual) children and the charitable work that she would perform at both the Pulsani house and at the hospice of S. Jacopo de Podio, it does not ascribe the impetus of that work to Bona being full of the Holy Spirit. And finally, even though both the S. Martino *vita* and B1 note that Bona wanted to take on the infirmities of the suffering, neither of these texts mentions (as B2 does) that she wanted to take on such suffering in her own body, or that such a response came from her being full of the Holy Spirit.

It is only in B2, therefore, that we see a narrative thread created that makes use of Bona's relationship to the Holy Spirit: all of Bona's experiences and actions spur from Christ blowing the Holy Spirit into her. In B2, it is because she is "full of the Holy Spirit" that Bona not only makes sense of Christ's oblique references while she is still in Jerusalem to her new role as charity worker, but also sets her sights on fulfilling such a role by assuming in her own body the suffering of others. In effect, B2 provides a cause and explanation for the plethora of charismatic activity that dominates the rest of Bona's life. While all three *vitae* mention that charismatic activity, only B2 provides its readers with a rationale for such behavior.

B2 continues to work with that narrative thread in its descriptions of Bona's extraordinary powers of prophecy and occult knowledge. After describing Bona's return from Pisa and the association she forged with S. Martino—she became a *devota* of the house, dedicating her time to her own spiritual progress through extensive fasts, night vigils, and constant prayer as well as to extending charity to pilgrims, widows, orphans, or to anyone else in need—B2 turns to describing her ability to know the secrets of both scripture and of the heart.[46] B2 sees a connection between the fact that Bona is full of the Holy

---

43. B2, cap. X, 121–22.
44. Ibid.
45. Zaccagnini, *La tradizione agiografica*, 33.
46. B2, cap. XIV, 123–24.

Spirit and her knowledge of these secrets.[47] Although the S. Martino *vita* offers a similar list of Bona's prophetic powers, it only mentions Bona's intense desire to unite with the Holy Spirit. Thus, where the S. Martino *vita*'s author sees Bona as seeking a connection to the Holy Spirit, the author of B2 not only describes this laywoman as already having such a connection but also sees it as responsible for awarding her prophetic and occult knowledge.[48]

In one of Bona's miracle stories, which takes place at S. Jacopo de Podio, the hospice Bona founded with the help of the Pulsani monks, a group of clerics who were known for the sweet and melodious quality of their singing voices began to sing for the congregation. While the clerics sang, Bona and a seven-year-old girl witnessed Christ and his twelve apostles descend upon the altar.[49] In another miracle, Bona asked Christ for an image that contained his likeness so that she might find consolation in it.[50] Christ obliged and Bona placed the image in S. Jacopo de Podio. One day at vespers, as Bona was in the church with another woman, the image began to speak.[51] The *vitae* report that both women went pale and Bona's companion began to yell for Paolo, the Pulsani abbot. When Paolo arrived, he noticed the women's lack of color but could not hear anything coming from the image. In response to his questioning about what had just taken place, Bona responded that she had just received a vision of the Trinity.[52]

In these episodes as well as in several others, girls and young women occupy a central place. Not only are they the ones who witness Bona's visionary and charismatic activity, but they are also portrayed (more so in B2 than in the S. Martino *vita*) as having looked to Bona as a model or guide for their own lay religious lives. For example, in an episode that appears in both redactions, a fifteen- or sixteen-year-old girl begged to meet the celebrated holy woman whom her father had long praised.[53] Once the father had arranged a meeting with Bona, who had begun to speak the words of God to the girl, B2 claims that Bona had asked to cut or tonsure (*tondantur*) the girl's braids.[54] While

---

47. Ibid.

48. A, cap. XXXVI, 182.

49. B2, cap. XXV, 131–32; A, cap. XXVII, 175–76. The episode is essentially the same in both redactions.

50. B2, cap XXVI, 132–33; A, cap. XXIX, 177. The episode is essentially the same in both redactions.

51. For more on the relationship between images and medieval women's visionary experiences, see Chiara Frugoni, "Female Mystics, Visions, and Iconography," in *Women and Religion in Medieval and Renaissance Italy*, ed. Bornstein and Rusconi, 130–64.

52. B2, cap XXVI, 132–33; A, cap. XXIX, 177.

53. B2, cap. XXXIV, 140–43; A, cap. XXXIV, 180–81.

54. B2, cap. XXXIV, 141: "Ego volo, filia mea, quod reste sive treccie tuorum capillorum penitus incidantur et tondantur."

the S. Martino *vita* includes this episode, it de-emphasizes Bona's active role in the shearing.[55] Nevertheless, both *vitae* make clear that through her contact with Bona, this young woman was initiated into a penitential life.

That life, however, would not be a long one. B2 describes how anxious the young woman's father was to get her back home after Bona had cut her hair. The young woman tried to resist her father's wishes, claiming that she wanted to remain with Bona, but she was finally moved to return home after Bona assured her that she would soon visit her there. When Bona did not immediately show up, the young woman fell into a depression, crying and neglecting her household duties.[56] Bona finally did arrive, but in a vision, accompanied by the same holy figures that had repeatedly appeared to the saint—Christ, Saint James, the Virgin Mary and her two sisters. Bona and her companions announced in the vision that in the middle of the next day, the girl would "pass from this vale of misery into the celestial kingdom."[57] Unaware of the fate that had been announced to his daughter, the father went to Bona to ask when she was going to visit his daughter as she had promised. While the Martino *vita* describes how Christ and his companions (including Bona) reappeared to the girl the next day, urging her to take the wine of communion (*vino communionem*) with her father and others in her house, B2 claims that Bona directly responded to the girl's father, telling him that he should give his daughter all of the sacraments.[58]

As this and other episodes demonstrate, B2 tends to see in Bona a religious as well as charismatic authority and agency absent in the S. Martino *vita*. Not only does Bona instruct the girl's father to give her all of the sacraments, she also asks to tonsure the girl. In another miracle account that also involves a

---

55. The S. Martino *vita* leaves it more ambiguous as to who actually cuts the girl's braids and does not use the word "tonsure." A, cap. XXXIV, 180: "Que cum ad beatam Bonam ipsam adduxisset, visa illa et audita, circa ipsam adeo est affecta, ut trecias, sibi valde dilectas, ab ipsa abscidi libentissime pateretur et, patris ac domus oblita, cum sancta Bona vellet ulterius indivisibiliter permanere."

56. B2, cap. XXXIV, 141. The S. Martino text leaves out most of these details, compressing into one sentence a description of the girl having her braids cut and later her anxiously waiting for Bona to arrive at her house.

57. B2, cap. XXXIV, 142: "Et Dominus Iesus Christus cum beato Iacobo apostolo et beata Virgine et sororibus et beata Bona dixerunt predicte puelle filie Syninbaldi: 'Die crastina, in meditate diei, te filia mea ex hac valle miserie subtracta ad celestia regna transibis.'" The S. Martino *vita* offers no significant difference here.

58. A, cap. XXXIV, 181: "Cumque inde, repleta gaudio, Dominum collaudaret, ecce iterum Dominus Iesus Christus cum quibus prius venerat, et cum beata Bona, apparuit et dicens ut cum patre et aliis domesticis de vino communionem faceret caritatis." B2, cap. XXXIV, 142: "Et tunc Dominus Iesu Christus dixit puelle: 'Voca patrem tuum et alios de familia, et fac cum eis caritatem de vino.' Et sic vocavit patrem et alios de familia. Et plena oba vel sypho vitreo vino, dicta puella bibit caritative cum eis." Both *vitae* conclude by noting that the girl had indeed drunk the communal wine with her household, taken the rest of the sacraments, and then died; see B2, cap. XXXIV, 142; A, cap. XXXIV, 181.

young woman, the author of the S. Martino *vita* inserts a rationale for some of Bona's more aggressive behavior. In this story, Bona heals a young woman who had been gravely injured after falling onto a marble table and piercing her chest.[59] A group of women rushed the injured woman to Bona, begging for the holy woman's help. Bona had at first wept alongside the women, but then quickly devised a more effective response. She turned to Abbot Paolo and implored him to make the sign of the cross over the injured woman. The abbot responded that he rarely did such a thing.[60] Bona then proceeded to take matters into her own hands. She touched the injured woman, asking her, "What happened, my child? What happened?" In response, the girl began to breathe, opened her eyes, and as if she had never fallen in the first place, replied that in fact nothing had happened.[61] Although the basic outlines of this episode are the same between the two *vitae*, only the S. Martino *vita* prefaces Bona's command that Paolo sign the girl with a defensive rationale: Bona was acting with an abundance of humility and reverence for the order of the sexes.[62] Bona's command that an abbot make the sign of the cross left the author of the S. Martino *vita* uncomfortable enough to need to reiterate that despite such actions, Bona knew her place in the religious and gender hierarchy.

Despite the differences between the two *vitae*, it is important to emphasize that the spiritual gifts ascribed to this female lay saint remain quite distinct from those claimed by another early thirteenth-century Pisan cult: that of Ranieri. Both the nature and the effects of Bona's spiritual gifts are more circumscribed than those ascribed to Ranieri. Her charisma does not reform or restore corrupt institutions or people. She is never called a new manifestation of Christ. She does not deliver priests from the hands of Satan. Nevertheless, each of the episodes in the *vitae* that are meant to illustrate her extraordinary piety and ultimately her sanctity do so through accounts of the miracles that come out of her touch and presence.

And yet, we cannot discount the role male agency plays in both Ubaldesca's and Bona's cults. As I have noted, both women's cults point to associations between these laywomen and religious institutions run by men as a means of legitimizing their relatively independent religious lives. Moreover, in Bona's *vitae* in particular, despite the fact that so many of her charismatic

---

59. B2, cap. XXIII, 130; A, cap. XXXIII, 179.

60. B2, cap. XXIII, 130: "Et dixit tunc beata Bona dicto Paulo abbati: 'Fili signa iuvenculam illam.' Qui respondens ait: 'Hoc domina mea minime faciam.'"

61. Ibid.: "Et beata Bona tetigit illam iuvenculam, et dixit: 'Quid habes filia mea? Quid habes?' Et illa suspirans, apertis occulis, dixit: 'Nichil habeo.' Et sic liberata est ac si non cecidisset"; A, cap. XXXIII, 179.

62. A, cap. XXXIII, 179.

acts involve women, men still play a crucial role circumscribing the production and effect of that charisma. For example, in one episode that appears in both the S. Martino *vita* and in B2, Christ appeared to Bona asking her to take an iron belt or girdle that encircled her (*circulum ferreum quo es precincta*) and give it to Giovanni, a priest from S. Martino, so that he could make it into a cross.[63] It seems likely that this was the same Giovanni identified elsewhere in the *vitae* as Bona's "spiritual father," and that the iron belt or girdle had functioned as some kind of chastity belt. The *vitae* describe Giovanni watching the belt transform into a cross as he placed it into a fire and seeing both a great light pour down from the sky and drops of "precious and glorious blood" fall onto the cross as he pulled it out of the flames. That blood, as the *vitae* maintain, was without doubt Christ's blood.[64] The *vitae* conclude this episode by noting that Bona delivered this miraculous cross to S. Jacopo de Podio.

Although the miraculously shape-shifting iron belt or girdle originally belonged to Bona, it is significant that the *vitae* present Christ asking a priest to bring about its transformation. Moreover, the *vitae* make clear that Giovanni was the one who witnessed the dripping blood. And finally, the assertion that these were "without doubt" drops of Christ's blood comes from Giovanni in the S. Martino *vita* and from the anonymous, but assumed male, author of B2. While Bona's role as a container of charisma might initiate these acts, her identity as a woman limits the extent to which her hagiographers are willing to imagine her role in their completion.

Nevertheless, there is still a resolutely female focus to both Ubaldesca's and Bona's cults. Ubaldesca serves the nuns of S. Giovannino for fifty-five years. Moreover, like Bona, the beneficiaries of her miracles are most often women. And it is with other women—and most often quite young women—that Bona receives miraculous visions and performs the majority of her charismatic acts. Especially in B2, Bona is portrayed taking an active role to initiate women into a committed penitential life. As we turn to consider the form that female lay sanctity would take by the mid-thirteenth century, we again see a resolutely female-dominated religious world but one that would be increasingly mitigated by male institutional authorities.

---

63. B2, cap. XVII, 126–27; A, cap XLVIII, 191–92.

64. The most significant difference between the two redactions in their account of this miracle is that in the Pulsani text it is the author who firmly believes the drops of blood to be Christ's blood; see B2, cap. XVII, 126: "Quem sanguinem credimus firmiter et indubitanter esse ex sanguine Domini nostri Iesu Christi." By contrast, in the S. Martino *vita* it is Giovanni who deems the blood to belong to Christ; see A, cap XLVIII, 192: "Ex cuius lucis splendore, gutta una sanguinis cecidit super crucem, ipso Iohanne presbitero intuente que gutta ex divino Christi corpore et ex eius pretioso sanguine creditur emanasse."

Although the extant *vitae* we have for both Ubaldesca and Bona come from the mid-thirteenth century, they describe laywomen who lived in the late twelfth century. And, at least for the case of Bona's *vitae*, they are redactions that depend upon an earlier source. To some extent then, we can classify these texts as reflecting a late twelfth- and early thirteenth-century understanding of female lay sanctity. Furthermore, just as we saw in Ranieri of Pisa's cult, these *vitae* all point to the laywomen's charismatic acts as the most compelling evidence for their sanctity. These women's *vitae* also present an understanding of a lay saint's charisma that is gender-specific: both in the women's limited mobility and the manner in which their religious identities depended on associations with established religious institutions. Moreover, especially in the case of Bona's *vitae*, male religious authorities were often presented as authenticating the miracles performed by a laywoman.

When we look at two female lay penitents who died in the mid-thirteenth century, Umiliana de' Cerchi of Florence (d. 1246) and Rose of Viterbo (d. 1251), we see how, over the thirteenth century, two paths emerged that further emphasized the role men played in the making of the female lay saint: the institutionally connected but institutionally mitigated female lay saint (Umiliana), and the institutionally independent but institutionally suspect female lay saint (Rose). In the remainder of this chapter, I shall show how in Umiliana's cult the mendicants' increasing role as the guardians of lay penitents (and by extension of lay saints) ushered in a turn toward an internal visionary life as key evidence for a laywoman's sanctity. With regard to Rose's cult, on the other hand, I will argue that the underlying threat an unaffiliated female lay penitential life posed kept her cult from expanding until the Franciscans began a late fourteenth-century promotional campaign to reconceive of their past connections to lay penitents.

Umiliana de' Cerchi of Florence

Umiliana de' Cerchi was the daughter of a wealthy and politically prominent Florentine family.[65] She married when she was sixteen years old, had a num-

---

65. On Umiliana, see Benvenuti Papi, "*In castro poenitentiae*," 58–98; Anna Benvenuti Papi, "Umiliana dei Cerchi, nascita di un culto nella Firenze del Dugento," *Studi Francescani* 77 (1980): 87–117; Bernard Schlager, "Foundresses of the Franciscan Life: Umiliana Cerchi and Margaret of Cortona," *Viator* 29 (1998), 141–66. Anne M. Schuchman, "'Within the Walls of Paradise': Space, and Community in the *Vita* of Umiliana de' Cerchi (1219–1246)," in *Negotiating Community and Difference in Medieval Europe: Gender, Power, Patronage and the Authority of Religion in Latin Christendom*, ed. Katherine

ber of children, and was a widow by the time she was twenty-one. In a *vita* begun by the Franciscan friar Vito da Cortona immediately after her death, we hear that Umiliana's interest in a penitential life began not long after she was married.[66] She no longer wanted to use makeup. The fine clothes that she only continued to wear "out of respect" for her husband had become a "source of torment." And finally, she began regularly to give away her and her husband's food and linens to Florence's poor and needy.[67]

It was becoming a widow, however—or more specifically, Umiliana's efforts not to be remarried—that Vito presents as propelling her into an even more committed penitential life. At first, after her husband's death, Umiliana continued to live with her in-laws, devoting ever-increasing time to wandering the city with scraps of food, linens, or whatever other kind of support and sustenance she could offer to those Florentines in need. Eventually, she returned to her father's home after (we might imagine) she had exhausted her in-laws good will and resources. Back in her childhood home, she lived increasingly like a hermit, even as her family pressured her to remarry. Once it became clear that she would refuse any marriage offer, Umiliana's father defrauded her of her dowry, leaving her with nothing to support her charity work. Umiliana eventually retreated to a room high up in her family's tower, dedicating the rest of her short life to penance, prayer, prophecy, and visionary experiences.

Although Umiliana's *vita* gives numerous descriptions of her activity distributing charity around the city of Florence, that aspect of her religious life seems to have waned as she had fewer and fewer resources upon which to draw. To some extent, Vito presents a spiritual trajectory for Umiliana's religious life similar to the portrait of Pier "Pettinaio" of Siena. Just as Pier's *vita* (also a Franciscan-authored text) saw his embrace of a contemplative life over an active one as proof of spiritual growth, Vito frames Umiliana's work providing charity for her fellow Florentines as only the first stage of a spiritual journey.

Allen Smith and Scott Wells (Leiden: Brill, 2009), 49–64; Anne M. Schuchman, "Politics and Prophecy in the Life of Umiliana dei Cerchi," *Florilegium* 17 (2000): 101–14; and Beverly Mayne Kienzle and Travis Allen Smith, "Preaching, Heresy, and the Writing of Female Hagiography," in *Beyond Catholicism: Heresy, Mysticism, and Apocalypse in Italian Culture*, ed. Fabrizio De Donno and Simon Gilson (New York: Palgrave Macmillan, 2014), 33–53.

66. *AASS*, May IV, 385–400. Vito's *vita* of Umiliana has been translated by both Webb, *Saints and Cities*, 97–140, and Anne M. Schuchman, "Within the Walls of Paradise: Umiliana de' Cerchi and the Changing Rhetoric of Sanctity" (PhD dissertation, New York University, 2004), 291–353. Excerpts of Schuchman's translation appear in Katherine L. Jansen, Joanna Drell, and Frances Andrews, eds., *Medieval Italy: Texts in Translation* (Philadelphia: University of Pennsylvania Press, 2009), 377–84. I rely on Diana Webb's translation for my discussion of Umiliana's *vita*.

67. Webb, *Saints and Cities*, 98.

The more contemplative existence—full of prayer, prophecy, and visions—that Umiliana would find in her father's tower represents, in Vito's rendering, the fullest development of her religious commitment. This distinction allows Vito essentially to divide his account of Umiliana's life into two parts: before and after her husband's death. This division helps to frame another transition Vito's text presents: the movement from an active and rather independent religious life to one that takes place largely in Umiliana's tower room, as well as inside of her head.[68]

Thus, Vito notes that from the moment she could no longer wander the streets of Florence offering charity, she became "inflamed by the divine love," and "burned to achieve the solitary life."[69] At first, Umiliana looked to a female Franciscan convent for the space to live a more contemplative life. But she was turned away, presumably for lack of funds. Vito has a different reading of this rejection, however. God, he writes, had other plans for Umiliana. He did not want her light to be hidden any longer and "therefore placed her high up on a candelabrum of life and example."[70] Despite the fact that she was living an increasingly cloistered life in her family's tower, Vito goes on essentially to argue that Umiliana's extraordinary example became public because she took on "the honorable habit of the Third Order," and thus became the "wondrous foundress of a new way of holy life."[71]

Although scholars of Vito's work have questioned how appropriate it is to identify Umiliana's Third Order status before that wing of the Franciscan Order had a solid institutional identity, I am more interested in how Vito uses the construction of an institutional identity for Umiliana in order to obscure what was essentially an independent lay religious life.[72] If we look more closely at the miracle accounts that dominate Vito's description of Umiliana's life once she returned to her father's tower, we can see the efforts he has made to use these stories as exempla not only of an ideal lay penitential life but also of an institutionally contained, charismatically mitigated, and non-threatening vision of female lay sanctity.[73]

---

68. Schuchman has written about the way in which Vito's rhetorical use of Umiliana's father's tower "erased evidence of Umiliana's lack of virginity as well as her participation in a community of laywomen"; see "'Within the Walls of Paradise': Space and Community," 50.

69. Webb, *Saints and Cities*, 105.

70. Ibid.

71. Ibid., 106.

72. More, "Institutionalizing Penitential Life," 305.

73. My point here connects to Schuchman's analysis. Where she sees Vito's rhetoric once Umiliana has returned to her father's tower as emphasizing "solitude rather than sorority for laywomen" because someone like Vito coming from an organized religious community might fail "to recognize these groups of laywomen as communities," I am seeing that rhetoric creating an institutional iden-

Thus, even though Vito presents Umiliana's religious life in her family's tower as increasingly limited in its physical scope, he frames her new existence both as moving toward a contemplative ideal and, paradoxically, as a liberation. For example, Vito writes that after her husband's death, Umiliana found the challenge of being a married penitent disappear. She became "freer than before," inviting more people to her (in-laws') table and spending more of her time in prayer.[74] Moreover, in a vision that she received as soon as she returned to her family's home, Umiliana saw herself and a crowd of children dressed in white, representing, as Vito informs his reader, "purity of life in the present" and the fact that she would one day "be surrounded by ranks of angels."[75] The significance Vito sees in Umiliana experiencing such a vision as she returned home is clear: her future glory was inexorably linked to her new life of enclosure and containment.

Despite Vito's claim that Umiliana had found freedom as a widow, the episodes he includes portray a religious life of increasing enclosure and containment. In short, they describe a physical existence that was far from free. It is within Umiliana's response to such changes that Vito sees evidence of sanctity. Thus, when Umiliana realized that her father had taken her dowry because she would not remarry, Vito writes that she did not complain, but bore it patiently. Vito elaborates that this meant that she would no longer be living in her father's house as a daughter, but rather as a "servant and handmaid."[76] And, Vito writes, although she no longer had much to give, Umiliana did her best to continue to visit the poor during the first year back home. However, by the second year, Umiliana had given up "long visits and reached unbelievable heights."[77] Vito's logic in putting together these two points (giving up long visits to the poor and reaching "unbelievable" spiritual heights) reveals a great deal about how he is framing Umiliana's version of an ideal lay religious life. At the same time that there is clearly a practical angle to Vito's point— lacking the means to devote herself to endless rounds of charitable giving allowed this laywoman to devote herself exclusively to her own spiritual progress—Vito is also crafting an argument about the kinds of religious heights a laywoman might reach if she removed herself from the hustle and bustle of the city to remain practically cloistered in her family home.

---

tity for Umiliana as a means of containing the charismatic claims surrounding her; see "'Within the Walls of Paradise': Space and Community," 58.

74. Webb, *Saints and Cities*, 101.

75. Ibid.

76. Ibid., 103.

77. Ibid., 105.

Umiliana's new way of life, Vito goes on to elaborate, was, in essence, indistinguishable from a monastic life. Umiliana's life of silence, observance, austerity, and poverty looked no different from that of a nun or monk.[78] While "some leave the world and their paternal home, and fleeing into the desert, fight for the Lord," Umiliana, "brought the desert into her father's house," and in a noble fight "defeated the world and vice in the midst of worldly things."[79]

But she clearly did not do this solely by herself. The reader is told that Umiliana was first urged to take up a penitential life by her "kinswoman" only a month after marrying.[80] The *vita*'s prologue, which lists those who had witnessed Umiliana's life, has led scholars to venture that this "kinswoman" was likely Monna Ravenna, a woman whom Vito describes as "thoroughly religious and honorable, and very well known" in Florence.[81] Although the prologue includes the names of three Franciscan friars, including Vito, women vastly outnumber men here (thirty-one of thirty-four witnesses are women).[82] The listing of witnesses was a common part of a dossier to aid in a canonization inquiry, suggesting that Vito had such hopes for Umiliana. But we might also read the great number of women named as witnesses as evidence of the female-dominated religious community in which Umiliana fashioned her early penitential life.[83] These were the Florentine women who had adopted the same kind of independent penitential life that Umiliana had first adopted.[84]

Since Vito was writing both before the mendicant friars had been charged with guardianship over lay penitents and before the lay wings of those orders had taken their full institutional shape, his portrait of Umiliana can be read as an attempt to craft an ideal model of a female lay religious life that would appeal to the friars. He does this by using Umiliana's story to articulate a new way of life for female lay penitents—while it might begin as an active life dedicated to charity, it turns increasingly toward prophecy, visions, and living miracles. Activities that, in Vito's rendering, create a distance between the female lay penitent and her charismatic power.

In a series of miracle accounts that carry the reader through the end of the *vita*, Vito repeatedly describes the miraculous acts that emerge out of Umili-

---

78. Ibid., 106.

79. Ibid.

80. Ibid., 98.

81. Ibid.

82. Schuchman, "'Within the Walls of Paradise': Space and Community," 33.

83. Benvenuti Papi, "Umiliana dei Cerchi," 110–17.

84. For more on these communities of lay religious women (often called *Pinzochere*) in Florence, see Anna Benvenuti Papi, "Mendicant Friars and Female Pinzochere in Tuscany: From Social Marginality to Models of Sanctity," in *Women and Religion in Medieval and Renaissance Italy*, ed. Bornstein and Rusconi, 84–103.

ana's great piety and penitence but is careful to clarify that these are charismatic acts that are performed through Umiliana and because of her saintly merits. On one hand, this is a hagiographic trope: it is not the saint who performs holy acts but God using the saint as his intermediary or receptacle.[85] On the other hand, however, in Vito's text, such an emphasis contributes to the spiritual trajectory he is setting up for his lay saint: the more she progresses in her religious commitment, the more distant she becomes not only from the outside world but also from the charismatic power her extraordinary penitential life provides.

In one account, Vito describes how another lay religious woman, Gisla of Mugello, was bothered by neighbors making a racket as she sought to pray in her house. Gisla was ready to leave her house, Vito writes, "unless she could be liberated from these annoyances."[86] Umiliana's first response when she heard about Gisla's situation was to feel compassion for her. Umiliana's compassion, Vito makes clear, spurred God into action: the noise stopped.[87] On another occasion, Vito describes how this same Gisla was being induced by the devil "to live entirely alone in solitude"—something that, Vito points out in the next sentence, "is dangerous for women."[88] Gisla asked Umiliana for help. Umiliana "petitioned the Lord" on Gisla's behalf and the temptation waned.[89] In addition to emphasizing that it was Umiliana's compassion and piety that sparked God to perform these miracles, these episodes also convey the idea that the devotional life of a religious laywoman should take place within the confines of her home. In both accounts, the miracles keep Gisla from leaving her home—with Umiliana's piety spurring God into action, neither noise nor the devil can lead a religious laywoman out of her proper context.

When another female lay religious, who was living in a hermitage outside of Florence, came to Umiliana suffering from a broken arm that had begun to wither, Vito again describes Umiliana feeling "great compassion." Umiliana told the woman that she would ask God to lessen her weakness and pain. As Umiliana spoke, the woman's hand began to regain its strength.[90] In another account, one of Umiliana's own daughters had come to visit her mother but "was struck dumb" and "fell down as if dead" as soon as she entered her mother's room. Vito describes how Umiliana "began to nurse her sorrowfully, as is the way of mothers," but to no avail—the girl lay lifeless and cold on the

85. Robert Bartlett, *Why Can the Dead Do Such Great Things? Saints and Worshippers from the Martyrs to the Reformation* (Princeton: Princeton University Press, 2013), 336.

86. Webb, *Saints and Cities*, 113.

87. Ibid.

88. Ibid.

89. Ibid.

90. Ibid., 113–14.

floor. Umiliana finally began to pray in front of an image she had of the Virgin Mary, asking that her daughter be brought back to life. After finishing her prayers and making the sign of the cross over her daughter, "a wondrously beautiful boy" emerged from the panel. The boy approached the lifeless girl and also made the sign of the cross, causing her to sit up "fit and well," after which the boy vanished.[91] As is the case with so many of the miracles that Vito recounts, his description of this episode seems simultaneously to celebrate and limit Umiliana's religious powers. Her piety is so great that it brings about a divine vision—the boy emerges from the image of the Virgin. But it is not Umiliana's own signing of her daughter that brings about the miracle; only the boy, who represents the Christ Child, had the power to effect this moment of charismatic healing.

In other miracle accounts, Vito describes more moments of supernatural change that are inspired by but not performed by Umiliana. In one, Umiliana asked a maidservant to bring her water. It was Lent, and as Vito notes, Umiliana had given up wine. When she found that the servant had in fact brought her wine, Umiliana again asked for water. After watching the servant take what appeared to be water from the well, Umiliana again tasted wine.[92] Vito is quick to qualify the origin of this charismatic act. Umiliana, he writes, "was dumbfounded" by what had happened because "she thought herself unworthy of such a gift." Nevertheless, noting that "God had done this for her twice . . . she gave warm thanks to God, who had deigned to show her this marvel."[93] And finally, in another instance when Umiliana had again asked a servant for some water, she was accidentally struck on the head with the pitcher of water. The wound on her head became increasingly painful as the days progressed, and one day, on the way to church, Umiliana "imprinted the sign of the Cross" on the injury. After doing so she felt "a hand which made the sign of the Cross in a like fashion," causing the wound to open, and release "bloody pus." The mysterious hand then "anointed the wound as if with some smooth and sweet-smelling ointment," leaving Umiliana "at once healed" with no scar and pain-free.[94] Umiliana might have been the first to sign her wound, but its miraculous healing, Vito's recounting makes clear, was the work of an unnamed, but presumably divine, other.

The distance Vito creates between Umiliana and her miracles underlines the idea that it is not the holy laywoman who is performing these miracles, but God. The boy's and the mysterious hand's signing bring a girl back to life

---

91. Ibid., 127.
92. Ibid., 130–31.
93. Ibid.
94. Ibid., 131–32.

and heal Umiliana's wound. Umiliana's compassion spurs God into action on behalf of another lay religious woman being driven out of her home, and her petitions to God induce him to heal another laywoman. Finally, Umiliana offers thanks to God for turning her water into wine. In these descriptions of miracles, Vito presents a new strategy for controlling and containing claims of lay religious power. While in his canonization bull for Omobono of Cremona, Innocent had entirely de-emphasized living miracles—making no mention of them and only referring to one postmortem miracle—here Vito establishes a distance between the charismatic act and the lay saint.

Scholars have framed Vito's and the Franciscans' interest in Umiliana as an attempt not only to promote their own reputation within Florence but also to co-opt a growing cadre of independent female lay religious.[95] A crucial part of that co-option, I believe, was a reframing of the proper context and result of an ideal lay religious life. Umiliana's life trajectory offered those friars an amenable canvas on which to work. Although Umiliana may have at first lived a more active life, after she returned to her father's house and lost her dowry, her life became essentially one of enclosure.

Finally, in Umiliana, the Franciscans had an opportunity to construct an ideal female lay penitential life that looked quite similar to that of a nun. At the same time that Umiliana existed within a network of lay religious women, as the witness list at the beginning of her *vita* makes clear, the circumstances of her life kept her from wandering the city freely. Defrauded of her dowry, Umiliana's world shrank to her room at the top of her father's tower. Umiliana and her female companions were part of the same lay penitential movement that spurred Ubaldesca and Bona into action at the end of the twelfth century. By the middle of the thirteenth century, however, the Franciscans had essentially become the institutional church's official emblems of such a life. As a result, an ideal female lay life looks different through the lens of a mendicant hagiographer than it had through the lenses of the various priests and religious who had written about the Pisan laywomen. Vito makes clear that the end result of an ideal female lay penitential life is enclosure and containment—a trend that we do not see in the mendicant hagiographies produced for male lay saints at this time. Attempting to make sense of that gender discrepancy dominates much of the work of the reminder of this study. In order to prepare for that work, I want to turn to the cult of a female lay penitent who seemingly defied all of the norms not only for a laywoman but also for a lay saint.

---

95. See the work of Benvenuti Papi, esp. "Umiliana dei Cerchi" and "Una santa vedova," in "*In castro poenitentia*"; as well as "Mendicant Friars and Female Pinzochere."

Rose of Viterbo

The early history of Rose of Viterbo's cult offers another example of a female lay penitent who lived what was essentially an independent lay religious life in the midst of an extensive network of other female lay penitents. In the fragmentary remains of Rose of Viterbo's first *vita*, likely written within a year of her 1251 death, the reader hears not only about Rose's conversion to a committed penitential life, which took place while she was a teenager still living with her parents and outside of any ecclesiastical oversight or setting, but also about her dramatic devotional behavior in both the streets and churches of Viterbo following that conversion. Rose's identity as a young unmarried laywoman likely made the ad hoc and independent nature of the lay penitential life she had adopted all the more threatening to church authorities. While we have extant documents showing that within a year of Rose's death, the papacy had begun a canonization proceeding, it was not successful. The portrait of an independent and dramatic lay penitential life found in Rose's first *vita* was likely not something Rome was interested in promoting in the thirteenth century.

Today, Rose is often written about and celebrated as an early member of the Franciscans' Third Order.[96] Rose's Franciscan identity is absent from the extant thirteenth-century sources, however. Those sources include the fragmentary remains of an anonymous *vita*, probably written within a few years of her death; two bulls issued by Innocent IV in 1252 initiating a canonization inquiry; and finally, a series of three papal charters, issued by Innocent IV and Alexander IV between 1253 and 1255, responding to the complaints of the Damianites (the female Franciscan convent in Viterbo) that a local cleric was establishing a monastery dedicated to Rose too close to their own convent.[97] None of these thirteenth-century sources make any mention of a connection between Rose and the Friars Minor.

The Franciscan appropriation and reimagining of the circumstances of Rose's life began with Friar Bartholomew of Pisa's late fourteenth-century *De conformitate vitae Beati Francisci ad vitam Domini Iesu*, where Rose is listed among

---

96. For example, see Abate, *S. Rosa da Viterbo*; Fausta Casolini, "Rosa da Viterbo," in *Bibliotheca sanctorum*, vol. 11 (1968), 413–26; and Joan Weisenbeck and Marlene Weisenbeck, "Rose of Viterbo: Preacher and Reconciler," in *Clare of Assisi: A Medieval and Modern Woman*, ed. Ingrid Peterson (St. Bonaventure, NY: Franciscan Institute, 1996), 145–55; also note the title of Abate's study of Rose: *S. Rosa da Viterbo, terziaria francescana (1233–1251)*.

97. Modern editions of these sources can also be found in Abate, *S. Rosa da Viterbo*, 117–19 and 160–64.

other saintly "members" of the Franciscan Third Order.[98] A second anonymous *vita*, which survives in its entirety and was written sometime in the fifteenth century, also does not identify Rose as having had a formal connection to the Franciscan Order. This second *vita* does, however, report that the saint had once tried, without success, to join the Viterban Damianite community.[99] By the late fifteenth century, the "Franciscanization" of Rose that had begun in Bartholomew's catalogue had reached its peak. In a second canonization attempt launched in 1457 by Pope Calixtus III, Rose is explicitly identified as having been a member of the Franciscan Third Order.[100] However, like the first attempt, this one also ended without an official declaration of Rose's sanctity.

Instead of establishing a connection between Rose and the Franciscan Order, the remaining fragments of Rose's first *vita* describe a remarkably independent and female-dominated lay religious life that Rose created during a few momentous weeks in June 1250 and pursued over the remainder of that year. The first *vita* recounts this time in Rose's life in a manner that Rosa Mincuzzi has noted has a marked "simplicity in its concept and format," and Giuseppe Abate has characterized as constituting a "primitive document" or "straight biography."[101] In short, Rose's first *vita* is unusually free of hagiographic rhetoric. Thus, in addition to not placing Rose within a Franciscan context, this *vita* also frames Rose's spiritual environment solely in terms of family, neighborhood, and city, with no mention of her having received any ecclesiastical support, association, or supervision. Although we cannot know if the sections missing from this *vita* contained a rhetorical or institutional frame, in the fragments that do survive, the reader is given an account of Rose's experiences in 1250 that reads more like a series of eye-witness accounts than a carefully constructed piece of hagiography. In each of the episodes, the reader is given details about how Rose designed and lived a religious life outside of the institutional church, offering an extraordinary glimpse into the networks of female lay religious who were crafting their own devotional lives and religious communities—activities that we can imagine left the church and communal authorities nervous.

The *vita* begins by describing a severe illness that Rose survived and the resulting visions of the dead she received. The text's presentation of these dramatic events in Rose's life lacks the reflective elaboration so common in medieval hagiography. Once Rose's visions stopped, she had announced to her

98. Bartholomew of Pisa, *De conformitate vitae Beati Francisci ad vitam Domini Iesu*, in *Analecta Franciscana*, vol. 4 (Rome: Quaracchi, 1906), 360–62.

99. A modern edition of that *vita* can also be found in Abate, *S. Rosa da Viterbo*, 124–45.

100. Abate, *S. Rosa da Viterbo*, 147.

101. Mincuzzi, *Santa Rosa da Viterbo*, 22; and Abate, *S. Rosa da Viterbo*, 137.

mother her intention to renounce all of her possessions and had asked for Lady Sita to clothe her and cut her hair.[102] Rose's request for both a tunic and cord has led some scholars to wonder if Lady Sita was associated with Viterbo's mendicant community, although, again, there is no explicit mention of the Franciscans in the extant excerpts.[103] Rose countered Sita's reticence to follow her requests by noting that the Virgin Mary had told her that Sita should use the haircloth that Sita kept at the head of her bed.[104] Rose's knowledge of the contents of Sita's bed seems to have been enough to convince her to agree. The episode ends with Sita successfully encouraging Rose to allow her family to witness her impending investiture.[105]

The *vita* makes clear how both Rose's illness and subsequent visions precipitated her desire to make a public commitment to living a penitential life—renouncing "the things of this world" and adopting clothing as well as a haircut that would make visible to her community her new identity. In doing so, the text does not shy away from conveying the independent and ad hoc nature of this transformation. Rose's conversion to and investment in a penitential life takes place in her family home, solely in the presence of her mother and another laywoman. Abate has argued that the ceremony described in the first *vita* should be seen as a preliminary one. Rose's official association with the Franciscan order, in his estimation, would have been overseen, approved, and adjudicated by two Franciscan lay ministers (one male and one female) and more likely would have followed the scenario outlined in the second *vita*, where Rose's investiture into a penitential habit takes place within a church.[106] However, Mincuzzi has countered convincingly that there is nothing preliminary about Rose's experience as it is described in the first *vita*.[107] Once she had convinced Sita to invest her with the tunic and the cord and to give her a cleric's haircut, the *vita* immediately moves to recounting how Rose then asked her mother to wake all of the women of the neighborhood. When her mother protested that this would leave Rose by herself, Rose reassured her that in fact

---

102. *Rosa Vita I*, 3, 228.

103. See Mincuzzi, *Santa Rosa da Viterbo*, 44.

104. *Rosa Vita I*, 3, 228.

105. The *vita* also reports that Rose's mother had a bit of trepidation. It reports that she told Rose that she did not have a cord, to which Rose chided her, saying: "You don't have the cord of an ass?" The chapter concludes by noting that both Rose's mother and Sita began to do as the young virgin had ordered. *Rosa Vita I*, 3, 228: "Et ipsa domina Sita respondit, et dixit: 'Filia, permitte venire consanguineous tuos.' Et Virgo respondit: 'Beata Virgo Maria praecipit mihi, quod te istigem. Facias, quae tibi dixi.' Et mater dixit ipsi: 'Filia, non habeo chordulam.' Et ipsa respondit: 'Non habes unam chordam asini?' Et mater fecit sicut ei praeceperat. Tunc dicta domina Sita fecit quidquid ei praeceperat ipsa Virgo."

106. Abate, *S. Rosa da Viterbo*, 196.

107. Mincuzzi, *Santa Rosa da Viterbo*, 54–55.

she would not be alone, since the Holy Spirit was with her.[108] Just as we saw in Bona's *vitae*, Rose's first *vita* sees the presence of the Holy Spirit within this laywoman as marking the beginning of her committed religious life. Thus, the first *vita* makes clear that this was not a preliminary event, but rather, an independent religious ceremony. Rose had initiated, designed, and carried out her own rite to become a lay penitent.[109]

In addition to its direct, almost staccato style of narration, Rose's first *vita* is also extraordinary for its heavy reliance upon Rose's mother as primary witness to this laywoman's religious experiences.[110] Mincuzzi has noted the way in which the text's style of narration allows "an unexplored female universe to emerge" from these fragments.[111] That universe comes through most clearly in the episodes recounting what took place after Rose's mother had followed her daughter's commands and brought all of the neighborhood women to her house. Rose had arranged the women into a circle outside of her house, placed herself in the middle, and made her announcement that it was only she who could see the most beautiful bride of Christ, who had instructed her to make a circuit of the city's churches.[112]

The *vita* does not give us any sense of these women's reaction to Rose's claim, but in subsequent episodes it makes clear that they began to follow Rose on her city pilgrimage, frequently gathering at her house before and after these processions, to the dismay of Rose's father. The text describes Rose's father as alternating between begging Rose to stop her antics and threatening her with dire consequences if she did not. But to each of her father's threats, which included cutting off all of her hair or tying her up, Rose responded that she was not worried about such punishments, since, as she reasoned, Christ had suffered in a similar manner.[113] Rose told her father that if he were to allow her to continue on her religious path, Christ would associate him with the angels and saints in paradise—an appeal that seems to have worked.[114] The next lines of the *vita* describe Rose's father telling her, through his tears, that she should act with the blessing of God. With her father's blessing secured, Rose

---

108. *Rosa Vita I*, 4, 228. Mincuzzi sees such comments from Rose as conveying that a consecration and "transmission of the divine spirit" had already taken place; see Mincuzzi, *Santa Rosa da Viterbo*, 54–55.

109. Mincuzzi also points out that if we turn to look at the 1221 *Memoriale propositi*, which was used by Franciscan penitents until Pope Nicholas IV's *Supra montem* superseded that penitential rule, we also see how Rose does not follow that rule's "four elements of initiation, that is, the test, the investiture, the trial year and the profession," see Mincuzzi, *Santa Rosa da Viterbo*, 47.

110. Abate, *S. Rosa da Viterbo*, 142–44; and Mincuzzi, *Santa Rosa da Viterbo*, 22.

111. Mincuzzi, *Santa Rosa da Viterbo*, 55.

112. *Rosa Vita I*, 5, 228–29.

113. Ibid., 6, 229.

114. Ibid.

asked her parents, her aunt, a priest, Lady Sita, and anyone else who was with her at the time to bless her "in the name of the father, the Son, and the Holy Spirit."[115] The *vita* thus again presents Rose as having initiated, designed, and carried out a religious experience that was usually the purview of church authorities. Rose not only picked the people she wanted a blessing from but also—in the course of asking them for that blessing—essentially performed the blessing herself.

Not everyone in Rose's orbit was pleased with her behavior, however. After recounting how Rose had won over her father, the *vita* describes how one day Rose became inconsolable when she caught sight of a crucifix. After she had herself carried to an unidentified church, she began to pull out her hair, hit her face, and rip her clothes, and finally collapsed on the church floor, crying out, "Father, who crucified you?"[116] A man the *vita* only identifies as "Lord G." proceeded to drag Rose out of the church and back to her home, where, the *vita* notes she continued to grieve, enduring what the text describes as a three-day "martyrdom."[117] When Rose emerged from her martyrdom, she asked her mother to bring her a herb. After her mother returned with a bunch of mint, Rose instructed her to place it on Rose's chest. The *vita* goes on to describe how, after leaving the mint on her chest for a short while, Rose grabbed her mother by the hand, and told her to take care of that mint since Christ had not only blessed it while it lay on her chest but had also, in the process, blessed one side of their house, which Rose announced, was to continue on as her monastery.[118]

In the final fragments of the first *vita*, we hear about the trouble Rose's independent and dramatic religious life had brought to her family. After her three-day martyrdom, Rose wandered through Viterbo extolling the name of Christ and the Virgin Mary, behavior that scholars have concluded was likely seen as public preaching.[119] The city's *podestà*, who the text notes was loyal to Emperor Frederick II, first informed Rose's mother and then her father that such antics had earned the entire family exile from the city. When Rose's dis-

115. Ibid., 6, 229–30: "Et tunc beata Virgo dixit patri, matri, avunculae et presbytero, et aliis ibidem adstantibus secum, ac praefatae dominae Sitae: 'Benedicte me in nomine Patris et Filii et Spiritus Sancti.'"

116. Ibid., 7, 230: "Praeterea, cum tunc Dominus noster Iesus Christus in cruce eidem Virgini apparuerit, et ipsa Virgo incontinenti incoepit extrahere sibi capillos, et percutere se in facie, ac pannos sibi dividere; et plorabat cum magna devotione, et fecit se portari ad ecclesiam, et prostravit se ante Crucem, et dicebat ei plorando: 'Pater, quis te crucifixit.'"

117. Ibid.: "Et, dum ita plorabat, surrexit quidam dominus G, et traxit ipsam de ecclesia, et duxit ad domum suam. Quae Virgo, cum ducta esset ad domum, tribus diebus se martyravit, semper plorans."

118. Ibid., 8, 230.

119. Pryds, "Proclaiming Sanctity," 159.

traught father begged the Podestà to reconsider what was, in essence, a death sentence, given that it was the middle of winter and snowing heavily in the mountains and valleys surrounding the city, the Podestà responded that this was precisely why he was expelling them.[120] The final paragraphs of the first *vita* describe how Rose and her family sought refuge in surrounding towns, and how Rose received an angelic vision informing her of the imminent death of Emperor Frederick II. The *vita* abruptly ends after noting that Rose had received this vision on the very night that the emperor had died, as the news coming from Viterbo would later confirm.

In addition to this first *vita*, the thirteenth-century evidence for Rose and the beginning of her cult also includes two bulls issued by Pope Innocent IV launching a canonization inquiry as well as another series of papal bulls (three in all) that attempt to mediate a dispute between the priest at Santa Maria del Poggio (where Rose was first buried) and the Viterban Poor Clares. In the first of these sources, *In sanctis suis*, issued in November 1252, Innocent responded to the requests he had received from Viterbo's bishop, clergy, council, and people. The pope asked the Dominican prior of Santa Maria in Gradi and the archpriest of the church of San Sisto to collect and examine evidence documenting Rose's life and miracles for the purposes of a canonization inquiry.[121] Two days later, the pope sent a *forma interrogatorii* to Viterbo, stipulating the procedure for questioning the witnesses describing Rose's life and miracles.[122] These two bulls suggest both that there was an active cult dedicated to Rose in the year after her death and that the papacy saw such a cult as being worthy of investigation. Unfortunately, none of the documents collected and examined to aid this investigation have survived.

Might it therefore make more sense to think of the fragmentary remains of Rose's first *vita* not as a fully constructed piece of hagiography but rather as the witness accounts that were gathered for Rose's first canonization attempt? The first *vita* stands out not only for being the narrative source that is chronologically closest to Rose's actual lifetime but also for its distinctive tone. The direct and play-by-play nature of the narrative reads more like witness testimony than a full *vita*. If this hypothesis were to hold, Rose's first *vita* is a text similar to Bona of Pisa's B2, also likely a set of notes and witness accounts. And just as B2 presents a more charismatically active and aggressive portrait of Bona than later redactions would, we see Rose's first *vita* describing what

---

120. *Rosa Vita I*, 9, 231.

121. Abate, *S. Rosa da Viterbo*, 225–26.

122. Ibid., 226–27. On the new use of *forma interrogatorii* in the thirteenth century, see Vauchez, *Sainthood*, 25–52.

appears to be a laywoman fashioning a unique independent life as a committed penitent. As witness accounts, Rose's first *vita* does not try to make sense of, reconceive, or ultimately contain Rose's religious life but instead simply describes how she designed her own penitential ceremony, cobbled together a network of other urban laywomen, and wandered the city encouraging others to follow her on her spiritual journey. Looking at these fragments from this perspective, we can begin to craft our own narrative to explain why the canonization attempt launched by Pope Innocent IV a year after Rose's death did not succeed.

That narrative must take into account the three papal documents, produced between 1253 and 1255, that respond to what appears to be an ongoing battle between Peter "Capotosto," the priest of Rose's parish church, Santa Maria del Poggio, and the nearby convent of Santa Maria in Viterbo, the city's female Franciscan house. These papal letters (the first issued by Innocent IV, the second and third by Alexander IV) illustrate that in the first years after Rose's death, Capotosto was working to found a monastery in Rose's name to the dismay of the Damianites.[123] The letters note how Capotosto had ignored earlier injunctions against his founding of a monastery within the same neighborhood as Santa Maria. Moreover, while the first two letters call on the prior of the church of San Matteo in Viterbo to get Capotosto to adhere to this earlier injunction, the final letter asks the bishop of Viterbo to end this dispute. The letters demonstrate that the original injunction not only forbade the creation of a new structure but also the use of an existing structure as a monastery. The only direct reference to Rose in these documents comes in the final letter. Here, Alexander IV noted that since the San Matteo prior had not followed the earlier papal directives to stop Capotosto, he was turning to the bishop of Viterbo, who was ordered to see to it that the "house" in which Capotosto had gathered "a group of religious women" and was calling "the Monastery of Saint Rose" be destroyed.[124]

It seems likely that Capotosto had established a convent dedicated to Rose in her family's home. Rose, as the first *vita* notes, had reported to her mother that Christ had blessed one part of her house specifically so it could become a monastery. Regardless of where this monastery was located, these thirteenth-century sources suggest several conclusions about Rose's early cult. To begin with, in the first years after her death a secular cleric from Rose's parish church

---

123. Abate has also transcribed and edited these documents; see his *S. Rosa da Viterbo*, 270–273.

124. Ibid., 271: "Petrus dictus Caputosto, presbyter Viterbien, in quadam domo, quam infra praedictum obtinet et quam Monasterium Sanctae Rosae nominat, quasdam mulieres religiosas nititur congregare in dictarum Abbatissae et Conventus praejudicium et gravamen, eodem Priore in executione mandati nostri procedere negligente . . . mandamus, quatenus dictam domum omnino demoliri faciens, procedas in aliis supradictis, juxta directarum ad eumdem Priorem continentiam litterarum."

was managing her cult. In addition, that cleric had gathered together other laywomen to form a monastery dedicated to Rose. Moreover, Rose's cult had caught enough of the interest of the papacy to warrant the launching of a canonization inquiry. And finally, Viterbo's female Franciscan community saw this new cult (and especially its manifestation in the construction of a new monastery) as significant competition.

By the fourteenth century, however, any tension between those supporting Rose's cult and those favoring the city's Damianites had seemingly disappeared. Rose's body now lay with the Poor Clares at Santa Maria. In what scholars generally refer to as Rose's second *vita*, produced in the fifteenth century, either before or in conjunction with Pope Callixtus III's canonization inquiry, we find an explanation for how Rose's body ended up with the Franciscans.[125] While Rose was still alive and living in her father's house, she had gone to Santa Maria and asked to be admitted. Although the abbess claimed that the monastery was full, Rose responded that she knew that was not true. In fact, she added, she knew that the sisters did not want her because they despised her.[126] Nevertheless, Rose said, again prophesizing, that while they might not want her living body, she knew that they would be glad to receive her corpse.[127] The second *vita* then turns to describing Rose's death and the fact that she was buried in the church of Santa Maria del Poggio, where her body would remain for eighteen months. After noting that during those months many miracles took place at Rose's tomb, the second *vita* claims that, thereafter, Rose began to appear to Pope Alexander IV in a series of visions, imploring him to move her body to the Damianite convent. After the third vision, Alexander gave in, and with the help of four cardinals moved Rose's body to Santa Maria.[128] While the second *vita* presents Alexander's decision to move Rose's body as a means to demonstrate the fulfillment of Rose's prophecy, it also underscores a connection that, by the fifteenth century, the Franciscan Order was aiming to establish between themselves and Rose's cult.

The extant thirteenth-century evidence suggests some alternate conclusions, however. Alexander's decision to move Rose's body might have been motivated instead by concern about the possible popular response to his order that her monastery, which was likely her former house, be destroyed. Moving Rose's body to Santa Maria also offered a means to end the competition between the two houses. In other words, in one move, Alexander could placate

---

125. Abate has also transcribed and edited this *vita*; see ibid., 232–53.
126. *Rosa Vita II*, 12, 243–44.
127. Ibid., 12, 244.
128. Ibid., 12, 244–45.

both Rose's devotees (by placing her remains in an exalted home) and the city's Poor Clares (by removing the competition represented by a monastery dedicated to new popular saint).[129]

As is true of much of the work on thirteenth-century religious laywomen—but not religious laymen—the question of institutional status has loomed large in the scholarly literature on Rose. Such questions regarding Rose, I believe, have been motivated more by the friars' efforts beginning in the late fourteenth century to connect her history to the development of the Franciscan Third Order than by the actual references to Rose and the friars found in any thirteenth-century sources.[130] These earlier sources either make no mention of an association between Rose and the Viterban Franciscans, or suggest tension between Viterbo's female Franciscan community and Rose's nascent cult and monastic institution. Instead of coming out of a place of genuine devotion, the Franciscans' interest in Rose seems more likely to have originated from the need to stop her cult from siphoning off resources from their own convent. Rose's body may have ended up in a female Franciscan convent, but as counter-intuitive as it might seem, this does not stand as clear evidence that the order was interested in promoting her cult in the mid to late thirteenth century.

We can make sense of the complexity of Rose's early cult if we keep in mind that Rose embodied a side of the lay penitential movement that church authorities were increasingly seeking to control and redefine. Not only was she an independent lay penitent, without any formal connection to a religious order, but she was also a woman. The information the first *vita* gives us about how informal, ad hoc, and independently designed Rose's initiation ceremony into a committed penitential life was makes clear the danger she represented. Rose orchestrated her own induction ceremony, complete with a tunic, a cord, and a haircut "like a cleric's." She had it performed by another laywoman, and gathered together a community of other Viterban women, who first assembled at her house and then followed her in her processions through the streets. Although scholars have commented upon the fact that this first (as well as the second) *vita* present Rose preaching in the streets of Viterbo, thus complicating

---

129. The transfer of Rose's body to Viterbo's Damianite convent within a decade of her death seems more to reflect a settlement in the dispute between Santa Maria del Poggio's priest and the city's Poor Clares than it does a Franciscan-led cult since there is no evidence that the friars promoted Rose before the fourteenth century; see Mincuzzi, "Santa Rosa da Viterbo," 7–20.

130. The exception here is Stanislao da Campagnola, who has argued that Rose was one of many women adopting independent lay religious lives that were only later appropriated by the Franciscans; see his "L'Ordine della penitenza nelle Cronache del'200," in *L'Ordine della penitenza di S. Francesco d'Assisi nel XIII secolo*, ed. O. Schmuki (Rome: Istituto Storico dei Cappuccini, 1973); cited in Mincuzzi, "Santa Rosa da Viterbo," 45, 117.

our understanding of the on-the-ground reality of bans against both lay people and women preaching, I would argue that even more startling is the clear independence of Rose's religious life.[131] Thus, even though Ranieri of Pisa might have been depicted as leading a religious life that functioned as a critique of the present state of the church, his cult still made clear that he wanted to work within and heal such an institutional structure. In Rose's first *vita*, by contrast, we see a committed lay penitential life that requires no ecclesiastical oversight. It is Rose who asks not only her parents but also a priest as well as others to bless her; it is Rose who directs her penitential investment ceremony; and it is Rose who leads others on a procession through the city and to various churches.

The first *vita* also illustrates that her behavior worried Viterbo's communal government. After the death of Frederick II and the return of both Rose's family and a Guelf government to Viterbo, we can imagine that the papacy had some interest in her cult. After all, Innocent III had used his interest in another pious layman to support Cremona's embrace of a Guelf-allied government, so it should come as no surprise that Innocent IV wanted to reap the same kinds of rewards in Viterbo from canonizing one of its contemporaries. But we must imagine that, faced with the information provided in the first *vita* (which we might more productively think of as notes made from witness accounts), the papacy found Rose too difficult, too independent, and ultimately too lay and female to support her cult. All that would change by the late fourteenth century, when the Franciscans had possession of her body and her second *vita* had reimagined those early ceremonies as having taken place within churches. Once Rose's body was resting within the Franciscan's convent in Viterbo, the independent aspect of her identity was dissolving; she belonged to the Franciscans. By the time she appeared in Bartholomew of Pisa's list of saintly Franciscan Tertiaries, Rose was an independent lay penitent no more.

In his study of Bona of Pisa's complex thirteenth-century hagiographic corpus, Zaccagnini has noted that it would be a mistake to label this laywoman's conversations with and visions of Christ and his companions as mystical dialogues.[132] Rather, Zaccagnini argues, these holy apparitions function as Bona's spiritual directors, offering her advice and keeping her company on her many pilgrimages and adventures. If we extend Zaccagnini's point, we can begin

---

131. See Pryds, "Proclaiming Sanctity."

132. Zaccagnini has noted the extent to which Bona's frequent visions of and conversations with Christ, Saint James, and the Virgin Mary and her two sisters has more of the flavor of a regular conversation than a mystical encounter. The *vitae* stress the extent to which Bona simply lives within the constant presence of God. Zaccagnini, *La tradizione agiografica*, 79.

to see the ways in which changes over the thirteenth century in the kinds of visionary activity ascribed to laywomen correspond to changes in ideals of female lay sanctity. At the same time that Bona's frequent visions of Christ and his companions punctuate the major moments of her religious life, they are not interactions that bring the reader into the saint's interior reality. By the late thirteenth century, once the mendicants had assumed guardianship over lay penitents, laywomen's visions had a resolutely internal focus. As we shall see in the *vitae* of Margaret of Cortona, Vanna of Orvieto, and Margaret of Città di Castello (shown, too, in the *vitae* of countless fourteenth-century female saints that are outside of the scope of this study), visions of Christ became a means of detailing a lay saint's internal reality—of describing the nature, extent, and progress of her spiritual life. We can see the very beginnings of this change in Vito da Cortona's *vita* of Umiliana de' Cerchi. In Vito's hands, Umiliana's sanctity is revealed in her growth from an active lay saint to a contemplative one, a transition that quite literally replaces the action of urban charity with a robust, but largely cloistered visionary life.

By contrast, Bona's conversations with Christ and his holy companions do not give the reader any sense of her internal spiritual state. Rather, they seem aimed at demonstrating the ways in which she was in the constant presence of Christ and his holy companions as she freely moved from one religious institution to the other and set off on one pilgrimage after the next. Instead of keeping her contained within her head and body, as I have shown Umiliana's visions ultimately do, Bona's visions grease the wheels of her independence. We also hear very little about Rose of Viterbo's visionary life in her first *vita*. Rose, like Bona, also constructed her committed lay religious life as an active urban one, but had a cult that was limited in its reach in the generation after her death precisely because she did not have the protection and promotion an institutional association would offer. The author of Rose's *vita* makes many references to what was clearly a potent visionary life. However, he (or she) does little with those experiences beyond presenting them in rather straightforward descriptions. Although this text's lack of a rhetorical frame suggests that it was more likely the notes of eye-witnesses to Rose's short but dramatic life than a fully formed piece of hagiography, it still seems significant that whoever first composed the descriptions of Rose's visionary life did not see them as a means for framing the content and shape of her sanctity. As we shall see in subsequent chapters, that would become increasingly rare in the cults of female lay saints as the mendicants became the main guardians of lay penitents and the patrons of lay saints. But before we see the change brought by the mendicants, we must first turn to the rise of a cult that seemingly broke all of the rules we have just identified for female lay saint: the cult dedicated to Zita of Lucca.

CHAPTER 5

Zita of Lucca
The Outlier

In 1308, Lucca's new *popolo*-dominated government, made up largely of the city's wealthiest merchants and artisans, added April 27, the feast day of the city's most famous domestic servant, Zita, to a long list of civic holidays.[1] It is likely that some of those advocating for the celebration of this day as a public holiday had known Zita personally. Whether they had seen her walk from her employer's house to the church of San Frediano, had stood next to her there while she prayed, had benefited from her frequent acts of civic charity, or had gathered together after her death, hoping to take away a piece of her clothing for themselves, these Lucchese were adding a contemporary to the ranks of civic saints. Like so many other communes in late medieval northern and central Italy, Lucca was turning the popular cult of a recently deceased layperson into a communal cult.[2]

---

1. For general scholarship on Zita, see Benvenuti Papi, *"In castro poenitentiae,"* 263–303; Michael Goodich, "Ancilla Dei: The Servant as Saint in the Late Middle Ages," in *Women of the Medieval World: Essays in Honor of John H. Mundy*, ed. Julius Kirshner and Suzanne F. Wemple (Oxford: Basil Blackwell, 1985), 119–36; and Vauchez, *Sainthood*, 210, 240–41, 244, and 421. Also, see F. P. Lusio, "L'anziano di S. Zita," in *Miscellanea lucchese di studi storici e letterari in memoria di Salvatore Bongi* (Lucca: Scuola Tipografica Artigianelli, 1931), 61–91; Americo Guerra, *Istoria della vita di Santa Zita vergine lucchese narrata secondo i documenti contemporanei* (Lucca: S. Paolino, 1875).

2. For a general history of Lucca in the Middle Ages, see Girolamo Tommasi, *Sommario della storia di Lucca dall'anno MIV all'anno MDCC* (Florence: G. P. Vieusseux, 1847); for thirteenth-century Lucca, see Giuseppe Matraia, *Lucca nel milleduecento* (1843; Lucca: M. Pacini Fazzi, 1983); for

Zita was not a native of the city that came to claim her as a patron but had arrived in Lucca from Monsagrati (a village in the surrounding countryside) at the age of twelve to work as a domestic servant for the Fatinelli, one of the city's leading merchant families. A *vita*, most likely written by a canon from her neighborhood church, San Frediano, within a decade of her death, reports that Zita had gained a reputation not only as a hardworking and loyal servant but also as a dedicated penitent. Zita's sanctity, the *vita* argues, derived in large part from her ability to serve her employers even though she spent much of her time rapt in prayer, making pilgrimages to shrines and churches outside of Lucca, and caring for the poor of her adopted city. By the end of her life, the constant care and concern Zita took to feed, shelter, and succor the poor and needy of Lucca, and the miracles that often resulted from that charity work, had won her a large following. So devoted to Zita were the Lucchese that, as her *vita* reports, when the news of her death spread through the city, a large crowd gathered in the square outside of San Frediano where her body lay, clamoring to touch her corpse or rip off a piece of her clothing for themselves.

The earliest source for the existence of Zita's cult is a miracle collection that was begun on April 28, 1278, the day after Zita's death. This collection survives in only one manuscript, which was produced in the fourteenth century and once belonged to Zita's employers, the Fatinelli family. This same manuscript contains the earliest copy of her *vita*, which reports that it was the notary Fatinello di Migliore (not a member of the Fatinelli family for whom Zita worked) who had transcribed 150 accounts of miracles performed at Zita's tomb.[3] Even though it is likely that Fatinello collected these accounts to one

---

fourteenth-century Lucca, see Louis Green, *Castruccio Castracani: A Study on the Origins and Character of a Fourteenth-Century Italian Despotism* (Oxford: Clarendon Press, 1986); Christine Meek, *The Commune of Lucca under Pisan Rule, 1342–1369* (Cambridge, MA: Medieval Academy of America, 1980); and Meek, *Lucca 1369–1400: Politics and Society in an Early Renaissance City-State* (Oxford: Oxford University Press, 1978).

3. Biblioteca Statale di Lucca, MS 3459. Unfortunately, this manuscript only contains 99 of the 150 miracles mentioned in the *vita*; for more on the Fatinelli copy, see Marco Paoli, *Arte e committenza privata a Lucca nel trecento e nel quattrocento: Produzione artistica e cultura libraria* (Lucca: M. Pacini Fazzi, 1986), 92–93. A transcription of Zita's *vita* as well as the miracle collection was prepared by Daniel Papebroch in 1673: *AASS*, April III, 502–32 [hereafter *De S. Zita*] (*BHL* 9019). Papebroch's text largely relies on a copy of the *vita* from the Tuscan monastery of Camaldoli (now held in Florence, Biblioteca Nazionale Centrale, Conventi Soppressi G.5, 1212, ff. 193–200v). Although he claims to have checked that copy with the earliest copy of the *vita* made for the Fatinelli family, Diana Webb has noted that his edition of the *vita* includes several transcription errors; see the introduction to her translation of the Lucca manuscript in her *Saints and Cities*, 160–90. Since the Bollandists' *AASS* text is the only published version of the Latin *vita*, I will draw on it for this chapter, but check it against Webb's translation. In my own translations, I have consulted Webb's work but unless otherwise noted, the translations that follow are my own.

day aid a canonization inquiry, there is no indication that such an inquiry was taken up by Rome until the late seventeenth century.[4] For at least three centuries, therefore, devotion to Zita remained a local Lucchese affair.

In the eighteenth century, the Lucchese priest and scholar Bartolommeo Fioriti argued that Iacopo, the prior of San Frediano during Zita's life, was the most likely author of her *vita*.[5] As the guardians of Zita's tomb and witnesses to almost all of her miracles, the San Frediano canons were her earliest patrons. Their support was not immediate, however. The *vita* reports that even though Zita's tomb began to emit a "tremendous fragrance," Prior Iacopo and his canons remained skeptical and held off promoting her cult, reasoning that "if the whole business was ill-founded and of merely human origin," it would soon end, but, if of divine origin, "no mortal would be able to resist it."[6] When her body appeared to resist decay and a "salutary liquid" began to seep from it, Iacopo and the canons were convinced and joined a host of other religious and communal authorities flocking to her tomb in San Frediano.[7]

---

4. Zita was canonized in 1696: see Vatican City, Archivio Segreto Vaticano (hereafter ASV), *Riti*, Proc. 1315. The canonization proceedings refer to medieval testamentary donations made both by various Lucchese to honor Zita's memory and by her employers, the Fatinelli family, to build a chapel in San Frediano to hold her body. These testamentary documents are, to my knowledge, no longer extant.

5. For example, see Bartolommeo Fioriti, *Vita, virtu', e miracoli di Santa Zita vergine lucchese* (Lucca, 1752), xiii; and Guerra, *Istoria*, 17. The *vita*'s author notes that even though Zita's life had not yet been publicly promoted or preached, each year more and more people gathered at her tomb on her feast day, suggesting that he was writing at least a few years after her 1278 death; see *De S. Zita*, 513. Webb has posited that the text might have been written in 1286 when the canons of San Frediano began a protracted battle with the Lucchese Franciscans over burial rights. She argues that the San Frediano canons may have used the *vita* to support Zita's burgeoning cult, giving their parishioners incentive to be buried at their parish church rather than in one of the increasingly popular mendicant churches; see *Saints and Cities*, 161–62. Guerra disagrees with Fioriti, claiming that Iacopo was already dead by the time of Zita's death. A number of charters produced in response to a struggle over burial rights between San Frediano and the Lucchese Franciscans show that Prior Iacopo was alive until at least 1291, see *Le pergamene del convento di S. Francesco in Lucca (sec. XII–XIX)*, ed. Vito Tirelli and Matilde Tirelli Carli (Rome: Ministero per i Beni Culturali e Ambientali . . . , 1993), 277–79. While the speculation does not seem outlandish, it is curious that the text refers to Prior Iacopo several times in the third person.

6. *De S. Zita*, 513: "Jacobus, Prior praefatae ecclesiae, suique Fratres, nullam vel modicam sanctitati hujus fidem accommodantes (quamvis magnae viri religionis existerent) praehabito prudentium et etiam religiosorum virorum, tam Praedicatorum quam Minorum Ordinis Fratum, consilio et collatione concordi, in lapideo sarcophago fecerunt concludi venerandum ejus corpus, redolens immensi odoris multa fragrantia, exspectantes de concordi praedictorum consilio rei exitum: ut videlicet, si opus idem foret fictitium et dumtaxat humanum, cito deficeret; si vero esset divinum et de providentia divina procederet, nemo mortalium posset illi resistere, sed invito omni contradictore immensum prosperaretur et cresceret: sicut de die in diem publice cernitur adimpletum." This is Webb's translation; see Webb, *Saints and Cities*, 187.

7. *De S. Zita*, 513: "Sicut revera testari possunt plures ex S.R.E. Cardinalibus, ac etiam Archiepiscopis, Episcopis et aliis venerabilibus viris quamplurimis, ex diversis partibus adventantibus, qui viderunt; nec non Principum secularium, Baronum ac Militum, et grandis popularium multitudo,

Despite such initial doubts, the author of the *vita* presents Zita as "the perfect laywoman," whom he deemed "worthy of imitation not only by other laypeople, but also by ecclesiastical persons, including nuns and regulars."[8] Although he states that all should follow Zita's example, his convoluted and highly rhetorical writing style was likely hard for anyone except the most educated to follow. We might wonder if the *vita*'s stylized nature is the result of its author's attempt to craft a narrative that could serve such a mixed audience, appealing at once to the particular intellectual interests of his fellow canons, as well as to a broader religious audience and an uneducated lay population.[9]

In contrast to the *vitae* of so many of the other lay saints venerated in the Italian communes, Zita's *vita* makes no reference to a conversion experience. The *vita* suggests that Zita's saintly behavior derived, in part, from her particularly pious family.[10] With no conversion experience to narrate, Zita's *vita* maintains a decidedly impersonal tone. The *vita*'s author presents Zita in a similarly unspecified manner. As the text is narrated overwhelmingly in the third person, the reader gets only the most cursory examples of Zita's direct speech, a stark contrast to the many reports of Rose of Viterbo's conversations with her mother and father in her first *vita*. Moreover, although the devotional rou-

---

occurrentium diversis temporibus: qui corporeis oculis conspexerunt, dum pia devotione ad venerationem ejus, citra tamen juris prohibitionem, saepius occurrerunt, et occurrere quotidie non desistunt; maxime autem ii, qui in suis necessitatibus ejus subventiones et beneficia persenserunt: quibus in maris terraeque periculis ad opitulandum adstitit devotius invocata." The incorruptibility, sweet smells, and oozing of liquids from saints' corpses was a common theme in medieval hagiography. On these phenomena, see Herbert Thurston, *The Physical Phenomena of Mysticism*, ed. J. H. Crehan (Chicago: H. Regnery, 1952), 233–82; Michel Bouvier, "De l'incorruptibilité des corps saints," in *Les miracles, miroirs des corps*, ed. Jacques Gélis and Odile Redon (Paris: Presses et Publications de l'Université de Paris-VIII, 1983), 193–221; Caroline Walker Bynum, *The Resurrection of the Body in Western Christianity, 300–1336* (New York: Columbia University Press, 1995), 206–12 and 221–24; and Bynum, "Bodily Miracles and the Resurrection of the Body in the High Middle Ages," in *Belief in History: Innovative Approaches to European and American Religion*, ed. Thomas Kselman (Notre Dame, IN: University of Notre Dame Press, 1991), 70.

8. *De S. Zita*, 510: "O quam perfectissima feminini sexus laica, nedum a quibuslibet secularibus, nec non et viris ecclesiasticis, sed etiam ab ipsis Regularibus et Sanctimonialibus imitanda!"

9. Webb has noted that its author clearly had access to the works of Gregory the Great, in particular, the *Moralia in Job* and the *Regula pastoralis*, both of which he quotes extensively but does not identify; see Webb, *Saints and Cities*, 191. Furthermore, the writings of Gregory, along with those of other Church Fathers, were central to the clerical reform movement in the eleventh and twelfth centuries and would certainly have been in heavy use at San Frediano. On this point, see Caroline Walker Bynum, *Jesus as Mother: Studies in the Spirituality of the High Middle Ages* (Berkeley: University of California Press, 1982), 47 and 53; and Charles Dereine, "Chanoines," in *Dictionnaire d'histoire et de géographie ecclésiastiques*, vol. 12 (Turnhout: Brepols, 1953), 377–78.

10. *De S. Zita*, 505. The Monsagrati family, the text points out, already had two members with saintly reputations: Zita's sister, Margherita, and her maternal uncle, Graziano, were both venerated in and around their rural village after they died.

tine described in Zita's *vita* suggests that she was a penitent, the text gives no indication that she followed a particular penitential rule or reported to a confessor. And finally, there is no suggestion in the text that its author ever talked with Zita about her religious experiences for the purpose of composing a written account—another trait that would become so common in the *vitae* of late thirteenth- and fourteenth-century Italian holy women.[11]

While several aspects of Zita's life and early cult do not fit into the trajectory of female lay saints' cults that we have studied thus far (or for that matter into the trajectory of later cults dedicated to laywomen), they do mirror certain themes in the cults of thirteenth-century laymen. First, the positive attitude we find in Zita's *vita* toward her work as a domestic servant fits what we have seen in the late thirteenth-century *vitae* of Omobono of Cremona, Facio of Cremona, and Pier "Pettinaio" of Siena. As *popolo* governments rose to power and became patrons of contemporary lay saints, lay work was no longer presented as something that inhibited a committed lay religious life, but rather as an endeavor that could enhance it. Second, Zita's dedication to providing charity to her fellow Lucchese underscores the primary place such work had assumed in defining an ideal lay religious life by the thirteenth century. Zita, unlike so many of the other female lay saints I have presented, was not connected either informally or formally with a mendicant order, although she did, like so many of the commune's male lay saints, have a strong parochial affiliation: San Frediano was her parish church. Thus, the roving and independent acts of charity that Zita performs for her fellow Lucchese ought to remind us more of communal Italy's male lay saints than its female ones. And third, the frenzy the Lucchese showed at Zita's death speaks to how primed that population was to see this pious laywoman as a new saint—an immediate popular reaction that we saw emphasized in the early cults of both Facio and Pier "Pettinaio."

Why was Zita, an unmarried laywoman, able to garner a civic cult on par with the cults awarded to laymen in the thirteenth century? Why did her civic cult grow in the generation after her death, while the cult of another mid thirteenth-century unmarried laywoman—Rose of Viterbo—did not? The answer, I will argue, can be found in a mixture of context and construction. On the one hand, the political context influencing the rising power of both Lucca's *popolo* government and the San Frediano canons helps to explain why a domestic servant like Zita, who worshipped at San Frediano, was the ideal candidate to be Lucca's newest patron saint. On the other hand, Zita's role as the

---

11. I am thinking here in particular of the *Legenda* of Margaret of Cortona, the *Memorial* of Angela of Foligno, and the *Legenda maior* of Catherine of Siena.

perfect candidate came as the result of the *vita*'s construction of her as an out-lier among the general lay population, and most importantly, among pious laywomen. Thus, Zita is not simply a pious parishioner as well as an attentive and obedient worker, but a model of lay religious restraint and practicality. Zita, as the *vita*'s author will repeatedly reiterate, knew the proper times, places, and manner for expressing her penitential commitment and zeal. In short, Zita was an anomaly, bucking all expectations about the behavior of a devout laywoman. Zita may have been a woman, but as the *vita* will constantly remind its readers, she did not act like one.

Given Zita's position as the outlier, it is ironic that she is also the lay saint in whose cult we see the most conservative and prescriptive definition of an ideal lay life. By locating Zita's sanctity in her ability to break out of various social, gender, and religious norms, the author of her *vita* ultimately reaffirms the existence and relevance of those roles. In the author's construction of Zita as an ideal laywoman, lay worker, and lay penitent, we can see the extent to which the promotion of contemporary lay sanctity could function to exert control over an ever growing and changing lay religious life. That construction also portrays Zita's sanctity as sanctioning the economic and social disparities of the commune. While Zita's concern for the throngs of hungry people who gathered outside of her employer's house, the poor who shivered in the winter outside of her neighborhood church, and the prostitutes who had nowhere to sleep might shine a light on the harsh conditions of city life, the miracles she performed in response to those situations produced practical solutions that in the end obscured the origins and blame for such problems. As a miracle worker, Zita does more to maintain the status quo than she does to articulate the charismatic powers of a holy laywoman.

The Pillars of a Holy Lay Life

Much of Zita's *vita* concentrates on the relationships Zita formed with her employers as well as the needy of Lucca. The author uses his exploration of those two relationships to emphasize how Zita's commitment to work—whether as a domestic servant, penitent, or charity provider—led to her sanctity. In effect, Zita's *vita* argues that her sanctity evolved out of an ability to overcome the limitations inherent in the life of a poor laywoman. As the text repeatedly demonstrates, Zita's energy, hard work, and courage allowed her to transform seeming impediments on the path to becoming a holy woman into devotional and charitable opportunities. No matter how much work she had in seeing to the needs of the Fatinelli family, Zita always had the time and energy to maintain an extensive routine of pilgrimage, penitence, prayer, and charity work. Conversely, no matter how rigorous her devotional activities may have been, they never kept her from fulfilling both her domestic and charitable duties.

Such a portrait of lay sanctity keeps Zita's early cult from making the kind of charismatic claims that were made in Ranieri of Pisa's cult. Zita's penitential commitment does not endow her with religious powers or gifts that could rival those of a priest. Moreover, unlike Rose of Viterbo, Zita's religious life remained firmly anchored within a social and ecclesiastical hierarchy. The miracles ascribed to Zita during her lifetime all take place either as she embarked on one of her many pilgrimages, adhered to her rigorous schedule of prayer, or handed out charity to her fellow Lucchese. Zita was, in sum, a lay saint in line with Innocent III's model of lay sanctity.

And yet, although the *vita* focuses on the ways in which each of Zita's devotional activities kept her firmly rooted in and concerned with the lay world, it also presents the miracles she performed while attending to that world as key evidence for her sanctity. In particular, Zita's *vita* celebrates her for gaining access into churches, onto routes, and through gates where she was at first blocked. It points to her ability to feed the poor through a variety of food multiplication miracles. And finally, the text highlights how in Zita's more dramatic moments of prayer, when she experienced miraculous visions, her ecstasies were ultimately private and controlled. Thus, in Zita's *vita*, the miracles of a living lay saint share a theme: they illuminate the extent to which Zita was unlike other members of the laity, and unlike other religious laywomen. Zita's miraculous acts repeatedly convey that this laywoman could do what was normally beyond the reach and against the nature of a poor but pious laywoman.

Pilgrimage

In the *vita*'s pilgrimage stories, the author draws the reader's attention to Zita's physical capability, overlooking any details about the internal spiritual life that precipitated these trips. To that end, in each of the recounted episodes, the reader learns more about the harrowing journeys to and from various churches than about what took place once Zita reached her destinations. In the text's first pilgrimage account, we hear about how Zita set off with a family companion—presumably another household servant—to visit the churches of S. Jacopo in Podio and S. Pier a Grado, both within the Pisan *contado*.[12] The

---

12. *De S. Zita*, 507. We might wonder about the extent to which Zita was imitating Ubaldesca or Bona of Pisa, both of whom are described in their *vitae* as having taken pilgrimages to these churches.

companion returned to Lucca after having visited the church of S. Jacopo. But Zita, refusing to leave unfinished what she had set out to achieve, continued on through Pisa toward the shore to S. Pier a Grado, the church built on the land where Peter was said to have once landed and where Ubaldesca of Pisa had turned water into wine for a thirsty pilgrim.[13] Even though the author makes clear how determined Zita had been to reach the church, he gives no information about what she did there and immediately turns to describing Zita's harrowing return home. On this journey, Zita refused offers of hospitality from those worried at seeing a woman walking alone at night. Exhausted and weak from the fasting that had accompanied her pilgrimage, she fainted when she finally reached the summit of Monte Pisano (about halfway back to Lucca). When Zita woke, she saw the Virgin Mary standing next to her with an outstretched hand, ready to lead her home. Energized by the sight of the Virgin, Zita accompanied her back to Lucca over a bridge where the two encountered gates that, although "according to custom [they] were bolted and locked," spontaneously opened to welcome them back into the city.[14]

In the *vita*'s descriptions of pilgrimages to churches closer to Lucca, the journey also remains the focus. The reader is told how one Saturday night Zita made her way to the church of Sant' Angelo in Monte later than usual, her domestic duties having kept her at the Fatinelli house. Before long, Zita found herself walking in the dark only a mile into the six-mile journey.[15] And, once again, as a woman alone at night on a rural road, her presence merited comment. A man passing her on horseback chided her for being out by herself at such an hour. In one of the few examples of Zita's direct speech in the *vita*, the author writes that she told the man to continue on his own way without worry for her since, "Christ leads me unharmed."[16] When the man arrived at the gate of Sant' Angelo and saw Zita praying there, having beaten him to the church even though he was on horseback and she was on foot, the *vita* reports

---

13. Ibid.

14. Ibid., 507–8: "Ad vocem cujus gratissimam Zita, non solum imperterrita mansit; sed exiliens, pio ac dulci famine, tantam fortitudinem, securitatem et confortationem recepit, quod omnis debilitas omnisque lassitude famis et sitis evanuit, et respondit continuo: Libenter: volo venire: eamus pariter. Dum igitur pariter commeantes pervenissent ad pontem tectum circa mediam noctem; ecce janua pontis, quae more solito clausa et firmata erat, ultro aperta est eis: quibus ingressis, per se iterum clausa fuit et obserata. Demum venientes ad portum civitatis, invenerunt eam similiter diligenter ferreis seris firmatam: quae modo simili in conspectu illarum seipsam patefecit in ictu oculi, liberum utrique prebens ingressum."

15. Ibid., 508.

16. Ibid.: "Qui dum cerneret eam, pedetentim se gressu raro et debili praecedentem, exorsus inquit: Quo, mulier stolida, pergis hac hora tardissima? te noctis jam tenebrae circumdantes in errorem sunt noxiam perducturae. Illa vero acsi nil penderet, respondit humiliter: Itote viam vestram, me Christus perducet incolumem."

that he began to imagine that she had been carried to the church by angels. When he asked her how she had managed to get to the church so quickly, the *vita* reports that Zita quoted Job, saying: "As it hath pleased the Lord, so it is done."[17] Zita, the *vita* makes clear, was simply following God's commands.

In the *vita's* final pilgrimage story, the reader is given a brief glimpse of what Zita did inside the churches to which she had undertaken such difficult journeys. In this account, we again hear how insistent Zita was to make her journey. Zita was on her way to the church dedicated to the Magdalene in Crebaria on that saint's feast day and would not be deterred from her goal no matter how dangerous the fighting between Pisa and Lucca had left the road. The author points out the courage Zita had to make such a journey; this was a road that had earned a reputation as a place where "one was frequently robbed of one's things . . . and sometimes had one's throat slit."[18] But, as the author notes, Zita always completed her tasks and thus would not abandon her pilgrimage.[19] When Zita arrived, she found the church closed. Undaunted by this seeming setback, Zita proceeded to pray at the church's door until she fell asleep. When she awoke and realized that she had slept through a wind and rainstorm, she watched the candle that she had brought to honor the Magdalene relight in her hands as the doors of the church opened. The story ends by noting that when the priest and several parishioners eventually arrived at the church, they were amazed to find Zita already inside, praying.[20]

With only the most limited sense of her devotional activities on those pilgrimages, the reader is left to wonder about the content of Zita's prayers in the church of the Magdalene as well as about what went on between her and the Virgin Mary during their long walk back to Lucca. But that is not what the *vita* wants its readers to notice about Zita's religious life. Gates and doors miraculously open for her. Limited to travel by foot, Zita can beat a man riding on horseback. Undaunted by a war-ravaged area, Zita wins entry into a church before the priest and other devotees. Thus, it is not the particular details or intensity of Zita's spiritual life that makes her holy, but rather, the determination and the freedom of movement that her courage and faith have afforded her. By framing her sanctity in this way—that is, by focusing on

---

17. Ibid.: "Quam cum admiratione permaxima exquireret idem eques, quomodo tam velociter se praecesserit et eo citius, pervenisset, inquit illud S. Job: Sicut Domino placuit, ita factum est."

18. Ibid., 509: "Quodam igitur tempore, dum adesset B. Mariae Magdalenae devota festivitas, Zita, more solito sibi pridem, accedere studuit ad ejus ecclesiam semotam a civitate Lucae milliariis pene decem in solitudine, quae Crebaria nuncupatur; quamvis propter guerrarum discrimina, quae Lucanos ac Pisanos graviter affligebant, nemo confideret ad eamdem ecclesiam properare; cum illis in partibus crebro spoliarentur, et aliquando jugularentur homines quilibet adeuntes."

19. Ibid.

20. Ibid.

Zita's practical, can-do attitude, and on the access and mobility such pluck and determination give her—the text essentially reframes the meaning of the miracles Zita performs. These miracles are not the result of what she believes or experiences internally but the result of her perseverance and the actions that resolve produces.

Penitence and Prayer

Claiming a similarity between Zita's name and the word for virginity "in the Roman language," the *vita* reports that Zita's purity extended far beyond her abstention from sexual activity.[21] Zita disciplined her body through self-flagellation so intensely "that she rarely felt sensual impulses."[22] Moreover, she refused any food beyond what was necessary to keep herself alive, and collected excess food to distribute to the poor and sick. Her body was so conditioned to fasting, the *vita*'s author maintains, that "it was hardly necessary for her to consume anything to support herself."[23] And while she may have looked plump, there was in fact nothing on her bones; her body was more akin to a ghost or spirit than to a human.[24] While, like so many medieval women, Zita used the manipulation of food as both expression and evidence of her penitential commitment, it is to her intense schedule of prayer that the *vita*'s author most frequently turns to prove her rigor. And while the *vita*'s author makes clear that Zita's prayers allowed her to reach ecstatic heights, he is careful to emphasize the extent to which her devotional life remained contained, controlled, and distinct from what he identifies as the typical behavior of a laywoman.

Unlike the silence we find regarding the content of Zita's devotional life during her many pilgrimages, the *vita* gives us some detail about the content and nature of Zita's prayers when she was at home. No matter how much her domestic duties for the Fatinelli constrained her time, Zita regularly got up at Matins to pray in San Frediano. And when she could not get to the church, Zita would spend her nights in the Fatinelli house praying in a "place of

---

21. Ibid., 509: "Reverendam insuper B. Zitam non eventu fatali credimus tale nomen fuisse sortitam, sed divino praesagio et dispositione gratiae supernaturalis, cui sunt futura praesentia: Zita nempe Romana lingua Virginem sonat."

22. Ibid., 507: "Tanta nempe disciplina et rigiditate felix Zita carnem crucifigebat cum vitiis, quod motus sensuales rarissime sentiebat . . ."

23. Ibid.: "et tam stricta fraenabat modestiae lege, ut aliqua vix sumeret necessaria sustentationi naturae."

24. Ibid.: "Et quia tunc castimonia ad perfectum munditiae candorem ducitur, cum per abstinentiam caro domatur; jejuniis crebris adeo se macerabat, ut licet videretur facie corpulenta, ossibus vix haereret. Pallebat os ejus jejuniis, et mens coelestibus desideriis aestuabat: ut plerumque nil minus quam corpus humanum, sed phantasma vel spiritus videretur."

solitude."[25] When she prayed in the Fatinelli house, Zita experienced spiritual ecstasies that left her "drunk with the overabundance of divine love," making it clear to others that she was experiencing an "angelic visitation."[26] Moreover, the reader is told that since she did not want to draw attention to the extensive time she spent in San Frediano or to her sometimes dramatic behavior there, she preferred to pray in the lower part of the church where, by herself, she could "shed tears, fill the place with groans, beat her chest with her hands or with a stone, and in different ways share all the secrets of her hidden thoughts with God."[27]

One place where Zita often found the privacy she craved was in San Frediano's cemetery, a place where she seems to have reached the greatest heights of ecstasy.[28] In a description of those ecstatic experiences, the *vita*'s author spares no rhetorical flourish. He writes that in that cemetery, in front of a certain crucifix, Zita regularly felt her soul melt "while she was sweetly and gently restored by the flesh of the Lamb." Filled with thoughts of Christ's passion "so intimately impressed on her innermost heart that it both burned her mind within with a fire of love and infused it with the wormwood of compassion," Zita could hardly "restrain her tearful groans." When she saw the marks of the wounds on the crucifix, she would imagine "how the bloody fluids burst forth from Christ's heavenly limbs," and how he "exhaled his spirit with them."[29] While the author's dramatic and flowery descriptions of Zita's experience praying in front of this crucifix are hard to ignore, it is noteworthy

---

25. Ibid., 508: "Ut autem quietius spiritualium consolationum immissiones exciperet, divini amoris exuberantia inebriata, loci solitudinem infra septa domus habitaculi sui quaerebat, et frequentius in ibi pernoctabat. Ubi ab his qui de familia erant tanta claritas saepe videbatur de nocte, ac si fons luminis sol oriretur ibiem; existimantibus his, quibus mens sanior inerat, eam tunc praesentia auctoris luminis vel visitatione Angelica consolari."

26. Ibid.

27. Ibid.: "Omni pene tempore vitae suae surgebat ad vigilias Matutinas, et saepius ad ecclesiam B. Fridiani sibi vicinam accedens, Officio matutinali intentissima permanebat; degensque solitaria in inferiori parte ecclesiae, admodum spatiosae, ibi suas orationes formabat, spargebat lacrymas, locum replebat gemitibus, tundebat manu vel lapide pectora, et cogitationis occultae secreta cuncta cum Deo multifarie conferebat."

28. Ibid.

29. Ibid., c. 18, 508: "Praecipue ante quamdam Dominicam crucem, jam pene vetustate consumptam, et ob hoc in diversorio coemiterii positam, consuevit orare: ibi liquefiebat anima ejus, cum de assati in clibano cruces Agni carnibus perdulciter et persuaviter reficeretur. Et ideo memoria Passionis Christi visceribus cordis ejus erat impressa medullitus, ut mentem ejus intrinsecus et incendio dilectionis aduret, et absynthio compassionis impleret. In cujus amore fontali eo aestuabat ardentius, quo de passione ejus doluit vehementius: et dum super crucifixo Domino plagas vulnerum oculis mentis interius quasi jugiter cerneret, vix exterius a lacrymosis gemitibus continere valebat; animadvertens videlicet virgineis visceribus, cum suspiriis inaestimabilibus, quomodo sanguinales fluvii ex coelestibus Jesu membris [prorumperent] et cum eis spiritus ille beatissimus ejulabat; nec prius a pectoris cessabat verberibus, donec invisibiliter Domino increpante rediret tranquillitas." I am using Webb's translation here; see Webb, *Saints and Cities*, 174.

that despite the fact that he gives his readers such arresting images ("bloody fluids burst[ing] forth from Christ's heavenly limbs"), he does not reveal what it meant for Zita to experience such a moment. The description of Zita's vision in front of the crucifix is thus dramatic but nonspecific. Without any hint of Zita's voice to qualify and particularize her experience, the author comes across as most interested in showing off his rhetorical flare.

In addition, the author also emphasizes the ultimate containment of Zita's dramatic visionary moment. As the *vita* makes clear in all of its descriptions of Zita's religious life, this laywoman knew the proper time and place for ecstatic visions. The dramatic visions she experienced in front of the cemetery crucifix were private experiences. Moreover, Zita's moments of spiritual frenzy are ultimately contained. At the climactic moment of her soul's melting, as she sees the blood bursting forth and cannot stop groaning, the reader is told that at God's chiding, tranquility returns.[30]

Immediately after describing this dramatic experience, the *vita's* author again comments on the physical dimensions of Zita's devotional life, reemphasizing its reserve, its restraint, and, above all, its distinction from the behavior of most female parishioners. Inside San Frediano, he writes, Zita conducted herself with "such modesty and silence" that not only did she try not to look anyone in the face but also that "nothing was on her mind or her lips except her prayers." This kept her from falling victim, the author notes, to the "presumptuous and foolish chatter" that so often emerges if the "the tongue is not at all restrained from idle talk."[31] When she did leave her graveyard crucifix and joined the other parishioners inside the church, she congregated with the men instead of the women. The women, the author laments, frequently stood out for their inane talking.[32]

We can imagine that Zita's restrained but rigorous spirituality was a model that a canon would have found particularly attractive for his congregation. Too much enthusiasm from a parishioner could be disruptive. In Rose of Viterbo's first *vita*, "Lord G." had felt compelled to drag Rose out of church as she wailed.[33] Moreover, in the generation after Zita, laywomen such as Margaret

---

30. *De S. Zita*, 508.

31. Ibid., 509: "Solita enim erat cunctis abire posterior, et ceteris prior introire: nihilominus quoque exclusa saepe, ante januam ecclesiae clausam, orationem suam faciebat . . . Tanto quoque silentio et pudore se in ecclesia coarctabat, ut non solum in cujusquam facie minime videre tentaret, sed nil aliud quam orationes ore et mente revolveret: nam saepe dum ob otiosis verbis nequaquam lingua compescitur, ad temeritatem quoque stultae loquacitatis effertur." I am relying on Webb's translation here; see Webb, *Saints and Cities*, 174–75.

32. *De S. Zita*, 509.

33. *Rosa Vita I*, 7, 230.

of Cortona and Angela of Foligno were often excluded from the church services that their ecstatic behavior tended to upstage.[34]

If the author of Zita's *vita* was aiming to present a compelling model of lay devotion, the particular attention he pays to what this saint did with her hands offered concrete actions that parishioners could imitate. In a paragraph exploring the spiritual rewards Zita found in prayer, the reader is told that Zita prayed with her hands in part as a way to make manifest the deep tenor of her devotion without "entirely forsaking the quiet."[35] In short, Zita's use of her hands allowed her to maintain her more circumscribed style of prayer. Augustine Thompson has looked at the influence Peter the Chanter's treatise on prayer had on lay devotion in the Italian communes and notes the importance Peter places on both bodily gestures—such as bowing and prostration—and hand gestures in lay prayer.[36] Although Zita's use of her hands to pray was not unusual, the author's concern to point out that her prayer was more effective precisely because she used her hands instead of her mouth seems again intent upon identifying ideal lay behavior in church.

These descriptions may also represent an attempt to reimagine the overall function of a lay saint's hands. Ranieri of Pisa's hands brought about healing miracles for his fellow Pisans, most often by blessing bread and water, turning them into thaumaturgic agents. Facio of Cremona's hands could not only craft masterful pieces of silver and gold but could also heal the sick. In Zita's *vita*, hands do not produce miracles as much as they function to identify proper lay behavior. Just as Zita kept herself separate from the noisy frenzy of other laywomen in church, opting to stand with the men instead of the talkative women, the use she makes of her hands keeps her devotional life restrained, quiet, and outside the realm of the charismatic.

Work

From his first description of Zita's working life, the *vita*'s author identifies a connection between the manual labor she performed for her employers, the

---

34. For examples of Margaret's upstaging, see chapter 6. In Angela of Foligno's *Memorial*, she is described as having been escorted out of San Francesco in Assisi by her confessor when she began to scream after feeling Christ leave her; see *Angela of Foligno: Complete Works*, trans. Paul Lachance (New York: Paulist Press, 1993), 136–37.

35. *De S. Zita*, 508: "Et ut ejus animae intellectus ab irradiatione divinae lucis purior redderetur, sic continuabat orare, ut etiam manibus operans, corde et ore obsecrationis verba ruminando depromeret; ne quietem funditus deserens, ignem superni amoris in se exstingueret."

36. Thompson, *Cities of God*, 344–57. For more on gestures in medieval prayer, see Jean-Claude Schmitt, *La raison des gestes dans l'Occident médiéval* (Paris: Gallimard, 1990).

Fatinelli family, and the charity that she was able to extend to the people of Lucca.[37] But while the author points to an economic impetus behind Zita's arrival in Lucca, noting that she came to support herself, he also wants his readers to understand that employment gave Zita the means to provide charity.[38] Just as we saw in Facio's *vita*, work is valued here for its potential to fund charity.

Zita worked for the Fatinelli family for nearly sixty years and is described throughout the *vita* as having been an ideal servant. She served all members of the family, rushed to attend to their every need, and never complained.[39] The *vita*'s author again uses descriptions of what the saint did with her hands as evidence for her saintly perfection. As a careful and attentive worker, Zita would "extend her hands eagerly" toward the poor, having gathered enough scraps of food and belongings (presumably collected from her employers) to feed and care for the growing number of needy Lucchese who daily gathered outside of the Fatinelli house seeking her help.[40] When she was left "empty-handed," she could still help by offering the poor "consoling words," something the author deems more useful for addressing the needs of her community than "the words of scripture."[41]

Zita's hard work as a domestic servant also distinguished her from other members of the laity. By keeping herself engaged in work, Zita could avoid what the text calls the "bite of burning serpents," a hazard the author sees as inherent in the "idleness and preoccupation" of worldly life.[42] Zita, the author argues, worked hard because "as it is written in the book of Wisdom,

---

37. *De S. Zita*, 505: "Ut autem juxta Apostolum ad ea, quae opus erant, sibi suis manibus ministraret; ne forte manducaret panem doloris, aut ut invalidis et egentibus afferret subsidia, tradidit se in domun civium Lucanorum degentium non longe a reverenda ecclesia S. Fridiani Lucani, in qua modo ejus corpus venerabile requiescit." This passage alludes to Acts 20:34: "ipsi scitis quoniam ad ea quae mihi opus errant et his qui mecum sunt ministraverunt manus istae"; and also to Psalm 126:2: "frustra vobis est de mane consurgere postquam sederitis qui manducatis panem idolorum."

38. *De S. Zita*, 505. It was common during the rapid economic expansion of cities in the thirteenth century for the poor to leave their rural villages for the city in search of work. See Benvenuti Papi, "*In castro poenitentiae*," 263–80; and Goodich, "Ancilla Dei," 119–36.

39. *De S. Zita*, 505.

40. See ibid., 505: "Itaque liquescebat gratia ejus ad infirmos et pauperes; extendebat quoque manus studiosius ad eosdem"; and ibid.: "Et ut se ad haec paratam facilius reperiret, non tantum decentia ad hoc opus, vel quae opportuna viderentur, cura pervigili praeparabat; sed etiam permodica fragmenta, vel vilia etiam, ex pulmentis et minutis solicite colligebat; observans intente, ne forte vacuum pauperem contingeret ab ea discedere."

41. Ibid.: "Quibus siquidem non poterat manum, saltem exhibebat affectum, exhortationibus ad patientiam aut verbis consolatoriis intersertis: egentis etenim cor doctrinae sermo non penetrat, si hunc apud ejus animum manus misericordiae non commendat: et illa vox cor audientis non penetrat, quae hoc quod sonuerit opere non conservat."

42. Ibid.: "Et si aliquando rei familiaris obsequia sibi non incumbebant, statim ad laborem manuum assidua recurrebat; devitans summopere, tamquam morsus serpentium ignitorum, omnem otiositatem, et curiositatem hujus volubilis temporis; arma videlicet hostis antiqui ad miseras animas captivandas."

'whatsoever thy hand is able to do, do it earnestly.'"[43] By simply attending to what needed to be done, Zita could keep herself insulated from the world. Zita, he claims at the conclusion of his first description of her working life, believed it "glorious to serve God, inglorious to serve the world."[44]

Although the *vita*'s author presents a harmonious and beneficial relationship between Zita's domestic and spiritual labor—by serving the Fatinelli, she could ultimately serve God—the subsequent episodes he uses to portray that relationship suggest a more complex interpretation of Zita's two commitments. First, the author notes that often when her mind was focusing on her prayers, "badly made things sprung from the work of her hands."[45] Zita could be so engaged in her prayers that "she seemed to have dedicated not only her heart and body but also her time and her work to God."[46] While this might seem another reason to celebrate Zita, the *vita*'s author notes how her spiritual dedication could get her into trouble. Zita's "excessive devotion," that is, the times when she found herself "suspended in ecstasy," could leave her unaware of her surroundings and forgetful of her domestic duties.[47] For example, the author describes a time when Zita became so engaged in her early morning prayers that she lost track of time and forgot about the bread she had been baking in the Fatinelli family's oven. The *vita* reports that when she finally remembered the bread, Zita rushed back to the Fatinelli house, berating herself for not having completed her domestic duties. Zita realized her good fortune, however, when "coming to the oven, she found the bread most beautifully done." Convinced that the lady of the house had taken over her duties, Zita sought her out to offer her gratitude. But it soon became clear to all in the house that "no mortal" had been attending to the bread, and that, instead, it had been finished "from heaven."[48]

---

43. Ibid.: "Implebat quoque sedula quod in libro scribitur Sapientiae, Quodcumque potest manus tua instanter operare." The author misidentifies the biblical passage. It is a quotation from Ecclesiastes 9:10. My English translation is taken from the Douay-Rheims translation.

44. *De S. Zita*, 505.

45. *De S. Zita*, 508: "Propter quod eveniebat aliquando, ut opera manuum ejus resultarent inepta, dum cor non apponeret operationi, sed magis orationi."

46. Ibid.: "Nam ambulans et sedans, laborans et vacans, intus et foris, adeo erat orationi mentis intenta, ut Deo videretur non solum quidquid erat cordis et corporis, verum etiam temporis et operis dedicasse." This is Webb's translation; see Webb, *Saints and Cities*, 173.

47. *De S. Zita*, 508: "Suspendebatur frequenter sancta in ecstasi, tanto devotionis excessu defixo synderesis apice in aeterna spectacula; ut super semetipsam rapta, et ultra humanum sensum aliquid sentiens, quae circa se agerentur omnino nesciret."

48. Ibid., 509: "Sed accedens ad arcam, invenit panes decentissime factos, quibus delatis ad clibanum, concito gradu rediit, gratias cum timore et pudore suae dominae matri familias relatura, quam existimabat panes confecisse praedictos; qui tamen coelitus facti fuerant, sicut postea signo certo certius est compertum; dum disquisitione praehabita diligenti nemo mortalium repertus est, qui confecisset eosdem."

Although the *vita* presents a happy ending to Zita's forgetfulness—she is both rescued and rewarded for ignoring her domestic duties—we are left to wonder about the lesson the *vita*'s audience was meant to take from this story. Should a pious laywoman (or layman) imitate Zita's spiritual commitment to the detriment of his or her worldly duties? Does Zita's example suggest that lay work could be finished "from heaven" if one exhibits a rigorous enough commitment to a contemplative life? By raising such questions, Zita's *vita* engages with the inherent tensions and difficulties of portraying a saintly lay life. How could Zita be both a good laywoman and a saint? How can one serve a domestic master and a spiritual one at the same time?

Charity

The *vita*'s author offers answers to these questions in his presentation of Zita's charity work. When Zita ignores her worldly duties, her great piety and penitential commitment allows her to perform miracles that ultimately serve and maintain her urban community. In this regard, Zita's *vita* seems to be working with notions of the civic value of lay sanctity that we saw most clearly articulated in the cult of Pier "Pettinaio" of Siena. Nowhere is this idea more clearly articulated than in the *vita*'s descriptions of Zita's charity work. When Zita is not working for the Fatinelli, praying, or making pilgrimages, she is offering charity to her fellow Lucchese. Each episode of Zita's charity work culminates in the performance of a miracle. Unlike the living miracles we saw male lay saints perform, Zita does not bring about bodily healings. Rather, Zita's miracles are of an entirely practical nature: they allow her to feed the hungry and clothe the poor without upsetting the conditions that have produced the starving and naked in the first place. Just as this *vita*'s presentation of Zita's penitential life aimed to use her as a model of the restrained and practical lay penitent—one whose prayers and visions remain private and controlled—its descriptions of the miracles that her charity work produced perform a similar articulation of the parameters of an ideal lay religious life. Zita is not a living manifestation of God. She does not have charismatic gifts that bring about physical healings. She is a laywoman, whose intense piety and commitment to charity creates a social harmony that maintains the economic and social divisions of her city.[49]

---

49. For more on the idea of charity as something that the elite use "to preserve political and social authority," see Trexler, "Charity and the Defense of Urban Elites"; as a means for "reaffirmation of the existing social distance between rich and poor," see Teofilo Ruiz, *From Heaven to Earth: The Reordering of Castilian Society, 1150–1350* (Princeton: Princeton University Press, 2004), 115; both of these

In an episode included early in the text, the author describes Zita mobbed by a throng of poor and starving Lucchese who had heard about her charitable reputation and had come to the Fatinelli house to seek her help. At first, Zita was concerned; she had given all that she had collected through her works of piety and was facing the crowd of starving poor with nothing to offer.[50] But, as the *vita* reports, having been "pierced by the sword of compassion" when she spotted a woman with several hungry children emerge from the crowd, Zita began to look again for anything she might be able to offer. Zita remembered her employers' storehouse of food, and began to distribute some of the Fatinelli family's large supply of beans. Over the next few days, Zita continued to offer the Fatinelli family's reserve to the hungry, "no matter how many came asking for alms."[51]

The *vita's* author notes that Zita was afraid of the punishment her employers would inflict on her once they discovered her transgression, but offers a justification for her actions:

> Not having the means to extend a helping hand to her [the starving woman], she was divinely directed, for in times of need everything is to be shared and the heavenly rather than the earthly Lord must be obeyed . . . For those who claim private rights in the common gift of God are wrong to consider themselves blameless. Almost every day they are killing as many poor dying people as those whose means of support they keep to themselves; as long as they fail to give out what they have received, they are bringing about the deaths of their neighbors.[52]

The author's insistence on both the righteousness of Zita's actions and the shame of those unwilling to imitate her example recalls Raimondo of Piacenza's

---

citations were found via Adam J. Davis, "The Social and Religious Meanings of Charity in Medieval Europe," *History Compass* 12 (2014): 935–50.

50. *De S. Zita*, 506.

51. Ibid.: "Quapropter diebus subsequentibus ex arca praefata largiebatur pauperibus, quotquot adveniebant eleemosynam postulantes."

52. Ibid.: "Sed dum advenisset quaedam miserabilis paupercula, cum parvulorum puerorum turba, circiter se et super se consistentium, et instanter ab eo eleemosynam postularet, deplorans se una cum illis paupertate pene incredibili laborare, imo nec ultra posse subsistere; continuo benignissima Dei famula compassionis extitit gladio perforata; nec habens unde posset illi manus porrigere adjutrices, edocta divinitus, quod videlicet necessitatis tempore communicanda sunt omnia, et plus esse coelesti Domino quam terreno parendum, constanter accessit ad quamdam arcam domini sui, continentem fabarum multitudinem copiosam, scilicet ad certam stariorum mensuram; et indigenti feminae cum liberis partem tribuit, ut famis posset periculum evitare; quoniam incassum se innocentes putant, qui commune Dei manus sibi privatim vendicant: qui tot pene quotidie perimunt, quot morientium pauperum apud se subsidia abscondunt; qui dum recepta non tribuunt, in proximorum nece versantur." This is Webb's translation; see Webb, *Saints and Cities*, 167–68.

haranguing of his civic neighbors. Just as in Raimondo's *vita*, Zita's charity is not simply an act of compassion and generosity, but also an act of social criticism. How could someone hoard excess food, the *vita* demands, when so many starve? Moreover, how could such provisions be one's particular property? In times of necessity, Zita's *vita* insists, "all things ought to be shared." And those who do not share, the author claims, quoting Gregory the Great's *Pastoral Care*, have their neighbor's blood on their hands.[53] On one hand, this episode ought to recall Innocent III's framing of lay sanctity as a balm for what ails the laity. He had celebrated Omobono not for bringing about healing miracles during his lifetime but for extending charity to his fellow lay population. But, if we look at how the author of Zita's *vita* concludes this episode, we see that this charity miracle ultimately functions to relieve certain segments of the lay population of responsibility or guilt.

At the conclusion of this episode, the reader is told that Zita was not punished for using the beans of the Fatinelli family to feed the poor. When the lord of the house ordered the box of beans to be assessed for its worth and then sold, it was found to be "divinely crowded with beans."[54] God had "marvelously protected his maidservant from all imminent harm in a supernatural way."[55] Just as we saw in the description of the miraculously baked bread, the *vita* presents Zita acting in a manner contrary to what one would expect from an ideal servant. Yet, in both episodes, she is protected from her moment of distraction (forgetting about the baking bread as she prayed) and defiance (giving away goods that were not rightly hers) by miracles that save her from rebuke and underscore her sanctity.

Such protecting miracles were common in late medieval *vitae* of female saints. Uncomfortable with their families' wealth, women were often portrayed by their hagiographers as offering those resources as charity.[56] But the portrayal of Zita's charitable actions in the *vita* does more than simply emphasize her commitment to using excess resources to aid her fellow Lucchese. It recasts the nature of her religious power. Her great penitential commitment

53. Gregory the Great, *Regula pastoralis*, in *Patrologiae cursus completus: Series latina*, vol. 77 (Paris: Migne, 1857–66), 3:19.

54. *De S. Zita*, 506: "Et ecce comperta est arca referta divinitus fabis, et in nullo earum inventa est diminuta mensura . . ."

55. Ibid.: "sicque Dominus, in quo confidebat, protexit mirifice ab omni imminente molestia famulam suam, miro et inexcogitato humanitus modo."

56. For example, Ida of Louvain (d. late thirteenth century) gave away her father's money as alms for the poor and Elizabeth of Hungary (d. 1231) gave as charity her husband's resources; see Bynum, *Holy Feast and Holy Fast*, 121–22, 135–36, 146, 170. In two later Italian examples, both Catherine of Siena (d. 1380) and Columba of Rieti (d. 1501) performed food multiplication miracles that restored items they had taken from their families, effectively protecting themselves from punishment.

does not render her a new Christ or give her a spiritual charisma on par with a priest's power, but instead allows her to see, address, and ultimately mollify the social and economic inequalities of Lucca.

The author's sharp criticism of anyone who would hoard food while others starved effectively reimagines the ultimate results of an ideal lay religious life. A saintly laywoman is not someone who adopts a religious or priestly identity, as we saw Rose do in her first *vita*, but someone who rights the wrongs brought about by her fellow lay population—an understanding of the ideal lay religious life that we first saw put forward in Raimondo of Piacenza's *vita*. At the same time, however, her actions recognize and respect the hierarchies that surround her. Even though the text criticizes the Fatinelli family for storing beans while their neighbors starve, the concluding miracle protects both Zita and the family from guilt: Zita does not have to confess her crime and the Fatinelli family have no need to punish her.

Immediately following the bean episode, the author describes another charitable act of Zita's that ends with a protecting miracle. The author claims that Zita was an imitator of Saint Martin and presents a miracle story as proof.[57] On a particularly cold Christmas Eve, the master of the Fatinelli house noticed Zita bundling up in her "cheap and flimsy clothes" to pray and attend services at San Frediano, as was her custom. He implored her to stay and keep warm with the family, remarking that she had already completed her fast. If she was intent on going, however, he insisted that she borrow his coat to protect her from the church's "moist and frigid marble pavement." Her master's kindness came with an ominous warning, however. "Pay attention Zita," he commanded, "that you don't give the cloak to someone . . . for if it is lost, I shall be much put out by my loss and you will suffer for it."[58]

But of course this was exactly what Zita did. As soon as she entered the church her attention was seized by "a certain half-dressed and murmuring

---

57. *De S. Zita*, 506: "Imitatrix siquidem extitit ancilla Dei Zita Apostolici viri B. Martini Pontificis, dum, prout legitur, vestire Christum Dominum meruit in ejus persona vel quempiam Angelorum."

58. Ibid.: "O Zita, quomodo sic properas ad ecclesiam hoc noctis in tempore frigidissimo, quo vix sub tecto et pannis consistentes rigoris gelidi, possumus perferre molestiam? cum tu maxime jejunio praecedenti confecto, vilique veste ac tenui cooperta, super humecta et frigida consessura sis marmora pavimenti? Nempe, aut tibi parcens, hoc in loco vacatura sanctis obsecrationibus dege; aut tuis humeris contra molestiam frigoris chlamydem meam cum pellibus superadde. Cumque Zita recusaret in nocte tantae solennitatis deesse sanctae ecclesiae, et assumpta pelliceata illius chlamyde ad ecclesiam properaret, replicans loqui pater-familias dixit, quodam praesago spiritu, prout sequentia indicant: Adverte, Zita, et diligenter cave, ne chlamydem recommendes alteri cuiquam, aut dimittas ubilibet; ne forte illa deperdita, ego rerum mearum carentia et damno afficiar, et tu a me gravem molestiam patiaris." This is Webb's translation; see Webb, *Saints and Cities*, 169.

pauper" whose "teeth were chattering" from the cold. She approached the shivering man and, disobeying her master, offered him her borrowed coat. The *vita* reports that Zita was careful to warn the man that he needed to return the coat to her before he left the church.[59] After the services, however, Zita was left searching for the pauper, convinced that his shame had led him to disappear with her cloak.[60] Returning home empty-handed, Zita's lord "reproached her with harsh words" and continued to berate her for several hours until the pauper appeared to them on the stairs of the Fatinelli house with the cloak on his arm.[61] As soon as Zita and her master began to speak to the pauper, he disappeared "like a flash of lightening," leaving them both with "a new and unfamiliar sensation of heavenly joy."[62]

Just as Saint Martin had figured out that the poor man with whom he had shared his cloak was Christ, it is clear that the author of Zita's *vita* wants his audience to understand that Zita and her master also realized the divine identity of their mysterious pauper. The story of the life and miracles of Saint Martin would have had a particular resonance for the *vita*'s Lucchese audience. In addition to the circulation of Sulpicius Severus's *vita* of Martin and the newer popular version found in Jacobus de Voragine's *Legenda aurea*, the Lucchese knew Martin as the titular saint of their cathedral.[63] By casting Zita as a new Saint Martin, the *vita* not only buttresses its claims for her sanctity but also, by giving readers a familiar narrative in which to place Zita, begins to merge her saintly identity with Lucca's civic identity.

Perhaps even more noteworthy is that in both this miracle story and the miraculous replenishment of the Fatinelli family's storehouse of beans, the *vita* draws attention to the fact that Zita was spared the consequences of her charitable impulses. The cloak returns, the beans are replenished, and there is no need for the Fatinelli to punish their servant. Even though stories of female saints' manipulation of the resources around them for charitable ends point to one of the few contexts in which medieval women could rebel, these protecting miracles seem to do more than simply protect Zi-

---

59. *De S. Zita*, 506.

60. Ibid., 507.

61. Ibid., 507: "O immensa divinae bonitatis clementia! Ecce siquidem hora tertia, adest in scala et domus medio pauper, venusta specie demulcens animum intuentium, et in ulnis deferens chlamydem praefatam . . ."

62. Ibid.: "Et subito, dum tam Zita quam pater-familias ipsum alloqui inchoassent, disparuit ab eis, velut fulgur coruscationis cujusdam, immisso in eorum corda coelitus quodam novo et inexperto gaudio, ex quo cum admiratione iaetabantur, et cum delectatione quadam diutius mirabantur."

63. On San Martino, see Clara Baracchini and Antonino Caleca, *Il duomo di Lucca* (Lucca: Baroni, 1973).

ta.[64] On the one hand, the miracles themselves criticize the social inequalities of the late medieval city. By placing the blame on the laity itself—they are the ones who are hoarding food while the poor starve—the *vita* repeats Innocent III's idea that lay sanctity can be the balm for what ails the laity. On the other hand, however, they also serve to protect the Fatinelli from harsh judgment.

Nevertheless, the Fatinelli come across in the *vita* as less than generous: Zita doles out her employers' excess as charity to those in need, while the Fatinelli, warm and secure in their house, remain as unaffected by and perhaps oblivious to the starving throngs outside as they were to the shivering paupers populating their neighborhood church. And yet, the miracles the *vita* narrates seem to serve a double purpose. They come to the practical rescue of the poor and the moral rescue of the wealthy. With Zita around, the *vita* ultimately argues, there is no need for the wealthy to change their ways; Zita's charity can mend the social problems of her day and remove any need for social change. The poor may be starving and cold while the rich are warm and hoard excess food—Zita's sanctity allows such disparities to exist in relative harmony. The *vita*'s focus on her charity work and its social utility also keeps her sanctity externally identified—Zita is not a lay saint who becomes a manifestation of Christ in order to reform the church, but a laywoman who rescues both the poor and morally suspect members of her civic community.

Zita's Cult

The *vita*'s author makes clear that in the final days of Zita's life, the spiritual rewards she enjoyed were both a result of her years of hard work and proof of her sanctity. Zita's commitment to "servitude or subjection" had "earned [her] the right to be swept up to the celestial dwellings and hailed by the resplendent heralds of sanctity." As Zita died, "she was carried to the love of the Creator by exertion in marvelous works," because, the author argues, "all ascent is in exertion, all descent in pleasure; by effort the steps lead upward, but by relaxation they lead downwards."[65] In the author's understanding, the "effort" Zita manifested toward her work substantiates her claim to sanctity:

---

64. Bynum explores food distribution as rebellion in the *vitae* of several late medieval women; see *Holy Feast and Holy Fast*, 119–22, 190–93, and 221–27.

65. *De S. Zita*, 512: "sed consideratione solicita, cautela quam amplissima, tunsionibus ac pressuris innumeris expolita, merebatur coaptari coelestibus aedificiis, amplificisque efferri praeconiis sanctitatis; et semper seipsa ferventior, rebus fugacibus spretis, in amorem Conditoris, mirabilium operum laboribus ferebatur. Omnis enim ascensus in labore est de intensione, descensus in voluptate: quia per annisum gressus ad superiora tenditur, per remissionem vero ad inferiora declinatur."

her manual labor was her spiritual progress. Moreover, at her death, the years of "exertion in marvelous works" carry her to a God whom the author portrays as committed to compensating those who have worked hard. This is a God "who does not cheat the laborers in the vineyard of penitence out of their daily penny, as the gospel trumpet proclaims, 'Come to me all you that labor, and are burdened.'"[66] In short, Zita's labor, her *vita's* author emphasizes, has earned her a place in heaven.

As word spread through the city of Zita's death, "both men and women of all ages" crowded into San Frediano's cloister and the adjacent streets.[67] The *vita* describes Zita's devotees jostling to remain as close to the body as possible, and, as a result, keeping the canons of San Frediano from completing the funeral service for several days. The enthusiasm of the Lucchese was so strong that, as the canons carried Zita's corpse into San Frediano, the crowd scrambled to rip off bits of Zita's clothes, leaving her body almost nude.[68] Concerned that this "irrational mob" might next start to pull Zita's body apart, the *vita's* author describes how "those of more substantial discipline" (most likely a reference to the canons) took Zita's body on a circuit of San Frediano, moving the body through the enclosed choir, the cloister, the cathedral chapter, the refectory, and the hospital. It was a fitting end to a life that so often transcended its sex and status; even after her death, Zita could get into places usually inaccessible to a laywoman.

The *vita's* author notes that in the first years after her death no one was "preaching the pre-eminent sanctity of her life and the excessive abundance of miracles" taking place at her tomb. Nevertheless, despite the lack of promotion, every year more and more people came on the anniversary of her death to "bear witness to her saintly merits."[69] The accounts of miracles that

---

66. Ibid.: "Fidelis et verax Deus omnipotens (qui laborantes in poenitentiae vinea diurno denario non defraudat, quin imo clamat evangelica tuba, Venite ad me omnes, qui laboratis et onerati estis) jam requiescere et reficere volens dilectam ancillam suam, ad coelestes Agni nuptias dignatus est eam hoc modo perducere." The *vita's* author is citing Matt. 20:1–2 and 11:28.

67. *De S. Zita*, 513: "tanta indigenarum convenit utriusque sexus et aetatis hominum innumera multitudo, ut ecclesiam dicti B. Fridiani, praegrande claustrum, et adjacentes plateas implerent . . ."

68. Ibid.

69. Ibid.: "Et quod est satis devota admiratione et miranda devotione dignum, licet de suæ præeminentia sanctitatis aut vitæ et miraculorum multiplicitate prænimia, nequaquam fautores, promotores, coadjutores, aut prædicatione promulgatores usquam locorum habuerit, imo contradictores quam plures; tamen non solum annuatim concursus infinitæ gentium multitudinis diversarum regionum, civitatum et diœcesium pene totius Italiæ, occurrentium anniversario die suæ glorificationis et transitus, ejusdem sanctitatis merita protestatur: sed etiam quotidianus visitationis excursus, ad sepulcrum ejus venientium, tam citra [quam ultra] montanorum, quibus præsto adest et affuit, in necessitatibus et periculis contingentibus invocata, eam apud Dominum insignem et exaudibilem, non voce solum, sed opere asserit, indiciis et subventionibus manifestis."

the notary Fatinello di Migliore collected between April 1278 and January 1279 attest to the immediate interest in Zita's cult. And, in almost every miracle account, the San Frediano canons are named as the primary witnesses. In several of these accounts, beneficiaries mention that they had come to seek a cure from Zita after hearing that she had been "sanctified."[70] Early modern scholars speculated that Bishop Paganello of Lucca must have authorized a civic canonization, but Paganello is not mentioned by name in either the *vita* or the miracle collection, and there is no outside documentation suggesting that he ever deemed Zita a saint.[71] Instead, the *vita* describes, without specifically naming, a number of prominent church and secular leaders (cardinals and archbishops, knights and barons) who came to witness the miracles taking place at Zita's San Frediano tomb.[72] The anonymity of these figures maintains the *vita*'s argument that Zita's cult was born from popular support.

But in spite of both the *vita*'s and the miracle collection's emphasis on the popular origins of Zita's cult, if we look more carefully at these sources as well as at Lucca's religious and political history during the Middle Ages, it becomes clear that the San Frediano canons had a significant hand in directing the beginnings of Zita's cult and did so in concert with the growth of the city's *popolo* regime. As was true of Pier "Pettinaio" of Siena's cult, Zita's Lucchese cult developed largely because of its political context and utility.

The Canons of San Frediano

Zita's own connection to San Frediano was itself circumstantial—she frequented it because it was the closest church to her employer's home. But Zita likely knew very little about the important place that her neighborhood church occupied in Lucca's history. Founded in the late sixth century by Bishop Frediano,

---

70. *De S. Zita, Miracula*, c. 35, 519; c. 63, c. 523–24; c. 69, 525; c. 83, 527–28; c. 90, 529–30. For example, in January 1279 testimony, a woman from Pisa described the successful cure of her arthritis at Zita's tomb during the previous summer. The notary added that this miracle took place after Zita "had been sanctified in Lucca." See *De S. Zita, Miracula*, c. 98, 531–32: "Jacobina, uxor Bonajunctae Pellicciarii, de S. Martino in Guasso longo civitatis Pisanae, et filia qu. Rodolphini Bursarii anno MCCLXXIX; decima die mensis Januarii, corporaliter ad sancta Dei Evangelia juravit et suo juramento dixit . . . Et dixit, quod hoc proximo praeterito anno in aestate, juxta festivitatem Ascensionis Domini, quando suprad. B. Zita Virgo sanctificaverat in civitate Lucana, ipsa vovit se Deo et supradictae, venire Lucam ad ejus corpus ad ejus laudem, et referre ei laudes et gratias, si ipsa sibi redderet sanitatem . . ."

71. Webb has posited that the *vita* might have been written in 1286 when the canons of San Frediano began a protracted battle with the Lucchese Franciscans over burial rights and that the author might have omitted any mention of Paganello if the bishop was not aiding the canons in this dispute; see *Saints and Cities*, 161–62. On the history of episcopal canonizations, see Vauchez, *Sainthood*, 22–57.

72. *De S. Zita*, 513.

an Irish monk and later bishop of Lucca, the church originally included a monastery that by the mid-eighth century had been replaced by secular clerics.[73] During the eleventh century, most notably under the influence of Bishop Anselm I (later Pope Alexander II, 1062–73), Lucca was one of the first Italian cities to embrace the papacy's calls for a reformed clergy. By 1100, most Lucchese churches had communities of reformed canons living a common life. Foremost among those communities were the canons at San Frediano.[74] Papal letters sent in the late eleventh and early twelfth century reveal that in return for their successful embrace of the papacy's reform program, the Frediani were repeatedly singled out for praise and reward. Paschal II offered the canons episcopal immunity and called them to Rome to help reform the Lateran canons, an honor that was extended again by Gelasius II and Calixtus II.[75]

In addition to the changes brought to the city by the reform papacy, a dramatic increase in pilgrimage traffic into the city during the eleventh and twelfth centuries also significantly affected San Frediano as well as other Lucchese churches. Located on a main pilgrimage route to Rome from northern Europe, the Via Francigena, Lucca enjoyed the economic benefit the increasing number of pilgrims brought into the city. To capitalize on that traffic, the city's cathedral of San Martino, as well as San Frediano, began immense rebuilding projects in the eleventh century, with both churches increasing the size of their naves and translating their most celebrated relics from crypts to high altars to attract and accommodate a flood of pilgrims. The large, three-nave church that Zita attended was completed in 1147. Its size now rivaled the cathedral's footprint, proof of the prestige San Frediano's community of reformed canons had achieved over the past century.

The rivalry between Lucca's two largest churches had a more complicated history than the competitive quest for pilgrimage profits might suggest. The prestige the canons of San Frediano enjoyed in the late eleventh and early twelfth centuries (their episcopal immunity and many invitations to Rome, for

---

73. On the history of San Frediano, see Romano Silva, *La Basilica di San Frediano in Lucca: Urbanistica, architettura, arredo* (Lucca: M. Pacini Fazzi, 1985); Giorgio Giorgi and Umberto Nicolai, *Le tre basiliche di S. Frediano nella storia e nell'arte* (Lucca: M. Pacini Fazzi, 1998); Diana Webb, "The Church of San Frediano in Lucca," *History Today* 44 (1994): 62–63. The last mention of San Frediano's monastery comes in a 762 charter and a 1042 charter refers to the "priests, deacons, and canons"; see Martino Giusti, "Le canoniche della città e diocesi di Lucca," *Studi Gregoriani* 3 (1948): 346.

74. On the history of the canons of San Frediano, see Dereine, "Chanoines"; Giusti, "Le canoniche"; Enrico Coturri, "La canonica di S. Frediano di Lucca dalla prima istituzione . . ." *Actum Luce* 3 (1974): 47–80.

75. See Charles Buchanan, "Spiritual and Spatial Authority in Medieval Lucca: Illuminated Manuscripts, Stational Liturgy and the Gregorian Reform," *Art History* 27 (2004): 723–44; Coturri, "La canonica di S. Frediano," 58–63; Giusti, "Le canoniche," 326–27; Silva, *La Basilica di San Frediano*, 26–29; and Paul Kehr, *Italia pontificia*, vol. 3 (Berlin, 1908), 414–28.

example) came—to some degree—at the expense of the reputation of the cathedral chapter. San Frediano's canons became the privileged Lucchese chapter only after San Martino's canons had lost favor with the papacy in 1079.[76] In that year, the cathedral canons had split into two factions, with one faction, led by Bishop Anselm II, willing to conform to the reforms called for by Pope Gregory VII, and another faction rejecting modifications to the canonical life. The cathedral canons who refused to reform eventually allied themselves with Lucchese nobles and citizens partial to the Imperial cause in Tuscany, contributing to the beginnings of Lucca's communal government, and further alienating the papacy.[77] In 1080, his attempts to reconcile the rebellious canons having failed, Bishop Anselm II fled to escape the city's increasingly powerful imperial faction. In 1081, Henry IV granted the Lucchese their first set of civic privileges, a step on the road to an independent civic government.

The conflict within the community of cathedral canons therefore not only set the stage for the development of the commune but also allowed for the canons of San Frediano to come to the attention of the papacy. By the early twelfth century, the papacy had redirected its attention away from the difficult San Martino canons toward the canons of San Frediano, repeatedly praising and rewarding the Frediani for their successful observance of the reformed canonical life.[78]

In the late eleventh century, however, the cathedral's lot began to change with the discovery of the *Volto Santo*. This larger than life-size wooden crucifix depicts a clothed, dark-skinned Christ figure that at the time was believed to have been carved by Nicodemus and to convey Christ's true likeness. A twelfth-century account dates the statue's first appearance in the city to the eighth century—it was believed to have been found by Lucchese fishermen after washing ashore—but no contemporary evidence attests to its presence in the city before c.1097.[79] The cult of the *Volto Santo* grew dramatically with the new influx of pilgrims through the city and the completion of a new chapel for the statue within San Martino. The popularity of the *Volto Santo* was the ammunition Lucca's cathedral needed to reassert its authority over San Frediano. Long seen as at

---

76. Charles Buchanan, "A Late Eleventh-Century Illustrated Hagiographic Lectionary from Lucca (Biblioteca Capitolare, Passionario C): Expression of Ecclesiastical Reform" (PhD dissertation, University of California at Santa Barbara, 1997), 237–42, and Buchanan, "Spiritual and Spatial Authority," 733.

77. Buchanan, "Spiritual and Spatial Authority," 729.

78. The history of this split has been well summarized in ibid., 728–29.

79. On the history of Lucca's *Volto Santo*, see *Lucca, il Volto Santo e la città medioevale*, Atti convegno internazionale di studi, Lucca, Palazzo Pubblico, 21–23 ottobre 1982 (Lucca: M. Pacini Fazzi, 1984); and Diana Webb, "The Holy Face of Lucca," *Anglo Norman Studies* 9 (1986): 227–37. For the scholarly debate over the date of the *Volto Santo*'s first appearance in Lucca, see Antonino Caleca, "Il Volto Santo, un problema critico," in *Il Volto Santo: Storia e culto*, ed. Clara Baracchini and Maria Teresa Filieri (Lucca: M. Pacini Fazzi, 1982), 59–69.

a disadvantage since it did not hold the relics of the city's favorite bishop-saint, Frediano, San Martino had found in the *Volto Santo* an attraction that could rival the remains of Lucca's beloved Irish bishop.[80] Here was the opportunity for San Martino to assert itself over San Frediano as the city's primary holy site. In 1120, the canons of San Frediano agreed to observe the celebration of the feasts of Saint Martin as well as Easter Monday at San Martino, feasts which had traditionally been celebrated at San Frediano.[81] By the early thirteenth century, the feast day dedicated to the *Volto Santo*, often referred to as the *Santa Croce*, had come to be associated with the newly sworn commune, and had achieved a status on par with the cults of the Virgin Mary in Siena and of John the Baptist in Florence.[82] In the city's earliest communal statutes (composed in the mid-thirteenth century), citywide processions of the sculpture on its feast day were in fact days to celebrate the commune.[83] The San Martino canons had found the means to reassert their primacy within the city through this growing cult.

The history of the rivalry between San Martino and San Frediano offers some concrete explanations for why the San Frediano canons were attracted to Zita's cult in the late thirteenth century. As a laywoman committed both to work and prayer, Zita presented the canons with the opportunity to explore and celebrate the merits of a mixed life—a balancing act that the canons knew well. Like Zita, they were required to participate in the business of the world without being entirely of it.[84] Moreover, Zita's tomb gave the canons the opportunity to attract a significant portion of the religious traffic (both from the Lucchese themselves and from pilgrims) away from the *Volto Santo* and San Martino. Zita, as the author of her *vita* was careful to point out, was a new Saint Martin. But in addition to attracting traffic away from San Martino and the *Volto Santo*, the canons could also use their patronage of Zita's cult to play to the ideals of an emerging political power in Lucca at the end of the thirteenth century: the *popolo*.

---

80. Buchanan, "Spiritual and Spatial Authority," 739. Buchanan's study of the extensive number of hagiographic lectionaries held by San Frediano as well as his analysis of the cathedral's thirteenth-century *Ordo officiorum*, which outlined the city's celebrated stational liturgy, both convincingly argue for the primary role San Frediano held in the promulgation and celebration of the cult of saints in the diocese from the Lombard period through the late eleventh and early twelfth centuries; also see Martino Giusti, "L'*Ordo officiorum* della cattedrale di Lucca," in *Miscellanea Giovanni Mercati*, vol. 2, *Letteratura medioevale* (Vatican City: Biblioteca Apostolica Vaticana, 1946).

81. Buchanan, "Spiritual and Spatial Authority," 739.

82. Webb, "The Holy Face of Lucca," 232–33, and 288. Raoul Manselli, "Lucca e Il Volto Santo," in *Lucca, Il Volto Santo e la città medioevale*, 13.

83. S. Bongi, S. and L. del Prete, *Statuto del Comune di Lucca dell'anno 1308. Memorie e documenti per servire all'istoria del Principato lucchese* (Lucca: Tipografia Giusti, 1857), book I, c. VII and XLII; and book IV, c. I.

84. On the role of regular canons within public life, see Joan Barclay Lloyd, *The Medieval Church and Canonry of S. Clemente in Rome* (Rome: San Clemente, 1989), 208–10.

Lucca's *Popolo*

Like so many other northern Italian cities during the late thirteenth century, Lucca was witnessing the rise of a *popolo*-dominated government.[85] In the statutes of 1308, we see Lucca's *popolo* at its zenith. Along with formally awarding civic bodies representing the *popolo* a majority of power, the statutes also articulated the political and judicial limitations that were to be placed on the urban nobility to protect the *popolo*'s new power. While Lucca was far from the only Italian commune to place such limitations upon its *grandi*, the city's reforms were aimed at a much larger proportion of the urban population than had been similar statutes in Florence, or in other communes.[86] Instead of placing restrictions solely upon the upper reaches of the urban magnates, the 1308 Lucchese statutes kept knights, their male offspring, the old landed nobility of the city, as well as 120 families deemed *potentes et casastici* from holding any real political power.

Over half of the San Martino canons came from families named as *potentes et casastici*.[87] These were the same families who had resisted the papal reform program in the eleventh century, allied themselves with the imperial cause, and eventually were instrumental in founding Lucca's first communal government. And by the early fourteenth century, in addition to being shut out of Lucca's new government, these canons once again found themselves at odds with the papacy. In 1301, Boniface VIII expelled six canons allied with a Guelph faction that had been strongly anti-*popolo*. In their place, he appointed new canons from families sympathetic to the new *popolo* government.[88] While there is no evidence that speaks to a specific connection between the San Frediano canons and Lucca's new *popolo* government, both the Frediani canons' long alliance with the papacy and their rivalry with San Martino suggest that they might well have imagined that a *popolo*-dominated commune would be receptive to Zita's cult.

---

85. On the rise of the *popolo* government in Lucca, see Green, *Castruccio Castracani*, 12–29; and Tommasi, *Sommario della storia di Lucca*, 140–64. On the rise of the rise of *popolo* governments throughout Italy, see Jones, *The Italian City-State*, 440–520. For the 1261 statutes in Lucca, see Tommasi, "Documenti," in *Sommario della storia di Lucca*, 15–16.

86. Green, *Castruccio Castracani*, 19–23. For work on the limitations placed on *grandi* or *magnati* in Florence, see Robert Davidsohn, *Storia di Firenze* (Florence: Sansoni, 1956–68), iii; also see Carol Lansing, *The Florentine Magnates: Lineage and Faction in a Medieval Commune* (Princeton: Princeton University Press, 1991).

87. *Statuto del Comune di Lucca dell'anno 1308*, book III, c. CLXX. Although the Lucca statutes did not completely exclude these families from participating in Lucca's government—they could still participate through the older representative council, the Consiglio del Comune—the statutes did limit the Lucchese magnates' legal rights and ability to bear arms.

88. Green, *Castruccio Castracani*, 193–94.

Several chapters of the 1308 statutes make clear that Lucca's *popolo* government was particularly interested in supporting and expanding Zita's cult. These chapters outline measures the commune was taking to ensure that that there would be sufficient guardians to keep order during feast days that excited the most attention in the civic population, delineating the fines to be levied if guardians should fail to fulfill their duties and naming the commune as having the ultimate authority to punish those caught.[89] Those days included the feasts of saints Martin and Regulus (an eighth-century saint whose relics were held in San Martino), the night of the raising of the *Volto Santo* in San Martino, as well as Zita's feast. A 1290 testament specifying that five Lucchese florins be given to benefit the poor each year on "the feast of Santa Zita" suggests that Zita's feast day had been celebrated at San Frediano for some time before the 1308 statutes.[90] Zita is also mentioned in a 1308 statute dedicated to civil administration. In a chapter outlining the days, times, and manner in which the city's *Podestà* and judges were required to adjudicate and render justice within the city, Zita's feast-day is named among the days when administrative business would not be conducted.[91] Zita had become a member of a list of saints, which included the Virgin Mary, the Apostles, and the city's other patrons, who marked the time in Lucca and gave the city a day off from work.

The cult of a pious servant whose *vita* emphasized not only her devotion to providing charity for Lucca's needy but also her ability to right the wrongs of her aristocratic employers was clearly a good fit for the new political regime. The extensive segment of the civic population excluded from Lucca's new government, much larger than the population of *potenti* kept out of popular governments in other Tuscan cities, suggests that the rise of the *popolo* brought a comprehensive restructuring of the city's political elite. By co-opting the cult of a laywoman who spent her life engaged in manual labor, prayer, and charity work, the *popolo*-dominated commune could both tap into the current religious enthusiasm of its citizens and be aligned with a saint who more closely resembled its values. One can also imagine how much the *vita*'s portrayal of the acts of charity that implicitly criticized Zita's wealthy employers—a family listed among the *potentes et casastici* and thus excluded from the new government—appealed to the *popolo* government. Here was a saint whose

---

89. *Statuto del Comune di Lucca dell'anno 1308*, book I, c. VII.

90. This testament made by Lando di Buonagiunta and recorded by the notary Ser Giunta Ranieri on August 11, 1290 unfortunately has, to my knowledge, not survived. It is transcribed by Fioriti, *Vita, virtu', e miracoli*, 137, and also appears in Zita's canonization proceedings; see ASV, *Riti*, Proc. 1315, 43v.

91. As Thompson has pointed out, there was no distinction between religious and secular time in the Italian communes; see *Cities of God*, 3 and 274–80.

reputation was based, in part, on her ability to point out the excesses of the powerful.

We must remember, however, that Lucca's *popolo* government was not made up of merchants and artisans who occupied a social status or economic position anywhere near as low as Zita's. In fact, as with so many *popolo* communes in thirteenth- and early fourteenth-century Italian cities, Lucca's new government was dominated by the wealthiest of workers. Nevertheless, the distinction between older, aristocratic families who had dominated Lucca's government until the mid-thirteenth century and the new merchant- and artisan-based government was a significant enough divide that a domestic servant could stand as an emblem for the *popolo*'s cause.

We might wonder, then, to what extent the author of Zita's *vita* was working to craft an image of a new popular cult in order to insert Zita into Lucca's saintly pantheon. While the San Frediano canon who wrote Zita's *vita* was not specifically aiming to have her appear as the city's newest patron in the yet to be drafted *popolo* statutes, the stirrings of a new political regime on the rise in the late thirteenth century had to have been unmistakable. It seems reasonable to assume that the *vita*'s presentation of Zita as the people's saint—one who specifically appealed to and thus represented working people—was, at least in part, a shrewd political maneuver. Zita could be the emblem for the city's revamped communal government, hailed by the people of Lucca, just as the *Volto Santo* had represented Lucca's first commune.

A Family Saint

During the fourteenth century, the civic government of Lucca changed hands several times. Although scholars have characterized the *popolo*'s 1308 statutes as the zenith of Lucca's constitutional development, this form of the city's government had a rather limited life.[92] On June 14, 1314, the White Guelphs, having allied themselves with both the Lucchese and Pisan Ghibelline parties, sacked the city and overthrew the *popolo* government. From 1314 until 1328, Lucca was ruled by despotic, or proto-Signorial regimes, first headed by Uguccione della Faggiuola, and then followed two years later by Castruccio Castracani.[93] Under Castracani's rule, Lucca enjoyed its broadest territorial expansion. Upon Castracani's death in 1328, however, Lucca entered a forty-year period under a series of foreign rulers, with Pisa's control of the city from 1342 until 1369 standing as the

---

92. Christine Meek, "Lucca," in *Medieval Italy: An Encyclopedia*, ed. Kleinhenz, vol. 2, 661.
93. For Lucca under della Faggiuola and Castracani, see Green, *Castruccio Castracani*, 30–78.

single longest occupation.[94] In 1369, with the aid of Charles IV, the Lucchese were once again able to become an independent commune and were to remain so until the late eighteenth century.

Throughout this chaotic period, Zita's cult continued to flourish. However, its identity as a cult representing the city itself faded. With the *popolo* government overthrown by the early fourteenth century, Zita's memory and sanctity came to be associated with her employers, the Fatinelli. In addition to the fact that the earliest manuscript containing Zita's *vita* belonged to the Fatinelli and was copied in the mid-fourteenth century, in 1321, the noble family began to build a chapel around the tomb of their former servant. At that time, Zita's tomb was located within San Frediano's cemetery, which lined the east side of the church. The Fatinelli family also took steps at this time to enclose the area around her tomb, a process that would eventually result in a fully enclosed annex to the original church.[95] In his 1382 will, Jacopo Fatinelli ordered that a panel painting be created depicting the *Volto Santo*, "Beata Zita," and several testators.[96] This painting was either never made or was lost, as no record of the completed panel survives. He also ordered that a daily mass be said by the canons at Zita's tomb for the good of his soul, and he left money for the embellishment of the chapel.[97] Moreover, starting in 1383, the Fatinelli family began to stipulate in their wills that they be buried in the chapel of their venerated servant.[98]

By the early fifteenth century, relations between the Fatinelli family and San Frediano's canons had become strained over who held the ultimate authority in the management of Zita's chapel. As Vauchez has noted, disputes between religious institutions and individual families were common at this time.[99] The Fatinelli felt they had a right to control the activities of a chapel that not only had been funded by them but also was dedicated to the woman who had spent nearly sixty years living with and caring for their family. In 1410 the Fatinelli and the canons reached an agreement whereby a rector, chosen by the Fatinelli from among the canons but approved by the church's prior, would be in

---

94. For the period before the Pisan occupation, see Green, *Lucca under Many Masters: A Fourteenth-Century Italian Commune in Crisis (1328–1342)* (Florence: L. S. Olschki, 1995); and for during the Pisan occupation, see Meek, *The Commune of Lucca under Pisan Rule*.

95. On the building of Zita's chapel in San Frediano, see Silva, *La Basilica di San Frediano*, 66–68; and Paoli, *Arte e committenza privata a Lucca*, 217–18 and 257–63.

96. Silva, *La Basilica di San Frediano*, 67; Silva cites *Scritti d'arte e d'antichita di Michele Ridolfi* (Florence, 1879), which I have been unable to locate.

97. See Vauchez, *Sainthood*, 240–41; ASV, *Riti*, Proc. 1315, 61r–63v; and Gerardo Mansi, *I patrizi di Lucca: Le antiche famiglie lucchesi e i loro stemmi* (Lucca: Titania, 1996). This testament has been transcribed, see Fioriti, *Vita, virtu', e miracoli*, 138–39.

98. See Vauchez, *Sainthood*, 241; and ASV, *Riti*, Proc. 1315, 43v–44r.

99. Vauchez, *Sainthood*, 240–41.

charge of the chapel.[100] The family then proceeded to have the chapel completely separated from the cemetery, making it a large side chapel off the main nave.[101] At this time, the Frediani canons also allowed the Fatinelli to place their coat of arms outside of the chapel's entrance, thus securing an association between the family and the pious servant in the minds of all who came to see her tomb.[102] The Fatinelli family's efforts to build a chapel in honor of Zita was a double-edged act of civic charity: although the Lucchese gained a more substantial location to venerate Zita, the Fatinelli also believed that they were garnering spiritual rewards through their generous patronage.[103] We might imagine that the family wanted an opportunity to restore the less-than-benevolent portrait of them in Zita's *vita*.

Even though the Fatinelli clearly made a push to cement an association between themselves and their pious servant, those efforts did not entirely eclipse her status as a civic saint. In the 1342 statutes, issued immediately after the beginning of Pisa's occupation of Lucca, Zita's name again appears among the saints' feast days recognized as civic holidays.[104] And although there seems no longer to have been the need to control rowdy worshippers on Zita's or other saints' feast days, the 1342 statutes specified that the commune was to set aside forty candles for the vigil of "Santa Zita" each year.[105] By the time Lucca issued a set of statutes in 1372 to mark the reestablishment of the city's independence three years earlier, Zita was again listed as a civic saint for whose feast day the regular business of the city was to stop.[106] The 1372 statutes also call for thirty pounds of wax to be donated by the commune to celebrate Zita's feast.[107] The only extant copy of the 1372 statutes was produced at the bequest of the Fatinelli family and bears their coat of arms on the first page.[108]

Although the continuing presence of Zita's name as one of Lucca's civic saints to some extent speaks to the endurance of her cult as a civic cult over

---

100. Ibid.

101. Silva, *La Basilica di San Frediano*, 70.

102. Paoli, *Arte e committenza privata a Lucca*, 217–18.

103. Similar to the merchant Enrico degli Scrovegni's decision to have the Scrovegni chapel built and decorated in an attempt to make up for his extensive involvement in usury; see Paoli, *Arte e committenza privata a Lucca*, 220–22.

104. Lucca, Archivio di Stato, Statuti 5 (1342), book IV, c. I. Pisa ruled Lucca without much change to the civic administrative structure that had been in place since the rise of the *popolo* regime.

105. Ibid., book II, c. XXI.

106. Ibid., book III, c. II.

107. Lucca, Archivio di Stato, *Statuti*, 6 (1372), book III, c. XCVI.

108. While some scholars believe that the manuscript containing these statutes was written in 1374, E. Lazzareschi concluded that the manuscript is a copy made as late as 1413. See E. Lazzareschi, "Angelo Puccinelli e gli altri pittori lucchesi del trecento," *Bollettino Storico Lucchese* 10 (1938): 138; also see Paoli, *Arte e committenza privata a Lucca*, 93.

the fourteenth century, the Fatinelli had successfully linked their history and memory with that of their former maid. Moreover, in addition to the spiritual benefits the family likely believed they would gain from being Zita's prime patrons, such efforts would have also helped to reestablish their overall reputation in Lucca's post-*popolo* political scene.

Thus the interest of the Fatinelli in Zita's cult over the fourteenth century has much in common not only with that shown by the San Frediano canons but also by Lucca's *popolo* governments. For each of these entities, Zita—or at least, the idea of Zita as a hardworking, energetic, charity-minded, practical yet visionary religious laywoman—served a particular political purpose. Patronizing her cult gave real political advantage to each benefactor—whether that was a tomb-site that could help San Frediano reassert itself as Lucca's main pilgrimage site, an emblem that could represent a newly articulated political identity for Lucca, or a connection that could restore and reassert a family's political and social power.

What is noteworthy here, and what helps explain the role of Zita's cult as the outlier among those dedicated to lay religious women in the Italian communes, is the fact that in each of these cases, the memory and reputation of a female laywoman was supported and protected by association with institutions identified with and controlled by males. Thus, despite being an unmarried lay penitent with no connection to a mendicant order, her cult was picked up by a religious order, a city, and finally, a powerful family—all of whom helped it to flourish from the time of her death and throughout the later Middle Ages. The success of Zita's medieval cult, therefore, depends on both political context and male associations. But as this chapter has shown, it also depends on a profoundly conservative construction of Zita's lay sanctity. Zita can be the anomaly because of the many things her hagiographer assures his reader she was not. She was a rigorously religious laywoman, but acted nothing like other devout laywomen. She was a visionary, but was not a public ecstatic. She was a miracle worker, but she was not another Christ. She was a charity worker, but she was not a revolutionary. Just as Innocent III's framing of lay sanctity in the canonization of Omobono worked to contain the more radical and powerful notion of an ideal lay religious life that had been expressed in twelfth-century cults like that of Ranieri of Pisa, the author of Zita's *vita* was undoubtedly constructing a portrait of the ideal female lay saint with a similar motivation. Zita was an ideal religious laywoman precisely because she was an anomaly, an outlier. Thus, not only was Zita nothing like Rose of Viterbo, or the women with whom she refused to associate in San Frediano, she was also certainly nothing like another Tuscan woman, Margaret of Cortona, in whose saintly ambition and actions we see the beginnings of the end of contemporary civic lay sanctity.

PART THREE

From Civic Saint to Lay Visionary

CHAPTER 6

Margaret of Cortona

Between Civic Saint and Franciscan Visionary

In the first part of this study, I explored the ways in which church authorities stepped into the emerging phenomenon of lay civic sanctity to define and to contain claims of lay charismatic power. In Part II, I explored how the use of both institutional affiliation and male conduits as well as the designation of one lay saint (Zita of Lucca) as a female anomaly stood as key factors in the construction of laywomen's sanctity. In these final two chapters, I turn to the late thirteenth and early fourteenth centuries, a time during which both the Franciscans and the Dominicans not only began more formal and concerted efforts to oversee the religious lives of lay penitents but also took significant steps toward the creation of institutionally distinct third or lay orders. The result of these changes, I argue, was the development of more complex methods for controlling lay claims of charismatic power that were primarily aimed at laywomen. While a layman's holy powers continued to be seen in his external acts, a laywoman's saintly charisma was increasingly found in the visionary heights she reached.

Although the Roman church would not canonize Margaret of Cortona until 1728, both the community of lay penitents with whom she had lived at the church of San Basilio and Cortona's commune wasted no time in establishing, managing, and developing her cult in the generation after her death in

1297. Visual and written sources document the attention that Cortona's lay penitents, bishops, and civic leaders paid to this former concubine, who had come to the city after the death of her lover had left her a homeless single mother.[1]

The earliest of those sources is a panel painting (often called a *vita*-panel by scholars) likely produced for San Basilio within a decade of Margaret's death. The panel as we shall see depicts a large, fully frontal portrait of the saint dressed in a penitent's habit, surrounded by eight smaller registers documenting the development of her religious life.[2] By the 1310s, Margaret's San Basilio tomb-site had gained a large funerary sculpture, most likely the work of the Sienese sculptor Gano di Fazio (d. 1317/18).[3] As news of the many miracles taking place at Margaret's tomb spread, San Basilio became a popular pilgrimage site, and by the late 1330s, this once-ruined church had been extensively rebuilt and was often referred to as Santa Margherita.[4] It was in the 1330s, and most likely at the behest of the commune, that San Basilio gained an extensive fresco cycle depicting scenes from Margaret's life and miracles.[5] The cycle, attributed by scholars to Ambrogio and Pietro Lorenzetti, is remarkable as the earliest known example in Italy of a cycle celebrating an uncanonized contemporary individual.[6] It is doubly remarkable for the fact that the subject was a laywoman.

Unfortunately, those frescoes were whitewashed in the late seventeenth century. Besides a few fragmentary remains, our knowledge of the cycle comes from watercolor copies made by Adriano Zabarelli during a papal visitation to Cortona in the seventeenth century (in conjunction with Margaret's can-

---

1. On Margaret of Cortona, see Cannon and Vauchez, *Margherita of Cortona*; Bornstein, "The Uses of the Body"; Doyno, "The Creation of a Franciscan Lay Saint"; and Mary Harvey Doyno, "'A Particular Light of Understanding': Margaret of Cortona, the Franciscans, and a Cortonese Cleric," in *History in the Comic Mode*, ed. Fulton and Holsinger, 68–78.

2. This painting is now held in the Museo Diocesano in Cortona. On the painting's provenance, see Joanna Cannon, "Beyond the Limitations of Visual Typology: Reconsidering the Function and Audience of Three *Vita* Panels of Women Saints c. 1300," in *Italian Panel Painting of the Duecento and Trecento*, ed. Victor M. Schmidt (New Haven: Yale University Press, 2002), 293.

3. This tomb sculpture remains in San Basilio (now called Santa Margherita) in Cortona. Cannon is also the authority here; see her "Popular Saints and Private Chantries: The Sienese Tomb-Altar of Margherita of Cortona and the Questions of Liturgical Use," in *Kunst und Liturgie im Mittelalter*, ed. Nicolas Bock, Sible de Blaauw, Christopher Luitpold Frommel, and Herbert Kessler (Rome: Bibliotheca Hertziana, 2000), 149–62. Cannon has noted that the miracle scenes illustrate two different types of miracles (curing of the lame and of the demonically possessed) rather than particular miracle events; see Cannon and Vauchez, *Margherita of Cortona*, 171.

4. On the use of a joint dedication to Basilio and Margaret, see Cannon and Vauchez, *Margherita of Cortona*, 45–47.

5. Cannon has done the most extensive study of these frescoes; see ibid.

6. Ibid., 175.

onization), and Joanna Cannon's detailed study of those reproductions.[7] In addition to these visual sources, evidence of Margaret's early cult can be found in the references to celebrations held on her feast day that we find in Cortona's first set of statutes as an independent commune. The 1325 statutes make clear that less than a generation after her death this former concubine had earned a thriving cult as civic patron of her adopted city.[8]

And yet, the source that offers the most extensive account of Margaret's life in Cortona and the beginnings of her cult is the *Legenda de vita et miraculis Beatae Margaritae de Cortona*. This account of Margaret's life from the time she arrived in Cortona until her 1297 death—more than three hundred pages in the latest modern edition—was written by her Franciscan guardian and confessor, Giunta da Bevegnati, and survives in only three medieval copies.[9] Giunta begins the *Legenda* by describing how in 1277 Margaret had "humbly offered herself on bended knees, with her hands joined and in tears to Friar Renaldo, custodian of Arezzo, for admission to the third order of the blessed father Francis."[10] This is an anachronistic description of what had been—coming more than ten years before Pope Nicholas IV's 1289 bull *Supra montem* stipulated that all lay penitents be placed under the Friars Minor guardianship—in reality, a much looser association.[11] We can imagine that as an unattached

---

7. Ibid., 79–154. Watercolor copies of the lost frescoes were made during a 1653 papal visitation to Cortona that culminated in Margaret's 1728 canonization. One set of these watercolors was inserted into Margaret's canonization proceedings; see ASV, *Riti*, Proc. 552.

8. Florence, Archivio di Stato (hereafter ASF), "Statuti comunità soggette," 279, ff. 95, 123, 140v–141v; these statutes, which mention Margaret's feast day, have been transcribed by Vauchez in Cannon and Vauchez, *Margherita of Cortona*, 227–30.

9. Iunctae Bevegnatis, *Legenda de vita et miraculis beatae Margaritae de Cortona*, ed. Fortunato Iozzelli (Grottaferrata: Editiones Collegii S. Bonaventurae ad Claras Aquas, 1997), 220–21 (hereafter cited as *Legenda*) (BHL 5314). All three manuscripts were written in the fourteenth century and all remain in Cortona; see Iozzelli's "Introduzione," in *Legenda*, 149–69. I would like to thank Thomas Renna, who shared an early draft of his translation of the *Legenda* with me. While I have benefited greatly from his work, unless otherwise indicated, the translations in this paper are my own. In the *Legenda*, Giunta writes that Margaret entered the Franciscan penitential order in 1277; see *Legenda*, 181. The eighteenth-century scholar and priest Lodovico Bargigli da Pelago, who published both an edition of Giunta's *Legenda* with extensive notes and a study of the context and content of the work, argued that Margaret had actually joined the Franciscans in 1275; see his *Antica leggenda della vita e de'miracoli di S. Margherita da Cortona scritta dal di lei confessore fr. Giunta Bevegnati dell'Ordine de'Minori* (Lucca, 1793), 17, n. 1. While most scholars have since followed da Pelago's dating, Iozzelli convincingly argues that 1277 is more likely the correct date; see Iozzelli, "Profilo biografico di Margherita da Cortona," in *Legenda*, 60, n. 32.

10. *Legenda*, 181: "Christo Deo deuota, mente pura, corde feruida, Margarita, anno a natiuitate Christi millesimo cc° lxxvii° quo se ordini beati Francisci, manibus iunctis, cum lacrimis coram fratre Ranaldo bone memorie aretino custode, genibus flexis, humiliter optulit et sponte in corpore et anima est oblata, assumptis etiam ordinis tertii beati patris Francisci cum magna precum instantia indumentis . . ."

11. Mariano D'Alatri has noted the attention Giunta pays to Margaret's physical posture. D'Alatri sees this focus as aimed at conveying the formality of Margaret's submission and entry into the Franciscans' lay wing; D'Alatri also points out that Giunta cannot quite purge his text of all evidence of

woman with a scandalous past, Margaret was drawn to the prestige and legitimacy the friars could offer her new religious identity. Unlike Zita of Lucca, Margaret did not have wealthy employers to shelter and protect her. An affiliation with the city's leading mendicant order could offer her a clear path to redeem herself from her past shame and give validity to her new life of penance.

The Cortonese Franciscans were quite wary of Margaret, however. Her sinful past and her identity as an illegitimate "widow" made the friars uneasy. In a "Testimony of Authenticity," likely written by Giunta and found at the end of the earliest surviving manuscript of the *Legenda*, we learn that Friar Giovanni da Castiglione, provincial Tuscany's "Inquisitor of the depraved heretics," had ordered the text to be compiled.[12] While Giovanni's title does not in itself mean that the friars formally charged Margaret with heresy, the suspicion and concern that were written into that title appear throughout the *Legenda*.[13]

Giunta notes early in the *Legenda* that it had taken Margaret several years to convince the friars that she was a worthy cause. "Why, O reader," he asks, "did the friars hesitate to give Margaret the habit of penance?"[14] He answers his own question by claiming that the order had rejected her several times because they had found her too pretty and too young to believe that she was truly devoted to the penitential life.[15] And while they finally relented after seeing that she was, as Giunta describes, "united inseparably to Christ," and hearing from her that she had changed her life for the better by fleeing "the world to join a community of religious people," the *Legenda* is full of episodes that reference the Franciscans' enduring doubts about her.[16]

---

the ambiguity of lay penitents' status; he describes other Cortonese penitents as having taken the habit of the "Brothers of Penance," and others the habit of "the Order of Penitents." See D'Alatri, "L'Ordine della penitenza nella leggenda di Margherita da Cortona." *Analecta Tertii Ordinis Regularis* 15 (1982): 69.

12. Archivio del Convento di S. Margherita, Cortona, codex 61. Also found in *Legenda*, "Appendix." Giunta also notes in the "Testimony" that the papal legate, Napoleone Orsini, had held a copy of the *Legenda* in Rome for several months, and that on February 15, 1308, in the Cortona palazzo of Lord Uguccio dei Casali, Orsini gave the text his approval.

13. By the mid-thirteenth century, responsibility for checking lay penitents for signs of heresy had shifted from bishops to the friars; see Iozzelli, "Introduzione," 9 and 66–69. See Mariano D'Alatri, "Genesi della regola di Niccoló IV: Aspetti storici," in *La "Supra montem" di Niccolo IV (1289): Genesi e difusione di una regola*, ed. R. Pazzelli and L. Temperini (Rome: Analecta TOR, 1988), 93–107.

14. *Legenda*, 184: "Quare, o lector, dare fratres habitum differebant?"

15. Ibid.

16. Ibid.: "'Sed postquam fratres inseparabiliter eam Christo adherere uiderunt, postquam in feruorem spiritus magis ac magis in Deum ascendere conspexerunt, postquam audierunt eam dicentem: 'Patres mei, quibus sum a Domino commendata, non hesitetis de me, quia si toto tempore uite mee moram in solitudine uasta contraherem, adeo Deum meum diligo, adeo mentem meam confortuait omnipotens, quod de nulla creatura nullaque temptatione timerem propter spem quam in Deum fixi, me ad suam gratiam reuocantem. At postquam me fugisse mundum uidistis, me religiosa-

Those misgivings seem to have come to a head sometime around 1288, when, at a provincial council meeting in Siena, the Tuscan Franciscans condemned Margaret as both delusional and a fraud, moving that Giunta only visit her once every eight days, and then, not long afterwards, ordering him to move to the order's convent in Siena.[17] Our only evidence for this condemnation comes from the *Legenda* itself. Giunta describes how the newly elected custodian of the Arezzo friars told Margaret that the order was "certain that her whole way of life, her revelations, and her consolations were nothing but deceptions," and that "she [had] pretended to have such consolations in order to become famous among the populace."[18] Giunta records Margaret's reaction: trembling and weeping, she begged Christ to help her, crying out that she could not do more than she was already doing either to fight against "the invisible enemies" or to deal with the friars, whose doubts about her were terrifying.[19] This was also likely the time when Margaret left her cell at San Francesco and moved to a new cell attached to the ruined church of San Basilio, located up a steep hill overlooking Cortona. Giunta claims that Margaret's move was the result of her wish for a break from the bustle of city life. But she did not find a quiet or solitary life at San Basilio, as a community of lay penitents joined her and would remain there after her death to manage her tomb and cult.[20]

Although this episode makes clear how suspicious and judgmental the Franciscans were of Margaret, for all of the passages suggesting that Giunta and his superiors were checking her for signs of heresy, demonic possession, and fraud, there are just as many passages in the *Legenda* celebrating her penitential

---

rum personarum consortio sociaui meamque uitam mutaui in melius per gratiam michi datam a Christo. Cur timetis? Cur me differtis induere?'"

17. Ibid., 376 and 249. Angela of Foligno's confessor and scribe, Friar A., also had his visits limited by the Franciscan provincial minister; see "The Memorial," in *Angela of Foligno: Complete Works*, chaps. 7 and 9.

18. *Legenda*, 249: "Cernens autem hostis noster antiquus aliquos fratres de ipsius perseuerantia dubitare, et ne consolationes ille per illusionem uel fictionem fierent ad acquirendam fame popularis celebritatem, cepit in cella dicere quod fratres, experientia docti, sapientia scripturarum illuminati et gratia Sancti Spiritus plenius illustrati, idcirco de ipsa ceperant dubitare, quia per eos cognoscebatur ueraciter quod tota uita, reuelatio et consolationes que uidebantur diuine, nil erant nisi decptio."

19. Ibid.: "Propter quod Margarita statim se in orationem prosternens, cum lacrimis et tremore dixit: 'Domine Iesu . . . qui scis omnia antequam fiant, bene nosti quod aliud agere modo non possum, tum quia pugno cum inuisbilibus hostibus certantibus contra me, tum quia fratres, quibus me commendasti, sua dubitatione me terrent.'"

20. Scholars have long assumed the move was likely a response to the Franciscan condemnation; see Roberto Rusconi, "Margherita da Cortona: Peccatrice redenta e patrona cittadina," in *Umbria: Sacra e civile*, ed. Menestò and Rusconi, 89–104; Bornstein, "The Uses of the Body," 167; and Nancy Caciola, *Discerning Spirits: Divine and Demonic Possession in the Middle Ages* (Ithaca, NY: Cornell University Press, 2003), 108.

commitment, visionary life, and avid community of devotees.[21] Such a dichotomy within the text suggests that, at some point, the agenda driving Giunta's writing had changed. Instead of assessing her orthodoxy, Giunta transitioned to using his writing about Margaret to convince his fellow friars, most of whom remained skeptical and wary, not only that she was a saint but also that her sanctity was derived in no small part from her identity as a member of the Franciscan Third Order.[22]

This chapter will argue that one result of Giunta's complex agenda in writing the *Legenda*—moving from checking Margaret's sincerity and orthodoxy to celebrating her Franciscan-identified sanctity—was the creation of a new model of an ideal lay life: the lay visionary. Giunta stakes his most powerful claims for Margaret's sanctity on the content, fervor, and results of her internal life. While we have already seen an interest in a lay saint's internal religious life—Pietro da Montarone had described Pier Pettinaio's graduation from an active to a contemplative life in his 1330s *vita*—Giunta's focus on Margaret's internal dialogue as evidence for her sanctity stands as the earliest as well as the most comprehensive example of such a point of view within late medieval Italian lay hagiography.

To some extent, such a focus should come as no surprise. If Giunta wanted to prove to his fellow friars that Margaret was not a heretic, was not delusional, and was not a fraud, what better way to do so than to mine her emotional and spiritual life? After all, the friars were most concerned about what was going on inside of Margaret. But Giunta's mode of investigation coupled with his need to convince his readers of Margaret's orthodoxy, authenticity, and ultimately her sanctity led him away from looking for evidence of an ideal lay life in extraordinary acts of piety that were externally directed. Giunta, instead, crafts a path to lay sanctity through thoughts, feelings, and visions.

Giunta's construction of a new model of lay sanctity—the lay visionary—becomes all the more apparent when we notice that not only the visual sources created to surround Margaret's tomb (the *vita*-panel, funerary monument, and fresco cycle) but also significant parts of the *Legenda* itself present a more traditional portrait of Margaret as communal lay saint. The *Legenda*'s alternate understanding of lay sanctity comes to us through Ser Badia, a secular cleric, who took over as Margaret's primary confessor after Giunta was transferred to Siena. Badia seems to have kept Giunta informed about Margaret's activi-

---

21. Elliott has explored the connections between hagiography and inquisition in texts associated with religious women in the later Middle Ages, see Dyan Elliott, *Proving Woman: Female Spirituality and Inquisitional Culture in the Later Middle Ages* (Princeton: Princeton University Press, 2004), 119–79.

22. Doyno, "The Creation of a Franciscan Lay Saint," 66.

ties through written reports. Although it is not clear whether or not Giunta rewrote Badia's dispatches or included them without alteration, we can say that at least two people, Giunta and Badia, contributed details about Margaret's life in Cortona—Giunta describing her life within the city before the Franciscan condemnation, and Badia her life after that condemnation, when she was living with a community of other lay penitents at San Basilio.[23]

In Badia's descriptions, Margaret looks more like the civic lay saints who had been appearing in other thirteenth-century communes. Instead of thinking about her own sinful past, her need for redemption and her spiritual progress, at San Basilio Margaret focuses on the sins and salvation of others. This portrait of an externally focused civic lay saint is mirrored in the visual sources. In the funerary monument and frescoes, Margaret's role as a miracle worker overshadows any references to her past identity and shame. And while the *vita*-panel emphasizes Margaret's prayer and penitence as a means to reflect and validate the actions of devotees at her tomb, this source also does not try to illustrate the depths of emotions and visionary activity that dominate Giunta's sections of the *Legenda*.

The uniting of civic and ecclesiastical authorities to support the burgeoning popular cult of a contemporary layperson, and as a result, a new civic patron, that we see in the visual evidence from San Basilio stands as the zenith of the phenomenon of the contemporary lay civic saint. But coming in the generation after *Supra montem*, this zenith was concomitant with the decline of lay civic sanctity. Giunta's construction of Margaret in the *Legenda* as a lay visionary was intended to make her more palatable for his wary Franciscan brothers. It had the additional effect, however, of illustrating a new means for controlling and containing lay charismatic claims. By focusing upon the lay penitent's quest for redemption, the evidence and site of meaning of lay civic sanctity had moved from performing miracles and cures for others to working on one's own religious progress. In short, lay charisma was something that took place within a lay saint and, in effect, it had been circumscribed once again.

Turning the Inside Out: Giunta's Creation of the Lay Franciscan Visionary

Giunta devotes the first chapter of the *Legenda* to describing Margaret's initial experiences in Cortona. In these descriptions, Giunta not only tries to

---

23. The *Legenda* does refer to Badia as having written some of Margaret's revelations: in one conversation with Margaret, Christ tells her not to worry if at times Badia could not believe the things he had written about her. See *Legenda*, 345.

solidify what was most likely an ambiguous relationship between Margaret and the Cortonese Franciscans but also makes clear the importance Margaret's internal life will play in proving her sanctity. Instead of focusing on Margaret's actions, from the first pages of the text, Giunta is interested in what Margaret felt and said as well as in how those feelings and words influenced others.

Giunta first introduces his readers to Margaret by describing the sadness, anxiety, and fear that dominated her existence as a lay penitent. He does this by bookending his account of Margaret's initial association with the Cortonese Franciscans with an extended report Christ had given her detailing the stages of her penitential calling. Giunta writes that Christ had told Margaret to remember the sorrow and desperation she felt when her father and stepmother had refused to offer her refuge after the death of her "enemy of salvation," a reference to her lover in Montepulciano.[24] Christ reminded Margaret how she had gone to Cortona and submitted to the obedience of the Friars Minor. It was here in Cortona, Christ recounted, that her heart was healed through her "filial fear" of the Franciscans. Thus, from the text's very first lines, Giunta asks his readers to pay attention to Margaret's emotional life.

Although Margaret's emotions take center stage at the beginning of the *Legenda*, the reader is given only a few details about what this new lay penitent actually did to prove her religious dedication. In that same initial conversation with Christ, the reader hears about the many ways in which Margaret began to subject her body to a rigorous routine of penance, denying herself the ornaments, foods, and comforts to which she had been accustomed.[25] But Giunta encloses these details within mentions of other emotions. He writes that Margaret had shared her "many gifts of fear, sorrow, and tears" with both the Franciscans and the Cortonese; she asked them with such "sorrowful groans and sighs" if she would be rescued from the exile of her sinful life that she "made the friars weep."[26] The idea that Margaret's emotions are contagious—her sorrow and fears "made the friars weep"—is a theme that Giunta will employ throughout the *Legenda*.

---

24. Ibid., 181: "Recordare quod, hoste tue salutis defuncto, ad patrem tuum, Lauianum, confecta doloribus, lacrimis irrigata, facie lacerata, nigris induta uestibus ualdeque confusa redisti."

25. Ibid., 182.

26. Ibid., 183: "Recordare copiosi muneris timoris, doloris et fletus continui quod tam copiose tibi largiri dignatus sum, ut non solum fratres minores, quibus te commendaui, cum lacrimarum interrogares profluuio, si ego tuus pater et dominus exulem factam in delictis, te de cetero ad misericordiam et patriam reuocarem, uerum etiam seculares interrogando cum fletibus dolorosis de hoc tuis amaris suspiriis ad fletus uberrimos commouebas."

But while she may have felt sorrow in her early days in Cortona, the emotions that Giunta ascribes to Margaret most often are fear and shame. For example, Christ reminds Margaret of how she would "blush" whenever she saw one of the friars "in church, in a house, or on the street." Christ asks Margaret: "Do you not remember how you would not dare to sit down or even speak to secular persons in the presence of the friars?"[27] Margaret's feelings of intimidation likely had some basis in the privileged position the friars held in thirteenth-century Cortona.[28] The Franciscans had first arrived in the city in 1250, when Elias of Cortona moved all of the friars he could convince to join him out of the hermitage known as the Celle, which had been founded by Francis and was located just outside of Cortona, and into the newly built church of San Francesco within the city walls.[29] San Francesco was one of the earliest Franciscan churches in Italy and stood just a few meters away from the Palazzo del Comune, the city's political and economic center.[30] Having established themselves in Cortona well before the arrival of other mendicant orders, the Cortonese Franciscans maintained their power in the city in no small part because of their central location.[31] As the most prominent religious order in the city, the Franciscans could offer Margaret a path to redeem herself from her past shame and give validity to her new life of penitence.

But that path was a treacherous one. Margaret's fear of the friars was a product not only of their power but also of the skepticism and concern that—the *Legenda* makes clear—the order maintained toward her well after her initial association with them. Giunta emphasizes that the friars had these feelings because of the specter of shame and dishonor that Margaret's very presence represented. For example, Christ tells Margaret that she need not bleach her soiled veil, the stench, he assures her, will not make the friars sick. Christ goes on to remind Margaret that when she first came to them with "the stench" of sins not one of them shrank from her, so they would hardly be concerned

---

27. Ibid., 182: "Nonne cum frater aliquis de ordine tui patris apparebat in ecclesia, domibus seu uia, pre reuerentia facies tua perfundebatur rubore, timens sedere uel loqui cum secularibus coram ipsis?"

28. For the history of the Franciscans in Cortona, see Giuseppina Inga, "Gli insediamenti mendicanti a Cortona," in *Cortona: Storia della città*, (Milan: Electa, 1976), 44–55; and Fortunato Iozzelli, "I francescani ad Arezzo e a Cortona nel duecento," in *La presenza francescana nella Toscana del '200: "Sabati francescani"—Ciclo di conferenze 1989–1990* (Florence: Convento S. Francesco, 1990), 121–42.

29. For the history of the Celle, see *Le Celle di Cortona, eremo francescano del 1211* (Cortona: Calosci, 1977).

30. Girolamo Mancini, *Cortona nel medio evo* (Florence, 1897), 45–55.

31. Of the four mendicant churches built in Cortona, only San Francesco and San Agostino are within the city walls. San Agostino, located in the southwest corner of the city, was finished by 1275. San Domenico and Santa Maria (both second half of the thirteenth century) were built just outside the city gates; see Inga, "Gli insediamenti mendicanti a Cortona," 44–45; and Iozzelli, "I francescani ad Arezzo e a Cortona," 138–40.

about her veil.[32] Giunta's account of these conversations between Margaret and Christ make clear that the possibility of shame, disgust, and dishonor was ever present for the Franciscans when they interacted with Margaret. After all, as Christ reminds us, Margaret was once covered with the stink of her sins. In Giunta's hands, then, Margaret's emotions not only reveal the tensions that existed between her and her guardians, but they also are the prime evidence of her sanctity. As Giunta will try to prove, it is Margaret's internal life—her feelings of shame, fear, and sorrow—that allow her to reach remarkable spiritual heights. Those feelings are the engines behind her sanctity. While a layman in the twelfth century might have manifested his sanctity through extraordinary acts of penance (as Ranieri of Pisa had), and a layman or laywoman in the thirteenth century did so through extraordinary acts of charity (as Raimondo of Piacenza, Facio of Cremona, and Zita of Lucca had), in Giunta's hands, the lay penitent is made holy by means of the content and fervor of her emotional life.

The tricky negotiation between attending to the demands of lay life and reaching toward spiritual ideals is a concern voiced in the *vitae* of all communal lay saints. By contrast, it makes only a brief appearance in Giunta's *Legenda*. Giunta reports that after Margaret had joined the Franciscans' order of penitents, she supported herself and her son by working as a midwife for the noblewomen of Cortona.[33] Although Giunta's emphasis on Margaret's decision to earn a living "by the work of her hands" might remind one of the repeated references in Zita's *vita* to the manual labor the Lucchese saint performed, Giunta is not particularly concerned with celebrating Margaret's ability to balance the demands of her work life with her spiritual life. In fact, Giunta discusses Margaret's working life only in the first few pages of the second chapter and seems to offer these details in the service of describing the harsh penitence to which she regularly subjected her body. In Giunta's account, charity is not the ultimate expression of Margaret's religious life but rather a means to an end. And unlike other communal lay saints, that end is not aiding others as much as it is the development of Margaret's own penitential and spiritual program.

Thus, when Giunta first mentions that Margaret worked as a midwife, he does so to emphasize the degree to which she fasted. Even though she had to

---

32. *Legenda*, 211: "A fratribus autem, quos tibi dedi in patres, nil recipias seruitii uel laboris quod ipsorum possit honoribus derogare. Iniungo etiam tibi ut capitis uelum de petiolis factum omni priuetur albedine. Et si times ne filiorum meorum fratrum minorum accedentium ad te stomaci sordem panni abhorreant, non de hoc oportet quod dubites, quia dum prius te misi ad eos et posui sub eorum sancta custodia, cum in tuis adhuc feteres defectibus, te propter amorem meum nullus abhorruit set in filiam receperunt. Quanto magis ergo faciam, quando te consecraui in tabernaculum meum, quod non uilipendent te ex fetore panniculi? Ibi pie consolabor te et uisitationes meas suauitate plenissimas degustabis."

33. Ibid., 186.

prepare delicious meals for the pregnant women she cared for, Giunta writes, Margaret would continue to fast as if it were Lent.[34] The other details Giunta provides about Margaret's working life serve a similar rhetorical purpose: while Margaret would bathe her patients, she would wash herself only in tears; and while other attendants would sing for the laboring women, Margaret would stand off to the side and cry, inducing in all those present great feelings of guilt and compunction.[35] At the same time that Giunta reassures his reader that Margaret was able to recite all of the canonical hours (even adding in a few extra prayers) without ignoring the women in labor around her, he notes that her duties as a midwife often left her unable to attend Mass and sermons.[36] In order for her to be able both to devote herself to the care of others and pursue her spiritual goals, Giunta reasons, Margaret would need a wealthy patron.[37] A noblewoman named Diabella filled that need, donating her house so that Margaret could found a "hospitium misericordie" or "domus misericordie."[38] In this house, Giunta tells us, Margaret founded not only a refuge for the city's poor but also a place dedicated to attending to sick friars, in gratitude for the care they had offered her.[39]

But again, Giunta seems minimally interested in Margaret's charity work. We hear how, after founding the *domus*, Margaret gave everything she could

---

34. Ibid.

35. Ibid., 186–87.

36. Ibid., 187.

37. Ibid.

38. While the text states that Margaret began her "domus misericordie" in Diabella's house, I am aware that the text also mentions in the previous sentence that Margaret needed to find a "largum dominum," in other words, a male patron. Relying on both da Pelago's conclusions, scholars have suggested that this might be a reference to either Uguccio dei Casali or his son, Guglielmino. This would move the beginning of Casali involvement with Margaret to a much earlier date. I have found no other information to confirm or deny connecting the Casali with Margaret's "largum dominum." For a good summary of the scholarship on this issue, see Iozzelli, "Introduzione," 74.

39. *Legenda*, 187. A fifteenth-century document suggests some confusion over which charitable institution Margaret founded in the city. This document claims that Margaret had founded Cortona's Fraternitas Sancte Marie de Misericordia, an organization that oversaw Cortona's Ospedale della Misericordia. This 1421 document, written by Uguccione di Lando, the prior of the Fraternitas Sancte Marie, has been transcribed by da Pelago, see *Registro*, in *Antica leggenda*, no. XXIV; see also Iozzelli, "Introduzione," 75; and Bruno Fresucci, "Attività sociale di S. Margherita," in *Cortona a Santa Margherita nel VII centenario della "conversione" 1272–1972* (Cortona: Calosci, 1973), 55–59. Two thirteenth-century documents, a charter offering Bishop Guglielmino of Arezzo's approval of the fraternity and its first statutes, make no mention of Margaret, however. For Bishop Guglielmino's charter, see Fresucci, "Attività sociale di S. Margherita," 56–57; and for the fraternity's statutes, see Piero Scapecchi, "Santa Margherita nella società cortonese del XIII secolo: Appunti sul 'Liber Fraternitatis Sancte Marie de Misericordia de Cortona' e altre fonti margaritiane," *Accademia Etrusca di Cortona Annuario* 28 (1997–98): 196–202. Scholars have been unable to determine when Margaret founded the "domus misericordie" mentioned in the *Legenda* but suspect that it was one of the charitable organizations or hospices managed by the Fraternitas Sancte Marie de Misericordia. See Iozzelli, "Introduzione," 72–77; and Cannon and Vauchez, *Margherita of Cortona*, 192–93.

to the poor, saved nothing for herself, and distributed food to the needy each year on the feast of John the Baptist.[40] Margaret may have founded one of Cortona's leading charitable institutions, but Giunta is most interested in Margaret's charity work because of its ability to illustrate her own radical transformation. Her attention to others is all the more noteworthy, Giunta seems to argue, in light of the amount of attention she had once given to herself. Thus, we hear how, as Margaret's reputation for charity spread, the poor stopped begging at the homes of the rich and came looking for alms at her cell instead.[41] Giunta notes that by begging in the streets and giving away every last bit of her and her son's food and possessions, Margaret had found, along with her frequent prayers and confessions, another means to "erase the memory of the worldly honor and vanity of her former life."[42]

Even though there are a few passing references in the rest of the text to Margaret's commitment to giving all that she had to the poor, Giunta's most extensive discussion of Margaret's charity work comes at the beginning of the chapter he titles "De perfecta conversione ipsius ad deum." The title indicates that, in Giunta's estimation, Margaret's charity work constituted the beginning of her religious life and not, as we have seen in so many of the *vitae* of lay saints who preceded her, the culmination and most perfect expression of that life. For Giunta, then, charity work functions as a barometer for the extent to which Margaret has transformed herself from a vain concubine to a devoted lay penitent.

Giunta does, however, mention that Margaret's reputation drew those looking for alms to her cell. But even in these accounts, the particular aid Margaret offers her fellow Cortonese seems to matter less than the way in which witnessing Margaret's devotional life could influence others' penitential progress. Giunta describes how, as word spread through Cortona of the intensity of Margaret's penitential life and of the visions she experienced, the Cortonese began to sit outside her cell near San Francesco, begging her to perform baptisms, and, when they heard she was experiencing a vision, rushing to her side so that they could witness her often dramatic behavior.

Giunta notes that Margaret resisted her new role as civic holy woman and longed to live as a recluse. Giunta's descriptions of this longing contribute to

---

40. *Legenda*, 188.

41. Ibid.

42. Ibid., 189: "In tam dolorosis amarisque fletibus et suspiriis nunc de suis defectibus, nunc de Iesu Christi passione conceptis posita, sciens quod uere dilectionis euidentissimum signum est operum exhibitio recta, ad exterminationem pristine uite uanique honoris seculi pro elimosina cepit ire per terram, nullius domum ingrediens nulliusque faciem hominis intuendo . . . Verumtamen tanta postea sibi ad pauperes inerat pietas maternalis, quod pro amore inopum panes integros recipere nullatenus recusabat. Hec est illa Margarita que capsam donans et uasa pauperibus tribuens, panem pro suo uictu in olla fracta et lapide tecta paupertatis amore recondidit."

the framing he does throughout the text of Margaret as a "new Magdalen."[43] He writes that Margaret had been so transformed after she received the habit of penance from the Friars Minor that she came to want "a solitary place where she could remain hidden and refrain from worldly conversation"; a place where she could be united with Christ, as a new Magdalen, through her meditation, prayers, tears, and fasts.[44] Medieval legends claimed that Mary Magdalen had lived as a recluse after Jesus's death; her status as a redeemed sinner made her all the more an appropriate model for Margaret.[45]

Giunta attributes Margaret's desire to become a recluse to the difficulties and distractions she encountered as her reputation as a visionary spread. It is significant that many of those distractions grew out of the growing sense that Margaret had a charisma that allowed her to heal, to baptize, and to exorcize. But as Cortona's holy woman, Margaret found that the demands on her time and alleged spiritual powers kept her from completing her schedule of prayer. Women would bother her both while she prayed inside of San Francesco and when she stayed within her cell near the church.[46] Giunta writes that a crowd of women often stood outside of Margaret's cell because there they would become inspired by "the ecstasies" that they saw and heard.[47] Requests for Margaret's presence at baptisms, healings, and exorcisms were constant, leaving her conflicted about what the right course of action might be; while she did not want to be a part of worldly occasions, she also worried that she might "lose merit" by declining such requests.[48] In one episode, Margaret berates herself for having eaten the figs (a particular weakness of hers) that a few devout ladies, who thought her penitential practices were too harsh, had prepared and

---

43. For Margaret as a "new Magdalen," see Benvenuti Papi, "In castro poenitentiae," 141–68; and see Katherine Ludwig Jansen, The Making of the Magdalen: Preaching and Popular Devotion in the Later Middle Ages (Princeton: Princeton University Press, 2000), 136, 261, 280, and passim.

44. Legenda, 185: "Recepto igitur a fratribus minoribus penitentie habitu, mox per Sancti Spiritus infusionem noua femina uisa est. Nam sic eam in se transformauit supernus ignis amoris, ut ex tunc antiori cura studeret perquirere qualiter se in solitario loco absconderet, tum ne cum hiis qui de terrenis rebus locuntur, loquendi haberet materiam, tum quia regi omnium seculorum ut noua Magdalena meditando, orando, flendo et ieiunando, sine medio iungi optabat."

45. On legends regarding Mary Magdalen's eremitical life, see Jansen, The Making of the Magdalen, 116–42.

46. Legenda, 197 and 371.

47. Ibid., 250: "Qua ex re sepe ad uocem flentis et in oratione cum Deo sepe loquentis, uicine domine cum magna deuotione currebant et extra celle hostiolum obseruantes cum inundantia lacrimarum orantem, seseque in uisis et auditis feruoribus ad diuinum amorem renouabant."

48. Ibid., 207: "Ne crebrescente fama honorabilior haberetur, curam cepit relinquere de pueris baptizandis, a quorum parentibus cum deuotione requirebatur. Agebat hoc propter discursum nimium quem spernebat. Dum uero super tali meditaretur proposito et tanti boni meritum perdere dubitaret, in magno perplexitatis agone posita, uidit uenientem ad se matrem filii procuratoris minorum fratrum, ut filium filii baptizaret."

brought to her cell.[49] In another episode, Giunta writes that one night, as Margaret thought about the necessity of solitude for dedicated prayer, she asked Christ to allow her to remain in her cell because too many pious women interrupted her meditations in San Francesco. Margaret believed that in her cell she could "be removed from the noise of the world" and relieved of the embarrassment she would feel if she were seen receiving divine consolations publicly.[50]

But as the *Legenda* reports, Christ denied Margaret's frequent requests to live as a recluse, reminding her that in order for her to taste his sufferings, as she had so often asked to do, she must, in preparation, experience hardships.[51] Those hardships included leaving her cell but remaining silent as she made her way through the city. She should not speak with secular people, Christ reminds her, because in the past she had been harmed by such conversations; instead, Christ encourages her to rely solely on her Franciscan guardians since they were responsible for her salvation.[52] Thus her role as the "new Magdalen" in the *Legenda* seems to rest more on her status as a redeemed sinner than as a recluse. Christ tells Margaret at one point that she cannot live as the Magdalen had lived because he did not intend for her to live in the desert; "Deserts are not relevant today," Christ explains to her, but "you can remain solitary in your own land, as if you were in a vast desert."[53] Again, it is the Franciscans who, Christ notes, will help Margaret reach this goal. If she relies upon her guardians, she will be able to live in silence in the midst of the city as if she were alone in the desert.[54] While the *Legenda* will eventually claim that Christ finally gave in to Margaret's requests, permitting her to flee the city and move

---

49. Ibid., 210.

50. Ibid., 197: "Nocte quadam in octaua Ephyphanie, dum sola in cella oraret, considerans quod orationi uacantibus solitudo necessaria est, petiit sibi concedi a Domino ne ulterius de cella exiret, tum quia deuote domine circumdabant eam in oratorio beati patris sui Francisci et sepe suis uerbis impediebant orantem, tum quia cella a strepitu mundanorum erat semota, tum quia corpus grauabatur nimis discurrere debilitatum langoribus ex penitentie austeritate contractis, tum etiam quia consolationes diuinas in publico recipere recusabat."

51. Ibid.

52. Ibid., 197–98: "Nam si hunc modum deuote seruaueris, tibi non solum pro te, uerum etiam pro meis fidelibus magna et utilissima reuelabo. Et caue ne timeas unquam creaturam aliquam plus quam me et nec oculum dirigas siue figas in uultus tecum loquentium personarum: quanto enim plus fueris a talium colloquiis separata, tanto tibi ero propinquior; et tanto menti tue ero domesticus et humanus, quanto cum seculo inueniam te siluestrem. De fratribus uero minoribus qui mittentur ad te, non intelligas hoc tibi mandari, quia ipsi sunt tue salutis occasio. Recordare quotiens dampnosa extitit familiaris allocutio secularium personarum, quot et quales penas inde traxeris et sustinebis adhuc, nisi plenius solito te correxeris."

53. Ibid., 211: "Tu etiam statum Magdalene quantum ad solitudinem cum desiderio postulasti et quamuis te in desertum non destinem, cum deserta non sint his apta temporibus, ita siluestris maneas intra terram, sicut si intra uasta deserta maneres. Ibique fratres minores, quorum te cure commisi, filia, et commicto, personam tibi assignent, que seruiat tuis necessitatibus cum silentio."

54. Ibid.

to San Basilio, in the first half of the text we repeatedly hear how it is the Cortonese friars who allow her to live a silent and solitary life in the midst of the city. To what extent, we might ask, was that silent and solitary life provided by her Franciscan guardians also one that aimed to contain her growing reputation for charismatic activities?

In order to begin to answer this question, we must first look more closely at the episodes that make up the bulk of Giunta's portion of the text. Here, we see that Margaret was rarely alone and far from silent. In fact, the majority of Giunta's text is given over to describing Margaret's dramatic, loud, and public visions. In Giunta's hands, Margaret's religious life is in effect a public spectacle. Even though Christ repeatedly tells Margaret not to speak to secular people, the intensity of her internal life consistently produces visionary experiences that are witnessed by others. On one hand, Giunta's descriptions of these episodes make clear that this was exactly the kind of behavior that concerned Margaret's Franciscan guardians. On the other hand, these displays of Margaret's internal reality—the moments when she is literally turned inside out, performing the dramas that were taking place inside of her—also function to construct a new understanding of lay sanctity. Instead of attending to the needs of the poor and sick of her community, the public and dramatic nature of Margaret's visions gives the Cortonese opportunities to consider their own transgressions, their own sins, and their own internal lives. By being a spectacle for the benefit of others, Margaret's internal life comes to have meaning for her civic community, leading it away from sin and toward salvation.

In one episode, the reader learns that Margaret had accused herself "outloud" of having both violated God's laws and brought scandal to her neighbors; she asked her fellow Cortonese if they thought God would ever forgive "the worst of sinners" such as herself.[55] Moreover, on one Good Friday, Giunta writes, Margaret ran through the streets of Cortona "as if she were drunk, weeping and groaning, like a mother who had just lost her son." Giunta recounts that Margaret stopped her circuit of the city when she reached the Franciscans' convent but would have continued on to other churches if her sense of decency and fear of the friars had not restrained her.[56]

---

55. Ibid., 217: "Ex suorum consideratione defectuum ad tam profundam humilitatem Dei famula Margarita descenderat, ut altissima uoce cum inconsolabili fletu exprimeret qualiter omnium conditorem offenderat et quibus modis per diuinorum inobedientiam preceptorum, corda dehedificauerat proximorum. Interpellabat non solum cum lacrimis et suspiriis sanctos pro suorum impetranda remissione peccaminum, uerum etiam seculares in limo mundialium uitiorum defixos interrogabat, ut ebria, si Deus, impiorum ultor, unquam parceret maxime peccatricum, dicens: 'Creditisne, karissimi patres et matres, quod Deus omnipotens exulem suam uelit de cetero in suam gratiam misericorditer reuocare?' Et hec dicendo, ita tremebat et infrigidabatur uniuersaliter cum sudore, sicut ad capitalem sententiam duceretur."
56. Ibid., 251.

In another episode, Giunta writes that one night, as Margaret thought about her own worthlessness, the devil began to tempt her with reports about her growing fame. The devil told Margaret that Christ had given her so many virtues that she had become famous among people of all ranks and reminded her of how many people were coming to visit her. Margaret's response to the devil's observations both confirms his words at the same time as it recasts their significance. After hearing the devil's taunts, Margaret passed part of the night in silence. Before the night was over, however, she got up and began to shout from the balcony of the house where she was staying: "Get up, people of Cortona, get up! Arise I tell you, and drive me out of town with stones, for I am a sinner who has transgressed against God and my neighbors!" As Margaret continued to weep and wail, Giunta reports that people came from all around to see her, and having "only admiration and compassion," they returned to their homes "inspired" and "full of remorse for their own sins."[57] It appears that Margaret had indeed become famous in her adopted city. Her public act became the impetus for those witnesses to reflect upon their own sins. Giunta's recounting of this episode calls attention to the potential danger of Margaret's growing reputation and fame as well as the practical influence her outbursts could have over her fellow Cortonese. Although Margaret's past sins might have the potential to corrupt her new religious identity, they also made Margaret's role as a penitent all the more powerful and inspirational to those around her.

And finally, in perhaps the most arresting of Margaret's visions, Giunta notes that one day Margaret had asked him not to leave his convent after she learned that she would experience a "mental crucifixion" inside San Francesco.[58] Giunta does not seem to have listened, describing in detail what he witnessed of her behavior. As "Margaret's soul became completely absorbed in God," she narrated to those around her each moment of Christ's Passion as it was unfolding in her head: "Now I see him being led from the palace of Pilate outside the city . . . Now the Jews insult and murmur against him . . . Now he

---

57. The text does not make clear what house Margaret was staying in, but it seems likely that this was the house of Marinaria and Raniera, the lay penitents who offered Margaret and her son refuge when they first arrived in Cortona. Ibid., 204: "At Margarita que solius eterni Dei querebat gloriam, nocturni silentii tempus expectans, cepit uicinis quiescentibus de solario sibi prestite domus Tarduli cum fletu clamare, dicens: 'Surgite, Cortonenses, surgite—dico—surgite et sine more dispendio cum lapidibus de uestra expellite me regione: nam ego sum illa peccatrix que hec et hec contra Deum et proximum egi.' Et descripta per ordinem cum innundantia lacrimarum, excitando uicinos undique, preterita uitia sua, pre admiratione, compassione et hedificatione plenissima onmes in suis compungebantur cubiculis, gratias Domino cum lacrimis referentes."

58. Ibid., 242–43: "Horaque predicta, dum uenisset ad locum, me suum confessorem et indignum baiulum requirens, humiliter pro speciali poposcit gratia quatenus nulla ratione locum fratrum egrederer, quia sicut sibi fuerat reuelatum a Domino debebat ad crucem die illa mentaliter crucifigi."

cries out in a loud voice and commends his spirit to God the father."[59] In addition to describing each moment of Christ's ordeal, Margaret experienced the drama of what she was seeing in her own body. Giunta writes that her movements were so striking that "we believed she was about to die." Margaret ground her teeth and twisted her body until she turned pale, her pulse stopped, and "her body became cold as ice."[60] When she finally completed her recounting of the Passion, Margaret lowered her head and did not move for several hours, leaving those around her convinced that she had died.[61] Giunta writes that not only had the friars witnessed and been affected by Margaret's vision, but the people of Cortona had also been moved. Many Cortonese left their work as well as infants in their cribs and the sick in their beds in order to witness Margaret's mental crucifixion.[62] When Margaret awoke, "as one who just rose from the dead," she was horrified to realize that she had experienced Christ's Passion "in front of the people, rather than in her cell."[63] Christ reassured Margaret that her vision had been a public affair precisely because she was a "mirror of sinners," who could inspire even the most obstinate of sinners to be saved. Nevertheless, she remained distraught.[64] Giunta's narration of the episode ends with him describing how Margaret was so upset that she began to run around the city asking those she passed if they had seen the crucified Christ; her state of anxiety and her entreaties were so powerful that she was unable to eat or sleep and moved those she encountered to tears.[65]

There is much in these episodes that highlights how skeptical and concerned the Franciscans were when it came to Margaret. The responsibility *Supra montem* gave them to oversee the religious lives of all lay penitents likely seemed

---

59. Ibid., 243–44: "Finitis itaque missarum sollempniis, prope horam tertiam anima illa Deo deuota, felle passionis potata et in Deum absorta, uidere cepit proditionis processum . . . Et dicebat: 'Nunc uideo eum de palatio extrahi, nunc extra portam duci et Simonem angariari . . . Nunc Iudei insultant et murmurant . . . Nunc indulget omnibus suis crucifixoribus et spiritum Deo Patri suo, uoce altissima, recommendat.'"

60. Ibid., 244: "In qua tam mira patuerunt signa doloris, ut in mortis articulo crederemus eam penitus constitutam. Pre nimio enim uehementique dolore stridebat dentibus, torquebatur ut uermis et discolorabatur ad instar cineris, perdebat pulsum, ammictebat loquelam, glaciabatur totaliter et ita sunt facte rauce fauces eius, ut uix posset intelligi cum redibat ad sensum."

61. Ibid., 245.

62. Ibid., 244.

63. Ibid., 245: "Set quia uersa retrorsum in oratorio uidit multitudinem personarum, extrema gaudii occupauit timor amarus et cepit uehementer affligi, quia Deus illum passionis dolorem in conspectu concesserat populorum et non in cella."

64. Ibid.: "At suorum amantium admirandus amator, Margarite sedans timorem dixit: 'De omnibus, que circa te et in te hodie acta sunt, non timeas neque dubites, quia te feci speculum peccatorum quantumcumque obstinatorum, ut agnoscant per te quam libenter impertior eis meam misericordiam, ut saluentur.'"

65. Ibid., 245–46.

more of a burden than an opportunity, especially when they had to deal with a lay penitent like Margaret. Her expression of a penitential commitment was public, dramatic, and often disturbing. But we have to wonder about the extent to which it was novel. After all, in the *vitae* of earlier lay saints, we see hints of behavior that could also be categorized as public spectacle: Ranieri of Pisa stripped off his clothes in the middle of Jerusalem's Church of the Holy Sepulchre; Bona of Pisa repeatedly claimed to have been visited by Christ, Saint James, the Virgin Mary, and other saints; Rose of Viterbo wandered around her city with a group of laywomen, preaching about sin and redemption and also experienced what is described in her first *vita* as a three-day martyrdom; and Pier "Pettinaio" of Siena regularly fell into ecstatic trances. If Margaret's dramatic and public expressions were part and parcel of the way in which lay religious enthusiasm was expressed in the late medieval communes, we ought not to ask why she behaved in such a manner, but rather ask why Giunta makes such behavior the focus of the *Legenda*. In other words, why does Margaret's charity work, the dominant currency of lay sanctity in the late thirteenth century, matter less to him than her internal life and visionary experiences?

One way to answer this question would be to return to a distinction made by Wolf in his study of Francis of Assisi. Francis, Wolf notes, comes across in the sources as more interested in becoming poor than in aiding the poor.[66] As a result, Francis presents a sharp contrast with the reigning model of an ideal lay life represented by someone like Raimondo of Piacenza, who was chided by Christ for spending too much time attending to his own spiritual progress through pilgrimages and not enough time helping the needy of his own city. This was the occasion that led Raimondo to return to Piacenza and dedicate his life to aiding that city's poor and needy. In chapter 2, I argued that Innocent III's canonization of Omobono of Cremona made possible what Wolf describes as Francis's "different path"—once the church had defined a religious life for the laity that did not threaten its own role as the guardian of charismatic authority, it could endorse a movement that had at its core ideals of self-transformation and charismatic power.

By focusing on Margaret's internal life—that is, by essentially turning her inside out and by making what is going on inside of her (her feelings of shame, the visions those feelings produce) the prime evidence of her sanctity, Giunta connects Margaret to Francis, and as a result, constructs her as a Franciscan saint. Francis wanted to become poor in order to live what he believed was the most

---

66. Wolf, *The Poverty of Riches*, 69–76.

authentic version of the *vita apostolica*; in Giunta's eyes, Margaret—as a lay member of the order—must become an embodiment of lay sin. She is a "mirror of sinners"—as she is so often called in the text—and can show her devotees their own missteps as well as a path for redemption. The impetus behind this new model of lay sanctity came out of Giunta's dual agenda in writing about Margaret. Giunta began the *Legenda* in an effort to check Margaret for signs of fraud and heresy. Once he was convinced of her authenticity and sanctity, he had to reframe his material in order to convince his fellow friars that Margaret's behavior spoke specifically to Franciscan ideals. His initial questioning of Margaret aided this reframing—he had already been more interested in what was going on inside of this lay saint than in the actions she performed for her civic community.

In creating this new model, Giunta finds examples of Margaret's spiritual gifts—her charisma—that are distinct from the kind of charismatic activity ascribed to other late medieval Italian lay saints. Margaret does not, for the most part, perform living miracles that respond to the needs of her fellow lay population. Instead, Giunta finds evidence of Margaret's charisma in the visions she earns from the intensity of her thoughts and feelings. At its core, this kind of charisma is both self-reflective and circular. Margaret's spiritual gifts do not lead her to reach outside of herself to help others but instead demonstrate and prove her own spiritual worth and acumen. Moreover, it is through the shame that Giunta claims Margaret feels about her past identity and behavior, and the lengths she goes to purge herself of the evidence of this past (her beauty, the fine clothes and food she once craved, and her vanity), that she earns the ability to engage in conversations with Christ and receive visions of his passion.

In the end, Giunta's characterization of lay sanctity is made all the more striking when compared with the portrait of Margaret in the second half of the text. After recounting the Franciscans' condemnation of Margaret, her move to San Basilio, and Badia's assumption of the role of primary confessor, the *Legenda* no longer describes what is going on inside of Margaret. Instead, the text presents a portrait of lay sanctity more akin to the model of the communal lay saint that emerged over the thirteenth century. In short, instead of hearing about Margaret's internal dialogue and efforts at a self-transformation, we hear about how her spiritual gifts allowed her to help her civic community.

Margaret as Lay Civic Saint: The Cure for Urban Life

In episodes likely witnessed if not written by Ser Badia, the secular cleric who took over as Margaret's confessor at San Basilio, we no longer hear about

Margaret's internal, emotional state. Instead, the text focuses on the ways in which Margaret's access to Christ allowed her to impart wisdom and warnings to her fellow Cortonese, to other Franciscans, and to the devotees who surrounded her at San Basilio. To some extent, the change in the tenor and shape of Margaret's religious life was likely the result of the Franciscans' condemnation. Not long after she was denounced, Margaret heard Christ tell her that while in the past she had proclaimed his Passion "in a loud voice and with inconsolable tears," she now remained silent "out of fear of being accused of vainglory." But while in that same conversation Christ had encouraged her to return to her more dramatic devotions and "not to fear the whispering of worldly people who were questioning the wonders" taking place in her, the second half of the *Legenda* makes clear that she did not do so.[67] Christ ends his conversation with Margaret by giving her an extensive description of the ways in which she should go about proclaiming the details of his life and Passion to others. From the wounds of Christ's circumcision, to his working of miracles, to his betrayal by Judas's kiss, and finally to his bloody death, Christ provides Margaret with a vivid narrative that she is to proclaim to others.[68] Unlike the account of her mental crucifixion that we found in the first half of the text, in which Giunta had recorded both Margaret's narration of each moment in Christ's Passion as it unfolded in her head and the reaction those around her saw taking place in her body—Margaret grinding her teeth, and twisting like a worm in agony—here, the reader is not given any sense of Margaret's physical state.[69] Rather than focusing on the effect of Christ's words, this passage emphasizes Margaret's role as the mouthpiece for Christ's story. She is not to reenact Christ's life but instead to proclaim its details to those around her.

Thus, in the second half of the *Legenda*, the evidence for Margaret's sanctity is found overwhelmingly in her role as Christ's agent. As the spokeswoman for Christ's complaints about contemporary urban life, Margaret relays information needed by those around her for their own salvation. Unlike earlier episodes, it is not the physical transformation taking place within Margaret that matters. Margaret's insides are not being turned out when she comes into contact with Christ. Instead, Christ's words remain the focus; the fact that they

---

67. *Legenda*, 254: "Passionem meam altis uocibus hactenus, inconsolabiliter flendo, solebas exprimere et nunc propter detrahentium metum, qui tui fletum doloris temere pro uana gloria fieri extimant, silentium tibi penitus indidisti. Ad fletum ergo pristinum reuerti non differas, quia propter secularium et mendaciter interpretantium bona, que in me fiunt, uerba uana et falsa duris cruciatibus punienda, passionem meam sub gutture non replices nec abscondas, quia nulla ratione debes timere proximum, ubi ex parte tua non datur peccandi set gloriam et gratiam promerendi occasio."

68. Ibid., 254–55.

69. Ibid., 244.

are being funneled through Margaret stands as evidence and confirmation of both her piety and her sanctity.

To that end, we hear the long series of questions and answers that Christ relayed to Margaret, in which he laments how the contemporary world continually reenacts his Passion with their sins. "Who are those who betray me, like Judas?" Christ asks Margaret. He answers His own question: "Those who talk, laugh, eat, drink, and dwell with other people, and then kill them for money."[70] As Margaret continues to convey Christ's invective, it becomes increasingly aimed at an urban audience. "Who are those who pull out my hair?" Christ asks, replying: "Goldsmiths, merchants, and artisans whose avarice drives them to concoct ever more clever ways to make illicit profits."[71] And "who are those who are not afraid to pull my beard and hit me in the face?" Miserable usurers, Christ responds, those who have "no hope of salvation."[72] And finally, he asks, "Who are those who are not afraid to spit in my face? Those who blaspheme my name and paint their faces with makeup."[73] In another spate of Christ's complaints that Margaret conveys, Christ tells her that he deplores "the married who debase the state of matrimony," claiming that "they should really be called adulterers." He is grieved by people's interest in the latest fashions in clothes and jewelry, which, he says, "fill the soul with obscene thoughts." And finally he finds "the use of perfumes, ornaments, and ribbons" offensive, noting that he takes no pleasure in the prayers, pilgrimages, almsgiving, fasts, and other good works performed by those who engage in such sins.[74] These charges and complaints could be read as a reminder of Margaret's past shame—Margaret had once loved painting her own face and parading up and down the streets of Montepulciano, as a nobleman's

---

70. Ibid., 257: "Qui sunt illi qui me produnt ut Iudas? Illi profecto sunt qui locuntur, rident, comedunt, bibunt et dormiunt cum hominibus et pro peccunia eos occidunt."

71. Ibid.: "Qui sunt illi qui modo tondent capillos meos? Aurifices, mercatores et artifices qui per auaritiam suam uariis modis et nouis lucrandi intendunt."

72. Ibid., 258: "Qui sunt illi qui genas meas et barbam euellere non formidant? Hii sunt miseri et a spe glorie separati feneratores."

73. Ibid.: "Qui sunt illi qui in faciem meam spuere non uerentur? Blasphemantes nomen meum et figmentis faciem suam pingentes."

74. Ibid., 398–99: "Conqueror tibi de illo innominabili uitio, quod in mea natiuitate puniui. Conqueror de coniugatis, qui matrimoniis tam uitiose utuntur, quod non uere coniuges, set adulteri nuncupantur. Conqueror de uana gloria nouiter adinuenta in indumentis et aliis ornamentis, que sunt occasio lucrorum illicitorum et faciunt intuentes peccare mortaliter, ymaginationes immunditie ipsorum mentibus inprimendo. Et ideo de huiusmodi loturis, ornamentis et ligaturis sepe mortaliter me offendunt: nam in facie sua ferunt audaciam et arma Sathane, necnon et in cordibus recondunt opera pessimi ducis et temptatoris. Et hinc est quod non solum eorum cogitationes, locutiones et opera terminantur ad ipsum, set inde oritur quod eorum orationes, peregrinationes, elemosine ac ieiunia, cum ceteris bonis operibus, minime michi placent."

concubine.[75] As a fallen laywomen who had so radically transformed her life, Margaret provided a powerful example of both the sinful snares of the lay world and the possibility of redemption that a life dedicated to penance offered. Giunta exploited these aspects of Margaret's past life in an effort to address the Franciscans' concerns; by making Margaret's internal, emotional state the focus of his writing he aimed not only to convince the friars that she was a saint but also that she was a new kind of saint—the lay Franciscan visionary. In Christ's invective, however, it is Christ's message that is the focus, not Margaret's past shame or present example.

In other passages found in the second half of the *Legenda*, which seem to describe moments in Margaret's life that took place at San Basilio, Christ continues to exclaim to Margaret about his disappointment in the present state of the world. In a vision that Margaret experienced in her cell during Advent, the saint claimed to have seen an angel with six wings in the midst of flames appear above her. As Margaret lay limp in the arms of her companions, Christ spoke to her, criticizing the sinful behavior of her contemporaries. Pointing out the sins of "bad virgins, married people, and widows" as well as "cheating merchants, and depraved usurers," Christ asked Margaret why people continued to injure him.[76] Although the text describes the physical reaction this vision caused in Margaret (she lay limp in her companions' arms), the real focus here is again the content of Christ's complaints.

Those complaints dominate the second half of the *Legenda* and continue to be particularly aimed at the sins perpetrated by the contemporary urban lay world. Christ tells Margaret the great offense notaries cause him when they add, change, or reduce the terms of wills or other contracts. Calling them "cruel and inflexible," Christ notes that these notaries have no concern for widows, orphans, or wards; rather, "their only concern is making money."[77] Counselors are no better received by Christ. In their desire to enrich their friends, they "neglect to defend the common good," Christ claims. And while they might appear to be working for the public interest, in reality they work

---

75. Ibid., 204.

76. Ibid., 394–95: "Conqueror de malis uirginibus, coniugatis et uiduis, de mercatoribus falsis et usurariis prauis, qui de suis offensis aspere punientur: nam qui in hoc seculo dilationem punitionis recipiunt, punientur durius in loco illo et tempore, quibus uoces eorum exaudiri non poterunt nec aliquorum suffragiis adiuuari. Quare, filia, meus populus me offendit, pro cuius amore iam tibi relata toleraui libenter, ut eorum sententiam retractarem?"

77. Ibid., 399: "Conqueror de notariis, qui offendunt me addendo, alterando, minuendo, differendo de hiis que audiunt in testamentis et aliis contractibus; qui crudelitate rigidi non compatiuntur uiduis, orphanis et pupillis, set solum peccunie cumulande intendunt."

"only for their private welfare, seeking fame and praise."[78] Christ concludes his tirade with an invective that seems to carry with it a condemnation of urban commercial activity in general. Christ complains to Margaret about "lying merchants" who, in their "wish to profit," conceal the flaws in their merchandise, those who "pass off inferior goods as being of higher quality and the sick for the healthy," and finally craftsmen "who defraud their customers with their weights and measures."[79]

At the conclusion of his long list of complaints, Christ tells Margaret that although he himself has endured insults and beatings, the sinners he mentioned "will not tolerate even a word of criticism," because, as he tells her, "they refuse to see me as their mirror and model of behavior and listen to sermons about me."[80] The phrase "mirror and model" appears throughout the *Legenda*. In several conversations, Christ tells Margaret that her penitential transformation has made her a mirror and model for the laity. Whether depicting Margaret as the "mirror of sinners," "a model of patience," or "a mirror in eternal life for all sinners," the text repeatedly emphasizes that her past has made her all the more able to show other laymen and laywomen the path to salvation.[81] But in those passages relaying moments witnessed and likely recorded by Giunta, Margaret's dramatic penitential extremes and visionary moments ultimately do not reflect common lay experiences but rather turn her own internal life inside out. In Badia's text, however, the complaints Christ relates to Margaret allows her to function more fully as that mirror: her sinful urban neighbors are encouraged to see a bit of themselves in her history and use her as a model of redemption.

---

78. Ibid.: "Conqueror tibi de prauis consiliariis, qui particularibus et priuatis amicitiis capti, comunem utilitatem impediunt et non defendunt: et si aliquando pro reipublice utilitate uidentur loqui, hoc ideo fideliter agere se ostendunt, ut laus et fama propterea in eorundem commodum conuertatur. Quare uerba eorum sub colore liciti proferuntur, ut etiam collegas opprimant et in contemptione confundant, maiorem legalitatem ad comune bonum mostrantes, opera uero nulla."

79. Ibid., 399–400: "Conqueror tibi de mercatoribus falsis, qui mendaciter et sine lege discretionis lucrari uolunt et rerum uitia etiam in herbis occultant. Conqueror de uendentibus panem et uinum, ceram et oleum, panum, repe et alia quecumque uenduntur cum malitia et proximorum deceptione; et de hiis qui uendunt mala pro bonis et infirma pro sanis. Conqueror et de hiis qui uendunt triticum, salem et oleum et de artificibus omnibus et de hiis qui offendunt in pondere et mensura."

80. Ibid., 400: "Nam merito hec fient, cum ego, Dei Filius, substinuerim pro eis tot uerba et uerbera et ipsi pro me nolunt unum solummodo uerbum pati. Et quare hoc? Quia in me, suum speculum, non attendunt, uerbum predicationis mee audire contempnunt, immitantes hostis antiqui dolos, actus et uoluntates."

81. Ibid., 327: "Verum lux uera sui comunicatiua nobis equaliter, dixit ei: 'Non loquar tecum, si emiseris assistentes, cum fecerim te speculum peccatorum'"; ibid., 395: "in qua etiam multas consolationes et tribulationes te noueris susceptura et in exemplum patientie tibi me pono . . ."; ibid., 401: "Et dico tibi quod tu eris unum speculum in uita eterna omnibus peccatoribus: necesse namque est ut misericordia mea demostretur in celo et in terra."

Thus, when Margaret parrots Christ's complaints about lying merchants, bad virgins, and evil counselors, the focus is not on how her religious experiences transform or affect her but on how she can influence others. As Christ's conduit, she no longer has the potential to dishonor and disgust those around her, but instead the potential to influence and transform her fellow city-dwellers. Margaret can offer both criticism of her contemporary world and represent the potential for its transformation. Moreover, in the episodes describing how some of those transformations take shape, Margaret acts more like other thirteenth-century communal lay saints—we see her performing miracles.

For example, the reader learns that during her lifetime, Margaret became known for releasing souls from purgatory through her prayers. On one occasion, the *Legenda* describes a visit Margaret received from the souls of two shoemakers who had been murdered before they had the chance to confess their sins. One of the shoemakers admitted to Margaret that he had been a dishonest businessman and had been guilty of feigning friendship and love. He begged Margaret to encourage his family and that of his fellow shoemaker to make satisfaction for their sins so that they might be released from purgatory.[82] Although the text does not tell us if Margaret or the families were successful, in another passage we learn that Margaret was able to help her friend Gilia move from purgatory to heaven.[83]

Margaret also transforms the lives of her fellow Cortonese through her ability to see into their souls and help them to make, or their confessors to elicit, a full confession.[84] In an extended conversation between Margaret and Christ, the reader learns that one of Margaret's companions had not fully confessed her sins. Christ tells Margaret that while this woman "believed that no serious sins remained in her soul," he would reveal to Margaret this woman's hidden sins so that Margaret could, in turn, reveal them to the woman's confessor, who is not named in this passage. Christ gives Margaret a long list of sins and ends by noting that even though this woman will receive the light of God's grace when she does make a full confession, she will never completely recognize the gift that Margaret's revelation has provided.[85]

The later chapters of the *Legenda* describe even more of the ways that Margaret could effect change in others. She serves as a source of guidance and

---

82. Ibid., 351.
83. See ibid., 391–92. The text also reports that Margaret told Marinaria (one of the women who had offered her refuge when she arrived in Cortona) that her son had been released from purgatory; see *Legenda*, 393–94.
84. Ibid., 351, 391–92, and 393–94.
85. See ibid., 354–58.

advice for several Franciscan friars, a dramatic change in the relationship we saw between Margaret and her often skeptical guardians in the first part of the text. In one passage, Christ gives Margaret advice to pass on to Friar Benigno, who was concerned that he was saying Mass and receiving the Eucharist too often. Through Margaret, Christ assures Benigno that he is pleased with his commitment to the poor and that as long as he confesses his sins, he may say Mass and presumably receive the Eucharist as often as he desires.[86] It is striking to see Margaret in this passage offering reassurance on a subject about which she was hesitant. Earlier in the text, Christ told Margaret not to worry if she was worthy to receive communion but to partake in it daily.[87] In fact, an entire chapter of the *Legenda* discusses Margaret's desire for frequent communion, her constant fear that she was unworthy to receive the sacrament, and finally Christ's assurances that her commitment to confession, prayer, and penance had redeemed her.[88] Conversely, this passage is also noteworthy for how little it depicts Margaret's internal life mattering. The focus of the *Legenda* has moved to documenting Margaret's help for others—she is no longer a lay Franciscan visionary as much as she is lay civic saint, attending to the needs and concerns of her urban community.

San Basilio: A Franciscan Community Apart

Between the time when Margaret left her cell in the city center and her death in 1297, the church of San Basilio not only began what would become a massive project of restoration and rebuilding but also became the center of a community of lay penitents who had followed Margaret up the hill and away from the San Francesco friars. In the earliest document we have connecting Margaret to San Basilio, Bishop Ildebrandino (1289–1312) reconfirmed the name of San Basilio on August 27, 1290, authorized the church to be rebuilt *ex novo*, and offered an indulgence to anyone who aided that rebuilding. We know from the *Legenda* that Margaret had previously sought this privilege from Ildebrandino's predecessor, Bishop Guglielmino.[89] Another charter issued by Cor-

---

86. Ibid., 375.
87. See ibid., 317–18.
88. See ibid., 319–47.
89. Bishop Guglielmino is the subject of much criticism in the text. In chapter 9, Christ instructs Margaret to tell the bishop to stop doing a number of things, including postponing the confirmation of the title of San Basilio; *Legenda*, 401–3. Moreover, in both the first and second half of the text Christ tells Margaret that there would soon be peace between Bishop Guglielmino of Arezzo and the people of Cortona; ibid., 219–20 and 303–6. Scholars have assumed that these passages refer to the peace

tona's commune in September of 1290, less than ten days after Ildebrandino's charter, names Badia as the rector of the newly reconfirmed church of San Basilio, and notes that the church stands on communal land.[90] These charters suggest that just a few years after the Franciscans had condemned her as delusional and a fraud, Margaret had found vital sources of support in the new bishop of Arezzo and Cortona's communal government. They also make clear that, at least seven years before her death, Margaret had begun to turn her new home at San Basilio into something much more than a place of solitude.

Although we have evidence that mentions the lay penitents who followed Margaret up the hill and remained there to manage her cult as part of a Franciscan community, it would be a mistake to see that community as a satellite of the community at Cortona's San Francesco. In November 1392, nearly a century after Margaret's death, the commune of Cortona granted control of the church, its adjacent houses, and Margaret's shrine to the San Francesco Franciscans.[91] This marked the end of nearly one hundred years of management by the community of penitents who began as Margaret's devotees. Even though late thirteenth- and early fourteenth-century sources identify these penitents as *mantellati* or *continenti*, by the mid-fourteenth century those living and working at San Basilio were called members of the Franciscan Third Order in extant sources.[92] But beyond a few references in the *Legenda* to those helping Margaret at her last cell, information about this community of lay penitents comes almost exclusively from a number of testaments and a series of episcopal and papal legatine charters and indulgences. These documents suggest that, even before her death, Margaret took part in the efforts to restore San Basilio and was aided by a community of devotees that included both lay penitents as well as clerics. These charters also portray this community of lay penitents as living together in a number of houses surrounding San Basilio, responsible for maintaining the church and Margaret's tomb, and overseeing both a hospital for the pilgrims who came to Margaret's tomb and the *domus*

---

agreement reached between the bishop and Cortona in 1277; see Cannon and Vauchez, *Margherita of Cortona*, 14; and Mancini, *Cortona nel medio evo*, 76.

90. This charter is transcribed by da Pelago, *Registro*, no. V. Also see D. M. Manni, *Osservazioni istoriche sopra i sigilli antichi de secoli bassi*, vol. 19 (Florence, 1757), 66; Scapecchi, "Santa Margherita nella società cortonese," 202; and Mario Sensi, "Margherita da Cortona nel contesto storico-sociale Cortonese," *Collectanea Franciscana* 69 (1999): 243–44.

91. ASF, Unione di vari luoghi pii di Cortona, November 25, 1392; this charter has also been transcribed by da Pelago, *Registro*, no. XXI.

92. Lodovico da Pelago, "Sommario della storia della chiesa e convento di Santa Margherita da Cortona, compilato e disposto per ordine cronologico dal P. Fra Lodovico da Pelago," MS, Archivio del Convento di S. Margherita, Cortona, 1290 and 1298. For charter referring to the penitents as members of the Franciscan third order, see ASF, Unione, July 2, 1336; July 10, 1336; November 15, 1360; August 10, 1363; April 17, 1370; and May 9, 1374.

misericordia, which the *Legenda* claims Margaret had founded.[93] And finally, these sources show how both the people of Cortona and church officials were aware of the distinction between them and the Franciscans at San Francesco, dividing their pious bequests and indulgences accordingly.[94]

In a will dated to September 27, 1290, Donna Santese vowed to bequeath money to a number of Cortonese churches as well as to those who were in service to the church of San Basilio.[95] Badia is named as the testament's executor, and is identified not only as the rector of San Basilio but also as associated with the *domus misericordiae*.[96] The next surviving document from San Basilio comes from nine months after Margaret's death. On November 28, 1297, Bishop Pietro of Chiusi, which was the diocese that included Laviano, Margaret's birthplace, offered an indulgence of forty days to anyone who donated money to aid the construction of the new church in which the body of the "beatissima Margherita" remained.[97] The bishop's indulgence mentions the miracles that had been taking place in San Basilio, stating that the blind had been made to see, the deaf to hear, and that many lame and infirm people had been liberated from their maladies at Margaret's tomb.[98]

On March 1, 1298, another charter issued by Bishop Ildebrandino promoted Felice, identified as a member of the *continenti*, into the priesthood.[99] We know from later charters as well as Giunta's chapter on miracles (see below) that Felice eventually succeeded Badia as rector of San Basilio.[100] In an additional charter issued in 1298, we see a mention of another individual who seems to have been a member of the community of penitents Margaret established at San Basilio: in his March 18, 1298 testament, Marzio offered himself and his belongings to God and the blessed Basilio, placing himself in the hands of Badia, who is again identified as the rector of the communal church of San

93. da Pelago, "Sommario," 1298, 1304, 1308; also see ASF, Unione, March 18, 1298; August 15, 1304; June 1, 1308; June 21, 1308.

94. Bornstein has also studied testamentary donations made to Margaret's cult; see "The Uses of the Body."

95. ASF, Unione, September 27, 1290; March 18, 1298; July 13, 1300.

96. Ibid., September 27, 1290.

97. Ibid., November 28, 1297; transcribed in da Pelago, *Registro*, no. VI.

98. Iozzelli discusses the way in which the types of miracles mentioned are meant to suggest the kinds of miracles performed by Christ; see Fortunato Iozzelli, "I miracoli nella 'Legenda' di Santa Margherita da Cortona," *Archivum Franciscanum Historicum* 86 (1993): 249. Vauchez has claimed this is the only episcopal document to identify Margaret as a *beatissima* or to mention her miracles; see Cannon and Vauchez, *Margherita of Cortona*, 30. In charters issued in the fourteenth century, other bishops and cardinal legates would be more cautious and not mention Margaret's yet-to-be approved cult so explicitly.

99. ASF, Unione, March 1, 1298.

100. We can assume that Badia had died by April 1306 when we have a charter that first identifies Felice as the rector of San Basilio; see ibid., April 25, 1306.

Basilio.[101] And finally, in a testament from July 18, 1300, Donna Giacobella bequeathed her Cortona house to San Basilio and its rector, Badia.[102]

Between July 1304 and June 1308, the papal legates Niccolò da Prato and Napoleone Orsini issued a number of charters offering indulgences to those who visited San Basilio or aided in the church's reconstruction. On July 13, 1304, Niccolò of Prato offered forty days' indulgence to anyone helping to build the church, and on September 16, 1306, he offered one hundred days of indulgence to anyone who visited the church on particular feast days.[103] Napoleone Orsini offered three indulgences in support of San Basilio between 1306 and 1308. In the first, issued on September 2, 1306, Orsini offered an indulgence of one year and forty days to anyone visiting San Basilio on feast days, including the feast of Cathedra Petri, which took place on February 22, the same day as Margaret's death.[104] At the end of that same month, Orsini expanded his previous decree and offered an indulgence of one year and forty days to anyone who visited San Basilio "confessed and penitent" on any day of the year.[105] And finally, on June 1, 1308, Orsini offered an indulgence to those who gave money or worked in favor of the hospital at San Basilio.[106]

We learn that the penitents who remained at San Basilio had come to live in houses surrounding the church from a charter issued on June 21, 1308 by Bishop Ildebrandino of Arezzo. The bishop offered an indulgence to anyone who helped construct houses for those penitents who were living at San Basilio, where the body of the *beatissima* Margaret remained and where many miracles had taken place.[107] A charter issued on August 15, 1304, tells us that although Buongiovanni del fu Ranieri Villani left his body to the Franciscans at San Francesco, he left the hospital he had founded in his house in the San Basilio neighborhood to the commune of Cortona.[108] In her May 15, 1307 testament, Domina Ranaldesca stipulated that ten soldi be left to the hospital at San Basilio (likely the same hospital founded in Buongiovanni's house). Like

---

101. Ibid., March 18, 1298. Da Pelago suggested that this is the same Marzio mentioned twice in the *Legenda*: Giunta includes him among those who witnessed Margaret's ecstasies after her eight-day confession, and Christ instructs Margaret to tell Marzio to stop murmuring and complaining about Christ's friends, although it is not made clear who those "friends" were; see da Pelago, *Dissertazioni*, in *Antica leggenda*, 63. For the passages of the *Legenda* that mention Marzio, see 194 and 316.

102. ASF, Unione, July 18, 1300.

103. Ibid., July 13, 1304; and September 16, 1306.

104. Ibid., September 2, 1306; on this charter, see Cannon and Vauchez, *Margherita of Cortona*, 30.

105. ASF, Unione, September 28, 1306.

106. Ibid., June 1, 1308.

107. Ibid., June 21, 1308.

108. This charter is discussed by Bornstein, "The Uses of the Body," 168; it is also mentioned in da Pelago, "Sommario," 1304.

Buongiovanni, Domina Ranaldesca also asked to be buried in San Francesco. Her pious bequests were even more spread across the various Franciscan institutions around the city than Buongiovanni's: in addition to her gift to the hospital at San Basilio, she left twenty soldi each to the *domus misericordiae* and the *fratres* staying at the Celle.[109]

The pairing in Domina Ranaldesca's testament of bequests to institutions associated with Margaret (the hospital at San Basilio and the *domus misericordiae*) and the Franciscan Celle has been one piece of evidence suggesting that both Margaret and her cult may have had a connection to the spiritual Franciscans.[110] In late thirteenth- and early fourteenth-century documents, friars still living at the Celle were often referred to as *fraticelli*, leading scholars to think about the extent to which we can see these *fraticelli* as associated with the Italian wing of the spiritual Franciscans.[111] Even though we do not have sources to determine definitively whether or not Margaret, Giunta, or the penitents at San Basilio were associated with spiritual Franciscans, we can say that, like the *fraticelli* at the Celle, the devotees who had followed Margaret up the hill constituted a Franciscan community distinct from the friars at San Francesco. The San Basilio community consisted of lay penitents as well as clerics, all of whom lived around the church and managed not only the charitable organizations associated with San Basilio but also the crowds of pilgrims coming to Margaret's tomb, drawn by the stories of the miraculous events taking place there.

---

109. ASF, Unione, May 17, 1307.

110. See for example, Livarius Oliger, "Documenta inedita ad historiam fraticellorum spectantia," *Archivum Franciscanum Historicum* 6 (1913): 290. The Celle had been a point of controversy for the Cortonese Franciscans for some time. In the mid-thirteenth century, one of Francis's first companions, Elias of Cortona, had left the Celle, the hermitage founded by Francis, to build the church of San Francesco in Cortona. A number of friars had refused to make the move with Elias and remained at the hermitage. For more on the possible connections between Margaret and the spiritual Franciscans, see Doyno, "The Creation of a Franciscan Lay Saint," 85–86.

111. See ASF, Unione, April 9, 1301; April 11, 1301; February 3, 1304; May 17, 1307; and November 10, 1318. For example, Mancini and Oliger have posited that while the friars at the Celle may have followed a more rigorous Franciscan life, they did own property and thus cannot be grouped together with other spirituals; see Oliger, "Documenta inedita," 290; and Mancini, *Cortona nel medio evo*, 89–90. Sensi rejects the notion that Celle friars' ownership of property supports such a conclusion and believes that these *fraticelli* did indeed have some connection to other groups of spiritual Franciscans in Italy; see Sensi, "Margherita da Cortona nel contesto storico-sociale," 257. Moreover, he points to a November 1318 papal bull in which John XXII expelled the friars from the Celle; see ASF, Unione, November 18, 1318. This expulsion came a year after Pope John XXII had issued the first of a series of papal bulls aimed at condemning the spirituals, and only six months after four spirituals were burned in Avignon. While in the November 1318 bull, John XXII names Felice, rector of San Basilio, as a patron of the *fraticelli*, Burr has questioned Sensi's argument, noting that if both the *fraticelli* and lay penitents at San Basilio had been part of the spiritual movement, the pope would have also taken action against the penitent community. Sensi answers this objection by pointing out that the San Basilio penitents were protected by the support they received from the commune; Burr, *The Spiritual Franciscans*, 333–34.

Margaret's Miracles

The miracles that the *Legenda* claims Margaret performed both during her lifetime and after her death are further evidence not only that Giunta felt the need to contain claims of Margaret's charisma while alive but also that the San Basilio lay penitents constituted a community apart from the San Francesco Franciscans. Giunta describes the miracles Margaret performed in two places: the body of the *Legenda* and a chapter that primarily focuses on Margaret's postmortem miracles that he added to the text around 1311. Although this added chapter made it into only one of the three extant manuscripts of the *Legenda*, all three mention it in their table of contents.[112] The added chapter contains accounts of eighty-three miracles, only fourteen of which are dated—the earliest to 1302, and the latest to 1311. And of the eighty-three reports, only three recount cures Margaret performed during her lifetime.

This is one more living miracle than we find in the body of the *Legenda*. There, Giunta includes only two stories of cures Margaret performed while alive. In the first, a boy from Borgo San Sepolcro who had been tormented by demons is brought to see Margaret in Cortona. When the boy was within the vicinity of Cortona's walls, Giunta notes, the devil could not "stand the defensive walls thrown up by Margaret's prayers" and withdrew from the boy.[113] In the other account, a man having an affair with a married woman tells his mother that the only way he can be cured of his sinful behavior is through bread taken from Margaret's table. When his mother finally obtains this bread, the son tastes it and "becomes a new man."[114]

In both accounts, Giunta describes these living miracles in a manner that seems intent on containing and reframing the charismatic power they ascribe to Margaret. Thus, in the first account, just after being told that the devil could not stand the defensive wall that Margaret's prayers built around the city, the

---

112. The last lines of the *Legenda* anticipate the added chapter: *Legenda*, 451: "In quo secundum promissa Dei, quia multis miraculis corruscauit, ideo restat undecimum scribendum capitulum, per decem diuisum capitula, de signis que Deus omnipotens, ad ipsius honorem, per propinqua remotaque loca peregit et agere non desinit." This miracle chapter is only found in one of the three extant fourteenth-century manuscripts of the *Legenda*: codex 61 in the Archivio del Convento di S. Margherita, the earliest manuscript and the one upon which Iozzelli bases his recent edition of the *Legenda*. Cannon has noted, however, that the other two manuscript copies list the chapter of miracles in their table of contents, suggesting that they had intended to contain the final chapter; see Cannon and Vauchez, *Margherita of Cortona*, 158.

113. *Legenda*, 220–21: "Hic puer nunc a monialibus, nunc a consanguineis et amicis adiuratus per quem sanctorum liberandus erat, interrogantibus semper una voce respondit quod virtute orationum et meritorum sororis Margerite, que morabatur Cortone, infestus demon expelleretur."

114. Ibid., 231: "Mox ut filius particulam panis sibi gustauit delatam, statim in novum conversus hominem, reonvatus spiritu mentis sue . . ."

reader hears about Margaret's claims of shame and humility: "Do not think for a moment that the most-high, eternal, and all-wise power of God performed this miracle because of my love . . . I am but a cesspool of vice."[115] In the second, not only does Giunta begin his description by noting that the story he was about to tell was "almost miraculous," but he also describes Margaret's attempts to distance herself from any claims of charismatic power. When the mother asks for the bread, Margaret at first refuses, claiming that "anything that comes into contact with me becomes contaminated." Margaret's elaborates on her point: "If I touch something that has power, it immediately loses this inherent power."[116] Margaret not only does not effect miraculous change through her touch, but she also claims to be an agent of negative charisma—she removes "inherent power."

In the added chapter of miracle accounts, even though Giunta does not seem as intent on limiting the claims of spiritual gifts that Margaret's miracles convey as he was in the body of the *Legenda*, the stories of Margaret's living cures still make up a minor part of the overall chapter. In the first of the three accounts, the mother of a child who has just died runs to Margaret's cell, begging for help. After describing how the two women wept together, the reader learns that Margaret told the woman to "go with confidence," since, as she assured her, "the lord has brought your child back to life."[117] In the second, Margaret saw in her mind a man in despair begin to hang himself. After rushing to the man with two companions, Margaret cut him down in time to save his life. The account concludes by noting that it was through Margaret's merits that the man's temptation disappeared.[118] And finally in the last account of a living miracle, we learn that a possessed girl, also from Borgo San Sepolcro, was brought in front of the predella of an unnamed altar. After Margaret prayed for the girl, the reader is told that the demons vanished.[119]

The remaining eighty accounts focus on the miracles performed through prayers to Margaret after her death. Giunta organizes these accounts according to types of cures, creating categories that adhere to a common typology

---

115. Ibid., 221: "'Cum sim uitiorum fex omnium, plena demeritis et uas abhominabile, uas detestabile et stabulum spurcitiarum fetulentum, numquam credatis quod summa et etera ac sapientissima uirtus, que numquam potest in suis errare operibus, hoc mei amore fecerit.'" I am relying on Renna's translation of this passage.

116. Ibid., 231: "'Quicquid michi uilissime omnium appositum fuerit, ex contactu mearum manuum adeo maculatur, quod si qua uirtus in rebus a me tactis prius extiterat, subito recedit et perditur.'" This is Renna's translation.

117. Ibid., 463: "'Vade secura, quia Dominus in hac hora tuum filium suscitauit: nam Dominus noster modo concessit, ut uiuum puerulum debeas reperire.'"

118. Ibid., 473–74.

119. Ibid., 460.

of miracles reported in late medieval collections.[120] For example, the reader learns about how Margaret restored sight to the blind, cured those suffering from hernias and kidney stones, liberated the possessed, and raised the dead. As was often the case in miracle collections written after the mid-thirteenth century, most of the miracles did not take place at Margaret's tomb.[121] Beneficiaries came to Margaret's tomb with wax and votive offerings in gratitude for their cure, fulfilling vows they had made after the miracle was performed.[122] We can be relatively sure that the decision to add a final chapter of miracles was a strategic move aimed at Margaret's canonization.[123] Adhering to the standard *forma interrogatorii* used in canonization proceedings in the early fourteenth century, the miracle stories portray Margaret's powers to heal and cure in a manner that conforms to conventional hagiographic style. This style is a marked departure from what we have seen in much of the *Legenda*.[124] All the hints and references to the ambivalence and doubts that surrounded Margaret's penitential transformation and visionary claims have disappeared. Instead, each of the eighty-three accounts straightforwardly describes and celebrates miracles performed through the merits of and prayers to Margaret. But while the content of the miracle accounts does not raise questions about the nature of Margaret's religious life, its descriptions of those who witnessed and were responsible for Margaret's developing cult ask us to think more about the influence Margaret's move to San Basilio had on those who came to champion her sanctity.

Cannon has argued that the mention in some of the miracle accounts that both members of the San Basilio community (several accounts mention Ser Badia or his successor as rector, Ser Felice) and friars from San Francesco served as witnesses demonstrates that the two communities in some sense had a

---

120. See Vauchez's table on the "Development of the typology of the miracles recorded in processes of canonization (1201–1417)," in *Sainthood*, 468.

121. Iozzelli, "I miracoli," 237–38. For more on the late medieval trend of miracles taking place away from the saint's tomb and the beneficiary vowing to visit the tomb if their request was granted, see Vauchez, *Sainthood*, 446.

122. While more beneficiaries came from the city and *contado* of Cortona than from any other area, the miracle accounts suggest that by the early fourteenth century, Margaret's *fama sanctitatis* was well diffused throughout the geographic area between Cortona, Perugia, and Arezzo. Most of the accounts do not provide enough information to allow identification of the professions and social status of the beneficiaries. However, we can say that more men appear in the accounts as beneficiaries than women and that Margaret seems to have been particularly associated with curing sick or injured children. Iozzelli notes that men would have been more likely than women to have had their accounts recorded and so these do not necessarily mean that men were more interested in Margaret's cures than women. Iozzelli also cites scholarship that has been done on the marked increase in cures of children in late medieval miracle collections; see Iozzelli, "I miracoli," 239, 243–44, and 249.

123. Vauchez, "Afterword," in Cannon and Vauchez, *Margherita of Cortona*, 222.

124. Ibid.

"shared supervision" over Margaret's growing cult.[125] For example, we learn that on May 27, 1310, a man from the village of Antria swore in the cloister of San Francesco in front of Giunta, Ser Felice, and other Cortonese that his wife had experienced such intense labor pains that she lost her sight and only had it restored after she vowed to walk barefoot to Margaret's tomb.[126] Another account, also from May 1310, reports that both Giunta and Ser Felice swore on the gospels that they had seen a man from Perugia suffering from a severe wasp sting recover after vowing to visit Margaret's tomb every year on her feast day.[127]

Cannon also argues that both the content and size of codex 61 (the manuscript containing the added miracle chapter) signal the end of that joint supervision. Although she contends that this was likely not Giunta's working copy, Cannon does see the codex's small size (ca. 24×16.5 cm) along with the presence of both the final chapter of miracle accounts and the report of Cardinal Napoleone Orsini's declaration of authenticity as suggesting that this was the copy intended to travel to Avignon to argue for Margaret's canonization.[128] Cortona's first communal statutes written in 1325 charged Ser Felice, then the rector of San Basilio, with the task of traveling to the papal palace in the hopes of having Margaret canonized. Cannon maintains that if this were indeed the copy intended for Felice to take with him on his journey, by 1325 "the promotion of Margherita's cult—together, perhaps, with this very copy of the Legenda—had passed from the Franciscan friars of Cortona into the hands of the rector and owners of the Church of S. Basilio," that is, the communal government.[129]

Although Cannon's conclusions about the possible intended use of codex 61 make sense, the absence of friars from San Francesco in the majority of the miracles reported in Giunta's added chapter suggests that the Cortonese Franciscans, once so wary of an association with Margaret, were still keeping their distance from her burgeoning cult. If we look more carefully at the miracles in the added chapter that provide us with any details about date, location, or witnesses, we can see evidence that even though Giunta and a few other friars were working with the community at San Basilio and Cortona's commune to promote Margaret's cult, the Franciscans at San Francesco were largely uninvolved in this effort.

Thus, of the eighty-three accounts, fourteen are dated and can be divided into two periods: eight accounts occurred between 1300 and 1304 and six from

---

125. Cannon and Vauchez, *Margherita of Cortona*, 157.
126. *Legenda*, 455–56: miracle 7.
127. Ibid., 461–62: miracle 34.
128. Cannon and Vauchez, *Margherita of Cortona*, 157–58.
129. Ibid., 158.

between 1310 and 1311. Of the 1300–1304 miracles, only three provide additional information about where and to whom they were reported. In 1304, Cardinal Orsini examined the claim of a woman from Città di Castello that prayers and vows to Margaret revived her five-year-old son after he fell from a high window.[130] In 1303, prayers and vows to Margaret again revived a child, this one having suffocated in his crib; Ser Badia and Ser Costanza as well as Suore Amata, Margherita, and Meliore (all likely members of the San Basilio lay penitential community) are all named as having witnessed the mother's claim.[131] And in 1304, in the oratory of San Francesco, the friars Giovanni of Castiglione, Matthew John, and Niccoluccio Anitaldi of Cortona all heard a mother's claim that her son had been saved from a fall when she invoked Margaret's name.[132] This 1304 miracle is the only one in the chapter that mentions any Franciscans besides Giunta.

Of the six miracles that we know occurred in 1310 or 1311, four list both Giunta and Felice as witnesses and three note that the claims took place in the oratory of San Francesco. Two of these accounts were written by notaries, a practice that was becoming increasingly common in Italian cities in the later Middle Ages and one that we have already seen in the collection of miracles in Zita of Lucca's *vita*. These two notarized claims of Margaret's miraculous healings were both taken in San Francesco in May 1310 and both name Giunta, Felice, and other Cortonese as witnesses.[133] Two other accounts that took place in May 1310 name Giunta and Felice as witnesses.[134] And finally, there are two miracle accounts dated to 1311. In one, we learn that in February of that year a woman named Mina, from the Porta San Vincenzo neighborhood in Cortona, claimed that Margaret had cured her three-month-old daughter of epilepsy.[135] And in the other, Ser Felice served as the only named witness to a claim that Margaret had healed sores on a boy's legs.[136]

Therefore, of the miracle claims that we know were made between 1300 and 1304, one was witnessed by a group of San Basilio penitents, one by a group of Franciscan friars, and one was examined by Cardinal Orsini. In the claims that were made in 1310 and 1311, the only witnesses that are named are Giunta, Ser Felice, and various Cortonese, who appear in four of the six accounts from this period. We can draw a few conclusions from this data—some more tentative

---

130. *Legenda*, 463: miracle 36.
131. Ibid., 463–64: miracle 38.
132. Ibid., 468: miracle 52. This is not the same Giovanni who had served as Margaret's confessor and Franciscan inquisitor, who the *Legenda* makes clear died before 1297.
133. Ibid., 455–56: miracle 7; and 461–62: miracle 34.
134. Ibid., 468: miracle 54; and 474: miracle 79.
135. Ibid., 469: miracle 55.
136. Ibid., 475: miracle 82.

than others—about the early history of Margaret's cult. To begin, it seems that the Franciscans were not overtly interested in promoting Margaret's cult in the first decade after her death. The fact that only one account mentions any other friars besides Giunta suggests that the friars were neither gathered around Margaret's tomb at San Basilio looking to collect miracle accounts nor questioning the beneficiaries of Margaret's miracles in their own church. As I have noted, most of these beneficiaries had vowed to visit Margaret's tomb if they or their family member were cured, so it seems likely that most of these accounts were recorded in San Basilio as beneficiaries came to fulfill their vows. Since Giunta indicates when he was present as a witness to claims (he names himself as a witness to five accounts), we can also conclude that someone other than Giunta first recorded most of these accounts. When Giunta does appear as a witness, he is always alongside Felice, and never in the company of any other friars.

The fact that Giunta's name only appears alongside members of the San Basilio community suggests that the other friars at San Francesco did not share or perhaps support his interest in Margaret. In addition, the fact that the friars from San Francesco appear in only one of the miracle accounts points to the idea that the Cortonese Franciscans were either not particularly interested in the events taking place at San Basilio or did not have access to those making miracle claims. We have already seen how the Franciscans shared their supervision of Margaret when Badia took over as her confessor after Giunta was sent to Siena. What remains unclear, however, is whether Giunta's Franciscan superiors sanctioned the relationship that Giunta cultivated with Badia in order to receive reports about Margaret's religious life. The portrait we see of those who served as witnesses to the many claims of miraculous cures that Margaret's devotees made after her death suggests that Giunta's interest in Margaret and the promotion of her sanctity met more support among the community of lay penitents and clerics at San Basilio than among the friars at San Francesco. To learn more about that community, we must turn to the visual sources created to surround Margaret's tomb.

Seeing Margaret: The *Vita*-Panel, Funerary Monument, and Fresco Cycle

The earliest of the visual sources that scholars believe was placed near Margaret's tomb in San Basilio is a painted *vita*-panel, now located in the Museo Diocesano in Cortona (figure 8).[137]

---

137. For more on late medieval *vita*-panels, see Cannon, "Beyond the Limitations of Visual Typology," 293.

Figure 8. "Vita Panel of Margaret of Cortona," ca. 1297, Cortona, Museo Diocesano. Scala/Art Resource, NY.

The panel's style of painting and the absence of depictions of any of the miracles mentioned in Giunta's final chapter have led scholars to believe that this painting was created in the first decade after Margaret's death, before Giunta had finished the *Legenda*.[138] Without a specific textual source to rely on it is likely that the *vita*-panel gives us a glimpse into how Margaret's lay sanctity was understood by those who had known her.[139] Just as we saw in Giunta's portion of the *Legenda*, the *vita*-panel pays more attention to Mar-

138. Cannon and Vauchez, *Margherita of Cortona*, 160–61.

139. Cannon argues that the panel should be treated as "a parallel" to the text of the *Legenda*; see Cannon and Vauchez, *Margherita of Cortona*, 163.

garet's private spiritual journey than to her role as a charismatic civic holy woman.[140] But unlike Giunta's portrait, the panel does not argue for an exclusive relationship between Margaret and the Cortonese Franciscans.[141] Its more flexible understanding of lay penitents' institutional status is reminiscent of Andrea Gallerani of Siena's reliquary shutters. And just as the Gallerani shutters had, Margaret's *vita*-panel both guides and reflects the devotional activity that was taking place among those who had come to venerate this lay saint's remains.

In the center of the panel, Margaret stands with a nimbus, clasping paternoster beads with her palms turned inward in a gesture that likely signifies her penitential conversion.[142] She wears a stripped habit, which identifies her as an independent lay penitent rather than a Franciscan tertiary.[143] The nine smaller-scale scenes surrounding the portrait focus on Margaret's entry into religious life, her spiritual progress, and her death. The first three scenes (beginning at the panel's top left corner and moving downward) depict Margaret's arrival in Cortona, her entry into the Franciscan penitential order, and her donation of her belongings to the poor. The fourth and fifth scenes portray Margaret twice resisting temptation. In the first, (the final cell on the left side) a figure dressed in red, likely a demon in disguise, tempts Margaret with a mirror. In the next scene, (the top-most cell on the panel's right side) which is badly damaged, Margaret is kneeling in front of a now hooved demon. Margaret turns her head away, suggesting that she has overcome the temptation in front of her.[144]

The final three scenes (moving downward from the hooved demon) again focus on Margaret's penitential progress. In the first, Christ appears to a kneeling Margaret with Saint Francis next to him, echoing Margaret's claim in the *Legenda* that Christ absolved all of Margaret's sins through her prayers to Francis and by Francis's own merits.[145] In the next scene, Margaret again kneels, this time in front of two clerics who administer the Eucharist to her. In the bottom right corner, Margaret kneels in front of Christ, who points upward and is accompanied by a female saint. Cannon has noted that this compresses

---

140. Ibid., 159–70.

141. Ibid., 166.

142. Laura Corti, "Esercizio sulla mano destra: Gestualità e santi nel medioevo," *Annali della Scuola Normale Superiore di Pisa*, serie IV (1996): 39–49; cited by Cannon and Vauchez, *Margherita of Cortona*, 165.

143. See Canon and Vauchez, *Margherita of Cortona*, 164–65, nn. 34 and 35; Caciola, *Discerning Spirits*, 110–11; and Fabio Bisogni, "L'abito di Margherita," in *Margherita da Cortona: Una storia emblematica devozione narrata per testi e immagini*, ed. Laura Corti and Riccardo Spinelli (Milan: Electra, 1998), 33–43.

144. Cannon challenges Kaftal's conclusions that these two scenes depict Margaret thwarting a suicide attempt and washing the feet of lepers; see Cannon and Vauchez, *Margherita of Cortona*, 163.

145. *Legenda*, 188.

three ideas present in the *Legenda* into one image: Margaret's vision of her throne in heaven, her vision of the Magdalen wearing a crown, and finally her understanding that just as the Magdalen is enthroned among other virgins in heaven, so she will be as well.[146] And finally, in the bottom register of the panel, a rectangular scene shows Margaret's corpse flanked by two figures, one clearly Franciscan and the other Dominican. The painting is too damaged to say definitively if these figures are meant to represent Francis and Dominic themselves.[147] Below Margaret's body are two more barely visible figures that Cannon believes are individuals seeking cures at Margaret's tomb.

In this the earliest depiction (either visual or textual) that we have of Margaret, she is portrayed as an independent lay penitent, who, while connected to and dependent upon both mendicants and clerics for access to a religious life, pursues her spiritual progress through her own interactions with demons, Christ, and the saints. By means of her gestures, her dress, and the narrative arc of her religious life, the *vita*-panel argues that more than a Franciscan tertiary, Margaret was foremost a lay penitent. The repeated depiction of Margaret kneeling and holding paternoster beads has led Cannon to wonder if the panel was encouraging those lay penitents viewing it to perform a particular prayer.[148] Regardless of the type of prayer the panel encourages, it is clear that as a whole this visual document emphasizes Margaret's penitential identity at the same time as it reflects and encourages the behavior of those coming to her tomb. The lay penitents who had gathered at San Basilio as well as those who came seeking the miraculous cures reported to be taking place at Margaret's tomb might, as the panel seems to argue that Margaret did, see the Franciscans as a legitimizing authority—a means for a lay penitent's religious life to receive an institutional stamp of approval. But the panel also seems to argue that a lay penitent's religious life might partake of a variety of authorities—Franciscans, Dominicans, secular clerics, saints, and Christ. We might wonder about the extent to which this flexibility was one impetus behind Giunta's efforts to claim that Margaret belonged so intrinsically to the Franciscans.

Margaret's ca. 1310 marble funerary monument, and a fresco cycle (now lost but known through watercolor copies made in the seventeenth century) completed in the 1330s by the Lorenzetti brothers provide the most extensive evidence of the civic cult that grew around Margaret in the generation after her death. In both sources, it is not Margaret's association with the Franciscans that is emphasized but rather the charismatic power that she wields. Above

---

146. Cannon and Vauchez, *Margherita of Cortona*, 164.
147. Ibid.
148. Ibid., 169.

FIGURE 9.   Gano di Fazio, "Funerary Monument of Margaret of Cortona," ca. 1320–30, Cremona, Santa Margherita. Alinari/Art Resource, NY.

all else, these artifacts celebrate Margaret for the miraculous cures she issued both during her lifetime and after her death.

The funerary monument depicts two angels holding open the lid of Margaret's tomb to reveal the saint's fully dressed and fully preserved body beneath (figure 9).[149]

Below Margaret's body, six rectangular reliefs include scenes from Margaret's life and miracles performed after her death. The four scenes depicting moments from Margaret's life largely repeat the narrative from the *vita*-panel: Margaret's entry into the Franciscan Order, her donation of her clothing to the poor, the absolution of her sins through the merits of Saint Francis, and finally Margaret's death and her soul's ascent into heaven. Below these panels are two more panels, one depicting the cure of those with various physical illnesses at Margaret's tomb and the other showing the cure of a possessed

149. Ibid., 66–74.

figure. In these reliefs the Franciscan presence is even further reduced from that seen in the *vita*-panel.[150] In the scene of her entry into the penitential order, the monument shows one friar cutting Margaret's hair. Beyond this, the only representations of Franciscans in the monument are of tertiaries: Margaret receives her penitential tunic from a figure whose dress suggests that he is a *mantellato* or a Franciscan tertiary. And in the scene depicting Margaret's death, a man wearing the same outfit as the *mantellato* in the scene of Margaret's profession stands next to her body.[151] At the other end of Margaret's deathbed stands a veiled woman, also likely a lay penitent. Thus, in a funerary monument that was originally placed on the wall above the niche containing Margaret's body, the Franciscans' role in Margaret's life and cult has been de-emphasized. While they are there at the beginning of her penitential life, the friars do not figure in the charity work and miracles that Margaret performs. Instead, next to her at each of those moments are other members of the San Basilio community of lay penitents.

In the watercolor copies of the frescoes that once covered the walls of San Basilio, there is a similar de-emphasis of the role the Friars Minor played in Margaret's life. These frescoes seem to have focused on the miracles that Margaret performed either during her life or after her death and, unlike the *vita*-panel, reference the *Legenda*'s added miracle chapter.[152] In addition to those miracle scenes, four frescoes told the story of Margaret's conversion to and perfection of a religious life; two depicted the events surrounding Margaret's funeral; one showed her association with the *domus misericordiae*; and finally, one documented Napoleone Orsini's investigation and authentication of the miracle accounts and the *Legenda* text as a whole.[153] Although it is clear that the Lorenzetti had access to Giunta's *Legenda*, they did not try to represent the many visions and conversations with Christ that Margaret claims to have had. Moreover, the frescoes seem to have stayed away from depicting important moments in Margaret's spiritual progress, a focus of the *vita*-panel.

Nevertheless, like the *vita*-panel, the frescoes presented an institutional diversity in those venerating Margaret after her death. In the fresco of Margaret's funeral, two Franciscans and two Dominicans appeared among what looks like various Cortonese.[154] In the scene of Margaret's entry into a religious life, a Franciscan cut Margaret's hair and was accompanied by four kneel-

150. Ibid., 170.
151. Ibid., 171.
152. Ibid., 147–54.
153. Ibid., 177–78.
154. For a reproduction of this image, see ibid., color plate IX.

ing figures, two women and two men, who likely represented other lay penitents.[155] And finally, in the fresco showing Napoleone Orsini's visit to Margaret's tomb when he came to Cortona to authenticate the *Legenda* and the miracle claims, no friars were included.[156] Although these frescoes did not pay much attention to Margaret's Franciscan guardians, they did provide the visitor to San Basilio with images representing members of the larger Cortonese community—just those people, we can imagine, who were the beneficiaries of Margaret's miracles and who were pushing for her canonization.

Seeking Canonization

At the same time that San Basilio was becoming a church dedicated to Margaret's burgeoning cult, the city of Cortona was changing. During the reign of Bishop Ildebrandino, who had played a significant role in helping Margaret rebuild the church of San Basilio and in promoting her cult after her death, Cortona had begun its march toward independence. As Ghibelline fortunes rose in central Italy during the early fourteenth century, Cortona's *popolo* party, with the Casali family at its head, began to draft the city's first communal statutes. After Guido Tarlati was made bishop of Arezzo in 1312, however, the two cities faced another period of tension. Bishop Tarlati was bent on increasing Arezzo's territory and wealth, and to that end he looked to Cortona. Tarlati was also loyal to imperial interests and, fortunately for Cortona, Pope John XXII excommunicated him in 1324. One year earlier, in 1323, the head of the Casali family, Ranieri Casali, had helped to expel Cortona's magnates in an effort to raise a *popolo*-led independent commune. In the strife that ensued, the Cortonese named Ranieri Casali to be *dominus generalis* for life, in an effort to bring peace to the city.[157] Finally, in 1325, John XXII voided all of the agreements that had bound Cortona to Arezzo and took land from the diocese of Arezzo, Chiusi, and Città di Castello in order to grant Cortona its own episcopal seat.[158]

These events paved the way for the commune, under the rule of Casali, to claim independence from all overlords and issue the city's first set of communal statutes. Thus, when Cortona finally achieved independence, its government looked more like a signorial regime under the Casali than a government run by a consortium of *popolani*. The Casali would go on to rule the city for

---

155. Ibid., color plate XVII.

156. Ibid., color plate I.

157. Ibid., 16.

158. Daniel Bornstein, "Parish Priests in Late Medieval Cortona: The Urban and Rural Clergy," *Quaderni di Storia Religiosa* 4 (1997): 166.

the rest of the fourteenth century, although by the end of the century Florence's increasing power would slowly chip away at Cortona's independence until the city officially became part of the Florentine territory in 1411.[159]

In communal deliberations from 1324 (the only year for which such documents survive), the commune voted to give money to aid in the enlargement of San Basilio (*pro ecclesia Sancti Basilii augmentanda*).[160] Cannon has suggested that this referred to an ongoing subvention to the church and stands as evidence that it was most likely the commune that funded the Lorenzetti brothers' work on the frescoes in the 1330s.[161] In 1325, after John XXII removed Cortona from the jurisdiction and control of the Arezzo bishop and made the city the seat of a new diocese, the commune issued its first set of civic statutes.[162] These statutes named Margaret as one of the city's patrons. As we have seen in the communal statutes of other cities where lay saints were venerated, Cortona's statutes decreed that on Margaret's feast day both civic officials and guild members were to lead a citywide procession.[163] If anyone spoke ill of Margaret, he or she would be punished.[164] And finally, the statutes make provisions for the current rector of San Basilio, Felice, to travel to Avignon at the commune's expense to advocate for Margaret's canonization.[165] We do not know if Felice ever made this trip, but if he did, he was not successful. It would not be until 1728 that Rome recognized Margaret as a saint.

Nevertheless, Margaret's cult continued to grow in Cortona throughout the fourteenth century. The Casali, who had been instrumental in pushing for Cortona's independent status, had by 1325 become the ruling family of the city. Napoleone Orsini's authentication of Margaret's *Legenda* in the Casali palace in 1308 gave the family the ability to associate their rule over Cortona with Margaret's memory.[166] Just as the Fatinelli had done in San Frediano to mark their devotion to Zita, the Casali made San Basilio their family mausoleum by the mid-fourteenth century.[167] In addition, the Cor-

---

159. Cannon and Vauchez, *Margherita of Cortona*, 16.

160. Cortona, Archivio storico del Comune di Cortona: Q1: "Deliberazioni comunitative 1323–1324," f. 29. Also cited in Cannon and Vauchez, *Margherita of Cortona*, 218.

161. Ibid.

162. ASF, "Statuti comunità soggette," 279, ff. 95, 140v–141v, and 123. These are transcribed in Cannon and Vauchez, *Margherita of Cortona*, 227–30.

163. ASF, "Statuti comunità soggette," 279, ff. 140v–141v.

164. Ibid., f. 123.

165. Ibid., f. 141v.

166. For more on this point, see Franco Cardini, "Agiografia e politica: Margherita da Cortona e le vicende di una città inquieta," *Studi Francescani* 76 (1979): 127–36; and Cardini, "Allegrezza Casali: Devota di S. Margherita, figura poco nota della spiritualità cortonese," *Studi Francescani* 72 (1975): 335–44.

167. See Cannon and Vauchez, *Margherita of Cortona*, 219.

tonese continued to make testamentary donations to the community of San Basilio. Many of the charters identify the pious gifts as going to both San Basilio and Santa Margherita.[168]

The history of the commune of Cortona compresses the transition we see in other medieval Italian communes from *popolo* government to signorial regime: in Cortona the events seemed to occur simultaneously. As a result, Margaret's role as a civic patron came to be associated with the idea both of an independent commune and a Casali-controlled city. But the role of the Casali as patrons to Cortona's newest saint was a relatively straightforward relationship; they gave her a prominent role as patron saint in the city's statutes and elected to make San Basilio, which by the mid-fourteenth century was commonly referred to as Santa Margherita, their family mausoleum.

By 1392, however, as Cortona's commune was being pulled into the Florentine orbit, and control of Margaret's church and tomb was granted to the Franciscans at San Francesco, both the rule of the Casali and Cortona's independence were fading. But when Margaret's body and cult finally passed into the hands of the Franciscans who had once been so wary of her, it no longer mattered that she was a fallen woman with a dramatic visionary life. By the end of the fourteenth century, Margaret was simply Cortona's saint.

The Lay Visionary

The visual material created to celebrate Margaret at San Basilio, produced likely from the combined resources of communal and episcopal authorities as well as from the pious bequests left to the church's community of lay penitents, stands as the zenith of the phenomenon of lay civic sanctity, but it came at the same time as the beginning of its decline. Over the fourteenth century, Giunta's articulation of a new kind of lay saint—the lay visionary—would become the dominant model of an ideal lay religious life. As we shall see in the next chapter, this new understanding of the lay saint would continue to locate evidence of holiness more in an internal or visionary life than in acts of civic charity, and it would be most often gendered female.

Nancy Caciola has argued that the *Legenda* often presents Margaret as consciously fashioning herself into a saint. In one passage, Giunta reports that she told a crowd of women mocking her transformation from a concubine to a lay penitent that one day they would come to visit her as pilgrims because "the

---

168. See, for example, ASF, Unione, August 10, 1363; May 9, 1374; April 17, 1387.

time will come when you will call me holy, because I will in fact be holy."[169] Although this sense of self-fashioning is arresting and raises questions about the value of sanctity actively and unabashedly sought, I am most interested in thinking about what kind of lay saint Margaret imagined becoming. How did her desire for the life of a recluse figure into that self-fashioning? On one hand, she likely had the models of the desert hermit saints and Mary Magdalen in mind. On the other hand, except for Zita of Lucca, Margaret would have had a hard time coming up with examples in communal Italy of unaffiliated single laywomen who had earned civic cults. Despite this, the female urban hermit was, by the late thirteenth century, an established phenomenon in Italian cities. Not only did Vito da Cortona celebrate Umiliana de' Cerchi of Florence for her spiritual progress into a reclusive life in her father's tower, women such as Verdiana of Castelfiorentino (d. 1241) and Fina of San Gimignano (d. 1253) earned cults for their lives as civic recluses.[170] Nevertheless, Margaret's identity as a lay penitent and illegitimate widow with no social connections beyond her Franciscan guardians conformed to no existing saintly models.

As Ser Badia's portions of the *Legenda*, the added chapter of miracles, and the visual sources produced to surround Margaret's tomb all make clear, Margaret's lay penitential community and first devotees did not see her either as a recluse or as a lay visionary. Instead, these early fourteenth-century Cortonese saw Margaret as a contemporary civic holy woman, who both during her lifetime and after her death revealed her sanctity primarily through the acts of miraculous healing she performed. Giunta's complex and changing agenda in writing the *Legenda*—from acting on feelings of suspicion to working to persuade his fellow friars of Margaret's sanctity—coupled with the fact that in the midst of that writing Pope Nicholas IV's bull *Supra montem* called for a radical change in the nature of the relationship between lay penitent and the friars, led him to produce a new model of lay sanctity. In Giunta's hands, an ideal layperson was someone who—in an effort to perform penance—reached so far and so completely into her emotional life that she was rewarded with di-

---

169. Caciola, *Discerning Spirits*, 102; and *Legenda*, 184: "Et ipsa dicebat: 'Adhuc tempus adueniet, in quo me nominabitis sanctam cum sancta fuero et uisitabitis me cum baculo peregrino, scarsellis pendendibus ad humeris uestris.'"

170. On urban recluses in medieval and Renaissance Italy, see Anna Benvenuti Papi, "Velut in sepulcro," in "*In castro poenitentiae*," 263–414; Giovanna Casagrande, "Oltre lo spazio istituzionale: Il fenomeno della reclusione volontaria," in *Religiosità penitenziale*, 17–74; Sensi, *Storia di bizzoche* and "Anchoresses and Penitents"; also see Gabriella Zarri, *Le sante vive: Profezie di corte e devozione femminile tra '400 e '500* (Turin: Rosenberg & Sellier, 1990). While Anneke B. Mulder-Bakker's work focuses on urban recluses in northern Europe, her introductory essay is a useful guide to the larger phenomenon of medieval urban recluses, see *Lives of the Anchoresses: The Rise of the Urban Recluse in Medieval Europe*, trans. Myra Heerspink Schulz (Philadelphia: University of Pennsylvania Press, 2005), 1–23.

vine visions. Such a framing of Margaret as a visionary, I have argued, produced a new understanding of lay religious experience; one in which the locus
and the evidence of the divine had moved inside. In order to understand this
change, we must also recognize that it came at the same time as lay penitents'
"lay" status was becoming a thing of the past and the mendicant third orders
were taking full institutional shape. It is to that transition and its effects on
civic lay sanctity that I shall now turn.

CHAPTER 7

Envisioning an Order

The Last Lay Saints

André Vauchez was not only the first scholar to identify the phenomenon of contemporary lay civic sanctity in the Italian communes but also the first to offer an explanation for its seeming disappearance in the fourteenth century. Pointing to the growth of the mendicant orders and "the diffusion of their spirituality," Vauchez argued that an extraordinary lay life became increasingly defined via "mystical and paramystical phenomena" rather than by an investment in charity or social and civic values.[1] Vauchez noted that by the late thirteenth century, the mendicants had begun a campaign to dominate local cults, focusing their attention overwhelmingly on women.[2] Whereas in an earlier model of lay sanctity, "the spirit of prayer went hand in hand with good works and the desire to pacify and moralize the society in which they lived," the mendicants promoted an ideal of the lay religious life that championed "the search for union with God through solitary meditation on the mysteries of salvation."[3]

This chapter argues for a new explanation for why and how the contemporary lay civic saint seemingly disappeared over the fourteenth century.

---

1. Vauchez, "A Twelfth-Century Novelty," 71–72.

2. Vauchez, *Sainthood*, 207–12.

3. Ibid. Vauchez also notes how, after 1270, the mendicants were motivated by a desire to wrest control of the cults of contemporary lay saints away from the secular clergy; see *Sainthood*, 206–8.

Instead of seeing mendicant spirituality as inherently oriented toward "mystical and paramystical phenomena," and thus as pushing lay sanctity in that direction (and favoring women's cults in the process), I argue that the stress placed on medieval gender and power norms by women's participation in the lay penitential movement as well as the cults they earned for their efforts ultimately led to the end of the contemporary lay civic saint. This chapter will extend the argument begun in chapters 5 and 6 that from the second half of the thirteenth century, hagiographers—who were increasingly mendicant friars—responded to the female lay penitents garnering saintly reputations by advocating for an ideal lay life in which visions trumped a commitment to civic issues and charitable works. I argue that this new conception of an ideal lay life was not simply an indication of the spiritual point of view of the mendicant hagiographers, but rather a means the church had adopted to solve the longstanding problem of the female lay penitent.

At the heart of my argument is the contention that gender played a crucial role in the development of new lay religious ideals in the late medieval Italian communes. Although a changing political context offers some explanation for why we see fewer cults dedicated to contemporary laypeople in the fourteenth century—as *popolo* regimes gave way to rising *signoria* governments, the contemporary lay saint had a less urgent political and social significance—it is not the full story. In the cults that did emerge over the first half of the fourteenth century, we see male lay saints continue to adhere to the model of the communal lay saint that was constructed over the thirteenth century, while women's cults adopted an entirely new vocabulary for sanctity. If we ascribe this change to inherent qualities in the mendicant orders and to those orders' particular interest in women's cults, we not only risk essentialism but we also overlook the ambivalent and sometimes contentious history between the mendicants and laywomen. As Catherine M. Mooney's study of Clare of Assisi and her community of lay penitents has shown, the issue of what to do with laywomen seeking to follow the *vita apostolica* was something that had long vexed and preoccupied the church.[4]

In recent years, other scholars such as Giovanna Casagrande, Alison More, and Maiju Lehmijoki-Gardner have argued that evidence that has long been read as documenting the creation of the mendicant "third" or lay orders would be more productively approached as regulatory measures, and thus not as sources illustrating institution building.[5] This evidence includes the 1221

---

4. Catherine M. Mooney, *Clare of Assisi and the Thirteenth-Century Church: Religious Women, Rules, and Resistance* (Philadelphia: University of Pennsylvania Press, 2016).

5. Casagrande "Un ordine per i laici"; More, *Fictive Orders*, as well as More, "Institutionalizing Penitential Life," 297–98; and Lehmijoki-Gardner, "Writing Religious Rules as an Interactive Process."

Memoriale propositi from Cardinal Hugolino (the future Pope Gregory IX), directed at the "Brothers and Sisters of Penance"; the 1286 *Ordinationes* by the Dominican friar Munio of Zamora, written for a community of *vestitae* or female lay penitents in Orvieto; and Pope Nicholas IV's 1289 bull, *Supra montem*, which repeated much of the *Memoriale propositi* but placed lay penitents under a stricter oversight that was to be managed by Franciscan friars. My work in this chapter builds on the findings of these scholars to suggest that the issuing of such regulatory directives demonstrates how the very idea of a lay penitent remained a troublesome issue for the church throughout the thirteenth century.

And yet, as my study of the canonization of Omobono of Cremona in 1199 and the many laymen's cults that formed over the thirteenth century has shown, both church and commune put their support behind a portrait of an ideal lay life that itself mitigated concerns about the laity's embrace of the *vita apostolica*. But as Clare of Assisi and her companions must have quickly realized when they sought to follow Francis's example, there were limits to what medieval society would tolerate in women seeking a penitential life. Mooney argues that Cardinal Hugolino created the Order of San Damiano as one solution to the problem of the female lay penitent.[6] My work in this chapter proposes that even though many regulatory measures were addressed to both laymen and laywomen, it is likely that a primary aim of these regulatory measures (especially *Supra montem*) was to solve the troublesome issue both of women's participation in the lay penitential movement and of the increasing number of cults they were earning for their efforts.

This chapter will identify a two-part solution that the church adopted over the thirteenth century to solve the problem of the female lay penitent and saint—a solution that, I will argue, ultimately regulated the lay penitent, and thus the lay saint, out of existence. The first part came in hagiographic sources. Initially Franciscan authors, and by the early fourteenth century, Dominican authors as well, had adopted a new paradigm for an ideal lay life that privileged visions over charity. Thus, as we saw first articulated in Vito da Cortona's *vita* for Umiliana de' Cerchi of Florence and then brought into much sharper focus in Giunta Bevegnati's *Legenda* for Margaret of Cortona, by emphasizing a laywoman's internal spiritual life—her visions, her emotions, or both—saintly charisma became something that no longer benefited others or brought the lay saint into the midst of the city as a charity worker and charismatic healer but instead became a barometer for the spiritual health of the

---

6. Mooney, *Clare of Assisi*, 54–66.

woman herself. In the first quarter of the fourteenth century, Dominican friars would use similar means to celebrate the lives of Giovanna of Orvieto (d. 1309) and Margaret of Città di Castello (1321).

The second part of the solution to the problem of the female lay penitent is to be found in regulatory measures that laid the groundwork for—but did not fully establish—the mendicant lay orders. Here again, the Franciscans appear to have taken a more prominent role at first in the late thirteenth century, with the Dominicans acting more in the late fourteenth and early fifteenth centuries. This chapter will argue that as both lay penitents and the church pushed the friars to take a more substantial and formal role as the guardians of lay penitents, mendicant hagiographers embraced an approach to female lay religious life that concomitantly celebrated and contained these women's charisma.

Integrating the cult of a female lay penitent into the norms of medieval society was of course not a new problem. As we saw in the early thirteenth-century cults that grew up around Ubaldesca and Bona of Pisa, institutional affiliation and male presence had long been seen as a crucial means for establishing laywomen's saintly charisma. Although the mendicants were therefore not the first to try to contain and control a female lay saint's charismatic claims, they became the dominant voice in such endeavors as the church increasingly charged them with the oversight of lay penitents. In short, an emphasis on visions as well as on one's internal spiritual state became a means by which hagiographers could check female lay religious power just as Innocent III's canonization of Omobono had worked to check an earlier version of lay charisma.[7]

This is not to suggest that by the late thirteenth and early fourteenth centuries, the promoters of laywomen's cults had invented a contemplative, visionary, or internal point of view—far from it. Such religious expression has a long and complex history. My account of Ranieri of Pisa and the many thirteenth-century communal lay saints is itself evidence not only of a small piece of that history but also of how a charismatic or visionary aspect of the ideal lay life was an ever-present part of lay sanctity. But just as I have argued that both church and commune were eager to limit as well as co-opt such notions of lay religious charisma and power over the thirteenth century, this chapter advocates for seeing a similar motivation behind hagiographers' promotion of laywomen's cults.

---

7. My argument here is inspired by other studies that have considered the variety of means by which women's spirituality and religious expression was checked or controlled during the Middle Ages; prime among those studies are Caciola, *Discerning Spirits*, and Elliott, *Proving Woman*.

Thus, I will show that while the cults of late thirteenth- and early fourteenth-century male saints, such as Giovanni of Urbino (d. 1309), Enrico of Treviso (d. 1315), and Peter Crisci of Foligno (d. 1323), continued to celebrate the attributes of an ideal lay religious life that we saw created over the thirteenth century, hagiographers writing about women at this time adopted new ways of containing and reconceiving lay charisma. In the cults that grew up around Giovanna of Orvieto and Margaret of Città di Castello we hear little about how these women served their civic communities but much about how their penitential commitments deepened their own spiritual lives. However, by contrast, in the cults that grew up around laymen there was still an interest in how a lay saint's charisma both served and was manifested in his civic community. In other words, while the men remained externally focused, the women turned ever more dramatically in on themselves.

In short, I argue that it was not a new mendicant-influenced spirituality replacing a more practical lay saint model that led to the end of the contemporary lay civic saint, but rather that the solutions the church adopted to address the problem of the female lay penitent—found both in hagiographic texts and regulatory measures—essentially regulated the civic lay saint out of existence. Anachronistic claims about Francis founding an order of lay penitents not only motivated the formal creation of the mendicant third orders but also eventually made moot the very category of the lay religious. And although some of the waning of the lay saint by the mid-fourteenth century can be ascribed to a changing civic context that no longer needed contemporary lay saints as emblems of a commune's political or social identity, a more substantial explanation is to be found in the work the church had done over the thirteenth and early fourteenth centuries to change the very definition of an ideal lay life. That work was in direct response to the fundamental problem of women seeking, finding, and being celebrated for their embrace of the *vita apostolica*.

A Changing Context: Fourteenth-Century Male Lay Saints

When Giovanni "Pilingotto" (the pilgrim) of Urbino died on June 1, 1304, he was buried in the city's Franciscan church.[8] Giovanni did not want to be separated in death, his hagiographer reports, from the man he most aimed to

---

8. *AASS, De Beato Pilingotto,* June I, 145–51 [hereafter *De Beato Pilingotto*] (*BHL* 6850). On Giovanni, see Vauchez, *Sainthood,* 187 and 208; and Thompson, *Cities of God,* 183, 187, 287, 293.

imitate during his lifetime: Francis of Assisi.[9] Vauchez has written about the many similarities between Giovanni and Francis—both men were the sons of wealthy cloth merchants, and both men renounced their family fortunes to take up lives of extreme penitence and works of charity.[10] And yet, this is the only mention of Francis in Giovanni's *vita*. Moreover, while scholars, including the Bollandist editors of his *vita*, often identify Giovanni as a member of the Franciscan Third Order, his *vita*, written by an anonymous contemporary of Giovanni's, makes no claims that the saint wore a tertiary habit or had any special connection with his city's Friars Minor during his lifetime.[11] As we have seen for other lay saints considered in this study, it was quite common for fourteenth-century Franciscan authors to portray the institutional identities of thirteenth-century lay penitents in ways that suggested not only that a fully formed Franciscan Third Order existed during those lay penitents' lifetimes but also that those saints were early members.[12] In Giovanni's case, despite the obvious similarities between Giovanni and Francis, as well as the hagiographer's work to create a rational for why this layman was buried in Urbino's church of San Francesco, this *vita* pays ultimately no attention to Giovanni's institutional status—a stark contrast to the hagiography produced for female lay saints at the turn of the fourteenth century.

Instead, Giovanni's *vita* focuses on the ways in which this young layman's penitential calling at first made him a spectacle but later a revered holy man in his city—another aspect of Giovanni's cult that contrasts with the cults of laywomen over the thirteenth century. Although the reactions of those witnessing Rose of Viterbo's and Margaret of Cortona's public penances ultimately forced them to flee (or in Rose's case, be exiled from) their initial penitential communities, the public's response to Giovanni was at first dubious but in the end became a means for demonstrating both his penitential zeal and his saintly reputation.

Before his *vita* builds a portrait of how the people of Urbino responded to Giovanni, however, it describes his virtues in a manner consistent with other contemporary male civic lay saints. Giovanni led such an upright religious life that he both resisted loquaciousness in order to free himself for prayer and made a regular circuit of his city's churches, finding the divine office to be like

---

9. *De Beato Pilingotto*, 149.

10. Vauchez, *Sainthood*, 208, n. 176.

11. *De Beato Pilingotto*, 145.

12. For example, the ca. 1333 *vita* for Pier "Pettinaio" of Siena claimed that he had been such a devoted member of the Franciscan Third Order that he had made his habit to mark his membership to his wider civic community.

spiritual food for the soul.[13] Giovanni's *vita* makes clear that this layman's conversion to a committed penitential life came as an obedient member of the institutional church; Giovanni was so aware of his lay religious responsibilities that he kept a journal of all of his sins so that he would be ready for confession each Friday.[14] Moreover, he adopted and stuck to a rigorous routine of fasting as well as contemplation.[15]

All of these aspects of Giovanni's upstanding religious life took place in the context of a privileged urban existence. Giovanni, after all, was, like Francis, the son of a successful merchant. Thus, while the *vita* notes that Giovanni despised all things earthly, the text pays particular attention to the way in which he demonstrated that point of view by rebuking his parents' wealth.[16] For example, during a lavish feast day celebration he smuggled meat under his cloak to feed the poor. Moreover, it was his parents whom the text repeatedly describes as having acted to protect him from both his extreme penitential behavior and the ridicule it earned him from his civic community.

Thus, during one Lent, Giovanni's contemplation on the Passion was so intense that he began not only to wear a sackcloth but also a rope around his neck as he made his usual circuit of the city's churches.[17] When he got to the cathedral, he placed himself in front of the altar dedicated to the Virgin, remaining there for so long and in such a deep state of prayer that, as his hagiographer writes, he was able to "penetrate divine love," and seemed almost to be present in heaven.[18] Giovanni's behavior sparked rumors in the city as the people of Urbino began to whisper that it was "as if this pious man had run to his own hanging."[19] Nevertheless, as the text reports, both the city's lay and religious population immediately rushed to the cathedral in order to see "this reported holy man."[20] The disparity of responses to Giovanni's actions as opposed to the actions taken by female lay saints is, again, striking. Giovanni's behavior earned him a few raised eyebrows but many more eager spectators. In contrast, Giunta forbade Margaret of Cortona to return to Mon-

---

13. *De Beato Pilingotto*, 146.

14. Ibid. Thompson mentions this part of Giovanni's *vita* in *Cities of God*, 287.

15. *De Beato Pilingotto*, 146.

16. Ibid.

17. Ibid.

18. Ibid.: "Versus Episcopatum iter arripuit, et ante altare Virginis gloriosae gradum figens, ipsam coepit genitricem invocare. Cumque in hac meditatione diu persisteret, tanta fuit illius anima ibi divini amoris dulcedine penetrata, ut per diem medium ibi permanens quasi abstractus, videretur in coelestibus habitare."

19. Ibid.: "Denique dum haec agerentur, rumor per civitatem insonuit, quasi vir pius ad suspendium cucurrisset; praesertim cum aliqui ad collum ejus funem viderent ligatum: et factus est consursus populorum ac religiosorum, eo quod vir bonus reputabatur."

20. Ibid.

tepulciano (where she had lived as a noble's concubine) with a rope around her neck to signal her new identity as a penitent; to do so would risk the loss of her association with the Cortonese Franciscans. Both Giovanni's gender and social status likely protected him from the kind of harsh responses that Margaret received to her dramatic behavior.

This was not the only time that Giovanni's penitential behavior earned comment. In each of the moments when his civic neighbors were skeptical about his behavior, the *vita* notes that his parents were there to rescue him from his more dramatic displays of penitence and piety. Thus, the *vita* notes that after his activities over that particular Lent, Giovanni's parents begged him to stop his dramatic ways.[21] In addition, in a section of the *vita* that describes Giovanni's great love of solitude and his desire for the desert (which he shared with our other lay saints), the author notes that Giovanni's parents had to keep "violently dragging him back" from what we can assume, but the text does not explicitly say, were attempts to live an eremitic life.[22] In another episode, Giovanni's hagiographer gives an extended description of the time that this young layman went out into the streets "with the fervor of the spirit rising."[23] When he arrived in Urbino's main market square, he tied himself with chains to the spot normally reserved for the public condemnation of thieves and robbers. The *vita* notes that the people of Urbino viewed Giovanni's behavior as that of a fool (*fatuus*) and that his parents ran to the market in order to rescue him; when they got to him, the *vita* points out, he was "half-dead from the cold."[24]

The term fool (*fatuus*) shows up again later in the *vita*. In an episode describing a time when Giovanni sat eating with two companions, we hear how the group began to talk about divine matters (*divinis colloquiis*), prompting Giovanni to yell (exactly why and in regards to what, we are not told): "This is Christ!" Giovanni's outburst clearly startled his companions, who told him to "be quiet, lest we are considered to be fools" (*ne fatui deputemur*).[25] But

---

21. Ibid., 146.

22. Ibid., 146–47: "Sed retractus violenter a parentibus, frequenter, impressa manens in caritate et humilitate, studuit Domino servire."

23. Ibid., 147: "de mane in die Veneris, tempore frigoris intensissimi, in fervore spiritus surgens, ad plateam magnam perrexit; et ibi se catenis ligavit ad locum ubi consueverunt latrones et fures vinculati ad spectacular detineri; et ibi tamdiu sic stetit, ut prae frigoris immanitate semimortuus ab omnibus cerneretur; accurrentes autem parentes ejus, ipsum ad domum reportaverunt."

24. Ibid.

25. Ibid.: "Et ut de multis unum referam, accidit ut die quadam, ipse cum duobus Christi famulis caritative insimul comedentes, corporalem cibum sumentes, fortiter coeperunt divinis colloquiis insistere: et usque ad finem perseverantes, tanto ardore mentis, contigit ut vir Dei in vocem prorumperet talem. His est, inquit, Christus. Illi exorantes eum dixerunt, Tace, Frater; tace, ne fatui deputemur."

Giovanni seemed to relish how uncomfortable his outbursts made others, telling his companions that he knew he was a glutton and that the only appropriate penance for him was to go into the streets to give the food from his own mouth to the poor and hungry.[26]

The threat of public ridicule that hung over so many lay penitents, whose more rigorous—and often, outrageous—penitential and spiritual displays made them a spectacle for their civic communities, plays a crucial role in the creation of Giovanni's civic cult. Instead of having to endure any real mockery, shame, or consequence for his actions (as did both Rose of Viterbo and Margaret of Cortona), Giovanni's *vita* makes clear that he must simply withstand being called a "fool." He will be rescued from any further public shaming by his attentive parents. The idea that Giovanni's civic neighbors interpreted his dramatic behavior as that of a fool seems an especially forgiving and generous assessment when placed next to the Cortonese Franciscans' skepticism and doubts about Margaret of Cortona. Margaret's *Legenda* reports that the Franciscans' condemnation of her left her shaking, terrified, and feeling as if she needed to physically distance herself from the friars. Giovanni, by contrast, seems to thrive from the reactions his outlandish penitential behavior earns him; if yelling out "This is Christ" made his companions uncomfortable, watching him offer his chewed food to others would only intensify such feelings.

It is in this *vita*'s most often referenced moment, however, that the author mines the skepticism about Giovanni's behavior to prove that this pious layman was indeed not a fool, but rather a saint. In 1300, Giovanni made a pilgrimage to Rome (the origin of his nickname "pilingotto"), along with two companions, in order to mark the jubilee year called for by Pope Boniface VIII. The *vita* describes this episode simply by noting that at one point Giovanni and his companions were spotted in Rome by an unknown man, who yelled out: "Is that not the saint from Urbino?"[27] Giovanni's public reputation had clearly changed. No longer the fool, Giovanni was now the saint from Urbino.

The *vita* emphasizes the shift in Giovanni's public reputation in its description of the response to his death. When he died, all the people of Urbino—men and women, clerics and religious—flocked to his tomb in the cathedral, eager to see and perhaps benefit from the many miracles that were being reported to take place there.[28] Before giving a list of those postmortem mira-

---

26. Ibid.

27. Ibid., 148: "Tempore enim Indulgentiae Romanae, ipse cum duobus sociis, pariter incedens, obviarunt viro cuidam ignoto. Quos cum ille vidisset, quasi alius per ipsum loquens, in vocem talem prorupit: Nonne hic est ille vir sanctus de Urbino?"

28. Ibid., 149.

cles (divided by the type of malady cured), the *vita* mentions that it was the commune that had paid for Giovanni's tomb. Thus, the *vita's* description of the reaction to his death not only reaffirms the change in Giovanni's public reputation, but it also conveys the idea that the commune of Urbino was ready and waiting to celebrate one of their own as a civic saint. The commune immediately stepped in to pay for the tomb, and a notary was ready to transcribe the accounts of miracles taking place there. But nowhere was a commune more poised and eager to launch a celebration of a contemporary lay saint than in the city of Treviso's response to the death of its local saint, Enrico.

On June 10, 1315, when Enrico of Treviso (sometimes called Enrico or Rigo of Bolzano, referring to his native city) died, the city of Treviso, where he had spent the majority of his adult life living as a penitent, exploded. His *vita*, written sometime after 1362 by Treviso's bishop, Pietro da Baono, records that as word spread of this lay penitent's death, the bishop saw a crowd "without number" begin to gather, shouting, "a saint has died!"[29] Cathedral officials carried Enrico's body from the house where he had died toward the cathedral. But as Pietro describes, the crowd grew so much that "the body could scarcely, and only with great effort, be carried behind the clergy." The people filling the streets were so overcome with emotion that they broke off some of the casket's panels, exposing the saint's body, which, Pietro notes, was "rocking to and fro" inside.[30]

Communal documents collected by the eighteenth-century Trevisan scholar Raimbaldo degli Azzoni Avogari make clear that it was not just the people of Treviso but also the city's government and cathedral authorities who were instrumental in launching a saintly cult for Enrico immediately on his death. Avogari includes documents detailing the communal deliberations that took place the day after Enrico's death, during which the commune issued a statement noting the city's wish that God "through his mercy and the prayers of the blessed Rigo and all the other saints of God will maintain [Treviso] in a good, peaceful and communal state."[31] Within two days of Enrico's death, the commune, the bishop and the city's *podestà* had jointly appointed a committee of three men to verify and document the miracles taking place at Enrico's tomb and to create twin written accounts of those miracles—one

29. For Enrico's *vita* and cult, see Webb, *Saints and Cities*, 242–56; and R. degli Azzoni Avogari, *Memorie del Beato Enrico, morto in Trivigi l'anno MCCCXV, corredate di documenti, con una dissertazione sopra San Liberale e sopra gli altri santi dei quali riposano i Sacri Corpori nella chiesa della già detta città* (Venice, 1760). The Latin *vita* can be found in *AASS*, June II, 365–69 (*BHL* 3807). In all of the references to Enrico's *vita* that follow, I will be relying on Webb's translation in *Saints and Cities*, 246–56.

30. Webb, *Saints and Cities*, 252.

31. Cited by Webb, *Saints and Cities*, 244 and taken from Avogari, *Memorie del Beato Enrico*, part 2, 2.

for the cathedral and one for the communal chancery.[32] In addition, communal deliberations from those first days after Enrico's death claim that to honor the layman, twenty-four prisoners were to be released.[33] By October of 1315, the commune was earmarking funds to pay for an image of Enrico (alongside new portraits of the Virgin Mary and St. Lucy) to be painted on the *palazzo pubblico*.[34] And finally, Enrico's *vita* concludes with Pietro noting that a chapel was ordered to be built within the cathedral to hold Enrico's remains "by decree of the bishop and chapter and commune."[35]

The combination of communal documents and Pietro's eyewitness account (he was a cathedral canon at the time of Enrico's death) make clear not only that Enrico's cult took off immediately after his death but also that its promotion was a collaborative effort involving the people, the commune, and the city's religious authorities. Although Diana Webb has noted the extent to which these sources portray how public the launching of this cult was, I would add that they also suggest both a highly organized and planned effort. In other words, neither commune nor episcopacy appear to have wasted any time in checking what we have come to see in this study were the necessary boxes for launching the cult of a lay contemporary: a popular surge of emotion toward the newly deceased, recognition and monetary support from both commune and episcopacy, and finally steps to enshrine the layman's memory within the political and visual fabric of the city.

If the immediate and well-organized effort to promote Enrico as a new patron for Treviso was something that was anticipated, and perhaps even planned, why does a *vita* for the saint not appear until the 1360s, at least forty-five years after his death? This, I would argue, also speaks to the extent to which the idea or model of the communal lay saint had been so well established over the thirteenth century. The people, the commune, and the episcopacy each had a role to play in the early days of making one of their own into a civic patron. The writing of a *vita*, in which devotees would get a description of the man as well as the quality and content of his religious life, was not a crucial piece of that early effort. The proof of Enrico's sanctity came in the highly organized response that the people, the episcopacy, and the commune all demonstrated—not through a description of his life and miracles.

---

32. Vauchez, *Sainthood*, 236–38; Vauchez is relying on Avogari's *Memorie del Beato Enrico* and Enrico's eighteenth-century canonization inquiry.

33. Vauchez, *Sainthood*, 236–38.

34. Ibid., 237.

35. Webb, *Saints and Cities*, 256. In the proceeding paragraphs, Pietro suggests that this all took place within a year of Enrico's death.

The decision in the 1360s finally to write a *vita* to celebrate Treviso's new-est saint was likely driven by Pietro's election to the episcopacy in 1359. And even though the *vita* does not appear to have been instrumental in establish-ing Enrico's initial cult, it does offer a glimpse into how his sanctity was un-derstood in the mid-fourteenth century. Focusing almost exclusively on the final years of Enrico's life, and on the first years of his cult, the *vita* begins with a rather boilerplate description of an ideal lay life.[36] Once Enrico had grown old, and "could no longer supply his physical needs in his accustomed man-ner," he adopted a more contemplative life, going to live with a notary and his wife. This couple, Pietro writes, had taken pity on the aged Enrico, pro-viding him with a room in their house, where he would maintain "a life of abstinence and penitence" until his death.[37] Enrico sustained himself largely through alms, gave his leftover foods to the poor, and had a body that Pietro describes as having been "much worn down with fasts, vigils and other austerities."[38]

Attached as an appendix to the *vita* is an account of the 356 postmortem miracles that devotees ascribed to Enrico between June 12 and July 5, 1315. Webb has noted that the combination of an extensive collection of miracles focused on bodily healings and the fact that Pietro's *vita* describes an elderly, rather contemplative layman gives the reader the sense that Enrico "was re-membered above all as a thaumaturge."[39] But that is primarily a postmortem reputation, as the *vita* only includes two miracles that Enrico performed dur-ing his lifetime.[40] In the first, onlookers were amazed to see Enrico emerge dry from a rainstorm. In the second, Enrico touched the injured finger of the tailor who made his hair shirts, immediately restoring the finger to "full health."[41]

If Pietro does not seem to have been concerned with portraying Enrico as a living miracle worker, he certainly was intent on establishing an account of the saint's obedience to and interest in the city's religious institutions. And it

---

36. A document describing the June 1381 investigation of Enrico's relics by Bishop Pietro claims that it was on becoming bishop, after having served as a longtime cathedral canon, that Pietro finally wrote Enrico's *vita*; Webb, *Saints and Cities*, 243.

37. Webb, *Saints and Cities*, 248.

38. Ibid., 247–48. Pietro also provides nearly no information about Enrico's earlier life. While he notes that Enrico had been married before he took up a penitential life, the bishop makes no mention of the saint's son, whom we know from other communal documents the city had begun to financially support after Enrico's death. Moreover, no mention is made of Enrico's working life; see Avogari, *Memorie del Beato Enrico*, part 2, 24–27.

39. Webb, *Saints and Cities*, 246.

40. Miracles from June 11 and part of June 12 are missing from Pietro's collection; Webb, *Saints and Cities*, 246.

41. Ibid., 250–51.

is here, in Pietro's account of Enrico's wanderings around the city of Treviso, that a more nuanced portrait of this saint emerges. The bishop describes how Enrico's last years were taken up primarily by his daily routine of visiting and praying in each of Treviso's churches. Pietro's description of these regular circuits does two seemingly contradictory things at once: it gives Enrico a particular religious affiliation at the same time as it connects him above all to the city of Treviso. Pietro writes that even though Enrico made it a point to visit each of the city's churches every day, he was a frequent visitor to the city's Augustinian church. Nevertheless, Pietro notes that despite Enrico's "close relationship" with the Augustinians and his decision "to be buried with them," either out of negligence on the friars' part or because Enrico was poor, the Augustinians "lost him."[42] Pietro seems to use this somewhat negative portrait of the Hermit Friars as an opportunity to praise the cathedral's religious hierarchy. While the Augustinians may have "lost" the opportunity to have Enrico's body, it was the cathedral deans' and canons' "practice," Pietro writes, "to go personally and collectively to the funerals of any of their parishioners, of whatever station in life." As a result, it was they who received Enrico's "body with all care, according to their custom."[43]

Although Pietro makes clear that the cathedral authorities showed particular loyalty to Enrico, he also emphasizes that Enrico was himself an emblem of loyalty and obedience to the city's episcopal authority. Enrico "always hastened to sermons, both in the cathedral and in the houses of the religious, never missing one if time permitted." He was such an "eager listener" at these sermons that, as Pietro writes, "he committed to memory as much as he could take in." Moreover, it was always the cathedral that received the majority of Enrico's devotional time. Pietro writes that once Enrico had made his circuit of all of Treviso's churches, he would always return to the cathedral, remaining mostly "in the corner under the portico, towards the bishop's palace, near a certain image of the Blessed Virgin Mary." There, Pietro writes, with his cap in his hand, Enrico would pray, "continuously and devoutly, gazing at the image." Pietro notes how the bishop at the time, Master Castellano, would sometimes send alms to Enrico there. Enrico, Pietro points out, "never missed the divine office in that church and was always early at matins." Moreover, he had "such a conscience that every day he wanted to confess his least sins with the priests of that church."[44]

---

42. Ibid., 249.
43. Ibid.
44. Ibid., 251.

Two aspects of Enrico's religious life stand out here. First, Enrico was effectively independent. He may have had a particular affection for the Augustinians, but because of either their incompetence or disinterest, he was not buried in their church and they, as an order, had no claim to him. Second, Pietro's text argues that Enrico was most loyal and most present at Treviso's cathedral and that the interest was mutual—it was the canons' and deans' "practice" to collect the bodies of any of their parishioners. Enrico ends up buried in the cathedral, Pietro's *vita* argues, not only because he had a burgeoning saintly reputation but also because the city's episcopal authority looked out for its own. The celebration of Enrico becomes a celebration of the episcopacy's care for and ultimate authority over Treviso's population.

The emphasis in the remainder of the *vita* on the popular surge of emotion at Enrico's death as well as on the steps taken collaboratively by communal and episcopal authorities completes Pietro's portrait of a perfectly organized cult launch. No matter the particular interest this layman might have shown in the Augustinians, it was with the city, represented by the cathedral, that Enrico was most meaningfully connected. On one hand, we can read this emphasis as a means both for establishing Enrico's civic cult and for articulating the ideal of the institutionally obedient lay saint—an ideal that we have seen emphasized in lay saints' cults since Innocent III's canonization of Omobono of Cremona. But, on the other hand, Pietro's handling of Enrico's religious affiliation is something particular to the male lay saint. In the cults that grew up around female lay penitents, religious affiliation mattered.

The limited information that survives about another early fourteenth-century male lay saint reinforces the sense of how different the trajectory of a layman's cult was from that of a laywoman. Born in 1243 to a wealthy and perhaps even noble Foligno family, Pietro Crisci (d. 1323) made a name for himself by the time he was thirty by giving away all of his goods to the poor and adopting a life of intense penance, poverty, and service.[45] The majority of that service was dedicated to his city's cathedral, where he lived in a cell within the *campanile*. However, as his *vita*, written during the first half of the fourteenth century by the Dominican Giovanni Gorini tells us, Pietro's service to the city's religious authority did not keep him from being suspected of heresy: Pietro was brought before an inquisitor in Spoleto but ultimately exonerated of all

---

45. On Peter Crisci, see Mario Sensi and Fortunato Frezza, *Pietro Crisci: Beato, confessore, compatrono di Foligno* (Foligno: Diocesi di Foligno, 2010); and Vauchez, *Sainthood*, 206–8. Vauchez uses Pietro as example of one of the very last male lay saints of the type that was so popular in the preceding century.

charges.[46] Even Angela of Foligno admitted early doubts about Pietro, noting in her *Memorial* that before her own penitential conversion she used to make fun of "a certain Pietruccio" but now understood that she "could not do otherwise than follow his example."[47] Although Pietro's religious life clearly raised some eyebrows, the ease with which his *vita* passes over this part of his life distinguishes him from female lay saints, who were viewed with persistent suspicion. Moreover, the mentions of Pietro's feast day in Foligno's statutes in the fourteenth century as well as the May 11, 1400 indulgence Pope Boniface IX offered to those participating in such celebrations make clear not only that Pietro had indeed been exonerated of all charges but also that his civic cult was active in the first century after his death.[48]

Even though the *vitae* of Giovanni, Enrico, and Pietro all demonstrate how much concerns such as civic engagement and charity (albeit in all but Giovanni's life solely in the form of alms or goods given to the poor) still mattered in the civic cults awarded to laymen in the early fourteenth-century communes, they also underline the flexibility that was tolerated in a layman's religious life and institutional status; a flexibility that was not available to laywomen.

The Problem of the Female Lay Penitent

In *The Life of Saint Francis*, written in the 1230s, the German friar Julian of Speyer describes how Francis wandered through the Spoleto Valley, providing "a plan of salvation to persons of every state and condition, age and sex, giving them all a rule of life." Francis's interest in providing a new religious life for all manifested in what Julian calls a "threefold army." In addition to founding armies of Lesser Brothers and Sisters, Julian claims that Francis also established "the Order of Penitents," which brought together "clerics and laity, virgins, unmarried, and married persons of both sexes."[49] Julian was not the first Franciscan and far from the last to claim that Francis had founded a lay penitential order. From the thirteenth century until the modern day, Franciscans and scholars have referred to this lay order in a manner suggesting that

---

46. *AASS*, July IV, 665–68 (*BHL* 6709); Vauchez sees these charges as evidence of the suspicion "regulars" (especially mendicant regulars) began to demonstrate toward contemporary lay saints after 1270; see Vauchez, *Sainthood*.

47. *Angela of Foligno: Complete Works*, 131.

48. As Vauchez points out, Peter was one of the uncanonized saints recognized by Pope Boniface IX in an attempt to reward areas that had remained loyal during the Great Schism; Vauchez, *Sainthood*, 90.

49. "The Life of Saint Francis by Julian of Speyer (1232–1235)," 378 and 385, in *Francis of Assisi: Early Documents*, vol. 1, ed. Regis J. Armstrong, J. A. Wayne Hellmann, and William J. Short (New York: New City Press, 1999); cited by Mooney, *Clare of Assisi*, 81.

it had a canonical status as well as an institutional identity on par with the Friars Minor and the female Franciscan community at San Damiano.[50]

And yet, to borrow More's succinct assessment, there is no evidence "of a penitential order, let alone one founded by Francis of Assisi in the thirteenth century."[51] The work of More, Casagrande, and Lehmijoki-Gardner has gone far in recent decades in prodding scholars to rethink the origins of the third orders.[52] In addition to identifying and unpacking how the mendicants created institutional narratives for their third orders long before those orders had canonical or legal status, these scholars have also encouraged a reassessment of evidence assumed to be reflective of already established lay orders. In particular, More has argued that the sources that past scholarship has held up as early versions of Franciscan-sponsored or at least Franciscan-informed lay penitential rules are, in point of fact, simply regulatory measures cobbled together from a variety of "penitential canons, legal formularies, and regulatory documents for penitential societies."[53]

One of those sources, Cardinal Hugolino's *Memoriale propositi*, can help us to construct a new narrative for the end of civic lay sanctity in the fourteenth century.[54] Soon after assuming the papal throne, Pope Honorius III placed Hugolino (later Pope Gregory IX) in charge of overseeing and organizing the many lay penitential groups across urban Italy. By 1220, he had also been made Cardinal Protector of the new Franciscan Order. Attempting to bring what Michael Cusato has described as "organization and structure" to the lay penitential life, Hugolino issued the *Memoriale propositi* in 1221, a rule (or as Augustine Thompson translates the title, "a record of an intended way of life") for the "Brothers and Sisters of Penance."[55] Thompson has noted that the *Memoriale*

---

50. Alison More, "Institutionalization of Disorder: The Franciscan Third Order and Canonical Change in the Sixteenth Century," *Franciscan Studies* 71 (2013): 147.

51. More, "Institutionalizing Penitential Life," 297–98.

52. Casagrande, "Un ordine per i laici"; Lehmijoki-Gardner, "Writing Religious Rules"; More, *Fictive Orders*, "Institutionalizing Penitential Life," and "Institutionalization of Disorder."

53. More, "Institutionalizing Penitential Life," 301. While several thirteenth-century Franciscan sources claim that Francis founded a lay order, the real push to establish historical evidence that such an order existed in connection with the Friars Minor came at the same time as the Dominican effort: in the late thirteenth and early fourteenth centuries in conjunction with the order's Observant reform movement; see More, "Institutionalizing Penitential Life," 312–15; and Doyno, "The Creation of a Franciscan Lay Saint," 87–90.

54. Meersseman has edited the *Memoriale propositi*; see *Dossier de l'ordre de la penitence*, 91–112. For an English translation, see Margaret Carney, Jean François Godet-Calogeras, and Suzanne M. Kush, eds., *History of the Third Order Regular Rule: A Sourcebook* (Saint Bonaventure, NY: Franciscan Institute), 62–72.

55. Michael Cusato, *The Early Franciscan Movement (1205–1239): History, Sources, Hermeneutics* (Spoleto: Centro Italiano di Studi sull'Alto Medioevo, 2009), 181; Thompson, *Cities of God*, 78.

propositi is not "a piece of original legislation" but rather an amalgamation of preexisting "legal formularies and canon law sources" that provided "the basic structure and strictures for the lay penitential life."[56] Addressed to those penitents who were living in their own houses, it gives restrictions on dress and ornamentation, forbids lay penitents from attending any "shameful entertainments, theaters, or dances," and delineates a set of eating regulations, as well as times and places to gather as a community.[57] The text also encourages lay penitents, "if they conveniently can," to find "one religious, instructed in the word of God, who would admonish and encourage them to penance, perseverance and the performance of works of mercy."[58] Finally, Hugolino demands that a lay penitent be "silent during the Mass and preaching"; that the lay penitent be "attentive to the Office, prayer, and sermon"; that a priest be allowed to say three masses for the benefit of the lay penitents each year; and finally, that lay penitents rely on a combination of local ministers, the bishop, and an unidentified "visitor" to resolve any problems or scandals within penitential communities, as well as to "dispense" any deserving penitents.[59]

Although the *Memoriale propositi* would form the basis for later, Franciscan sponsored and identified lay penitential rules, Hugolino's text makes no explicit mention of any mendicant orders.[60] Moreover, as More has noted, while this document provided guidelines for a lay penitential life, "it neither constituted a religious order, nor gave those who followed it any claim to being canonically recognized as religious."[61] However, while the *Memoriale propositi* clearly did not establish a Franciscan-affiliated lay order, we would be misguided to distance Hugolino's regulatory work with lay penitents from similar work he did with Francis's first female followers. As Mooney has argued, Clare and her companions were themselves part of the wider lay penitential movement.[62] Hugolino's creation of the Order of San Damiano in the 1210s and early 1220s, as well as his efforts to absorb Clare's community of female lay penitents into that order had at its heart a similar desire to provide "organ-

56. Thompson, *Cities of God*, 78.

57. Carney et al., *History of the Third Order Regular Rule*, 63.

58. Ibid., 67.

59. Ibid., 63–71.

60. Cusato, *The Early Franciscan Movement*, 182–83. Cusato has argued that Francis's shorter version of his "Letter to the Faithful" functions as a kind of "supplementary word" aimed at turning Hugolino's rather "generic rule" into something that spoke more specifically to lay penitents with Franciscan associations.

61. More, "Institutionalizing Penitential Life," 301.

62. Mooney, *Clare of Assisi*, 2–3.

ization and structure" (Cusato's words) to the lay penitential life as found in his *Memoriale propositi*.[63]

And yet, to use Cusato's words is to characterize Hugolino's work in a rather passive and benign manner, especially when it comes to Clare and her companions. Mooney shows that by placing Clare and her fellow female lay penitents in the Order of San Damiano, Hugolino was essentially strong-arming her into an institutional setting at odds with the kind of religious life she and her fellow female penitents sought.[64] If we consider the issuing of the *Memoriale propositi* as part and parcel of the same effort to contain and control lay penitents that led Hugolino to create the Order of San Damiano, we can begin to see that despite the church's efforts to incorporate various lay penitential groups (for example, the Humiliati at the beginning of the thirteenth century and the Franciscans a decade later), it remained concerned about how to respond to the multitude of other lay penitents, both those living on their own and those living in communities. Even though Hugolino did not decide that the answer to that concern was to incorporate lay penitents into a canonically distinct order, he did see a need to articulate a set of normative guidelines to regulate them.

Attempting to define an appropriate lay penitential life is, of course, also the work of lay saints' cults. By creating an ideal portrait of a lay penitent, lay saints' cults provided models for other laymen and laywomen to follow. Nevertheless, many communal lay saints' cults celebrate individuals who did not scrupulously adhere to the guidelines articulated in the *Memoriale propositi*. An explanation for this discrepancy can be found in the arguments of the previous chapters. The ideal layman constructed by Pope Innocent III began to change in the context of the rising *popolo* communes. Even though Innocent's portrait of a contemporary lay saint emphasized charity, prayer, and the struggle against heresy over the performance of charismatic acts, *popolo* communes' interest in capitalizing upon this new saintly type allowed for the return of the lay saint as living miracle worker. As the cults dedicated to contemporary laymen over the thirteenth century have illustrated, when the pious layman was associated primarily with his city and its concerns, not only could he maintain an independent religious identity but he could also be credited with extraordinary living charisma.

With that argument in mind, it makes sense to think of Hugolino's *Memoriale propositi* as providing a normative path for lay penitents, while the many lay saints' cults that emerged in communal Italy constructed an ideal path. The

---

63. Ibid., 11.
64. Ibid., 66.

ideal lay saint could act in ways contrary to the norm precisely because he or she lived a religious life that was extraordinary, outside of what the *Memoriale propositi* had demarcated as acceptable. Pope Nicholas IV's issuing of the bull *Supra montem* in 1289 suggests, however, that at some point church officials found that normative model to be lacking. More has noted an overall shift in the attitude of canonical sources regarding lay penitents in the second half of the thirteenth century. She writes that while the *Memoriale propositi* is characteristic of the "more inclusive attitude" we see in the first half of the century, "when regulation was often only quasi-official," by the 1240s, "stricter directives for the spiritual care of penitents" began to be issued.[65]

Nicholas's *Supra montem* stands as the culmination of that trend.[66] As the first papally approved penitential rule, it is, in essence, a doubling down on the restrictions outlined in the *Memoriale propositi*. It also stands out for its articulation of an historical and ongoing association between the Franciscans and lay penitents.[67] The bull states that it was Francis who had originally founded a lay penitential order, and the friars who should have the primary role in overseeing the committed lay penitential life. Thus, while there are several sections in *Supra montem* that appear to be taken from the *Memoriale propositi*, most of these describe the basic structure of a committed lay penitential life.[68] But whereas the *Memoriale propositi* provided only a rather vague description of the oversight of a lay penitential community, *Supra montem* makes both the identity and responsibilities of those overseers clear. Nicholas's bull elaborates not only that a "visitor" be part of the initiation process for new lay penitents—a process that the bull notes was to take place "at some religious place, or in a church"—but also that because, as the bull rationalizes, "this present form of life took its origin from the aforementioned blessed Francis," such "visitors and instructors should be taken from the Order of Friars Minor."[69] And finally, to make clear that the control was being given exclusively to the Franciscans, the bull clarifies that it is the order's "custodes or guardians" who will appoint the said visitor. As the bull unnecessarily elabo-

---

65. More, "Institutionalizing Penitential Life," 300 and 302.

66. For the bull itself and scholarly assessment of its construction and content, see *La "Supra montem" di Niccolo IV*, ed. Pazzelli, and Temperini. For an English translation, see Carney et al., *History of the Third Order Regular Rule*, 73–85.

67. More has also noted that we ought to see *Supra montem* as a response to the legislation of the 1274 Second Council of Lyon outlawing orders founded after 1215; here was a means for establishing that the Franciscan Third Order had existed since the birth of the Franciscan Order and that it thus predated 1215. See More, *Fictive Orders*, 36–37.

68. That is, restrictions on dress, as well as the schedule of prayer and fasting that a lay penitent should follow.

69. Carney et al., *History of the Third Order Regular Rule*, 75 and 81.

rates, "we do not want a congregation of this kind to be visited by a lay person."[70]

On one hand, the differences between the 1221 *Memoriale propositi* and the 1289 *Supra montem* speak to the astonishingly quick growth of Franciscan Order over those years. By 1289, a Franciscan pope could call on his fellow friars, whose power and presence in the Italian communes was indisputable, to be the prime guardians of lay penitents. But, on the other hand, the added oversight, control, and concern that lay penitents be managed not by other laypersons but instead by church authorities, and in particular, by the Franciscans, indicates that the church saw the present state of the lay penitential life as too lax, too independent, and too unregulated. And yet, if, as I have argued, two viable paths—a normative and ideal one—had been articulated for and followed by lay penitents over the thirteenth century, why was there need for a stricter and more institutionally identified normative model in 1289?

The answer is to be found in the strain placed on these models by women's participation in both the lay penitential movement and the phenomenon of contemporary lay civic sanctity. The ideal path for the lay penitent—that of civic lay saint—was a path that, as we have seen, was overwhelmingly filled by men. A male lay penitent could have his religious ambitions subsumed into or represented by his civic identity. Civic engagement, whether through charity work or a rigorous adherence to civic statutes, became a means by which laymen were increasingly acclaimed for expressing their religious ideals. Moreover, men's cults not only tolerated but also often celebrated a lay saint's independence or ambiguous institutional status. Finally, several laymen's cults applauded lay devotional and charitable associations that these men both participated in and led.

In laywomen's cults, however, institutional identity and oversight was crucial. The women who earned civic cults—although they were never as robust as men's cults—did so in association with established (and often male-dominated) religious orders. Only Zita, who had the protection of her employers, seems to have been able to exist outside of such parameters. Moreover, in the instances where laywomen formed or participated in lay penitential communities—for example, in the cases of Rose of Viterbo, Umiliana de' Cerchi of Florence, or Margaret of Cortona—we see either a negative response (Rose) or a concerted effort in the *vitae* to reconstruct their identity in relationship to established religious authorities (Umiliana and Margaret).

The rise of the contemporary lay saint in the thirteenth-century communes therefore suggests that there was much less concern about how male lay

---

70. Ibid., 83.

penitents organized their religious lives than there was about laywomen. *Supra montem*'s effort not only to intensify those normative guidelines but also to clarify lay penitents' institutional identity and sponsorship suggests that this new regulatory effort was primarily directed at lay penitential women. As more women took up the lay penitential life and were increasingly celebrated for their efforts, the need for clearer and more stringent regulations emerged. Might *Supra montem* then be another attempt by the papacy, not wholly unlike Hugolino's creation of the Order of San Damiano, to solve the problem of the female lay penitent?

Like Hugolino's work with Clare's lay penitential community, *Supra montem* placed lay penitents under a rule, and laid the groundwork for the anachronistic claim that such a rule pertained to an "order of penitents" created by Francis. If the fundamental problem of the female lay penitent was the threat that she could take up an independent religious life, Nicholas had essentially solved that problem by regulating the lay penitent out of existence. To be a lay penitent according to *Supra montem* meant to be a Franciscan penitent. As I have argued, the texts celebrating both Umiliana de' Cerchi of Florence and Margaret of Cortona were essentially attempts by Franciscan friars to solve this same problem of the female lay penitent. The Franciscan authors of those hagiographies found a solution by outlining a new understanding of a perfected lay life and connecting that way of life to an established religious order. While this process ultimately circumscribed these women's charismatic power, *Supra montem* gave the church's stamp of approval to such an approach. And yet, as my exploration of the cults awarded to Giovanni of Urbino, Enrico of Treviso, and Peter Crisci of Foligno illustrate, such a new reality did not seem to apply to men.

A second answer for why, in 1289, the church decided that a stricter and more institutionally distinct normative path for lay penitents was needed can be found in the mendicants' growing role as the mentors and arbiters of the lay penitential life. Even though Pier "Pettinaio" of Siena did seem to construct his religious life in the orbit of his city's friars, this was a move much more common among laywomen. Umiliana de' Cerchi of Florence, Margaret of Cortona, and Rose of Viterbo all had religious lives that brought them (in varying degrees and manners) into contact with the friars. As the friars were the most visible and celebrated embodiment of the *vita apostolica* in the communes, we can imagine that for laywomen in particular, a connection to these new orders represented the potential for their lives as female lay penitents, inherently problematic, to garner protection, patronage, and prestige. Margaret of Cortona's *Legenda* makes such a motivation explicit—this former concubine sorely needed the benefit an association to the friars promised.

Moreover, Lehmijoki-Gardner's argument that a community of *vestitae* (lay-women associated with the Dominicans) in Orvieto requested that the Dominican Munio of Zamora write the *Ordinationes* demonstrates that by the 1280s female lay penitents were also turning to the Order of Preachers to find a similar protection and legitimacy for their way of life.[71]

However, as we saw in Margaret's *Legenda*, the Franciscans, at least, could be reluctant arbiters of lay penitents, especially when those lay penitents were women.[72] This reluctance had a long history.[73] In his *Earlier Rule*, Francis had prohibited his friars from receiving any woman into obedience.[74] But the anxiety about associating with female lay penitents is nowhere more clearly articulated than in a section of the anonymously authored Franciscan text entitled *Determinations of Questions Concerning the Rule* (ca. 1260). In "Why the friars should not promote the Order of Penitents," the reader is given a list of the potential problems and dangers the friars risked by associating with lay penitents.[75] While the majority of the author's points converge around issues of control and liability (what if a penitent was to be called before an ecclesiastical or secular court?), they also repeatedly touch on the particular dangers this friar saw in associations with laywomen. Lay penitents, and especially female lay penitents, the author's many rhetorical questions make clear, present the order with an untenable situation. Thus, he reasons that if the friars attach themselves to those who are excessively helpless (most often women or Beguines), they will become not only spiritually but also financially responsible for their charges.[76] In addition, an association with lay penitents leaves the order vulnerable to charges of heresy and sexual misconduct. Imagine the disaster that would befall the order, the author speculates, if a penitent who had been accused of fornication or adultery implicated a friar as her accomplice.

---

71. Lehmijoki-Gardner, "Writing Religious Rules."

72. See More, "Institutionalizing Penitential Life," 302; and Doyno, "The Creation of a Franciscan Lay Saint," 76–79.

73. More, *Fictive Orders*, 39.

74. *Francis of Assisi: Early Documents*, ed. Armstrong et al., 72–73.

75. Bonaventure of Bagnoregio [pseud.], *Determinationes quaestionum circa regulam fratrum minorum*, in *Bonaventurae opera omnia*, vol. 8 (Quaracchi, 1923), 368–69. This section concerning the friars' interaction with lay penitents also appears in Meersseman, *Dossier de l'ordre de la pénitence*, 123–24. On the text's authorship, see Ignatius Brady, "The Writings of Saint Bonaventure Regarding the Franciscan Order," *Miscellanea Francescana* 75 (1975): 107. For a brief summary of the author's explanations for the order's decline, see David Burr, *Olivi and Franciscan Poverty: The Origins of the Usus Pauper Controversy* (Philadelphia: University of Pennsylvania Press, 1989), 3–4 and 7; also see Neslihan Şenocak, *The Poor and the Perfect: The Rise of Learning in the Franciscan Order, 1209–1310* (Ithaca, NY: Cornell University Press, 2012), 193–94.

76. Bonaventure of Bagnoregio, *Determinationes*, 368–69.

Who would seem more likely to be responsible for a female penitent's pregnancy than the friars with whom she had spent all of her time?[77]

If the *Determinations* argues that some Franciscans saw connections to female lay penitents as a distracting and potentially dangerous enterprise, then perhaps *Supra montem* was not an acknowledgment and celebration of the relationship that already existed between the friars and lay penitents but rather an attempt to mandate such a connection. Is it possible that as more female lay penitents turned to the mendicant friars to protect and legitimize their way of life, a Franciscan pope understood that his fellow Friars Minor needed a substantial nudge to formalize those relationships?

Such a formalization ultimately brought to an end the idea of the lay penitent. By creating an anachronistic history for the lay penitential life, Nicholas's bull sowed the seeds for the formal creation of the mendicant third orders. The Franciscans would formalize that order over the fourteenth century, while the Dominicans did not follow suit until the very beginning of the fifteenth century.[78] But at the same time that this new norm was redefining a lay penitent as a Franciscan penitent, a new lay religious ideal—itself an attempt to solve the problem of the female lay penitent—was also emerging. The remainder of this chapter will argue that this new ideal of the female lay saint as visionary was the solution increasingly adopted to describe exemplary lay penitent women. This solution was already forming in the mendicant voices describing Umiliana de' Cerchi of Florence's and Margaret of Cortona's sanctity, and it ultimately moved the site of an ideal lay life out of the city streets and into women's bodies.

Giovanna of Orvieto

Giovanna (or Vanna) of Orvieto was a member of the same community of *vestitae* who had requested a set of guidelines for their religious lives from Munio of Zamora (the *Ordinationes*).[79] Giovanna had likely come to a committed penitential life through the sad circumstances of her childhood. She was born around 1264 in Carnaiola, a small town about twenty miles north of Orvieto. At five years old, she was an orphan; by twelve, she had run away to

---

77. Ibid.

78. More, "Institutionalizing Penitential Life," 308–15; and Lehmijoki-Gardner, "Writing Religious Rules," 662.

79. This biographical information draws on Lehmijoki-Gardner's introduction to her translation of Vanna's *Legenda*; see *Dominican Penitent Women*, 59–61.

Orvieto to escape an impending marriage her relatives had arranged. In Orvieto, Giovanna supported herself by working as both a dressmaker and a domestic servant. She lived for some time with a wealthy woman, Ghisla, who was also a member of the city's *vestitae*. Ghisla is mentioned several times in the *Legenda* written for Giovanna not long after her 1306 death.[80] While scholars had long held that Giovanna's *Legenda* was the work of the Dominican friar Giacomo Scalza (d. ca. 1343), in the most recent edition of the text, Emore Paoli has argued that such an attribution is far from certain.[81]

Despite lingering questions about the identity of its author, the *Legenda* makes clear that the young lay penitent Giovanna had found a committed religious life among a community of other female penitents with an association to the Dominican Order close enough to seek guidance from one of its celebrated friars.[82] Thus, whether or not a Dominican wrote this text, whoever constructed it must have had an awareness of the Dominican context in which she lived.

The *Legenda* begins with remarks that seem aimed at simultaneously celebrating and circumscribing Giovanna's charisma. Drawing on 1 Corinthians 12, the *vita*'s author notes that "by distributing certain gifts of the Holy Spirit," God makes clear who his chosen ones are.[83] The author elaborates that these gifts include "the utterance of wisdom by the Spirit . . . the gift of healing, and . . . the spirit of prophecy." After noting that such gifts are given to each person "according to the choosing of the Holy Spirit," the author introduces the text's protagonist: Giovanna, a "most holy virgin," to whom God had distributed abundantly "almost all kinds of gifts of celestial grace."[84] The author's use of "almost" (*quasi*) leads the reader to wonder which gifts of celestial grace Giovanna had not received. Although the author's mere mention of these gifts is a hagiographic trope—whom else but the saints would Christians associate with those chosen ones that Paul identifies in his letter to the Corinthians?—nevertheless, the author introduces Giovanna by placing parameters on her charismatic power: Giovanna had many but not all of God's gifts of grace.

The first chapter of Giovanna's *Legenda* ends with an explicit statement of its motive: we are to keep Giovanna "in front of our mental eyes as a path laid

80. *La Legenda di Vanna da Orvieto*, ed. Emore Paoli and Luigi G. G. Ricci (Spoleto: Centro Italiano di Studi sull'Alto Medioevo, 1996) (*BHL* 4289). In the references that follow, I shall be using Lehmijoki-Gardner's translation of Giovanna's *Legenda*; see *Dominican Penitent Women*, 61–86.

81. Paoli advocates for treating the author as anonymous until further work provides a more convincing attribution; see Emore Paoli, "'Pulcerrima vocor ab omnibus et non Vanna,'" in *La Legenda di Vanna da Orvieto*, ed. Paoli and Ricci, 5–16.

82. Lehmijoki-Gardner, *Dominican Penitent Women*, 60–61.

83. Ibid., 63.

84. Ibid.

out to us."[85] Giovanna's path shares a number of saintly qualities with that described in Zita of Lucca's *vita*. Like Zita, the beginnings of Giovanna's religious life are to be found, her hagiographer maintains, in her youth. Giovanna had lost her mother at three, and her father when she was five. It was at this time that "she began to show the signs of her future sanctity."[86] When another child taunted her for not having a mother, Giovanna pointed to an angel painted on a church wall and claimed that "this angel is my mother."[87] And like Zita, Giovanna both laid the foundation for her future sanctity and worked to maintain her virginity by dedicating herself to a life of work. As her hagiographer writes, knowing that "idleness is the root of sensual desire, she wished that the devil would always find her in some kind of occupation, and thus she wanted to engage in manual labor."[88] That manual labor was dressmaking. The *Legenda* recounts how Giovanna placed herself with a female dressmaker in order to learn the craft.

But this text also makes clear that such an affiliation was not enough to protect her; men harassed her as she made her way back and forth from her work to her hospice in Orvieto.[89] Again, there are similarities to Zita's life. Zita's *vita* described the harassment she endured from fellow servants in her employer's home. But while Zita protected herself by redoubling her focus on both her prayers and her manual labor, Giovanna's *Legenda* identifies a different path for the female lay penitent. Even though the text reports that each of the offending men ended up meeting an early death, Giovanna came to see "that it was not safe to live among scorpions," and thus began "to think how she could reject the world, not only in her heart, which she had already done, but also through external acts."[90] Giovanna thus chooses to take "the habit of the *vestitae* of Saint Dominic."[91]

Such an act did not stop her relatives, however. They soon resumed their efforts to have her marry, forcing Giovanna and a companion to flee to a nearby village. There, Giovanna's committed penitential life took its full shape: "she subjected her body to fasts and vigils," she "spent her nights praying to God," and as "she persevered in her prayers and holy meditations, she was enraptured with the bliss of divine consolations."[92] At some point, Giovanna made

---

85. Ibid., 64.

86. Ibid.

87. Ibid.

88. Ibid.

89. Lehmijoki-Gardner notes that the Latin used here to describe those accommodations (*hospitium*) could refer to a private home as well as a hospice; see *Dominican Penitent Women*, 262, n. 13.

90. Ibid., 65.

91. Ibid.

92. Ibid.

her way back to Orvieto and spent the next twenty-two years reaping the benefits or "bliss" of those divine consolations.[93] The majority of the remainder of the *Legenda* describes the visions, prophecies, and postmortem miracles that stand as evidence of both Giovanna's divine consolations and her sanctity. Thus, the *Legenda* posits that Giovanna's life as a committed lay penitent—in which she demonstrated her extraordinary piety and sanctity—only came once she had attached herself to a lay penitential community. A community, as we have seen, that had turned thirty years earlier to a noted Friar Preacher for guidance and legitimation. At the beginning of the fourteenth century, a full lay penitential life for a woman is one that takes place in community. The quasi-independent lives fashioned by our thirteenth-century lay saints seem no longer to be an option.

In addition to framing Giovanna's religious life as part of a larger Dominican lay penitential community, the remainder of the *Legenda* paints a picture of lay sanctity in language that aims to contain Giovanna's moments of extraordinary spiritual exuberance. The manner of describing lay sanctity found in this description of Giovanna ought to recall the portrait of Zita of Lucca. To that end, Giovanna's virginity provides the first opportunity for such a rendering of an ideal lay life. Giovanna had "fought with all her might to keep her chastity, the incomparable treasure of the soul, intact," fleeing from anything that might have "tarnished it." God saw her determination, and "used his mercy to keep her always intact," removing "everything that stood in the way of her chastity."[94] The two uses of the Latin *conservare* (to preserve or keep) set the stage for many of the *Legenda*'s subsequent descriptions of Giovanna's religious life: while she reaches extraordinary heights of spiritual engagement, that activity always takes place within her. Like her commitment to her virginity, Giovanna is repeatedly portrayed preserving the content and drama of her religious life within her body. The gifts she receives for her ardent prayers and mediations—the bliss of her divine consolations—are more often than not an internal rather than an external reality.

Thus, from the moment she took the habit of a *vestita*, Giovanna's devotional life becomes an immobile enterprise. The *Legenda* describes her as remaining every day "in prayer without moving from morning until Sext or None."[95] Moreover, from the very beginning of her life living as a lay penitent, Giovanna "shone like a guiding star wrapped in all virtues."[96] Although the author is clearly asking his readers to see Giovanna as a model or "guiding star"

---

93. Ibid., 66.
94. Ibid., 64.
95. Ibid., 66.
96. Ibid.

for other lay penitents, by describing her as "wrapped in all virtues," he also gives the sense that what made this young woman extraordinary, what marked her as a saint, was a quality that existed within her—a reality that was contained, wrapped up, and essentially controlled.

In listing Giovanna's many virtues, the author adds that Giovanna was "in all her manners" mature and "well-ordered."[97] But despite the fact that Giovanna was mature, well ordered, wrapped in virtues, and literally immobile from morning until evening, the reader also hears about a dramatic spiritual drama that was taking place within her. Giovanna's "heart burned so intensely" during her prayers and celestial contemplations that she could not wear clothes; "divine love" had "created such a heat in the virgin's mind that her entire body was overcome by extreme sweating."[98] Giovanna, the text's author is quick to assure his reader, took measures to prepare for such moments. Besides the fact that she always kept a cloth near her to mop up her sweat, "when she wanted to reach the heights of prayers and contemplation, she went to her usual place of prayer, a cell located in the attic of the house in which she lived."[99] Thus, just like Zita of Lucca, Giovanna knew the proper place to reach her spiritual heights. Zita's *vita* celebrated her for having experienced her ecstatic visions either in a hidden part of San Frediano, or privately in her room in her employer's house. Giovanna similarly planned for her ecstatic moments. Since they might make her sweat profusely she comes prepared with a sweat-rag, and is careful to keep herself separate from others. Such moments of divine love, the author makes clear, are private affairs.

In the many subsequent descriptions of Giovanna's raptures, the author repeatedly emphasizes how in the midst of such great spiritual heights reached by this laywoman, she always either cordoned herself off from others or was able to remain as she did during her daily prayers, "impassive and immobile."[100] Thus, during the feast of the apostles Peter and Paul, Giovanna meditated so intensely on their passions that she "experienced an immediate rapture," which rendered her unable to move. The author writes that Giovanna's body was "fixed immobile in the same way that the apostle was suspended on the Cross." And when she focused on Peter's death, her body came to imitate his martyrdom as "her body lay prostrate and her neck stretched out." Her immobilization was so complete that "if she would have been seen by someone who did not know, the person would have deemed her dead. She did not move or feel

---

97. Ibid.
98. Ibid., 66–67.
99. Ibid.
100. Ibid., 67.

anything. Just like a corpse, she did not breathe." In fact, Giovanna was so still during these raptures that, "one could see swarms of mosquitoes move freely on her uncovered and unmoving eyes." Her eyes, the author notes, "did not seem to belong to a living person, but to one who had just died."[101]

A similar spiritual immobilization overtook Giovanna each Good Friday. Her hagiographer describes how each year Giovanna experienced an "intense meditation of Christ's brutal suffering."[102] But that intensity did not show itself in writhing and yelling, as was true of so many of Margaret of Cortona's visionary experiences. Instead, Giovanna's mind was "absorbed in the bitterness of the Passion," leaving her not in control of her senses and her body in the shape of a cross. The *Legenda*'s author writes that her body "remained rigid, pale, and insensible in the same way that the body of the Lord had been when it was attached to the cross for ridicule." But while her body remained immobile, those who were around her could hear what the author describes as a "painful stretching . . . in what seemed to be such a powerful collapse of the bones that her limbs were loosened." Giovanna would remain like this from morning until dusk, her body "stretched out in such forceful immobility" that, as her hagiographer notes, it would have been easier to cut or break her limbs than to move them.[103] Although Giovanna's Good Friday experiences were clearly not private ones, her hagiographer is still at pains to emphasize the extent to which the visionary drama she endures was internal. Not only does Giovanna's body not move, but it is also only the sound of her limbs being "loosened" that reveals the internal reality to her audience. That internal reality is emphasized again in the descriptions of her meditations on both Holy Saturday and Resurrection Sunday. Giovanna was "instantaneously enraptured to such a degree" that it was clear she was "given the gift of tasting the glory of the Savior." The outward evidence of this experience, the author notes, came when Giovanna's "face appeared translucent and her eyes shone."[104]

And finally, the text recounts the times Giovanna appeared to levitate. On the feast of the Assumption of Mary, we can imagine again in imitation of the Virgin's assent to Heaven, Giovanna's body elevated "about a cubit" above the ground. Moreover, after hearing a reading on the feast of Saint Catherine, Giovanna "burst out with these words: 'Raise, Saint Catherine.'" Immediately, she found herself "freed of her bodily weight," and for a moment "elevated

---

101. Ibid.
102. Ibid., 68.
103. Ibid.
104. Ibid.

in the air."[105] Both descriptions of Giovanna's visionary experiences emphasize the distinction between an internal and external reality. Describing the
proof of her rapture as she meditated on Christ's resurrection as a translucent face and shining eyes, the text's author relates that a great spiritual drama
is taking place inside of her (her enrapture and her "gift of tasting the glory
of the Savior"). And finally, when the reader is given a bit of Giovanna's speech,
it comes in a moment in which she "bursts out," emphasizing how much is
being kept confined within her.

Similar to the portrait of Margaret of Cortona in her own *Legenda*, Giovanna's living miracles take a back seat to the postmortem wonders this text ascribes to her. In fact, Giovanna's *Legenda* only includes accounts of three living
miracles, two of which take place through messages and prayers Giovanna and
her devotees exchanged at a distance. Moreover, these miracles appear in a
chapter dedicated to Giovanna's "spirit of prophecy," indicating that her hagiographer saw these events more as demonstrating her ability to see the future
than her ability to heal and effect miraculous change. Thus, after hearing about
how Giovanna predicted whom the Dominicans of Orvieto would choose as
their next prior and which of her fellow *vestitae* had not followed the orders
of their prioress, the text offers three instances of the miraculous healing and
protection that Giovanna preformed during her lifetime. In the first, after a
noble lady sent a messenger to Giovanna asking her to pray for her ill son,
Giovanna completed her prayers and sent a return message: "Know that your
son is healed," she assured the woman.[106] The second miracle also depends
on messengers. A woman who was convinced that her in-laws faced "imminent danger" sent a request that Giovanna pray for them. Giovanna did, telling the woman (again through a messenger) that she should not be afraid
because her in-laws would be "saved" from such danger.[107] And finally, in the
only living miracle that involves Giovanna's touch, the *Legenda* reports that
she took the barley water a boy with tertian fever had been drinking, held it
up, and announced, "You will no longer drink this water." Her words, her
hagiographer argues, were "proven true by the healing that followed."[108]

The chapter ends by noting how "especially miraculous" it was that
Giovanna saw the miracles that she would perform after her death. The author gives one example. Giovanna had once announced to her matron that
she could see that she would be in a certain man's house three times. The *Leg-*

105. Ibid., 69.
106. Ibid., 73.
107. Ibid.
108. Ibid.

enda goes on to note how, after she died, three miracles in fact did take place "through her divine powers in that very room."[109] However, those miracles took place when Giovanna had come "spiritually to the room that she had never visited corporally."[110] The author further distances Giovanna's physical being from the miraculous acts he ascribes to her by placing accounts of her living miracles in a chapter devoted to prophecy. By categorizing these events as examples of Giovanna's gift of prophecy, the author argues that these incidents demonstrate the great spiritual knowledge that existed within Giovanna. Instead of drawing his readers' attention to what Giovanna did, he focuses on what she thought and the miraculous results of those thoughts. And finally, most of Giovanna's contact with her devotees comes through a messenger. In the only miracle in which Giovanna is actually present, she holds the water a sick boy has been drinking but is not described as touching the boy himself. Giovanna's charisma is not one that is transferred via her touch or her living presence.

In the seventh chapter, which describes Giovanna's "numerous virtues," the author notes that even though Giovanna was "strong in the virtues, she wanted to keep herself in the cellar of profound humility," so that she would not be carried away "by waves of vainglory."[111] In order to guard against such "vainglory," Giovanna often called herself "miserable, sinner, the worst of all women, or the devil."[112] When she was called a "lady," Giovanna responded, "Watch out, because I am not a lady."[113] Moreover, when Giovanna struggled with diabolic spirits, we hear how the devil "frequently appeared to her disguised as a religious woman, or an Ethiopian, or as a handsome young man," a grouping of types the *Legenda* clearly sees as sharing a questionable or suspicious nature.[114] And finally, in the *Legenda*'s account of the translation of Giovanna's body, we hear the clearest articulation of how Giovanna was a laywoman set apart from other laywomen. The text describes a vision of Fra Simon, a layman who belonged to a community of male lay penitents. During Matins, Giovanna appeared to Simon "in a bright light and in the company of two virgins." She instructed him to go to her "matron" and inform her that she was not content "because the secular ladies rant on about venial and

---

109. Ibid., 74.
110. Ibid.
111. Ibid., 71.
112. Ibid., 71–72.
113. Ibid.
114. Lehmijoki-Gardner also comments on the pairing of the devil with a "religious woman," noting "the ambiguous status of religious laywomen" at this time; ibid., 264, n. 29.

mortal sins here, something which is painful for me to hear."[115] The account ends with an extended description of Giovanna's translation to a new tomb, which was observed by various Dominican friars as well as *vestitae* (including Giovanna's prioress and matron, Ghisla) and featured the discovery of Giovanna's incorrupt, sweet-smelling, and oil-soaked body.

In her translation of Giovanna's *Legenda*, Lehmijoki-Gardner notes two moments when the author addresses his audience either as "brothers" or in the masculine case. These gender-specific references suggest that the text was written (at least partially) for a group of Dominican friars, or religious laymen.[116] If Giovanna's *Legenda* was aimed primarily at a male audience, it becomes hard not to read other references in the text to Giovanna's gender as making a similar argument to that found in Zita of Lucca's *vita*: Giovanna, like Zita, is a woman unlike other women, making her piety and sanctity all the more noteworthy. Thus, just as Zita's *vita* celebrated her for her care not to congregate with other female parishioners who liked to gossip and indulge in a dramatic devotional manner, Giovanna's *Legenda* uses the idea that she was not content to stay in a tomb with other "secular ladies" who "rant on" as further evidence of her sanctity. Undergirding that evidence is the idea that Giovanna is distinct from other women. She is a laywoman who recognizes the liabilities of her gender—her ranting that she was a "miserable sinner, the worst of all women" recalls the focus Giunta Bevegnati placed on Margaret of Cortona's own sense of shame and dishonor. To be a female lay saint in these hagiographies meant both to recognize and to defy the weakness, shame, and vainglory ascribed to all women.

But unlike the cases of both Zita and Margaret, we have very little information about Giovanna's civic cult. As her *Legenda* reports, Giovanna was buried "at the convent of the Friars Preachers of Orvieto."[117] Within a year, the odor of sanctity emanating from her body as well as the many miracles performed in her name led the Dominicans to translate her body into their church.[118] The *Legenda* notes that the decision to move Giovanna's body was one made not only by the order's provincial and convent priors but also by "other friars." The translation itself, the author is careful to record, was witnessed by the provincial prior, the convent's prior, four other friars, the abbot of San Severo, along with three of his friars, and finally also by Ghisla and three of her *vestitae*.[119]

---

115. Ibid., 82.
116. Ibid., 70, 72 and 264 (nn. 24 and 25).
117. Ibid., 75.
118. Ibid., 82–86.
119. Ibid., 83.

We know from communal records that on May 7, 1307—a year after Giovanna's death—Orvieto's communal government, the Council of Seven, offered twenty pounds of wax to mark the feast day of "soror Vanna."[120] In addition, civic statutes produced in 1314 and 1350 show that this donation was renewed until at least mid-century.[121] Although there is therefore some evidence that there was a civic cult dedicated to Giovanna in the first generations after her death, by the end of the fourteenth century the efforts of Thomas Caffarini of Siena, the Dominican friar who was not only involved in the effort to canonize Catherine of Siena but also led the charge to create a formal Dominican order of penitents, would put to an end any notions that Giovanna's sanctity had ever truly belonged to her civic community. In Caffarini's translation of Giovanna's *Legenda*, this ideal laywoman was transformed into a Dominican penitent—her piety and sanctity deeply connected to that institutional identity.[122] The *Legenda*'s unrelenting focus on Giovanna's internal spiritual life lent itself well to Caffarini's project. Caffarini would also translate the *vita* of another early fourteenth-century female lay saint, Margaret of Città di Castello. In the fourteenth-century Latin *vitae* of Margaret that Caffarini used to construct his Italian translation, he would find an understanding of the ideal lay life that was equally as amenable to his goals.

Margaret of Città di Castello

Whereas in Giovanna's *Legenda* a vision by one of her devotees reveals that she was not happy being buried in a communal grave, in the two *vitae* written for Margaret of Città di Castello, it is the people of this Umbrian commune who make clear their objections about the location of Margaret's tomb. When Margaret died on April 13, 1320, her *vitae* report that an outcry from the city convinced the Friars Preachers to place the body of this pious laywoman in their church instead of in their cemetery cloister.[123] Margaret had earned a reputation for the great intensity of her penitential commitment as well as the public manifestations of her "celestial grace" and visionary gifts.[124] But the story of this Margaret inverts a key component of the contemporary lay civic

120. Paoli, "'Pulcerrima vocor ab omnibus et non Vanna,'" 16–17.

121. Ibid.

122. *Leggenda della beata Giovanna (detta Vanna) d'Orvieto suora dell'Ordine della penitenza di S. Domenico*, ed. Luigi Passarini (Rome: Tipografia Sinimberghi, 1879); also see Lehmijoki-Gardner, *Dominican Penitent Women*, 261, n. 6.

123. For both Margaret's *Recensio maior* and the *Recensio minor*, see *Le Legendae di Margherita da Città di Castello*, ed. Maria Cristiana Lungarotti (Spoleto: Centro Italiano di Studi sull'Alto Medioevo, 1994) (BHL: 5313); *Recensio maior*, XXIV, 75.

124. *Recensio maior*, XXI, 76–77.

saint paradigm: instead of giving up wealth and privilege to help her city's neediest, Margaret could not have survived but for the kindness of strangers.

Margaret was the blind, deaf, deformed (likely as the result of a severely curved spine), and dwarf daughter of a noble family connected to the castle of Mertola in the Marche region.[125] As a young child, Margaret's parents responded to their daughter's disabilities by hiding her in a cell attached to a church.[126] Here, Margaret adopted a strict penitential life. As her *vitae* report, from the time she was seven she began a regular routine of wearing hair shirts, fasting, and surviving between those fasts solely on bread and water.[127] At some point when she was still quite young, Margaret's parents took her to Città di Castello in an attempt to have her cured at the shrine of a saintly Franciscan friar. When this proved fruitless, they abandoned her in the city.[128]

Margaret wandered through Città di Castello begging for provisions to survive. She was eventually taken in by the aptly named convent of Santa Margherita but seems to have quickly annoyed the nuns, who kicked her out for upstaging them in her extreme demonstrations of piety.[129] Although Margaret's *vitae* mention that several people offered her provisions, the generosity of one pious couple in particular seems to have saved her. This couple gave Margaret a room in their house. Margaret remained there for the rest of her short life (she died in her early thirties), dedicated to pursuing penance, experiencing visions, and performing miracles.[130]

Our knowledge about Margaret comes from two fourteenth-century Latin *vitae*, both of which likely rely on a lost original text.[131] While the *vitae* do not differ in the basic narrative they give of Margaret's life and death, they differ significantly in length, tone, and in the institutional affiliation they suggest for their authors.[132] The longer text, which scholars call the *Recensio maior* is divided into fifty-six chapters, with the first eight dedicated to an extended prologue that considers the nature of sanctity and the role of miracles. The mention by the author of the *maior* that he was ordered to write a life of Margaret by his superior, as well as his rather negative assessment of Dominicans (accusing them of promoting saints for financial gain) have led Ernesto Menestò

---

125. Ibid., IX, 67–68.

126. Ibid., X, 68.

127. Ibid., XI, 68–69.

128. Ibid., XII and XIV, 69–70.

129. Ibid., XV and XVI, 70–71.

130. Ibid., XVII, 71–72.

131. Maria Cristiana Lungarotti, "Le due redazione della *Legenda di Margherita da Città di Castello*," in *Le Legendae*, 1–31.

132. Lungarotti, "Le due redazione," 4–7.

to conclude that this *vita* was probably the work of a cleric who belonged to a community of canons.[133] The shorter *vita*, which scholars call the *Recensio minor*, recounts all the same episodes from Margaret's life and postmortem miracles found in the *maior* but does so in a much pithier and more direct manner.[134] The *minor* contains only fifteen chapters and has none of the introductory material included in the *maior*. The author of this version emphasizes the connection between Margaret and the Dominicans during her lifetime; this, along with the fact that it was found in its earliest manuscript copy between *vitae* of Giovanna of Orvieto and Catherine of Siena, has led scholars to conclude that this redaction was the work of a Dominican friar.[135]

Although we do not know the institutional affiliation of the author of the lost original version of Margaret's *vita*, the fact that both a secular cleric and a Dominican friar produced redactions of that text over the fourteenth century tells us that Margaret's institutional identity was far from fixed. Unlike Giovanna, she does not seem to have been a member of a lay penitential community; her religious life was, to some extent (and uncharacteristically for a woman), independent.

Like so many other late thirteenth-century lay saints, the postmortem miracles ascribed to Margaret far outnumber her living ones. But in both of her living miracles, it is Margaret's touch that brings about the miraculous change. In the first, she extinguished a fire in the house of the couple who had taken her in simply by placing her mantle on top of it.[136] In the second, a tumor on a woman's eye vanished after Margaret placed her hand on it.[137] The remaining miracles (at least thirty-four individual accounts) are all postmortem healings—many of which describe parents taking their mute or paralyzed children to be healed at Margaret's tomb.[138] With so little attention given to her living miracles, Margaret's *vitae* pay much more attention to her intense penitential routine and its bodily results to prove her sanctity. Thus, we hear how Margaret demonstrated such fervor in her prayer that she regularly appeared to levitate off the ground (by a measure of *unius cubiti*, her *vitae*

---

133. Enrico Menestò, "La 'Legenda' di Margherita da Città di Castello," in *Il movimento religioso femminile in Umbria nei secoli XIII–XIV*, ed. Roberto Rusconi (Spoleto: Centro Italiano di Studi sull' Alto Medioevo, 1984), 277; also see Lungarotti, "Le due redazione," 7.

134. Lungarotti notes that whereas the author of the *maior* uses verb forms and grammatical constructions that suggest more distance between Margaret's narrative and the text's audience, the *minor* author adopts a more "instinctive" and "immediate" style, using verbs that suggest more proximity to the events of Margaret's life; see Lungarotti, "Le due redazione," 27–30.

135. Ibid., 4.

136. *Recensio maior*, XVIII, 72.

137. Ibid., XIX, 72.

138. For these postmortem miracles, see ibid., XXIII–LVI, 74–90; and *Recensio minor*, 99–112.

report).[139] Moreover, at night, when she would subject herself to a rigorous penitential program, she seemed dead to those around her, as if her body was putrefying.[140]

Her *vitae* also emphasize how these displays of penitential piety came in the midst of the obedience she regularly manifested towards the institutional church. Margaret, the *vitae* reports, went every day to the city's Dominican church, wanting to confess as often as possible so that she might receive an infusion of "celestial grace" by "virtue of the sacraments."[141] In addition, every day she said the Office of the Cross, the Office of the Virgin, as well as the entire Psalter, which she had miraculously learned.[142] Her knowledge was so great (and so miraculously obtained) that she even corrected the grammar of her benefactors' children.[143]

Even though many aspects of Margaret's religious life might seem familiar after our exploration of other lay saints' cults, it is in the account of her embalming—itself a miracle story—that her cult not only assumes a more distinct identity but does its most trenchant work to mitigate aspects of her life that seem opposed to the norms of a female lay penitential life.[144] The *vitae* report that through the joint financial support of the Dominicans and the commune, and before she was buried within the city's Dominican church, she was publicly embalmed (in the Church of San Domenico) and later subjected to an autopsy of her exhumed organs.[145] The *vitae* describe that as her entrails were removed the earth shook, a result of an immense earthquake marking this momentous event.[146] After her entrails were buried in the church's cemetery, multiple claims of the miracles taking place there led the friars to exhume those remains for a more detailed investigation. That autopsy, which also appears to have taken place within the church's sacristy and was witnessed

---

139. *Recensio maior*, XX, 73.

140. Ibid., XXI, 73.

141. Ibid., XXI, 73: "Ad ecclesiam Predicatorum, quorum habitum defferebat, omni die solicite properabat, et cum confessorum copiam habere poterat, etiam diebus singulis confiteri volebat, novam sperans semper recipere gratie celestis infustionem illius sacramenti virtute."

142. Ibid., XXI, 73.

143. Ibid.

144. On this episode, see the work of Katherine Park. She has studied the embalming and exhuming of Margaret's corpse in several works; see her "Impressed Images: Reproducing Wonders," in *Picturing Science, Producing Art*, ed. Caroline A. Jones and Peter Galison (New York: Routledge, 1998), 254–71; Park, "The Life of the Corpse: Division and Dissection in Late Medieval Europe," *Journal of the History of Medicine and Allied Sciences* 50 (1995): 111–32; and Park, "The Criminal and the Saintly Body: Autopsy and Dissection in Renaissance Italy," *Renaissance Quarterly* 47 (1994): 1–33.

145. On the public nature of the embalming and the fact that Margaret's corpse was likely left uncovered for all present to watch her autopsy, see Park, "The Life of the Corpse," 129.

146. *Recensio maior*, XXV, 75–76.

by three named friars along with what the *vitae* describe as many other clerics, seculars, and doctors (two of whom are also named), led to the discovery
of three engraved stones within Margaret's heart.[147]

Those religious and secular witnesses (all men) then interpreted the images
they had found. They determined that the beautiful woman with a golden
crown engraved on the first stone was an image of the Virgin. On the second
stone, the men saw a child in a cradle surrounded by animals, interpreting this
as an image of the baby Jesus. And, on the third stone, the witnesses concluded
that a bearded man on horseback with a young woman in a Dominican habit
kneeling below him was clearly a representation of Saint Joseph and Margaret herself. Finally, on the back of this final stone was an image of a white dove,
which they said represented the Holy Spirit.[148]

Katherine Park has pointed to this arresting episode as key evidence for how
often female religious (and women in general) in the Middle Ages had their
bodies described as impressionable, "open to the reception of sensible images
and apt to conform themselves to forms received from the outside."[149] Park
argues that what Margaret had experienced as part of her visionary life had
become part of her internal reality, pointing to the claim in the *vitae* that Margaret had declared to "persons worthy of belief" that "if you knew what I carry
in my heart, you would be struck with wonder."[150]

We can also read this episode as vividly illustrating the way in which the experience of female lay spirituality and sanctity had become increasingly constructed as an internal phenomenon over the late thirteenth and early
fourteenth centuries—one that literally manifested itself as an internal rather
than an external drama. Inside of Margaret was the key evidence of her sanctity. The telling in the *vitae* of this miraculous end of Margaret's narrative sets
up the idea that no matter how she organized her external religious life, what
was of most importance was the evidence created within her body. Moreover,
this miracle emphasizes that no matter how independent a life she may have
led, the image of Margaret within her heart establishes her institutional affiliation: she was a Dominican, the interpretation of the image on the stones makes
clear. Finally, the fact that these stones were found and interpreted by a group
of male authorities (both religious and secular) further dispels any notion a
reader might have formed that Margaret lived a lay penitential life outside of
the medieval power and gender structure.

---

147. In the *Recensio maior* this account is found in XXVI, 76–77; in the *Recensio minor*, 99–100.
148. *Recensio maior*, XXVI, 77.
149. Park, "Impressed Images," 265.
150. I am using Park's translation here; ibid., 255.

With this reading of the miraculous heart stones in mind, it is possible to see other aspects of the telling of Margaret's narrative as intended to mitigate her seemingly independent existence. Both *vitae* use the many confined physical places where Margaret stayed to punctuate the text's narrative trajectory. As a young child, Margaret is placed in a cell by her parents; after her abandonment, she first finds refuge in the convent of Santa Margherita, and then later with a pious couple. And it is within the contained space of her body that the most miraculous event of Margaret's religious life takes place. Thus, even though Margaret spent much of her life wandering and begging in Città di Castello, she does so moving from one contained space to the next.

Finally, part of the *Recensio maior*'s more extensive introduction is a chapter dedicated to describing Margaret's disabilities. Although the author aims to celebrate the vast discrepancy between Margaret's physical weakness and her spiritual strength, he also remains focused on how much her physical disabilities limited and contained her. Margaret was born "deprived of her corporeal eyes so that she would not see the world." Margaret's small stature, the author notes, leaves her able to "enjoy those things hidden deeply." And even though she remains "on the earth," her disability keeps her only looking "toward heaven."[151]

The Lay Saint has argued that between the twelfth and fourteenth centuries the charismatic power to effect miraculous change that the cults of lay saints posited grew out of an extraordinary commitment to a penitential life challenged the church's expanding notions of its power and authority. And yet, as I have shown, it was both church and civic authorities that most vigorously promoted the cults of these contemporary lay holy men and holy women. Ever since Vauchez's groundbreaking studies of lay civic sanctity, scholars have understood that promotion as part and parcel of the church's recognition of the late medieval explosion of lay religious enthusiasm. According to this point of view, contemporary lay civic patrons in the Italian communes were both the evidence of and the reward for the extraordinary lay religious zeal that marked late medieval urban life.

I have taken a different approach, arguing that the appearance of lay civic cults—found in *vitae*, *Legenda*, accounts of miracles, visual memorials, as well as communal records—was neither simply an indication of lay religious en-

---

151. *Recensio maior*, IX, 68: "Hec enim oculis corporeis privata nascitur ne mundum videat; que iam lumine divino vescitur, ut in terra stans celum tantum aspitiat. Hec parvula corpore formatur, ut mente in yma defossa sublimi humilitate perfruatur, per quam in gloria nunc exaltata iudicatur." I thank Anna Trumbore Jones for help translating this tricky passage.

thusiasm nor of the church's recognition of that zeal, but rather an illustration both of the radical assertions standing at the heart of the laity's embrace of the *vita apostolica* and of the church's efforts to restrain and manage such claims.

This study began by looking at how one pious merchant's embrace of the *vita apostolica* was celebrated in terms that threatened the church's authority. Ranieri of Pisa's extraordinary dedication to penance earned him a charismatic authority that could reform a corrupt church and heal the sick. By the early thirteenth century, however, the papacy had stepped in to recalibrate that portrait. In Pope Innocent III's 1199 canonization of the merchant Omobono of Cremona, an extraordinarily pious lay life was one that healed a compromised lay population through civic charity and the fight against heresy, not one that fixed the church.

Despite this, we have heard little about heretics in this study. Even though battling heresy was a part of Innocent's prescription for an ideal lay life, such a struggle has not figured widely (save for a few miracle stories) in the cults I have studied. We might read this discrepancy as speaking to the particular context of late twelfth-century Cremona: it was, as Innocent was well aware, a center of Cathar activity. But might Innocent have meant something much broader? Was the real heretic the charismatic layman himself? The layman who had garnered a saintly reputation for healing both priests and parishioners through his touch? After all, a key aspect of Innocent's recalibration of lay ideals in Omobono's canonization bull was to establish that there was something inherently lacking in the very state of being a layperson—that to be a layman meant to be a "thorn" in need of reform.

And yet, as the preceding chapters have also shown, over the thirteenth century, it was the *female* lay penitent who most exemplified and exaggerated notions of the intrinsic shortcomings of the laity. Just as Clare of Assisi could not fully take up the way of life that Innocent had approved for Francis, female lay penitents ultimately could not imitate Omobono's model of the ideal lay life. I have argued that this problem was first approached through a variety of workarounds that emphasized laywomen's connections to religious orders or other male-dominated institutions, and continually aimed to mitigate a woman's role in charismatic acts. But it was also tackled through a spate of thirteenth-century lay penitential regulatory measures that, while addressed to both laymen and laywomen, seem to have been more aimed at dealing with those lay penitents who most challenged both the church's and the broader culture's notions of power, gender, and religious authority: the female lay penitent.

As the Friars Minor were increasingly cajoled over the mid to late thirteenth century into overcoming their inherent ambivalence toward female lay penitents—either by the papacy (in the case of the Franciscan Pope Nicholas IV's *Supra montem*) or by the growing number of laywomen garnering saintly reputations who were themselves claiming an association to their order—those friars began to take a leading role in creating a new definition of an ideal lay life. Instead of emphasizing an active, charity-driven, and civic-minded lay life, the Franciscans promoted a lay ideal that privileged an internal spiritual life, dominated by visions and somatic expressions of charisma.

Nevertheless, in the final two examples of lay sanctity explored in this study—that of Giovanna of Orvieto and Margaret of Città di Castello—the primary institutional association—no matter how embryonic—had changed. Unlike Rose, Umiliana, and Margaret of Cortona, these two women—Giovanna and Margaret of Città di Castello—existed within a largely Dominican rather than a Franciscan orbit. To what extent, we might ask, did this distinct religious context influence how an ideal lay life was being conceived? One way of answering this question would be to point out particularities in hagiographic themes. For example, Giovanna's struggles with the Devil take a form that is reminiscent of the Desert Fathers' struggles—an immensely important model for the Dominicans.[152] But despite there being certain so-called Dominican themes in these texts, Giovanna's and Margaret's expressions of an ideal lay life still fundamentally connect to the broad development of lay sanctity that I have been tracing in this study.

Thus, we might make more sense of the appearance of Dominican instead of Franciscan friars promoting and managing Giovanna's and Margaret's cults by considering the extent to which the burden of solving the problem of the female lay penitent had, by the late thirteenth century, shifted from being primarily a Franciscan responsibility to a Dominican one as well. The distinct institutional development of the two orders offers some clues for this trajectory. Although the early Dominicans had a complex and sometimes antagonistic relationship with women wanting to join their order, over the thirteenth century, those difficulties, by and large, did not extend to lay penitents.[153] Unlike the Franciscans, the Dominicans did not emerge from the lay penitential movement. The Friars Preachers were from their inception a clerical order;

---

152. See Alain Boureau, *Satan the Heretic: The Birth of Demonology in the Medieval West*, trans. Teresa Lavender Fagan (Chicago: University of Chicago Press, 2006).

153. See Maria Pia Alberzoni, "Giordano di Sassonia e il monastero d. S. Agneses di Bologna," in *Institution und Charisma: Festschrift für Gert Melville zum 65 Geburgstag*, ed. F. J. Felten, A. Kehnel, and S. Weinfurter (Cologne: Böhlau, 2009), 513–27; and G. Cariboni, "Domenico e la vita religiosa femminile: Tra realtà e finzione istituzionale," in *Domenico di Caleruega e la nascita dell'Ordine dei frati predicatori* (Spoleto: Centro Italiano di Studi sull'Alto Medioevo, 2005), 327–60.

they did not have to contend, as had Francis and many of his first friars, with a "hybrid" status (a tonsured layman living outside of a monastery).[154]

From their inception, therefore, the Dominicans were a population more distinct from lay penitents than were the Franciscans. And even though the meteoric rise of the Franciscan Order without doubt had much to do with the papacy's interest in charging the Friars Minor with the oversight of lay penitents, we might also see in that duty an attempt to further distinguish Franciscans from lay penitents. What better way of making clear that Francis and his friars were on a different path, that they had a different position within the church, that they had different privileges and opportunities than other lay penitents, than to place them as the arbiters of those penitents?

It is this history that made questions about what was an acceptable, as well as an ideal, form of the lay penitential life primarily one for the Franciscans to answer—especially in regards to laywomen who were garnering cults—over the first three-quarters of the thirteenth century. By the late thirteenth century, however, as the Dominican presence in the communes grew along with instances of women taking up as well as excelling at the lay penitential life, we see more examples of female lay penitents seeking out the Friars Preachers to legitimize, authorize, and perhaps even protect their way of life.[155] But, it was not until the Dominicans were faced with a lay penitent like Catherine of Siena, whose reputation for sanctity and charisma could rival that of Francis of Assisi, that they were finally forced to craft a fully considered and concrete approach to the problem of the female lay penitent.

---

154. Şenocak, *The Poor and the Perfect*, 41.

155. One of the earliest examples, as I have discussed above, being the request of Giovanna's Orvieto *vestitae* in 1286 that Munio of Zamora write a set of guidelines for their lay penitential lives; see Lehmijoki-Gardner, "Writing Religious Rules."

Epilogue

In 1395 the Dominican master general, Raymond of Capua, finally completed the *Legenda maior sive Legenda admirabilis virginis Catherine de Senis*.[1] This was the culmination of at least a decade of writing by Catherine of Siena's last Dominican confessor (Catherine had died in 1380). Scholars have studied how meticulously Raymond constructed a portrait of Catherine to emphasize the penitential extremes to which she subjected her body, her Christocentric piety, her resolute connection to the Dominican order, and her role as a public prophet. But in light of the conclusions drawn in this study, we can also see that in Raymond's as well as other Dominican promoters' hands, Catherine's life was not only a means (as scholars have long argued) for promoting the papacy during a period of schism as well as encouraging reform of the Dominican Order, but also an opportunity to bring to full fruition the ideas and ideals about what constituted a holy lay life that had developed between the mid-twelfth and fourteenth centuries.

As F. Thomas Luongo has argued, the very idea of Catherine—an unmarried laywoman who had a rigorous penitential commitment yet lived outside of a convent—raised a tension that her first Dominican hagiographers were

---

1. Raimondo da Capua, *Legenda maior sive Legenda admirabilis virginis Catherine de Senis*, ed. Silvia Nocentini (Florence: Sismel, 2013).

particularly anxious to allay.[2] That tension was essentially the problem of the female lay penitent. A problem that I have shown in the preceding chapters fundamentally shaped how church authorities portrayed an ideal lay life over the second half of the thirteenth century. And just as we saw emphasized repeatedly in the cults awarded to laywomen once the mendicants became the primary guardians of the lay penitential life in the later thirteenth century, Raymond presents Catherine's sanctity, and most importantly her charismatic power, in a manner that is overwhelmingly manifested within and limited to her physical body. In short, we can see in Raymond's construction an echo of the norms of lay, and specifically female, lay sanctity that grew up over the thirteenth and early fourteenth centuries.

For example, when Raymond describes how Catherine's family, in their ever-present desire to see her married, punished her by giving her more household tasks and not allowing her to withdraw to pray, he writes that Catherine regained her resolve by means of "an impulse of the Holy Spirit." That impulse, as he goes on to describe, induced her to make "for herself a secret cell within her own heart," and to decide "never to go forth from it no matter what the business on which she was engaged."[3] When Catherine was finally successful in her ambition to withdraw and managed to live as a recluse for a number of years in her family home, Raymond notes that she "kept close within the cloister of her tiny room, never leaving it except to go to church," having, "found a desert within her own home, and her solitude in the midst of people."[4] Thus, at the same time that Raymond acknowledges Catherine's charismatic authority, he aims to mitigate that power. While Catherine might have access to the Holy Spirit, she has no agency in its use (she regains her penitential resolve by "an impulse of the Holy Spirit"). To some extent, then, we are back in the world of Bona of Pisa and Rose of Viterbo; two female lay saints whose early cults claimed that they had a direct connection to the Holy Spirit (Christ blows it into Bona, while Rose tells her mother that she is "full of it"). But we are also, just as we saw in later redactions of Bona of Pisa's *vita*, back in a world where a male church authority has taken pains to insert a divide between that charismatic power and the laywoman herself.

In addition, Raymond's portrait of Catherine allows us again to see how a laywoman's desire for desert seclusion (something Margaret of Cortona had also sought) must find a compromise within the reality of her crowded urban community. And again, we have a hagiographer who articulates that com-

2. F. Thomas Luongo, *The Saintly Politics of Catherine of Siena* (Ithaca, NY: Cornell University Press, 2006), 23–25.

3. Raimondo da Capua, *Legenda maior*, I, 4: 49.

4. Ibid., I, 9: 83; I am using More's translation here; see her *Fictive Orders*, 75.

promise by drawing upon monastic allusions. Just as Vito of Cortona described Umiliana de' Cerchi's period of reclusion as constituting a new kind of monasticism, for Raymond, Catherine's room is a "cloister." And finally, we are back in a realm where female lay spirituality is primarily an internal experience. Catherine creates an interior cell within her own heart, and never, "no matter what business she was engaged in," Raymond maintains, emerged from it.

Raymond's efforts (of which I have named only a few) to mitigate and contain Catherine's penitential life and instances of charismatic authority are all the more significant if we compare them to another account of her life. In the anonymously authored *I miracoli di Caterina di Iacopo da Siena*, written during Catherine's 1374 stay in Florence during the Dominican's General Chapter, the reader is given a portrait of this lay penitent that draws a sharp contrast to Raymond's construction.[5] Although Luongo has cautioned against seeing Raymond's *Legenda* and the *Miracoli* as entirely independent accounts of Catherine's life, we can—just as we did for the many redactions of Bona of Pisa's *vita*—see some significant differences in how these two texts describe both the content and trajectory of Catherine's religious life.[6]

To begin, the *Miracoli* claims that Catherine adopted a penitential life in her early twenties rather than in her teens, as Raymond would maintain—evidence that not just widows and very young women were adopting this way of life, but women whose virginity and marriage prospects might have been more at risk. Moreover, the *Miracoli* places an emphasis on and gives an agency to both Catherine's independence and her charismatic acts. In the *Miracoli*, Catherine travels within as well as outside of Siena either by herself or accompanied by other female penitents. She often eats not in the company of her family, as Raymond asserts, but with her community of lay penitents. In addition, instead of favoring miraculous acts that ensued from Catherine's extraordinary charity work, as Raymond and other Dominican writers would, the *Miracoli* pays particular attention to the healing miracles that she brought about through her touch. Finally, the *Miracoli* does little to qualify Catherine's desire for a solitary life. The anonymous author notes that Catherine had always wanted to live as a recluse, writing that when she finally had the chance to stay "in the

---

5. On the *Miracoli*, see Lehmijoki-Gardner, *Dominican Penitent Women*, 87–104; Luongo, *The Saintly Politics of Catherine of Siena*, esp. 23–55; and André Vauchez, *Catherine of Siena: A Life of Passion and Purpose*, trans. Michael F. Cusato (New York: Paulist Press, 2018), 32–33. Vauchez points to the possibility that the author of the *Miracoli* was Niccolò Soderini, citing André Duval, "Sainte Catherine, dominicaine," *La Vie Spirituelle*, nos. 640–41 (1980): 828–51.

6. Luongo notes that both texts pull from the now lost notebooks of Tommaso della Fonte, Catherine's first Dominican confessor; see F. Thomas Luongo, "Cloistering Catherine: Religious Identity in Raymond of Capua's *Legenda maior* of Catherine of Siena," *Studies in Medieval and Renaissance History* 3 (2005): 39.

upper part of the house in a room that was appointed to her," she ended up remaining there "enclosed for about seven years," performing a "rigorous penance."[7] The *Miracoli*'s concise and matter of fact description of this period of Catherine's life differs from Raymond's account. There is no attempt to characterize Catherine's seclusion as monastic, no reference to an interior cell in which she was further enclosed. Instead, in the *Miracoli*, Catherine simply wanted to live as a recluse and for about seven years, she did.

But Catherine's saintly fame has not been based solely on the rigor of her religious life. From her earliest cult to the modern day, Catherine has been celebrated for being a laywoman who both criticized and advised the papacy during a moment of chaos and controversy. This political engagement again connects her to the tradition of the medieval communal lay saint. But unlike the cults that grew up around thirteenth-century lay saints, Catherine's political activism was on the whole universal as opposed to local. As André Vauchez has noted, Catherine "was not trying to become a local or civic saint" and in fact maintained a rather contentious relationship with Siena's commune throughout her life.[8] With Siena's regime of the Nine long gone and much of the idealism that marked Pier's Siena having faded, Catherine both witnessed and participated in a more fractured urban political life.

Despite the fact that she did not organize her life to earn a reputation as a civic lay saint along the lines of Pier "Pettinaio," Catherine expresses in her letters an understanding of the world that marries political and religious matters in a manner quite similar to her city's comb-maker's cult. Noting how this put her "perfectly in conformity with the Thomistic tradition, which privileged the search for the 'common good,'" Vauchez has argued that Catherine ultimately saw justice as the "supreme value," believing that "political institutions must ensure [that it] prevails by way of law."[9] Catherine's lived philosophy is thus an extension—on a much larger stage—of ideas emphasized in Pier's cult. Just as the comb-maker's sanctity was not only illustrated in his punctilious adherence to the rules and regulations of his city but also served as a guarantor of his city's greatness or *grandezza*, Catherine's religious life was one that championed the church's laws in order to ensure its justice.

And yet, although she championed the justice the church provided, Catherine was also keenly aware of the profound problems facing that institution. In a 1376 letter to Bérenger, the abbot of Lézat and Tuscan papal envoy, Cath-

---

7. Lehmijoki-Gardner, *Dominican Penitent Women*, 92–93.

8. These are Vauchez's words; see his *Catherine of Siena*, 30. For more on Catherine's political life within Siena, see Luongo, *The Saintly Politics*.

9. Vauchez, *Catherine of Siena*, 68.

erine writes that the only means she saw for responding to the church's present state of corruption and decay was "to raze it to its foundations."[10] This is a stunning statement, reminiscent of the radical ideas we saw expressed in Ranieri of Pisa's cult. Although Ranieri was never credited with advocating for the destruction of the church, his vision that God had told him that the priests had been placed in the hands of Satan conveys a similar pessimism about the state of the church. Despite such a dire assessment, however, Ranieri's cult maintained a belief in the fundamental enterprise of the church; it was through this extraordinary layman's penitential rigor that all Christians would be released from Satan's grip and that the church would heal itself.

The solution that Ranieri's penitential life offered for fixing a compromised clergy and church was the first of many strategic appropriations of lay charismatic authority throughout the thirteenth century. Benincasa, the author of Ranieri's *vita*, set the precedent of lay sanctity as a force that heals the ills of institutions without tearing them down. To some extent, the charismatic authority that Catherine offered was no different; scholars have noted how the papacy in particular drew on Catherine's saintly reputation to aid its own renewal and legitimation.[11] But if we dig a little deeper, we can see that it was not just the papacy but also the Dominican Order that profited from Catherine's charisma. Moreover, we can see how the use by the Friars Preachers of Catherine ultimately did raze something to its foundation: the independent lay penitent.

I have shown how the female lay saint exacerbated tensions intrinsic in the very idea of lay sanctity. The idea that a laywoman could earn charismatic authority through an exemplary embrace of a penitential life simply intensified concerns already present among church authorities that spiritual gifts—charisma—was something available outside of an institutional context. And although the regulatory measures aimed at lay penitents over the thirteenth century began the process of solving these tensions by making the category of the lay penitent moot—by 1289 a lay penitent was a Franciscan lay penitent—it was not until the Dominicans were faced with a lay charismatic authority as big and bold as Catherine's that we see that process completed.

In addition to Raymond's monumental *Legenda*, the evidence for how the Dominicans used Catherine finally to solve the problem of the female lay penitent and lay saint comes in the dizzying amount of text produced over the first quarter of the fifteenth century by Thomas Caffarini, another Dominican friar pivotal in promoting Catherine. In addition to producing the *Processo castellano*, a diocesan collection of twenty-three testimonies providing evidence for Catherine's

---

10. Ibid., 42–43.

11. Ibid., 67; Luongo, *The Saintly Politics*.

sanctity (of which none came from a woman), Caffarini completed an abbreviated version (the *Legenda minor*) of Raymond's *Legenda*, and the *Supplemento*, a collection of stories about Catherine that had not yet appeared in earlier texts.[12] This was also the period in which he produced the vernacular translations of Giovanna of Orvieto's and Margherita of Città di Castello's *vitae*, as well as a Latin *Legenda* and vernacular translation for a contemporary female lay penitent, Maria of Venice (d. 1399), a treatise on the Dominican lay penitential life, and finally a history of his order's recent Observant reform movement.

Although Caffarini's whirlwind of productivity is quite diverse, there is meaning and significance in its grouping. His efforts to push for Catherine of Siena's canonization went hand in hand with his efforts to create a model of the ideal female lay penitent. Moreover, his efforts to win papal approval of a Dominican Penitential Order and Rule came at the same time that he was working to record the history of his order's recent reform movement. Although Caffarini did not manage to get Catherine canonized during his lifetime—she was finally canonized in 1461 by Pius II—I would argue that the complex and multilayered work he produced over the first quarter of the fifteenth century stands as the most concentrated, most radical, and ultimately the most effective example of the strategic appropriation of lay charisma.

Catherine, her Dominican promoters understood, could only garner a papal stamp of approval—the first for a lay saint since 1199—once the essential category of the independent lay penitent was no longer a reality. As I have noted, Caffarini did not include any female witnesses in the *Processo castellano*. In addition, none of the texts that Caffarini wrote or compiled make any mention of the *Miracoli*. In promoting a new contemporary lay saint, female lay penitents were nowhere to be seen. To garner a papal stamp of approval for an ideal lay life, Caffarini and his fellow Dominican friars understood that the aspect of lay sanctity that most accentuated the inherent tensions of lay charismatic authority, the female lay penitent, had to be absent. Innocent III might have forged a path in his canonization of Omobono for laymen wanting to take up the *vita apostolica* outside of church orders, but it was only when that category had essentially been regulated out of existence, once the Franciscan and Dominican third orders were institutional realities, that we can ironically claim a path to sanctity had been created for a laywoman.

---

12. On Thomas Caffarini's early fifteenth-century texts, see Silvia Nocentini, "Lo 'Scriptorium' di Tommaso Caffarini a Venezia," *Hagiographica* 12 (2005): 79–144; also see F. Thomas Luongo, "The Historical Reception of Catherine of Siena," in *A Companion to Catherine of Siena*, ed. Carolyn Muessig, George Ferzoco, and Beverly Mayne Kienzle (Leiden: Brill, 2012), 27–29; and O. Visani "Nota su Tommaso d'Antonio Nacci Caffarini," *Rivista di Storia e Letteratura Religiosa* 9, no. 2 (1973): 227–97.

BIBLIOGRAPHY

Unpublished Primary Sources

Cortona, Archivio del Convento di Santa Margherita
    Lodovico Bargigli da Pelago, "Sommario della storia della chiesa e convento di
        Santa Margherita da Cortona, compilato e disposto per ordine cronologico
        dal P. Fra Lodovico da Pelago," 1781
Cortona, Archivio storico del Comune di Cortona
    Q1: "Deliberazioni comunitative 1323–1324"
Florence, Archivio di Stato
    Unione di vari luoghi pii di Cortona
    Statuti comunità soggette, 279
Florence, Biblioteca Nazionale
    Conventi Soppressi G.5, 1212, ff. 193–200v
    Codice II, I, 122, and Codice miniato II. I. 212
Lucca, Archivio di Stato
    Statuti del Comune di Lucca, 3 (1331), 5 (1342), 6 (1372)
Lucca, Biblioteca Statale di Lucca
    MS 3459
Pesaro, Biblioteca Oliveriana
    MS 1300, ff. 168c–171a
Rome, Biblioteca Vallicelliana
    Stampati: S. II. 45
Siena, Archivio di Stato
    Deliberazioni del Consiglio Generale (1285, 1289, 1329)
    Libri dell'entrata e dell'uscita della repubblica di Siena detti del Camarlingo e dei
        quattro provveditori della Biccherna (1258, 1265, 1282, 1286, 1292, 1296,
        1307, 1331, 1354, 1369)
    MS B.82, n. 515
Siena, Biblioteca Comunale degli Intronati
    K. VII. 2
Vatican City, Archivio Segreto Vaticano
    Riti, Proc. 552, 1315, and 3327
Venice, Biblioteca Marciana
    MS. Lat. 2798

Published Primary Sources

Abate, Giuseppe. *S. Rosa da Viterbo, terziaria francescana (1233–1251): Fonti storiche della vita e loro revisione critica.* Rome: Miscellanea Francescana, 1952.

Acta Sanctorum quotquot Toto Orbe Coluntur . . . Editio nova. Edited by Jean Bolland et al. Paris: Palmé, etc., 1863–.

Angela of Foligno. *Angela of Foligno: Complete Works.* Translated by Paul Lachance. New York: Paulist Press, 1993.

Avogari, R. degli Azzoni. *Memorie del Beato Enrico, morto in Trivigi l'anno MCCCXV, corredate di documenti, con una dissertazione sopra San Liberale e sopra gli altri santi dei quali riposano i Sacri Corpori nella chiesa della già detta città.* Venice, 1760.

Bartholomew of Pisa. *De conformitate vitae Beati Francisci ad vitam Domini Iesu.* In *Analecta Franciscana,* vol. 4, 359–61. Rome: Quaracchi, 1906.

Bartolomeo da Trento. *Liber epilogorum in gesta sanctorum.* Edited by Emore Paoli. Florence: Sismel, 2001.

Bevegnatis, Iunctae. *Legenda de vita et miraculis beatae Margaritae de Cortona.* Edited by Fortunato Iozzelli. Bibliotheca Franciscana Ascetica Medii Aevi 13. Grottaferrata: Editiones Collegii S. Bonaventurae ad Claras Aquas, 1997.

Bonaventure of Bagnoregio [pseud.]. *Determinationes quaestionum circa regulam fratrum minorum.* In *Bonaventurae opera omnia,* vol. 8. Quaracchi, 1923.

Bongi, S., and L. del Prete. *Statuto del Comune di Lucca dell'anno 1308. Memorie e documenti per servire all'istoria del Principato lucchese.* Lucca: Tipografia Giusti, 1857.

Cenci, C. "San Pietro Pettinaio presentato da un predicatore senese contemporaneo." *Studi Francescani* 87 (1990): 5–30.

Codex diplomaticus Cremonae, 715–1334. Volume 1. Edited by Lorenzo Astegiano. Turin, 1896.

Dante Alighieri. *The Divine Comedy of Dante Alighieri: Purgatorio.* Translated by Allen Mandelbaum. New York: Bantam, 1982.

da Pelago, Lodovico Bargigli. *Antica leggenda della vita e de'miracoli di S. Margherita da Cortona scritta dal di lei confessore fr. Giunta Bevegnati dell'Ordine de'Minori.* 2 vols. Lucca, 1793.

Die Register Innocenz' III. Volume I. Edited by O. Hageneder and A. Haidacher. Vienna, 1964.

Francis of Assisi: Early Documents. Edited by Regis J. Armstrong, J. A. Wayne Hellmann, and William J. Short. New York: New City Press, 1999.

Grégoire, Réginald. *San Ranieri di Pisa (1117–1160) in un ritratto agiografico inedito del secolo XIII.* Pisa: Pacini, 1990.

Gregory the Great. *Regula pastoralis.* In *Patrologiae cursus completus: Series latina,* vol. 77. Paris: Migne, 1857–66.

Hippolytus of Rome. *The Treatise on the Apostolic Tradition.* Ridgefield: Morehouse, 1992.

Jacobus de Voragine. *The Golden Legend: Readings on the Saints.* Translated by William Granger Ryan. Princeton: Princeton University Press, 1993.

La Legenda di Vanna da Orvieto. Edited by Emore Paoli and Luigi G. G. Ricci. Spoleto: Centro Italiano di Studi sull'Alto Medioevo, 1996.

Leggenda della beata Giovanna (detta Vanna) d' Orvieto suora dell'Ordine della penitenza di S. Domenico. Edited by Luigi Passarini. Rome: Tipografia Sinimberghi, 1879.

Lehmijoki-Gardner, Maiju, ed. *Dominican Penitent Women.* New York: Paulist Press, 2005.

Le Legendae di Margherita di Città di Castello. Edited by Maria Cristiana Lungarotti. Spoleto: Centro Italiano di Studi sull'Alto Medioevo, 1994.

Le pergamene del convento di S. Francesco in Lucca (sec. XII–XIX). Edited by Vito Tirelli and Matilde Tirelli Carli. Rome: Ministero per i Beni Culturali e Ambientali, 1993.

Les sermons et la visite pastorale de Federico Visconti archevêque de Pise (1253–1277). Edited by Nicole Bériou and Isabelle le Masne de Chermont. Rome: École Française de Rome, 2001.

Libri dell'entrata e dell'uscita della repubblica di Siena detti del camarlingo e dei Quattro provveditori della Biccherna, books 11 (1251), 19 (1258). Siena: Accademia Senese degli Intronati, 1963.

L'obituario della cattedrale di Cremona (obituarium ecclesias cremonensis). Edited by Francesco Novati. Milan: Bortolotti, 1881.

Meersseman, Gilles Gérard. *Dossier de l'ordre de la pénitence au XIIIe siècle.* Spicilegium Friburgense 7. Fribourg: Éditions universitaires, 1961.

Monumenta Germaniae Historica, Scriptores, vol. 31. Edited by O. Holder-Egger. Hanover, 1903.

Piazzi, Daniele. *Omobono di Cremona: Biografie dal XIII al XVI secolo, edizione, traduzione e commento.* Cremona: Diocesi di Cremona, 1991.

Raimondo da Capua. *Legenda maior sive Legenda admirabilis virginis Catherine de Senis.* Edited by Silvia Nocentini. Florence: Sismel, 2013.

Sacchetti, Franco. *Opera.* Edited by A. Borlenghi. Milan: Rizzoli, 1957.

Statuta et ordinamenta comunis Cremonae facta et compilata currente anno MCCCXXXIX. Edited by Ugo Gualazzini. Milan: Giuffrè, 1952.

Ubertino da Casale. *Arbor vitae crucifixae Iesu.* Venice, 1485. Reprint, Turin: Bottega d'Erasmo, 1961.

Un santo laico dell'età postgregoriana: Allucio da Pescia (1070 ca.–1134): Religione e società nei territori di Lucca e della Valdinievole. Edited by C. Violante. Rome: Jouvence, 1991.

Vauchez, André. "Sainteté laïque au XIIIe siècle: La vie du bienheureux Facio de Crémone (v. 1196–1272)." *Mélanges de l'École Française de Rome* 84 (1972): 13–53.

Vita del Beato Pier Pettinajo senese del terz'ordine di San Francesco volgarizeata da una leggenda latin del 1333 per F. Serafino Ferri Agostiniano di Lecceto l'anno 1508. Edited by Luigi de Angelis. Siena, 1802.

Secondary Sources

Agricoli, Carlo. *Pier Pettinaio nella Siena duecentesca: Biografia ragionata in cerca di trace nella Siena di otto secoli fa.* Siena: Il Leccio, 2014.

Alberzoni, Maria Pia. "Giordano di Sassonia e il monastero d. S. Agneses di Bologna." In *Institution und Charisma: Festschrift für Gert Melville zum 65*

Geburgstag, edited by F. J. Felten, A. Kehnel, and S. Weinfurter, 513–27. Cologne: Böhlau, 2009.

Amann, E., and A. Michel. "Pénitence." In *Dictionnaire de théologie catholique*, vol. 12, 722–845. Paris, 1933.

Amico, Rosalia. *Il monastero di S. Giovanni gerosolimitano in Pisa: Studio storico introduttivo: Inventario dell'Archivio e appendice di documenti*. Pisa: ETS, 2007.

Andrews, Frances. "Albertano of Brescia, Rolandino of Padua and the Rhetoric of Legitimation." In *Building Legitimacy: Political Discourses and Forms of Legitimacy in Medieval Societies*, edited by Isabel Alfonso, Hugh Kennedy, and Julio Escalona Monge, 319–40. Leiden: Brill, 2004.

——. *The Early Humiliati*. Cambridge: Cambridge University Press, 1999.

——. "Living Like the Laity? The Negotiation of Religious Status in the Cities of Late Medieval Italy." *Transactions of the Royal Historical Society* 20 (2010): 27–55.

——. "Monastic Observance and Communal Life: Siena and the Employment of Religious." In *Pope, Church and City: Essays in Honour of Brenda M. Bolton*, edited by Frances Andrews, Christoph Egger, and Constance Rousseau. Leiden: Brill, 2004.

Andrews, Frances, and Maria Agata Pincelli, eds. *Churchmen and Urban Government in Late Medieval Italy c.1200–c.1450: Cases and Contexts*. Cambridge: Cambridge University Press, 2013.

Aporti, F. *Memorie di storia ecclesiastica di Cremona*. Volume 1. Cremona, 1835.

Artifoni, E. "Tensioni sociali e istituzioni nel mondo comunale." In *La storia: I grandi problemi dal medioevo all'età contemporanea*, vol. 2, *Il medioevo*, edited by N. Tranfaglia and M. Firpo, 461–91. Turin: UTET, 1986.

Ascher, Mario, and Patrizia Turrini, eds. *La misericordia di Siena attraverso i secoli: Dalla domus misericordiae all'arciconfraternita di misericordia*. Siena: Protagon Editori Toscani, 2004.

Astell, Ann W., ed. *Lay Sanctity, Medieval and Modern: A Search for Models*. Notre Dame, IN: University of Notre Dame Press, 2000.

Baldwin, J. W. *Masters, Princes, and Merchants: The Social Views of Peter the Chanter and His Circle*. Princeton: Princeton University Press, 1970.

——. *The Medieval Theories of the Just Price: Romanists, Canonists, and Theologians in the Twelfth and Thirteenth Centuries*. Philadelphia: American Philosophical Society, 1959.

Baracchini, Clara, and Antonino Caleca. *Il duomo di Lucca*. Lucca: Baroni, 1973.

Bardotti Biasion, G. "Gano di Fazio e la tomba-altare di Santa Margherita da Cortona." *Prospettiva* 37 (1984): 2–19.

Barone, Guilia, and Jacques Dalarun, eds. *Angèle de Foligno: Le dossier*. Rome: École Française de Rome, 1999.

Bartlett, Robert. *Why Can the Dead Do Such Great Things? Saints and Worshippers from the Martyrs to the Reformation*. Princeton: Princeton University Press, 2013.

Becker, Marvin B. "Three Cases Concerning the Restitution of Usury in Florence." *Journal of Economic History* 17 (1957): 445–50.

Bellosi, L. "Per un contesto cimabuesco senese: a) Guido da Siena e il probabile Dietisalvi di Speme." *Prospettiva* 61 (1991): 6–20.

Benvenuti Papi, Anna. "Donne sulla strada: L'itineranza religiosa femminile nel medioevo." In *Donne in viaggio: Viaggio religioso politico metaforico*, edited by M. L. Silvestre and A. Valerio, 74–86. Bari: Laterza, 1999.

——. *"In castro poenitentiae": Santità e società femminile nel'Italia medievale*. Italia Sacra 45. Rome: Herder, 1990.

——. "Marguerite de Cortone." In *Histoire des saints et de la sainteté chrétienne*, vol. 7, *Une Église éclatée, 1275–1545*, edited by André Vauchez, 178–83. Paris: Hachette, 1986.

——. "Umiliana dei Cerchi, nascita di un culto nella Firenze del Dugento." *Studi Francescani* 77 (1980): 87–117.

Bibliotheca hagiographica latina antiquae et mediae aetatis. 2 vols. Brussels, 1898–1901. Supplementary vol. Brussels, 1987.

Bibliotheca sanctorum. 12 vols. Rome: Istituto Giovanni XXIII nella Pontificia Università Lateranense, 1961–69.

Bigwood, Georges. *Les livres des comptes des Gallerani*. 2 vols. Brussels: Palais des Académies, 1961–62.

Bisogni, Fabio. "L'abito di Margherita." In *Margherita da Cortona: Una storia emblematica devozione narrata per testi e immagini*, edited by Laura Corti and Riccardo Spinelli, 33–43. Milan: Electra, 1998.

Boesch Gaiano, Sofia. "Lavoro, povertà, santità fra nuove realtà sociali e luoghi comuni agiografici." In *Cultura e società nell'Italia medievale: Studi per Paolo Brezzi*, 117–129. Rome: Istituto Storico Italian per il Medio Evo, 1988.

Bolton, Brenda. *Innocent III: Studies on Papal Authority and Pastoral Care*. Aldershot: Routledge, 1995.

——. "Innocent III and the *Humiliati*. In *Innocent III: Vicar of Christ or Lord of the World?*, edited by James M. Powell, 114–20. Washington, DC: Catholic University of America Press, 1994.

——. "Signs, Wonders, Miracles: Supporting the Faith in Medieval Rome." In *Signs, Wonders, Miracles: Representations of Divine Power in the Life of the Church*, edited by Kate Cooper and Jeremy Gregory, 157–78. Martlesham: Boydell & Brewer, 2005.

Bonometti, Pietro, ed. *Omobono: La figura del santo nell'iconografia, secoli XIII–XIX*. Milan: Silvana, 1999.

Bornstein, Daniel. "Parish Priests in Late Medieval Cortona: The Urban and Rural Clergy." *Quaderni di Storia Religiosa* 4 (1997): 165–93.

——. "The Uses of the Body: The Church and the Cult of Santa Margherita da Cortona." *Church History* 62 (1993): 163–77.

Bornstein, Daniel, and Roberto Rusconi, eds. *Women and Religion in Medieval and Renaissance Italy*. Chicago: University of Chicago Press, 1996.

Boureau, Alain. *Satan the Heretic: The Birth of Demonology in the Medieval West*. Translated by Teresa Lavender Fagan. Chicago: University of Chicago Press, 2006.

Bouvier, Michel. "De l'incorruptibilité des corps saints." In *Les miracles, miroirs des corps*, edited by Jacques Gélis and Odile Redon, 193–221. Paris: Presses et Publications de l'Université de Paris-VIII, 1983.

Bowsky, William. *The Finance of the Commune of Siena, 1287–1355*. Oxford: Clarendon Press, 1970.

——. *A Medieval Italian Commune: Siena under the Nine, 1287–1355*. Berkeley: University of California Press, 1981.

Boyle, Leonard E. "Sicardus of Cremona." In *New Catholic Encyclopedia*, vol. 8, 190–91. New York: McGraw-Hill, 1967.

Brady, Ignatius. "The Writings of Saint Bonaventure Regarding the Franciscan Order." *Miscellanea Francescana* 75 (1975).

Brundage, James A. "Usury." In *The Dictionary of the Middle Ages*, vol. 12, edited by Joseph R. Strayer. New York: Charles Scribner's Sons, 1982.

Buchanan, Charles. "A Late Eleventh-Century Illustrated Hagiographic Lectionary from Lucca (Biblioteca Capitolare, Passionario C): Expression of Ecclesiastical Reform." PhD dissertation, University of California at Santa Barbara, 1997.

——. "Spiritual and Spatial Authority in Medieval Lucca: Illuminated Manuscripts, Stational Liturgy and the Gregorian Reform." *Art History* 27 (2004): 723–44.

Burr, David. *Olivi and Franciscan Poverty: The Origins of the Usus Pauper Controversy*. Philadelphia: University of Pennsylvania Press, 1989.

——. *The Spiritual Franciscans: From Protest to Persecution in the Century after Saint Francis*. University Park: Pennsylvania State University Press, 2001.

Bynum, Caroline Walker. "Bodily Miracles and the Resurrection of the Body in the High Middle Ages." In *Belief in History: Innovative Approaches to European and American Religion*, edited by Thomas Kselman, 68–106. Notre Dame, IN: University of Notre Dame Press, 1991.

——. *Holy Feast and Holy Fast: The Religious Significance of Food to Medieval Women*. Berkeley: University of California Press, 1987.

——. *Jesus as Mother: Studies in the Spirituality of the High Middle Ages*. Berkeley: University of California Press, 1982.

——. *The Resurrection of the Body in Western Christianity, 300–1336*. New York: Columbia University Press, 1995.

Caciola, Nancy. *Discerning Spirits: Divine and Demonic Possession in the Middle Ages*. Ithaca, NY: Cornell University Press, 2003.

——. "Through a Glass Darkly: Recent Work on Sanctity and Society." *Comparative Studies in Society and History*, 38 (1996): 301–9.

Caleca, Antonino. "Il Volto Santo, un problema critico." In *Il Volto Santo: Storia e culto*, edited by Clara Baracchini and Maria Teresa Filieri, 59–69. Lucca: M. Pacini Fazzi, 1982.

Canetti, Luigi. *Gloriosa civitas: Culto dei santi e società cittadina a Piacenza nel medioevo*. Bologna: Pàtron, 1993.

Cannon, Joanna. "Beyond the Limitations of Visual Typology: Reconsidering the Function and Audience of Three *Vita* Panels of Women Saints c. 1300." In *Italian Panel Painting of the Duecento and Trecento*, edited by Victor M. Schmidt, 291–313. Washington DC: National Gallery of Art, 2002.

——. "Dominic *alter Christus*? Representations of the Founder in and after the *Arco di San Domenico*." In *Christ among the Medieval Dominicans: Representations of Christ in the Texts and Images of the Order of Preachers*, edited by Kent Emery Jr. and Joseph Wawrykow, 26–48. Notre Dame, IN: University of Notre Dame Press, 1998.

———. "Marguerite et les Cortonais: Iconographie d'un 'culte civique' au XIVᵉ siècle." In *La religion civique à l'époque médiévale et moderne (Chrétienté et Islam)*, edited by A. Vauchez, 403–13. Paris: École Française de Rome, 1995.

———. "Popular Saints and Private Chantries: The Sienese Tomb-Altar of Margherita of Cortona and Questions of Liturgical Use." In *Kunst und Liturgie im Mittelalter: Akten des internationalen Kongresses der Bibliotheca Hertziana und des Nederlands Instituut te Rome*, edited by Nicolas Bock, Sible de Blaauw, Christopher Luitpold Frommel and Herbert Kessler, 149–62. Rome: Bibliotheca Hertziana, 2000.

Cannon, Joanna, and André Vauchez. *Margherita of Cortona and the Lorenzetti: Sienese Art and the Cult of a Holy Woman in Medieval Tuscany*. University Park: Pennsylvania State University Press, 1999.

Cannon, Joanna, and Beth Williamson, eds. *Art, Politics, and Civic Religion in Central Italy, 1261–1352*. Aldershot: Ashgate, 2000.

Cappelli, Silvio, ed. *Santa Rosa: Tradizione e culto*. Rome: Vecchiarelli, 1999.

Cardini, Franco. "Agiografia e politica: Margherita da Cortona e le vicende di una città inquieta," *Studi Francescani* 76 (1979): 127–36.

———. "Allegrezza Casali: Devota di S. Margherita, figura poco nota della spiritualità cortonese." *Studi Francescani* 72 (1975): 335–44.

Cariboni, Guido. "Domenico e la vita religiosa femminile: Tra realtà e finzione istituzionale." In *Domenico di Caleruega e la nascita dell'Ordine dei frati predicatori*, 327–60. Spoleto: Centro Italiano di Studi sull'Alto Medioevo, 2005.

Carney, Margaret, Jean François Godet-Calogeras, and Suzanne M. Kush, eds. *History of the Third Order Regular Rule: A Sourcebook*. Saint Bonaventure, NY: Franciscan Institute.

Casagrande, Giovanna. "Un ordine per i laici: Penitenza e penitenti nel Duecento." In *Francesco d'Assisi e il primo secolo di storia francescana*, edited by Maria Pia Alberzoni et al., 237–55. Turin: Einaudi, 1997.

———. *Religiosità penitenziale e città al tempo dei comuni*. Rome: Istituto Storico dei Cappuccini, 1995.

Castelli, Patrizia and Maria Luisa Ceccarelli Lemut, eds. *Intercessor Rainerius ad patrem: Il Santo di una città marinara del XII secolo*. Pacini: Pisa, 2011.

———, eds. *L'Invenzione di Ranieri il taumaturgo tra XII e XIV secolo: Agiografia ed immagini*, ed. Patrizia Castelli and Maria Luisa Ceccarelli. Pacini: Pisa, 2013.

Cenci, C. "Fonte anonima di un anonimo predicatore francescano senese." *Archivum Franciscanum Historicum* 87 (1994): 135–39.

———. "'San' Pietro Pettinaio presentato da fr. Bindo da Siena." *Archivum Franciscanum Historicum* 99 (2006): 189–211.

Chenu, M.-D. "Monks, Canons, and Laymen in Search of the Apostolic Life." In *Nature, Man and Society in the Twelfth Century: Essays on New Theological Perspectives in the Latin West*, 202–38. Toronto: University of Toronto Press, 1997.

Clark, Allison. "Spaces of Reclusion: Notarial Records of Urban Eremiticism in Medieval Siena." In *Rhetoric of the Anchorhold: Space, Place and Body within the Discourses of Enclosure*, edited by Liz Herbert McAvoy. Cardiff: University of Wales Press, 2008.

Coakley, John. *Women, Men, and Spiritual Power: Female Saints and Their Male Collaborators*. New York: Columbia University Press, 2006.

Cohn, Samuel K. *Death and Property in Siena, 1205–1800*. Baltimore: Johns Hopkins University Press, 1988.

Congar, Yves. "Laïc au Moyen Âge." In *Dictionnaire de spiritualité*, 79–108. Paris: Beauchesne, 1976.

Constable, Giles. "The Interpretation of Mary and Martha." In *Three Studies in Medieval Religious and Social Thought*. Cambridge: Cambridge University Press, 1995, 3–141.

——. "Opposition to Pilgrimage in the Middle Ages." *Studia Gratiana* 19 (1976): 125–46.

——. *The Reformation of the Twelfth Century*. Cambridge: Cambridge University Press, 1996.

Cornell du Houx, Adrian. "Journeys to Holiness: Lay Sanctity in the Central Middle Ages, c.970–c.1120." PhD dissertation, University of Lancaster, 2015.

Corti, Laura. "Esercizio sulla mano destra: Gestualità e santi nel medioevo." *Annali della Scuola Normale Superiore di Pisa*, series 4 (1996): 39–49.

Coturri, Enrico. "La canonica di S. Frediano di Lucca dalla prima istituzione (metà del sec. XI) alla unione alla congregazione riformata di Fregionaia (1517)." *Actum Luce* 3 (1974): 47–80.

Cristofani, F. "Memorie del B. Pietro Pettinagno da Siena." *Miscellanea Francescana* 5 (1890): 34–52.

Cusato, Michael. *The Early Franciscan Movement (1205–1239): History, Sources, Hermeneutics*. Spoleto: Centro Italiano di Studi sull'Alto Medioevo, 2009.

da Campagnola, Stanislao. "L'Ordine della penitenza nelle Cronache del'200." In *L'Ordine della penitenza di S. Francesco d'Assisi nel XIII secolo*, ed. O. Schmuki. Rome: Istituto Storico dei Cappuccini, 1973.

Dalarun, Jacques. "Angèle de Foligno a-t-elle existé?" In *"Alla signorina": Mélanges offerts à Noëlle de La Blanchardière*. Rome: École Française de Rome, 1995.

——. *"Dieu changea de sexe pour ainsi dire": La religion faite femme, XIᵉ–XVᵉ siècle*. Paris: Fayard, 2008.

D'Alatri, Mariano. *Aetas poenitentialis: L'antico Ordine francescano della penitenza*. Rome: Istituto Storico dei Cappuccini, 1993.

——, ed. *I frati penitenti di San Francesco nella società del due e trecento*. Rome: Istituto Storico dei Cappuccini, 1977.

——. *Il movimento francescano della penitenza nella società medioevale*. Rome: Istituto Storico dei Cappuccini, 1980.

——. *L'Inquisizione francescana*. Rome: Istituto Storico dei Cappuccini, 1996.

——. "L'Ordine della penitenza nella leggenda di Margherita da Cortona." *Analecta Tertii Ordinis Regularis* 15 (1982): 67–80.

Davidsohn, Robert. *Storia di Firenze*. Florence: Sansoni, 1956–68.

Davis, Adam J. "The Social and Religious Meanings of Charity in Medieval Europe." *History Compass* 12 (2014): 935–50.

de Lagarde, Georges. *La naissance de l'esprit laïque au déclin du Moyen Âge*. 3rd ed. 5 vols. Louvain: Nauwelaerts, 1956–63.

Delaruelle, Étienne. *La piété populaire au Moyen Âge*. Turin: Bottega d'Erasmo, 1975.

Dereine, Charles. "Chanoines." In *Dictionnaire d'histoire et de géographie ecclésiastiques*, vol. 12 (Turnhout: Brepols, 1953), cols. 353–405.

——. "Vie commune, règle de Saint Augustin et chanoines réguliers au XIᵉ siècle." *Revue d'Histoire Ecclésiastique* 41 (1946): 365–406.

Ditchfield, Simon. *Liturgy, Sanctity, and History in Tridentine Italy: Pietro Maria Campi and the Preservation of the Particular.* Cambridge: Cambridge University Press, 1995.

Doyno, Mary Harvey. "The Creation of a Franciscan Lay Saint: Margaret of Cortona and Her *Legenda.*" *Past and Present* 228 (2015): 88–90.

Elliott, Dyan. *Proving Woman: Female Spirituality and Inquisitional Culture in the Later Middle Ages.* Princeton: Princeton University Press, 2004.

——. *Spiritual Marriage: Sexual Abstinence in Medieval Wedlock.* Princeton: Princeton University Press, 1993.

Epstein, Steven. *Wills and Wealth in Medieval Genoa, 1150–1250.* Cambridge, MA: Harvard University Press, 1984.

Fioriti, Bartolommeo. *Vita, virtu', e miracoli di Santa Zita vergine lucchese.* Lucca, 1752.

Fontaine, Jacques. "The Practice of Christian Life: The Birth of the Laity." In *Christian Spirituality: Origins to the Twelfth Century*, edited by Bernard McGinn and John Meyendorff, 453–91. New York: Crossroad, 1985.

Fresucci, Bruno. "Attività sociale di S. Margherita." In *Cortona a Santa Margherita nel VII centenario della "conversione" 1272–1972*, 55–59. Cortona: Calosci, 1973.

Frugoni, Chiara. "The City and the 'New' Saints." In *City States in Classical Antiquity and Medieval Italy: Athens and Rome, Florence and Venice*, edited by Anthony Molho, Kurt Raaflaub, and Julia Emlen, 71–91. Stuttgart: Franz Steiner, 1991.

——. *A Distant City: Images of Urban Experience in the Medieval World.* Translated by William McCuaig. Princeton: Princeton University Press, 1991.

Fulton, Rachel, and Bruce W. Holsinger, eds. *History in the Comic Mode: Medieval Communities and the Matter of Person.* New York: Columbia University Press, 2007.

Galassi, F. L. "Buying a Passport to Heaven: Usury, Restitution and the Merchants of Medieval Genoa." *Religion* 22 (1992): 313–26.

Gilchrist, John. *The Church and Economic Activity in the Middle Ages.* London: Macmillan, 1969.

Gill, Katherine Jane. "Penitents, *Pinzochere* and *Mantellate*: Varieties of Women's Religious Communities in Central Italy, c. 1300–1520." PhD dissertation, Princeton University, 1994.

Giorgi, Giorgio, and Umberto Nicolai. *Le tre basiliche di S. Frediano nella storia e nell'arte.* Lucca: M. Pacini Fazzi, 1998.

Giusti, Martino. "Le canoniche della città e diocesi di Lucca." *Studi Gregoriani* 3 (1948): 321–67.

——. "*L'Ordo officiorum* della cattedrale di Lucca." In *Miscellanea Giovanni Mercati*, vol. 2, *Letteratura medioevale.* Vatican City: Biblioteca Apostolica Vaticana, 1946.

——. "Notizie sulle canoniche lucchesi al tempo della Riforma gregoriana." In *La vita comune del clero nei secoli XI e XII*, vol. 2, 434–54. Milan: Società Editrice Vita e Pensiero, 1959.

Goffen, Rona. "*Nostra Conversatio in Caelis Est*: Observations on the *Sacra Conversazione* in the Trecento." *Art Bulletin* 61 (1979): 198–222.

Golinelli, Paolo. "Antichi e nuovi culti al sorgere dei communi nel nord-Italia." *Hagiographica* 1 (1994): 159–80.

——. *Città e culto dei santi nel medioevo italiano*. Bologna: CLUEB, 1996.

——, ed. *Il pubblico dei santi: Forme e livelli di ricezione dei messaggi agiografici*. Rome: Viella, 2000.

——. *Indiscreta sanctitas: Studi sul rapporto tra culti, poteri, societa nel pieno medioevo*. Rome: Istituto Storico Italiano per il Medio Evo, 1988.

Goodich, Michael. "Ancilla Dei: The Servant as Saint in the Late Middle Ages." In *Women of the Medieval World: Essays in Honor of John F. Mundy*, edited by Julius Kirshner and Suzanne F. Wemple, 119–36. Oxford: Basil Blackwell, 1985.

——. "A Profile of Thirteenth-Century Sainthood." *Comparative Studies in Society and History* 18 (1976): 429–37.

——. *Vita Perfecta: The Ideal of Sainthood in the Thirteenth Century*. Monographien zur Geschichte des Mittelalters, 25. Stuttgart: Anton Hiersemann, 1982.

Green, Louis. *Castruccio Castracani: A Study on the Origins and Character of a Fourteenth-Century Italian Despotism*. Oxford: Clarendon Press, 1986.

——. *Lucca under Many Masters: A Fourteenth-Century Italian Commune in Crisis (1382–1342)*. Quaderni di Rinascimento, 30. Florence: L. S. Olschki, 1995.

Grégoire, Réginald. "Temi tipologici della vita di Sant'Allucio (†1134)." In *Un santo laico dell'età postgregoriana: Allucio da Pescia (1070 ca.–1134): Religione e società nei territori di Lucca e della Valdinievole*, edited by C. Violante, 15–54. Rome: Jouvence, 1991.

Grieco, Holly J. "Pastoral Care, Inquisition, and Mendicancy in the Medieval Franciscan Order." In *The Origin, Development, and Refinement of Medieval Religious Mendicancies*, edited by Donald Prudlo, 117–56. Leiden: Brill, 2011.

Grundmann, Herbert. *Religious Movements in the Middle Ages*. Translated by Steven Rowan. Notre Dame, IN: University of Notre Dame Press, 1995.

Gualazzini, U. *Il "populus" di Cremona e l'autonomia del comune*. Bologna: Zanichelli, 1940.

Guarnieri, Romana. "Pinzochere." In *Dizionario degli istituti di perfezione*, edited by Guerrino Pelliccia and Giancarlo Rocca, 1721–49. Rome: Paoline, 1980.

Guerra, Americo. *Istoria della vita di santa Zita vergine lucchese, narrata secondo i documenti contemporanei*. Lucca: S. Paolino, 1875.

Henderson, John. *Piety and Charity in Late Medieval Florence*. Oxford: Oxford University Press, 1994.

Hyde, J. K. *Society and Politics in Medieval Italy: The Evolution of Civil Life, 1000–1350*. London: Macmillan, 1973.

Inga, Giuseppina. "Gli insediamenti mendicanti a Cortona." In *Cortona: Storia della città*, 44–55. Milan: Electa, 1976.

Iozzelli, Fortunato. "I francescani ad Arezzo e a Cortona nel duecento." In *La presenza francescana nella Toscana del '200: "Sabati francescani"—ciclo di conferenze 1989–1990*, 121–42. Florence: Convento S. Francesco, 1990.

——. "I miracoli nella 'Legenda' di Santa Margherita da Cortona." *Archivum Franciscanum Historicum* 86 (1993): 217–76.

Jacobelli, Maria Caterina. *Una donna senza volto*. Rome: Borla, 1992.

Jansen, Katherine L. *The Making of the Magdalen: Preaching and Popular Devotion in the Later Middle Ages*. Princeton: Princeton University Press, 2000.

Jansen, Katherine L., Joanna Drell, and Frances Andrews, eds. *Medieval Italy: Texts in Translation*. Philadelphia: University of Pennsylvania Press, 2009.

Jones, Philip J. *The Italian City-State: From Commune to Signoria*. Oxford: Clarendon Press, 1997.

Kaftal, George. *Iconography of the Saints in Tuscan Painting*. Florence: Sansoni, 1952.

Karras, Ruth Mazo. "Prostitution in Medieval Europe." In *Handbook of Medieval Sexuality*, ed. Vern L. Bullough and James Brundage, 243–60. New York: Garland Press, 1996.

Kaye, Joel. *Economy and Nature in the Fourteenth Century: Money, Market Exchange, and the Emergence of Scientific Thought*. Cambridge: Cambridge University Press, 1998.

Kempers, Bram. "Icons, Altarpieces, and Civic Ritual in Siena Cathedral, 1100–1530." In *City and Spectacle in Medieval Europe*, edited by Barbara A. Hanawalt and Kathryn L. Reyerson, 89–136. Minneapolis: University of Minnesota Press, 1994.

Kienzle, Beverly M. "Holiness and Obedience: Denouncement of Twelfth-Century Waldensian Lay Preaching." In *The Devil, Heresy and Witchcraft in the Middle Ages: Essays in Honor of Jeffrey B. Russell*, edited by Alberto Ferreiro, 259–78. Leiden: Brill, 1998.

Kienzle, Beverly M., and Travis Allen Smith. "Preaching, Heresy, and the Writing of Female Hagiography." In *Beyond Catholicism: Heresy, Mysticism, and Apocalypse in Italian Culture*, edited by Fabrizio De Donno and Simon Gilson, 33–53. New York: Palgrave Macmillan, 2014.

Kirshner, Julius, and Kimberly Lo Prete. "Peter John Olivi's Treatises on Contracts of Sale, Usury and Restitution: Minorite Economics or Minor Works?" *Quaderni Fiorentini per la Storia del Pensiero Giurdico Moderno* 13 (1984): 233–86.

Klaniczay, Gábor. "Legends as Life-Strategies for Aspirant Saints in the Later Middle Ages." *Journal of Folklore Research* 26 (1989): 151–71.

Kleinberg, Aviad. *Prophets in Their Own Country: Living Saints and the Making of Sainthood in the Later Middle Ages*. Chicago: University of Chicago Press, 1992.

——. "Shared Sainthood." In *Modelli di santità e modelli di comportamento: Contrasti, intersezioni, complementarità*, edited by Guilia Barone, Marina Caffiero, and Francesco Scorza Barcellona, 167–76. Turin: Rosenberg & Sellier, 1995.

Koenig, John Cortland. "The Popolo of Northern Italy (1196–1274): A Political Analysis." PhD dissertation, University of California, Los Angeles, 1977.

——. "Prisoner Offerings, Patron Saints, and State Cults at Siena and Other Italian Cities from 1250 to 1550." *Bullettino Senese di Storia Patria* 108 (2001): 222–96.

Kuefler, Matthew. *The Making and Unmaking of a Saint: Hagiography and Memory in the Cult of Gerald of Aurillac*. Philadelphia: University of Pennsylvania Press, 2014.

Lansing, Carol. *The Florentine Magnates: Lineage and Faction in a Medieval Commune*. Princeton: Princeton University Press, 1991.

Lazzareschi, E. "Angelo Puccinelli e gli altri pittori lucchesi del trecento." *Bollettino Storico Lucchese* 10 (1938): 153–54.

Le Celle di Cortona, eremo francescano del 1211. Cortona: Calosci, 1977.

Leclercq, Jean, François Vandenbroucke, and Louis Bouyer, *The Spirituality of the Middle Ages.* London: Burns & Oates, 1969.

Lehmijoki-Gardner, Maiju. *Worldly Saints: Social Interaction of Dominican Penitent Women in Italy, 1200–1500.* Bibliotheca Historica 25. Helsinki: Suomen Historiallinen Seura, 1999.

——. "Writing Religious Rules as an Interactive Process: Dominican Penitent Women and the Making of Their *Regula.*" *Speculum* 79 (2004): 660–87.

Lisini, A. "Notizie sul B. Pier Pettinagno." In *Miscellanea storica senese,* vol. 4. Siena: C. Nava, 1896, 42–45.

Little, Lester K. *Indispensable Immigrants: The Wine Porters of Northern Italy and Their Saint, 1200–1800.* Manchester: University of Manchester Press, 2015.

——. *Religious Poverty and the Profit Economy in Medieval Europe.* Ithaca, NY: Cornell University Press, 1978.

Lloyd, Joan Barclay. *The Medieval Church and Canonry of S. Clemente in Rome.* Rome: San Clemente, 1989.

Lobrichon, Guy. *La religion des laïcs en Occident: XIᵉ–XVᵉ siècles.* Paris: Hachette, 1994.

Lucca, il Volto Santo e la civiltà medioevale. Atti convegno internazionale di studi, Palazzo Pubblico, Lucca, 21–23 ottobre 1982. Lucca: M. Pacini Fazzi, 1984.

Luongo F. Thomas. "Cloistering Catherine: Religious Identity in Raymond of Capua's *Legenda maior* of Catherine of Siena." *Studies in Medieval and Renaissance History* 3 (2005): 25–69.

——. "The Historical Reception of Catherine of Siena." In *A Companion to Catherine of Siena,* edited by Carolyn Muessig, George Ferzoco, and Beverly Kienzle, 23–45. Leiden: Brill, 2012.

——. *The Saintly Politics of Catherine of Siena.* Ithaca, NY: Cornell University Press, 2006.

Lusio, F. P. "L'anziano di S. Zita." In *Miscellanea lucchese di studi storici e letterari in memoria di Salvatore Bongi,* 61–91. Lucca: Scuola Tipografica Artigianelli, 1931.

Luttrell, Anthony. "Saint Ubaldesca di Calcinaia." *Ordines Militares: Yearbook for the Study of the Military Orders* 18 (2013): 287–91.

Maginnis, Hayden B. J. *The World of the Early Sienese Painter.* University Park: Pennsylvania University Press, 2001.

Mancini, Augusto. *Storia di Lucca.* Florence: Sansoni, 1950.

Mancini, Girolamo. *Cortona nel medio evo.* Florence, 1897. Reprint, Rome, 1969.

Manni, D. M. *Osservazioni istoriche sopra i sigilli antichi de secoli bassi.* Volume 19. Florence, 1757.

Mansi, Gerardo. *I patrizi di Lucca: Le antiche famiglie lucchesi e i loro stemmi.* Lucca: Titania, 1996.

Martines, Lauro. *Power and Imagination: City-States in Renaissance Italy.* Baltimore: Johns Hopkins University Press, 1979.

Matraia, Giuseppe. *Lucca nel milleduecento.* Lucca: M. Pacini Fazzi, 1983; originally published in 1843.

McDonnell, Ernest W. "The *Vita Apostolica*: Diversity or Dissent." *Church History* 24 (1955): 15–31.

Meek, Christine. *The Commune of Lucca under Pisan Rule, 1342–1369*. Cambridge, MA: Medieval Academy of America, 1980.

——. "Lucca." In *Medieval Italy: An Encyclopedia*, edited by Christopher Kleinhenz, vol. 2. New York: Routledge, 2004.

——. *Lucca 1369–1400: Politics and Society in an Early Renaissance City-State*. Oxford: Oxford University Press, 1978.

Meersseman, Gilles Gérard. *Ordo fraternitatis: Confraternite e pietà dei laici nel medioevo*. Italia Sacra 24–26. Rome: Herder, 1977.

Menestò, Enrico, and Roberto Rusconi, eds. *Umbria: sacra e civile*. Turin: Nuova Eri Edizioni Rai, 1989.

Miller, Maureen C. *The Bishop's Palace: Architecture and Authority in Medieval Europe*. Ithaca, NY: Cornell University Press, 2000.

——. *The Formation of a Medieval Church: Ecclesiastical Change in Verona, 950–1150*. Ithaca, NY: Cornell University Press, 1993.

——. "Religion Makes a Difference: Clerical and Lay Cultures in the Courts of Northern Italy, 1000–1300." *American Historical Review* 105 (2000): 1095–130.

Miller, Tanya Stabler, *The Beguines of Medieval Paris*. Philadelphia: University of Pennsylvania Press, 2017.

Mincuzzi, Rosa. "Santa Rosa da Viterbo: Penitente del XIII secolo." *Analecta Tertii Ordinis Regularis Sancti Francisci* 31 (2000): 7–120.

Mooney, Catherine M. "The Authorial Role of Brother A. in the Composition of Angela of Foligno's Revelations." In *Creative Women in Medieval and Early Modern Italy: A Religious and Artistic Renaissance*, edited by E. Ann Matter and John Coakley, 34–63. Philadelphia: University of Pennsylvania Press, 1994.

——. *Clare of Assisi and the Thirteenth-Century Church: Religious Women, Rules, and Resistance*. Philadelphia: University of Pennsylvania Press, 2016.

——, ed. *Gendered Voices: Medieval Saints and Their Interpreters*. Philadelphia: University of Pennsylvania Press, 1999.

——. "Nuns, Tertiaries, and Quasi-Religious: The Religious Identities of Late Medieval Holy Women." *Medieval Feminist Forum* 42 (2006): 84–85.

More, Alison. *Fictive Orders and Feminine Religious Identities, 1200–1600*. Oxford: Oxford University Press, 2018.

——. "Institutionalization of Disorder: The Franciscan Third Order and Canonical Change in the Sixteenth Century." *Franciscan Studies* 71 (2013): 147–62.

——. "Institutionalizing Penitential Life in Later Medieval and Early Modern Europe: Third Orders, Rules, and Canonical Legitimacy." *Church History* 83 (2014): 297–323.

Morris, Colin. "San Ranieri of Pisa: The Power and Limitations of Sanctity in Twelfth-Century Italy." *Journal of Ecclesiastical History* 25 (1994): 588–99.

Mulder-Bakker, Anneke B. *Lives of the Anchoresses: The Rise of the Urban Recluse in Medieval Europe*. Translated by Myra Heerspink Schulz. Philadelphia: University of Pennsylvania Press, 2005.

Murray, Alexander. "Archbishop and Mendicants in Thirteenth-Century Pisa." In *Conscience and Authority in the Medieval Church*. Oxford: Oxford University Press, 2015.

Nelson, Benjamin N. "The Usurer and the Merchant Prince: Italian Businessmen and the Ecclesiastical Law of Restitution, 1100–1550." *Journal of Economic History* 7 (1947): 104–22.

Niermayer, J. F. *Mediae Latinitatis Lexicon Minus: A Medieval Latin–French/English Dictionary*. Leiden: Brill, 1976.

Nocentini, Silvia. "Lo 'scriptorium' di Tommaso Caffarini a Venezia." *Hagiographica* 12 (2005): 79–144.

——, ed. *Verdiana da Castelfiorentino: Contesto storico, tradizione agiografica e iconografia*. Florence: Sismel, 2011.

Norman, Diana. "Santi cittadini": Vecchietta and the Civic Pantheon in Mid-Fifteenth-Century Siena." In *Art as Politics in Late Medieval and Renaissance Siena*, edited by T. B. Smith and J. B. Steinhoff, 115–40. Abingdon-on-Thames: Routledge, 2012.

——. *Siena and the Virgin: Art and Politics in a Late Medieval City-State*. New Haven: Yale University Press, 1999.

——. "When Charity Fails: Andrea Gallerani and Memory of the Misericordia in Siena." In *The Kindness of Strangers: Charity in the Pre-Modern Mediterranean*, edited by Dionysios Stathakopoulos, 91–118. London: Centre for Hellenic Studies, 2007.

Occhipinti, Elisa. *L'Italia dei comuni. Secoli XI–XIII*. Rome: Carocci, 2000.

Oliger, Livarius. "Documenta inedita ad historiam fraticellorum spectantia," *Archivum Franciscanum Historicum* 6 (1913): 267–90.

Orselli, A. M. *L'Idea e il culto del santo patrono cittadino nella letteratura latina cristiana*. Bologna: Zanichelli, 1965.

Osheim, Duane J. "Conversion, *Conversi*, and the Christian Life in Late Medieval Tuscany." *Speculum* 58, no. 2 (1983): 368–90.

Paciocco, Roberto. "'Virtus morum' e 'virtus signorum.' La teoria della santità nelle lettere di canonizzazione di Innocenzo III." *Nuova Rivista Storica* 70 (1986): 597–610.

Paoli, Marco. *Arte e committenza privata a Lucca nel trecento e nel quattrocento: Produzione artistica e cultura libraria*. Lucca: M. Pacini Fazzi, 1986.

Park, Katherine. "The Criminal and the Saintly Body: Autopsy and Dissection in Renaissance Italy." *Renaissance Quarterly* 47 (1994).

——. "Impressed Images: Reproducing Wonders." In *Picturing Science, Producing Art*, edited by Caroline A. Jones and Peter Galison. New York: Routledge, 1998.

——. "The Life of the Corpse: Division and Dissection in Late Medieval Europe." *Journal of the History of Medicine and Allied Sciences* 50 (1995): 111–32.

Parsons, Gerald. *The Cult of Catherine of Siena: A Study in Civil Religion*. Aldershot: Ashgate, 2008.

——. *Siena, Civil Religion and the Sienese*. Aldershot: Ashgate, 2004.

Pazzelli, Raffaele. *St. Francis and the Third Order: The Franciscan and Pre-Franciscan Penitential Movement*. Chicago: Franciscan Herald Press, 1989.

Pazzelli, Raffaele, and Lino Temperini, eds. *La "Supra montem" di Niccolo IV (1289): Genesi e diffusione di una regola*. Rome: Analecta TOR, 1988.

——, eds. *Prime manifestazioni di vita comunitaria maschile e femminile nel movimento francescano della penitenza (1215–1447)*. Roma: Commissione Storica Internazionale TOR, 1982.

Pecci, Giovanni Antonio. *Storia del vescovado della città di Siena*. Lucca, 1748.

Pellegrini, Luigi. "Female Religious Experience and Society in Thirteenth-Century Italy." In *Monks and Nuns, Saints and Outcasts: Religion in Medieval Society, Essays in Honor of Lester K. Little*, edited by Sharon Farmer and Barbara H. Rosenwein, 97–122. Ithaca, NY: Cornell University Press, 2000.

Peterson, Janine Larmon. *Suspect Saints and Holy Heretics: Disputed Sanctity and Communal Identity in Late Medieval Italy*. Ithaca, NY: Cornell University Press, 2019.

Peyer, Hans Conrad. *Città e santi patroni nell'Italia medievale*. Edited by Anna Benvenuti. Florence: Le Lettere, 1998.

Poggi, Giovanni. "Raimondo Palmerio e il suo ospedale nella Piacenza del sec. XII." *Rivista di Storia della Medicina* 12 (1968): 212–16.

Pompei, Alfonso. "Il movimento penitenziale nei secoli XII–XIII." In *L'Ordine della penitenza di San Francesco d'Assisi nel secolo XIII*, edited by O. Schmucki, 9–40. Rome: Istituto Storico dei Cappuccini, 1973.

Pryds, Darleen. "Proclaiming Sanctity through Proscribed Acts: The Case of Rose of Viterbo." In *Women Preachers and Prophets through Two Millennia of Christianity*, edited by Beverly Mayne Kienzle and Pamela J. Walker. Berkeley: University of California Press, 1998.

Puerari, Alfredo. *Il Duomo di Cremona*. Milan: Cassa di Risparmio delle Provincine Lombarde, 1971.

Pugliese, O. Z. "The Good Works of the Florentine 'Buonomini di San Martino': An Example of Renaissance Pragmatism." In *Crossing the Boundaries: Christian Piety and the Arts in Italian Medieval and Renaissance Confraternities*, edited by K. Eisenbichler, 108–20. Kalamazoo: Medieval Institute, 1990.

Raitt, Jill, ed. *Christian Spirituality: High Middle Ages and Reformation*. New York: Crossroad, 1987.

Roest, Bert. *Franciscan Literature of Religious Instruction before the Council of Trent*. Leiden: Brill, 2004.

——. *Reading the Book of History: Intellectual Contexts and Educational Functions of Franciscan Historiography, 1226–ca.1350*. Groningen: Stichting Drukkerij C. Regenboog, 1996.

Romagnoli, Alessandra Bartolomei. "Pier Pettinaio e i modelli di santità degli ordini mendicanti a Siena tra duecento e trecento." *Hagiographica* 21 (2014): 109–54.

Ronzani, Mauro. "La 'Chiesa del comune' nelle città dell'Italia centro-settentrionale (secoli XII–XIV)." *Società e Storia* 6 (1983): 499–534.

Rossiaud, Jacques. *Medieval Prostitution*. Translated by Lydia G. Cochrane. Oxford: Basil Blackwell, 1988.

Ruiz, Teofilo. *From Heaven to Earth: The Reordering of Castilian Society, 1150–1350*. Princeton: Princeton University Press, 2004.

Rusconi, Roberto, ed. *Il movimento religioso femminile in Umbria nei secoli XIII–XIV*. Spoleto: Centro Italiano di Studi sull' Alto Medioevo, 1984.

——. *Predicazione e vita religiosa nella società Italiana*. Turin: Loescher, 1981.

Scapecchi, Piero. "Santa Margherita nella società cortonese del XIII secolo: Appunti sul 'Liber Fraternitatis Sancte Marie de Misericordia de Cortona' e alter fonti margaritiane." *Accademia Etrusca di Cortona Annuario* 28 (1997–98): 183–206.

Schlager, Bernard. "Foundresses of the Franciscan Life: Umiliana Cerchi and Margaret of Cortona." *Viator* 29 (1998): 141–66.

Schmitt, Jean-Claude. *La raison des gestes dans l'Occident médiéval*. Paris: Gallimard, 1990.

Schuchman, Anne M. "Politics and Prophecy in the Life of Umiliana dei Cerchi." *Florilegium* 17 (2000): 101–14.

——. "'Within the Walls of Paradise': Space, and Community in the *Vita* of Umiliana de' Cerchi (1219–1246)." In *Negotiating Community and Difference in Medieval Europe: Gender, Power, Patronage and the Authority of Religion in Latin Christendom*, edited by Katherine Allen Smith and Scott Wells, 49–64. Leiden: Brill, 2009.

——. "Within the Walls of Paradise: Umiliana de' Cerchi and the Changing Rhetoric of Sanctity." PhD dissertation, New York University, 2004.

Sella, Barbara. "Cremona." In *Medieval Italy: An Encyclopedia*, edited by Christopher Kleinhenz, vol. 1, 265. New York: Routledge, 2004.

——. "Piety and Poor Relief: Confraternities in Medieval Cremona, c. 1334–1499." PhD dissertation, University of Toronto, 1996.

Şenocak, Neslihan. *The Poor and the Perfect: The Rise of Learning in the Franciscan Order, 1209–1310*. Ithaca, NY: Cornell University Press, 2012.

Sensi, Mario. "Margherita da Cortona nel contesto storico-sociale Cortonese." *Collectanea Franciscana* 69 (1999): 223–62.

——. *Storie di bizzoche tra Umbria e Marche*. Rome: Edizioni di Storia e Letteratura, 1995.

Sensi, Mario, and Fortunato Frezza. *Pietro Crisci: Beato, confessore, compatrono di Foligno*. Foligno: Diocesi di Foligno, 2010.

Silva, Romano. *La Basilica di San Frediano in Lucca: Urbanistica, architettura, arredo*. Lucca: M. Pacini Fazzi, 1985.

Simons, Walter. *Cities of Ladies: Beguine Communities in the Medieval Low Countries, 1200–1565*. Philadelphia: University of Pennsylvania Press, 2001.

Skinner, Quentin. "Ambrogio Lorenzetti: The Artist as Political Philosopher." *Proceedings of the British Academy* 72 (1986): 1–56.

——. "Ambrogio Lorenzetti's *Buon Governo* Frescoes: Two Old Questions, Two New Answers." *Journal of the Warburg and Courtauld Institutes* 62 (1999): 1–28.

——. "Machiavelli's *Discorsi* and the Pre-Humanist Origins of Republican Ideas." In *Machiavelli and Republicanism*, edited by Gisela Bock, Quentin Skinner, and Maurizio Viroli. Cambridge: Cambridge University Press, 1990.

Soldi, F. *La carità di Cremona*. Cremona: Pizzorni, 1959.

Starn, Randolph. "The Republican Regime of the 'Room of Peace' in Siena, 1338–40." *Representations* 18 (1987): 1–32.

Storia di Piacenza. Volume 2. Piacenza: Cassa di Risparmio di Piacenza, 1980.

Stubblebine, James. *Guido da Siena*. Princeton: Princeton University Press, 1964.

Tanzi, Marco, and Andrea Mosconi. *Il Palazzo Comunale di Cremona e le sue collezioni d'arte*. Milan: Electa, 1981.

Temi e problemi nella mistica femminile trecentesca: Convegni del centro di studi sulla spiritualità medievale. Todi: Presso l'Accademia Tudertina, 1983.

Temperini, Lino, ed. *Santi e santità nel movimento penitenziale francescano dal duecento al cinquecento*. Rome: Analecta Tor, 1998.

Thompson, Augustine. *Cities of God: The Religion of the Italian Communes, 1125–1350*. University Park: Pennsylvania State University Press, 2005.

Thurston, Herbert. *The Physical Phenomena of Mysticism*. Edited by J. H. Crehan. Chicago: H. Regnery, 1952.

Tommasi, Girolamo. *Sommario della storia di Lucca dall'anno MIV all'anno MDCC*. Archivio Storico Italiano 10. Florence: G. P. Vieusseux, 1847; reprint, Lucca: M. Pacini Fazzi, 1969.

Trexler, Richard. "Charity and the Defense of Urban Elites in the Italian Communes." In *The Rich, the Well-Born and the Powerful*, edited by F. C. Jaher, 64–109. Urbana: University of Illinois Press, 1973.

van Os, Henk. *The Art of Devotion in the Late Middle Ages in Europe, 1300–1500*. Princeton: Princeton University Press, 1994.

——. *Vecchietta and the Sacristy of the Siena Hospital Church: A Study in Renaissance Religious Symbolism*. The Hague: Ministerie van Cultuur, 1974.

Vauchez, André. *Catherine of Siena: A Life of Passion and Purpose*. Translated by Michael F. Cusato. New York: Paulist Press, 2018.

——. *Esperienze religiose nel Medioevo*. Rome: Viella, 2003.

——. *Francis of Assisi: The Life and Afterlife of a Medieval Saint*. Translated by Michael F. Cusato. New Haven: Yale University Press, 2012.

——. "La canonisation de Saint Homobon." In *Innocenzo III: Urbs et orbis*, vol. 1, edited by Andrea Sommerlechner, 435–55. Rome: Instituto Storico Italiano per il Medioevo, 2003.

——. "La commune de Sienne, les ordres mendiants et le culte des saints: Histoire et enseignements d'une crise (novembre 1328–avril 1329)." *Mélanges de l'École Française de Rome* 89 (1977): 757–67.

——. "La difficile émergence d'une sainteté des laïcs à Venice aux XIIᵉ et XIIIᵉ siècles." In *Genova, Venezia, il Levante nei secoli XII–XIV*, ed. G. Ortalli and D. Puncuh, 335–48. Venice: Istituto Veneto di Scienze, Lettere ed Arti, 2001.

——, ed. *La religion civique à l'époque médiévale et moderne (Chrétienté et Islam)*. Paris: École Française de Rome, 1995.

——. *The Laity in the Middle Ages: Religious Belief and Devotional Practices*. Translated by Margery J. Schneider. Edited by Daniel E. Bornstein. Notre Dame, IN: University of Notre Dame Press, 1993. Originally published as *Les laïcs au Moyen Âge: Pratiques et experiences religieuses*. Paris: Cerf, 1987.

——. "Lay People's Sanctity in Western Europe: Evolution of a Pattern." In *Images of Sainthood in Medieval Europe*, edited by Renate Blumenfeld-Kosinski and Timea Szell, 21–32. Ithaca, NY: Cornell University Press, 1991.

——. "Le culte de saint Homebon du XIIᵉ au XVIᵉ siècle: Intentions des promoteurs et modalités de sa réception." In *Il pubblico dei santi: Forme e livelli di recezione dei messaggi agiografici*, edited by Paolo Golinelli, 129–39. Rome: Viella, 2000.

——. "Le 'trafiquant céleste': Saint Homebon de Crémone (†1197), marchand et 'père des pauvres.'" In *Horizons marins, itinéraires spirituels (Vᵉ–XVIIIᵉ)*, ed. H. Dubois, J.-C. Hocquet, and A. Vauchez, 115–22. Paris: Sorbonne, 1987.

——. *Omobono di Cremona (†1197): Laico e santo, profilo storico*. Cremona: Nuova Editrice Cremonese, 2001.

——. *Ordini mendicanti e società italiana XIII–XV secolo*. Milan: Mondadori, 1990.

——. "Patronage des saints et religion civique dans l'Italie communale à la fin du Moyen Âge." In *Patronage and Public in the Trecento*, edited by Vincent Moleta, 59–80. Florence: Leo S. Olschki, 1986.

——. "Raimondo Zanfogni, detto Palmerio." In *Bibliotheca sanctorum*, vol. 11, 26–27. Rome: Istituto Giovanni XXIII nella Pontificia Università lateranense, 1961–70.

——. *Sainthood in the Later Middle Ages*. Translated by Jean Birrell. Cambridge: Cambridge University Press, 1997.

——. *Saints, prophètes et visionnaires: Le pouvoir surnaturel au Moyen Âge*. Paris: Albin Michel, 1999.

——, ed. *Storia dell'Italia religiosa*, vol. 1, *L'antichità e il medioevo*. Bari: Laterza, 1993.

Visani, O. "Nota su Tommaso d'Antonio Nacci Caffarini." *Rivista di Storia e Letteratura Religiosa* 9, no. 2 (1973): 227–97.

Waley, Daniel. *The Italian City-Republics*. 3rd ed. New York: Longman, 1988.

——. *Medieval Orvieto: The Political History of an Italian City-State, 1157–1334*. Cambridge: Cambridge University Press, 1952.

——. *Siena and the Sienese in the Thirteenth Century*. Cambridge: Cambridge University Press, 1991.

Warr, Cordelia. "Religious Habits and Visual Propaganda: The Vision of the Blessed Reginald of Orléans." *Journal of Medieval History* 28 (2002): 43–72.

Webb, Diana. "The Church of San Frediano in Lucca." *History Today* 44 (1994): 62–63.

——. "Friends of the Family: Some Miracles for Children by Italian Friars." In *The Church and Childhood*, edited by Diana Wood, 183–95. Oxford: Blackwell, 1994.

——. "The Holy Face of Lucca." *Anglo Norman Studies* 9 (1986): 227–37.

——. *Patrons and Defenders: The Saints in the Italian City States*. London: I. B. Tauris, 1996.

——. "The Pope and the Cities: Heresy and Anticlericalism in Innocent III's Italy." In *The Church and Sovereignty c.590–1918: Essays in Honor of Michael Wilkes*, ed. Diana Wood, 135–52. Oxford: Basil Blackwell, 1991.

——. "Raimondo and the Magdalen: A Twelfth-Century Italian Pilgrim in Provence." *Journal of Medieval History* 26 (2000): 1–18.

——. "A Saint and His Money: Perceptions of Urban Wealth in the Lives of Italian Saints." In *The Church and Wealth*, edited by W. J. Sheils and Diana Wood, 61–73. Oxford: Basil Blackwell, 1987.

——, ed. *Saints and Cities in Medieval Italy: Selected Sources Translated and Annotated*. Manchester: Manchester University Press, 2007.

Weinstein, Donald, and Rudolph M. Bell. *Saints and Society: The Two Worlds of Western Christendom, 1000–1700*. Chicago: University of Chicago Press, 1982.

Weisenbeck, Joan, and Marlene Weisenbeck. "Rose of Viterbo: Preacher and Reconciler." In *Clare of Assisi: A Medieval and Modern Woman*, edited by Ingrid Peterson. Clarefest Selected Papers 8. St. Bonaventure, NY: Franciscan Institute, 1996.

Wolf, Kenneth Baxter. *The Poverty of Riches: St. Francis of Assisi Reconsidered*. Oxford: Oxford University Press, 2003.

Young, Bonnie. "A Saint on a Holy-Water Font." *Metropolitan Museum of Art Bulletin* (1965): 362–66.

Zaccagnini, Gabriele. *La tradizione agiografica medievale di santa Bona da Pisa*. Pisa: ETS, 2004.

———. *La "vita" di san Ranieri (secolo XII): Analisi storica, agiografica e filologica del testo di Benincasa: Edizione critica dal codice C181 dell'Archivio Capitolare di Pisa*. Pisa: ETS, 2008.

———. *Ubaldesca, una santa laica nella Pisa dei secoli XII–XIII*. Piccola Biblioteca Gisem 6. Pisa: ETS, 1995.

Zarri, Gabriella. *Le sante vive: Profezie di corte e devozione femminile tra '400 e '500*. Turin: Rosenberg & Sellier, 1990.

Zorzi, Andrea. "The Popolo." In *Italy in the Age of the Renaissance, 1300–1550*, edited by John M. Najemy, 145–64. Oxford: Oxford University Press, 2004.

INDEX

CPSIA information can be obtained
at www.ICGtesting.com
Printed in the USA
BVHW031111310819
557206BV00001B/14/P